PHILADELPHIA'S
PHILOSOPHER
MECHANICS

HISTORY OF TECHNOLOGY

General Editor   Thomas P. Hughes

Advisory Editors   Bern Dibner
Melvin Kranzberg
Lynn White, Jr.

PHILADELPHIA'S PHILOSOPHER MECHANICS

A HISTORY OF THE FRANKLIN INSTITUTE
1824–1865

By Bruce Sinclair

THE JOHNS HOPKINS UNIVERSITY PRESS
Baltimore and London

This book has been brought to publication with the generous assistance of the Andrew W. Mellon Foundation.

The Johns Hopkins University Press, Baltimore, Maryland 21218
The Johns Hopkins University Press Ltd., London

Library of Congress Catalog Card Number 74-6843
ISBN 0-8018-1636-X

Library of Congress Cataloging in Publication data will be found on the last printed page of this book.

Z66221

B. T. S.

H. E. S.

TABLE OF CONTENTS

	Preface	ix
I	The Progress of the Age	1
II	"For the Promotion of the Mechanic Arts": The Founding of the Franklin Institute	28
III	A Period of Transition	50
IV	A Program for Economic Development	82
V	Education at the Institute	108
VI	Research, Kindred Spirits, and the Rise of Science	135
VII	Government, Science, and the Institute	170
VIII	The Grand Lever: The Journal of the Franklin Institute	195
IX	The Financial Rack	217
X	In Search of a Mission	241
XI	Industrial Technology and the Franklin Institute	280
XII	Consolidating a Technical Community	308
	Bibliography	326
	Index	345

ILLUSTRATIONS

Noble Ambitions   20

A Community of Craftsmen   73

The Science of Technology   160

A Center of Industry   268

PREFACE

Technology has been a central force in the American experience. Americans have long believed that they possessed a mechanical talent, that they had some inherent ability to make things work, and better than anyone else. Over a long period of time, they have closely tied that self-image to a democratic ideology. American technology was better because of political freedom. And since technical knowledge gave anyone a chance for wealth and esteem, it provided a mechanism to maintain a free and open society. The combination of these elements, each reinforcing the other, indicated the nation's special mission to the world: America's technology would prove the virtue of her political system.

That formulation has only recently been challenged. As we begin to examine more critically our long-held assumptions about progress, it is worth looking at the process by which the United States developed a modern technological capacity. Institutions are particularly valuable subjects for analysis. They reflect the rhetoric which surrounds self-conscious social inventions; and their successes and failures reveal what lies behind pronouncement. Of all the institutions established during the first half of the nineteenth century to advance technology, none was more successful than the Franklin Institute of the State of Pennsylvania, for the Promotion of the Mechanic Arts, founded in Philadelphia in 1824. Societies like it, many of them also using Franklin's name, soon sprang up in other cities. But the Philadelphia organization is especially interesting because it so quickly assumed for itself the mantle of national leadership. It began as a mechanics' institute in the first bloom of that movement in America, but unlike institutes in New York, Boston, Baltimore, Cincinnati, and elsewhere, the Franklin Institute was distinguished by a varied and active program of teaching, research, and publication. Almost from the outset, it aimed to represent the best of American mechanics' institutes.

On public occasions leaders of the Institute frequently hearkened back to its beginnings and to the democratic impulses which gave it an early vitality. But in that sense the Institute was not what it seemed to be. Educational reforms initially designed to benefit poor and disadvantaged artisans usually served a more literate clientele. A mechanics' magazine, begun in a self-improvement vein to provide useful information, was soon altered to the degree that its contents became incomprehensible to ordinary workingmen. Furthermore, the Institute was always directed by men who by circumstances of birth or natural endowment had different interests from the majority of those the society presumed to aid.

And yet, during the years 1824–1865, the period covered by this study, the Franklin Institute became the most important technical organization in the country. From its varied activities Americans learned the most rational and effective means of advancing their technology. They discovered that progress did not rest on native ingenuity, however free it might be. They came to realize that government had a legitimate interest in technology and the responsibility for control when public welfare was at issue. Perhaps most crucial for industrial development and economic independence commensurate with the country's political status, the Institute's efforts revealed that specialization was just as important in technology as in science, with the same emphasis on professional standards of research and publication.

In the decades before the Civil War, when specialized societies or public agencies concerned with technology did not exist, the Philadelphia organization performed the functions of a national technical institution. It served as a focal point for ingenious mechanics and industrialists; for scientists and engineers; and, indeed, for all those who felt that America's fate was inextricably linked with technology.

This book began as a doctoral dissertation in the history of science and technology program at what was then the Case Institute of Technology. It is a pleasure to acknowledge the support and encouragement I received there: from Professor Melvin Kranzberg, the great and infectious spirit at that time; and particularly from Professor Edwin Layton, who gave me—as he does all his students—enormous amounts of time and thoughtful criticism. He read the manuscript again, when it had swollen to more than twice its original size, which cost him more labor than anyone has a right to expect from his teacher. Other very good friends troubled themselves to read it: Professor Carroll W. Pursell, Jr., of the University of California, Santa Barbara, and Dr. Michal McMahon, Archivist of the Franklin Institute. Dr. Joseph Hepburn, with his wide knowledge of Philadelphia institutions, saved me from more than one blunder.

I am grateful for the financial aid which made it possible for me to travel to Philadelphia and to spend time with the remarkably rich historical materials of that city. Dr. Bowen C. Dees, president of the

Franklin Institute, was steadfast in his support. I hope he appreciates the inclusion of that quotation from a letter John C. Trautwine wrote to William Hamilton, when he said of his own book: "I find it requires as many *years* to prepare it, as I had thought months." The Bureau of General Research at Kansas State University generously provided me with research assistance. I also benefited from a travel grant from the American Philosophical Society. And when this work was still a dissertation in progress, I gratefully received aid from the National Science Foundation.

I want to thank the librarians and archivists at the American Philosophical Society, the Academy of Natural Sciences, the Library Company of Philadelphia, the Historical Society of Pennsylvania, the University of Pennsylvania, the Smithsonian Institution, the National Archives, and especially the Franklin Institute and its library director, Emerson Hilker.

Portions of chapter 5 have been adapted from my article in *Nineteenth-Century American Science: A Reappraisal*, edited by George Daniels (Evanston: Northwestern University Press, 1972). Also, portions of my article which appeared in *Technology and Culture* 10 (January 1969): 20–34 appear in revised form in chapter 12.

Another set of obligations which one incurs in a piece of research and writing which stretches over a period of years is to family and friends for their affection and confidence. I have been lucky beyond naming them all, but I do want to mention my colleague at the University of Toronto, Professor Mary P. Winsor. The greatest debt of all is to my parents, who always believed education was the door to freedom, and to whom this book is dedicated.

PHILADELPHIA'S
PHILOSOPHER
MECHANICS

I

THE PROGRESS
OF THE AGE

> . . . to establish that equality so particularly
> recognized in our Bill of Rights.
>
> *The Mechanics' Press* (Baltimore),
> November 19, 1825

The history of the Franklin Institute reflects the contrast between what it promised and what it became. The organization began as a mechanics' institute. Initially, it shared the ideas of most mechanics' institutes in the United States and carried on the same kind of programs. In a very short time, however, it became so different that only with difficulty could one describe it in the same terms as all those apparently similar societies which sprang up in the 1820's. Often pointed out as the most successful association of its type, the Franklin Institute quickly developed as the most untypical. But at the beginning, and at least at a rhetorical level, the society was simply part of a larger movement dedicated to the improvement of the human condition.

Few periods of American history have been so passionately committed to reform as the early decades of the nineteenth century. In those years before the Civil War, Americans campaigned zealously for prison reform, the abolition of Negro slavery, temperance, women's rights, trade unionism, the diffusion of knowledge, humane treatment of the poor and the insane, and for the recasting of society along any one of several different lines. It was a time, as Emerson once remarked, when you could hardly meet someone who did not have a new plan for the world in his vest pocket. Faith in man's ability to alter his environment, rationally and for the better, never stood higher.[1]

Bold ideas for human improvement catch the imagination, and many were drawn to utopian experiments and reform crusades. But to a

---

[1] John T. Flanagan, "Emerson and Communism," *New England Quarterly* 10 (June 1937): 244. The best single treatment of the extraordinary intellectual vitality of that era is still Alice Felt Tyler's republished study, *Freedom's Ferment: Phases of American Social History from the Colonial Period to the Outbreak of the Civil War* (New York: Harper and Row, 1965).

degree that has yet to be fully understood, the majority of Americans in those years placed their faith in democratic ideals and the applications of science.[2] They saw in that combination the potential for political freedom, the end of class privilege, and a basis for equal economic opportunity. And they had some cause for optimism. By the early 1820's, the depression which had followed the War of 1812 was over. Peace had removed the last substantial British check to westward migration, and Americans spilled over the mountains in their search for new opportunity and new wealth. Those manufacturers who had survived the depression sensed a dawning era of prosperity, with expanding markets in the West, the South, and in Latin America. The increasing use of machinery in manufacturing processes only heightened ambitions for the future. Inventiveness lightened the burden of labor, increased productivity, and made goods cheaper. It also elevated the condition of the laborer and raised his standard of living.

Americans became aware that they possessed a certain mechanical ingenuity, and it seemed to suggest their national destiny. Eli Whitney's cotton gin, Robert Fulton's steamboat, and New York's Erie Canal were transformed into highly evocative symbols of the future. A Phi Beta Kappa orator at Yale in 1825 nicely caught these feelings when he claimed:

The present is, pre-eminently, an age of inquiry, and of enterprize, of discovery, of invention, and of universal improvement. It is an age, full of destiny; and, if we are just to ourselves, of most auspicious augury to our country.[3]

The way to that bright future was science. The word had a broad meaning in the early nineteenth century. It defined a body of knowledge, an intellectual style, and a mode of communication. It meant systematic learning about nature, pursued in a rational manner and transmitted openly. Because it was freely available in written form rather than the esoteric secret of an exclusive minority, science had great potential for crafts and craftsmen. And in that respect science also implied a technology inspired by scientific principles. The period did not see science as something fractured into such categories as pure or applied; it was seen as a continuous spectrum. Knowledge offered a range of possibilities, and even if intellectualism for its own sake stood at one end and directly practical utility stood at the other, the extremes were still linked by progressive shadings.

[2] A. Hunter Dupree persuasively argues that "science is a thread woven into the very fabric of American civilization from the beginning" ("The History of American Science—A Field Finds Itself," *American Historical Review* 71 [April 1966]: 863–74).

[3] James Gould, *An Oration, Pronounced at New Haven, before the Connecticut Alpha of the Phi Beta Kappa Society, September 13, 1825* (New Haven, 1825), p. 29.

That broad definition made science applicable to a wide range of concerns. It had an obvious importance for material advance. Science would provide the principles for more new inventions, the engineering talent for the construction of roads, bridges, and canals. Science would give the farmer new agricultural techniques and create new uses for his products. It would yield the knowledge for the further development of steam and other power sources, the expertise required to exploit the iron, coal, and mineral resources of a developing nation.[4]

In addition to those considerations, science also had ideological implications for Americans of the early nineteenth century. Science was almost always thought about in terms of education, and there it became intertwined with democratic ideals. Science was "useful knowledge," a term widely popular in the 1820's and used consciously in opposition to that idle learning which characterized the aristocracies of the Old World, where education was restricted by class lines. If it were made widely available, useful knowledge—training in science and its applications—would give any individual the chance to advance as far as his talents would take him. That was not only democracy's goal but its best warranty for survival. Since useful knowledge was also the key to the country's natural abundance, it would become America's mission to the world to demonstrate that democracy was the political system best designed to produce wealth and freedom for its citizens. Technology, as Hugo Meier has persuasively argued, "proved to be a catalyst, blending the ideas of republicanism with the rising democratic spirit in the early national period."[5]

It was in that curiously mixed context of egalitarianism and opportunism that The Franklin Institute of the State of Pennsylvania, for the Promotion of the Mechanic Arts was established in Philadelphia in 1824. Its founders built into the organization most of their attitudes and aspirations and, consequently, some of the contradictions which lay in that gulf between idealism and self-interest. They were reformers in an era of reform, democrats in the age of Jackson, and entrepreneurs at a time of burgeoning economic opportunity. While the pattern for its structure apparently came from mechanics' institutes in Great Britain, the Philadelphia organization embodied ideals already ingrained in the

4 Arthur A. Ekirch, Jr., *The Idea of Progress in America, 1815–1860* (New York: Columbia University Press, 1944), pp. 106ff. And what made that vision even more attractive was the conviction that "the present generation has introduced a *new era* in science, and productive industry" (Gould, *An Oration, Pronounced at New Haven*, p. 29).

5 Hugo A. Meier, "Technology and Democracy, 1800–1860," *Mississippi Valley Historical Review* 43 (March 1957): 618.

American character. In its beginnings, the Institute looked back to the folklore of self-improvement and to Benjamin Franklin, its archetypal hero. At the same time, it pointed forward to the exploitation of a continent. Although it was begun for the purpose of diffusing useful knowledge, with all its democratic connotations, there were seeds within the society which would grow to a new form of intellectual elitism. All of these diverse elements were present at the Institute's conception, and it came to life bearing the marks of a mixed parentage.

The story of the Franklin Institute's founding has been told in a number of commemorative sketches of the organization's history.[6] Samuel Vaughan Merrick, a young man employed in his Uncle John Vaughan's mercantile establishment, was placed in charge of a bankrupt fire-engine factory whose financial obligations the uncle had assumed.[7] The transition from commercial pursuits suddenly made him aware of his lack of technical knowledge and conscious that in status-minded Philadelphia manufacturing was not esteemed as highly as the more traditional avenues to wealth. To mend at least the first defect, Merrick sought admission to a mechanics' association in the city whose members met periodically to improve themselves through the discussion of technical and scientific subjects. He was blackballed, however, reputedly because of the ill will of one of its members.

At that point Merrick determined to establish his own society, where he and others like him might learn the science upon which their arts and crafts were based and, not incidentally, elevate themselves socially, too. As Merrick pursued that object, he made the acquaintance of

---

[6] The first of such anniversary sketches, *Commemorative Exercises at the Fiftieth Anniversary of the Franklin Institute of the State of Pennsylvania for the Promotion of the Mechanic Arts* (Philadelphia: The Franklin Institute, 1874), provides good detail of the Institute's beginnings. Another valuable brief study is William H. Wahl, *The Franklin Institute of the State of Pennsylvania for the Promotion of the Mechanic Arts: A Sketch of its Organization and History* (Philadelphia: The Franklin Institute, 1895).

[7] The factory, "back of St. James's Church, North Seventh Street," was originally established by Jacob Perkins, a mechanic of remarkable talents, who conducted the business with various partners, one of whom was Dr. Thomas P. Jones, long-time editor of the *Journal of the Franklin Institute*. After Perkins left Philadelphia for England in 1819, the firm fell on hard times. Merrick took over its management, perhaps in 1820, in partnership with John Agnew, and the new concern was styled S. V. Merrick & Co. Eugene S. Ferguson, ed., *Early Engineering Reminiscences [1815–40] of George Escol Sellers* (Washington, D.C.: Smithsonian Institution, 1965), pp. 7, 16. An illustrated catalogue of the reorganized firm is in the collections of the Library Company of Philadelphia under the title *A Description of the Patent Improved Fire Engines and other Hydraulic Machines, Invented by Jacob Perkins, and Manufactured by S. V. Merrick & Co.* For Perkins, see Greville Bathe and Dorothy Bathe, *Jacob Perkins* (Philadelphia: Historical Society of Pennsylvania, 1943).

another young man, Professor William H. Keating, who had just returned to Philadelphia from an education in the scientific and technical schools of Europe.[8] Keating was similarly inspired with the idea of founding an institution devoted to the practical applications of science. The two matured their plans, and late in 1823 they held the preliminary meetings which led to the establishment of the Franklin Institute. Chance may well have played some role in Merrick's motives to form a technical society and in his association with Keating, but it does not explain the immediate success of their plan.

The key is in the Institute's own understanding of its past. And those unspoken issues—personified in the actions of the central characters—connect the society's beginnings to the mechanics' institute movement in Great Britain and America. The first and most fundamental ingredient, common to both the Philadelphia enterprise and the mechanics' institute movement, was the conviction that knowledge should be open to all who seek it; learning should be restricted neither by closed societies nor by exclusive universities. Related to that issue was the idea that mechanics should not be relegated to a subordinate social position simply because of their occupation. The third element behind the vitality of the movement was the sometimes vague but powerful conception of the "scientific mechanic," the workman directed by theory and experience rather than solely by craft tradition or blind empiricism. These elements were bound together by an interpretation of human history reiterated in countless speeches at mechanics' institutes, lyceums, and other reform-oriented associations. Time was, the story usually ran, when tyrants maintained their power by suppressing knowledge. Ignorance, fear, and superstition were the common lot of mankind in those days, and artisans suffered the same maladies. The crafts were practiced in secrecy. Guild restrictions limited production and blocked technical advancement. Science was locked away in remote towers, accessible only to the privileged or to closet philosophers.

Francis Bacon, speakers like Edward Everett were fond of reminding their audiences, ended the old despotism.[9] By redirecting science toward

---

[8] Details of Keating's life are available in the *Dictionary of American Biography* (New York: Charles Scribner's Sons, 1943), and in Wyndham D. Miles, "A Versatile Explorer: A Sketch of William H. Keating," *Minnesota History* 36 (1959): 294–99.

[9] In one of Everett's favorite talks, "On the Importance of Scientific Knowledge to Practical Men, and on the Encouragement to its Pursuits," he juxtaposed the old tyranny with the present "age of improvement." It was, he claimed, "an age in which investigation is active and successful, in every quarter; and in which, what has been effected, however wonderful, is but the brilliant promise of what may be further done." Edward Everett, *Importance of Practical Education and Useful Knowledge* (Boston: Marsh, Capen, Lyon and Webb, 1840), p. 99.

the improvement of the human condition, he opened the long-closed door separating theory and practice. Reason gradually came to prevail, and men discovered that education and freedom led to prosperity and happiness. That formulation gave mechanics' institutes an essential role to play in the historical process. Bacon had made the philosopher aware of the lessons to be learned in the workshop. Mechanics' institutes would make the philosopher and the mechanic the same person.

The man usually regarded as the father of the mechanics' institute was George Birkbeck, a philanthropically-minded Quaker physician from Yorkshire. For a time Birkbeck taught natural philosophy at Anderson's Institution in Glasgow, a school which already emphasized practical education in science. Birkbeck discovered that the ordinary workmen of the city had a strong desire to learn the principles of science but were without any means of obtaining that kind of education. He decided to provide it himself. In 1800 he announced that he would deliver a series of free lectures, entitled "The Mechanical Properties of Solid and Fluid Bodies," replete with experiments and "conducted with the greatest simplicity of expression and familiarity of illustration, solely for persons engaged in the practical exercise of the mechanic arts."[10]

The lectures were a great success. By the fifth meeting, the audience had swelled to five hundred, and Birkbeck continued to give special lectures to workmen until he left for London in 1804 to establish himself in medical practice. The series was maintained by Andrew Ure, Birkbeck's successor, and the mechanics' class at Anderson's Institution continued until 1823. At that time, the mechanics themselves decided to establish their own organization, and the Glasgow Mechanics' Institution was formed. Completely controlled by workingmen, who hired a lecturer and a lecture room, set up courses in natural philosophy, mathematics, chemistry, and mechanics, and started a library and museum, it represented the basic aims of all subsequent mechanics' institutes.[11]

The Glasgow society was soon known in London, where the editor of the recently begun *Mechanics' Magazine* proposed a similar organization. Birkbeck, then resident in London, actively supported the idea, and a mechanics' institute with him as its first president was established early the following year. One of the features of the Glasgow institute

[10] Thomas Kelly, *George Birkbeck, Pioneer of Adult Education* (Liverpool: At the University Press, 1957), p. 29. A lively account of Birkbeck's role in founding the mechanics' institute movement is presented by Timothy Claxton in his *Memoir of a Mechanic, Being a Sketch of the Life of Timothy Claxton, Written by Himself, Together with Miscellaneous Papers* (Boston: George W. Light, 1839), pp. 104ff.

[11] Thomas Kelly, *A History of Adult Education in Great Britain from the Middle Ages to the Twentieth Century* (Liverpool: At the University Press, 1962), p. 120.

was its complete independence from the wealthier classes, who had traditionally supported, and controlled, benevolences for the less fortunate.
Workingclass control became a hotly disputed issue in the London
institute, however, and finally was settled only by compromise. To tap
the purses of the wealthy, it was decided to admit to membership anyone
sympathetic to the cause, but to maintain control, a constitutional clause
stipulated that two-thirds of the managing committee should be workingmen. It was ultimately an unsatisfactory settlement; money and
power proved inseparable.[12] But at the time it seemed like a good idea,
and it became a characteristic of mechanics' institutes.

Despite the attacks of those who called it a "genteel humbug" or of
those who saw it as a radical assault on the established order, the London Mechanics' Institute prospered, and along with the Glasgow institute, it served as a model for literally hundreds of societies formed
throughout Britain within the next few years.[13] Their purpose, as the
constitution of the London institute proclaimed, was "the instruction of
mechanics, at a cheap rate, in the principles of the arts they practise."
To achieve that aim, they envisioned "lectureships on the different Arts
and Sciences, a Library of Reference and Circulation, a Reading Room,
a Museum of Models, a School of Design, and an Experimental Workshop and Laboratory, provided with all necessary instruments and
apparatus."[14] Few institutes ever developed all those features, and there
were critics, by mid-century, who thought that the movement had failed
to reach its objectives.[15]

To those looking back later, Birkbeck was the central figure in the
drama. And for Americans, who always felt comfortable in the assurances of old-world precedent, Birkbeck, Glasgow, and London were the
proofs they urged in support of their own ambitions. They might just
as reasonably have looked for examples among themselves. The mechanics' institute began simultaneously in Britain and the United States. The
London society and the Franklin Institute were established at practically
the same time, and there is reason to believe that the New York

---

[12] Charles A. Bennett, *History of Manual and Industrial Education up to 1870*
(Peoria, Ill.: The Manual Arts Press, 1926), p. 304; Kelly, *A History of Adult Educa-
tion*, p. 121. J. W. Hudson published a list of British institutes in his *History of Adult
Education* (1851; reprint London: The Woburn Press, 1969).

[13] For samples of adverse comment on the London Mechanics' Institute, see *The
Mechanics' Weekly Journal* (London), November 29, December 13, 1823; January 10,
31, 1824.

[14] *The Mechanics' Weekly Journal*, November 15, 1823, published a full account
of the meeting which established the London institution.

[15] James Hole, *An Essay on the History and Management of Literary, Scientific
& Mechanics' Institutions* (London: Longman, Brown, Green and Longmans, 1853),
p. 17.

Mechanic and Scientific Institution, incorporated in the spring of 1822, provided the stimulus to Glasgow artisans for their own organization.[16] Birkbeck's idea that workingmen had the intellectual capacity to learn the principles of science was not new to Americans. It had been a chief component of their dogma of self-improvement for years. And to secure those objects, they had been experimenting with voluntary associations for an equally long time.

The interest Americans had in science and its applications stemmed from a variety of impulses. Certainly one of the most important was a profound awareness of the need for specialized knowledge in order to develop the country's resources. And that feeling, which sprang first from America's geographic position, was strongly reinforced by the war for independence. Consciousness of that need linked a variety of organizations whose activities and membership might otherwise have been quite different. All of America's scientific societies, for example, directed their activities toward that end as well as toward the more abstract aim of advancing knowledge. From its commencement in 1743, the American Philosophical Society was dedicated to the study of geography, agriculture, geology, and all other subjects which would, to use Franklin's words, "tend to increase the power of man over matter, and multiply the conveniences or pleasures of life."[17] Throughout the remainder of the eighteenth century and into the nineteenth century, its members considered methods to facilitate transportation, improve agriculture, and advance industry.[18] The American Academy of Arts and Sciences,

[16] In an obvious reference to John Griscom, one of the founders of the New York society, the anonymous author of an early account of the Institute argued: "Justice requires us to state, that even before Dr. Birkbeck had invited the attention of the mechanics of London to this subject, and it is even said, prior to the formation of any association of mechanics for mutual instruction in Europe, a public spirited gentleman of New York, advantageously known by his scientific and literary publications, as well as by his success in popular lecturing, resolved upon an attempt to unite the Mechanics of his flourishing city, into an institution whose object should be the promotion of the Mechanic Arts, by lectures and by other judicious measures" ("Observations on the Rise and Progress of the Franklin Institute," *The Franklin Journal and American Mechanics' Magazine* 1 [February 1826]: 69).

The purposes of the New York organization are described in *Charter, Constitution, and By-Laws of the New-York Mechanic and Scientific Institution* (New York: New York Mechanic and Scientific Institution, 1822). J. W. Hudson, in his *History of Adult Education*, claimed that the establishment of the Liverpool Mechanics and Apprentices' Library was "*Prompted by the example of New York.*" Originally published in 1851, Hudson's study was reprinted in London, in 1969, by The Woburn Press. See p. 45.

[17] Brooke Hindle, *The Pursuit of Science in Revolutionary America* (Chapel Hill: University of North Carolina Press, 1956), p. 69.

[18] Whitfield J. Bell, Jr., "The American Philosophical Society as a National Academy of Sciences, 1780–1846," *Ithaca* 9 (1962): 167.

founded in Boston in 1780, included among its concerns "improvements in agriculture, arts, manufactures and commerce," and in addition, the application of knowledge to determine uses for the country's natural resources. In very much the same fashion, the Connecticut Academy of Arts and Sciences was chartered in 1799 "to promote, diffuse and preserve the knowledge of those Arts and Sciences, which are the support of Agriculture, Manufactures, and Commerce."[19]

The American passion for self-improvement was another source of interest in useful knowledge. And as in so many other instances, Benjamin Franklin's personal history offered dramatic inspiration. His 1727 Junto, a small group of intellectually ambitious young men who sought mutual instruction in the consideration of scientific questions or current issues, was but one example to those who wished to better themselves.[20] More structured learning was available in evening schools, which since colonial times had dispensed a varied intellectual fare, more often than not directed especially toward eager apprentices. Beyond such basic subjects as reading, writing, and arithmetic, evening schools emphasized instruction in algebra, geometry, and trigonometry, navigation, surveying, geography, and astronomy.[21] At a time when craft organizations had lost their effectiveness as educational instruments, self-improvement became increasingly important and increasingly popular. The locus of responsibility for education shifted from society to the individual.[22] And in the early decades of the nineteenth century, self-improvement was almost entirely centered on useful knowledge.

Popular lectures in science also fed the urge for self-improvement in America's towns and cities. It was from just such a performance that Franklin's interest in electricity was first aroused, and the number and variety multiplied with time. John Griscom, one of the founders of the New York Mechanic and Scientific Institution, became well known for his lectures in chemistry.[23] Dr. Thomas P. Jones, who later became edi-

[19] Ralph S. Bates, *Scientific Societies in the United States*, 3rd ed. (Cambridge, Mass.: The M.I.T. Press, 1965), p. 10.

[20] Leonard W. Larabee et al., eds., *The Autobiography of Benjamin Franklin* (New Haven: Yale University Press, 1964), pp. 116ff.

[21] For a detailed treatment of this form of education, see Robert F. Seybolt, *The Evening School in Colonial America* (Urbana: University of Illinois Press, 1925).

[22] Bernard Bailyn, *Education in the Forming of American Society: Needs and Opportunities for Study* (Chapel Hill: University of North Carolina Press, 1960), pp. 98-99.

[23] John H. Griscom, *Memoir of John Griscom, LL.D., late professor of chemistry and natural philosophy; with an account of the New York High School; Society for the Prevention of Pauperism; the House of Refuge; and other institutions. Compiled from an autobiography and other sources* (New York: Carter and Brothers, 1859).

tor of the *Journal of the Franklin Institute,* developed his reputation in
science as a public lecturer. His talks, which included crowd-pleasing
demonstrations, covered a wide range of subjects and encompassed the
applications as well as the principles of science.[24]

It was relatively easy for those seeking knowledge to find it in the
cities. Men of commerce with a bent for philosophical experiments
could join informally with skilled craftsmen of similar interests. There
were libraries and lecture platforms and easier communication with a
larger world than a rural villager might enjoy. But zeal for self-improvement in useful knowledge was not limited to urban centers; beginning
in the mid-1820's, the lyceum movement gave rural Americans the
opportunity to advance themselves through the study of science and its
applications.

Lyceums are often associated with general lectures on a wide variety
of topics which aimed as much at entertainment as at education.[25] But
in its first stages, the lyceum movement was clearly a vehicle for self-
improvement, particularly in the sciences. Its founder was Josiah Holbrook, who was to lyceums what Birkbeck was to mechanics' institutes.
Holbrook went to Yale in 1806, developed a strong interest in science,
and served as Benjamin Silliman's laboratory assistant when Silliman
was America's outstanding scientist. Holbrook carried on a school of
his own for a short period, giving instruction in the practical uses of
science. In 1826 he published a plan for a much more ambitious undertaking, along somewhat the same lines, entitled the American Lyceum
of Science and the Arts. The primary activity of the lyceum would be
meetings and discussion on "any branch of Natural Philosophy, such as
Mechanics, Hydraulics, Pneumatics, [and] Optics, Chemistry, Mineralogy, Botany, the Mathematics, History, Geography, Astronomy, Agriculture, Morals, Domestic or Political Economy, or any other subject of
useful information."[26] The central element of Holbrook's idea was to
make it possible for citizens in even the smallest village to cultivate
knowledge. Lectures formed the mainstay of lyceum efforts, but considerable emphasis was also placed on mutual instruction. Classes were

[24] Benjamin Silliman, for instance, was guaranteed $1,500 to deliver a set of
lectures in New Orleans in 1845, where he was received by the "largest, most intelligent, and fashionable audience ever seen convened in the city" (Carl Bode, *The
American Lyceum: Town Meeting of the Mind* [New York: Oxford University Press,
1956], p. 85).

[25] Bode, *The American Lyceum,* is a good general survey of the entire lyceum
movement.

[26] Josiah Holbrook, *The American Lyceum of Science and the Arts, composed of
Associations for Mutual Instruction, and designed for the General Diffusion of Useful
and Practical Knowledge* (Worcester, Mass.: S. B. Manning, 1826), p. 3.

established to teach scientific subjects using chemical and philosophical apparatus, study guides, and outlines of experiments to be performed. Holbrook's plan gave further direction to the strong interest Americans had in science and self-improvement, and by the 1830's lyceums were widely established over the settled parts of the country. In time, the preponderance of scientific subjects was replaced, but for two decades the lyceum served the interests of all those "disposed to improve each other in useful knowledge."

If any additional impulse were needed beyond that mixture of altruism and self-concern which already impelled Americans to search for knowledge, it was provided by a sense of cultural inferiority to Europe. When Bostonians attempted to organize a scientific library for the city in 1826, they argued that a national talent for "the quick invention and skillfull application of practical principles in the arts" made it particularly humiliating and frustrating to look abroad any-time one wanted a scientific or technical work.[27] The *American Journal of Education* interested itself in all proposals to advance the study of useful knowledge and the condition of those who would be instructed. And its columns continually confronted readers, in one way or another, with the question: "Shall we suffer Europe to march before us in that career of improvements which we have claimed as peculiarly our own?"[28]

Democratic idealism and a vision of national mission, the challenge of an undeveloped continent, and a sense of ingenious native talent—those were some of the elements behind the mechanics' institute movement in America. In that respect the movement was never isolated, never of concern only to a limited number of skilled artisans concentrated in a few cities. The mechanics' institute expressed in institutional form the hopes and ambitions of most Americans. The early nineteenth century was a period of remarkable social inventiveness in which a wide variety of organizations were created. And the fact that lyceums, libraries, and institutes sprang up almost simultaneously throughout the country demonstrates how well they embodied widely held convictions. To that extent, also, mechanics' institutes in America differed from those abroad.

In Great Britain the formation of mechanics' institutes involved distinct social issues. They were attempts by workingmen, aided by sympathetic political radicals, to create educational agencies which artisans themselves would manage. In Glasgow, and to a lesser extent

[27] *American Journal of Education* 1 (March 1826): 180.
[28] Ibid., 1 (February 1826): 157.

in London, workingmen recognized that, however well meant, support
from the wealthier classes would inevitably bring a conflict in objectives.
Birkbeck shared that understanding, and one of his organizing principles was that institutes should be controlled by the men for whose
benefit they were established. That idea was potentially threatening to
established society, and according to the editor of the *American Journal
of Education*, the rapid growth of mechanics' institutes in Great Britain
was beginning to make "the wealthy and the highly educated feel
uneasy for their rank."[29] In the Old World, mechanics' institutes
reflected a growing sense of class consciousness, which involved an awareness by workingmen that they would always be workingmen.

The opposite was true in America. Some of the mechanics' institutes
in this country incorporated into their constitutions the idea of artisan
control. The Boston Mechanics' Institution, founded in 1827, the Maryland Institute, established in 1825, and the Franklin Institute all had
constitutional provisions that at least three-fourths of the members of
their boards of directors should be practical mechanics or manufacturers. An 1825 Massachusetts legislative committee reporting on the need
for education in "the practical arts and sciences" also worded its message in class terms: "Now it must be observed, that this system of instruction is for the *Common Mechanics*, the *working men*, the *day laborers*;
in the language of Dr. Birkbeck, 'the unwashed artificers.' "[30]

For the great majority of American mechanics' institutes, however,
reform consisted of the elimination of class distinctions rather than
their solidification. The aim of most, certainly including the Franklin
Institute, was to broaden the avenues of opportunity rather than to close
class ranks. When the Maryland Institute was established—in frank
imitation of its Philadelphia neighbor—its educational program was
seen as a means "to establish that equality so particularly recognized
in our Bill of Rights."[31] The same objectives were described in a circular letter sent by Peter A. Browne, corresponding secretary of the
Franklin Institute, to all friends of the mechanic arts. One of the
Institute's major goals, Browne claimed, was "by instructing the labouring part of the community, to elevate them to their proper rank in a
republican society."[32] Behind all these pronouncements was the recognition "that opportunities beyond the expectation of birth lay all about

29 Ibid., 1 (January 1826): 6.
30 Ibid., 1 (January 1826): 157.
31 *The Mechanics' Press* (Baltimore), November 19, 1825.
32 *Letter from the Corresponding Secretary of the Franklin Institute of the State
of Pennsylvania, for the Promotion of the Mechanic Arts*, Philadelphia, December 15,
1824, p. 14.

and could be reached by effort."[33] That faith constituted the most important difference between American mechanics' institutes and their foreign counterparts.

American institutes also differed in their diversity. They varied in their educational approach, in their choice of emphasis within a set of objectives, in their involvement with such current issues as the tariff question or the temperance movement, and in those other ways which were as much a matter of time and location as anything else. In the first wave of interest, scores of institutes were established throughout the country. But in the harsh light of economic reality, few survived for very long. The Paterson, New Jersey Mechanics' Society, for example, never recovered from the burden of paying for the new hall it constructed in the flush of enthusiasm. The Maryland Institute, after a promising early career, burned in 1835 and was not revived until 1847.[34] In New York, the Mechanic and Scientific Institution, probably the first of its kind in the United States, enjoyed an existence of only two or three years before "members of the society quarreled among themselves, which led to the breaking up of the institution."[35] New Yorkers established another mechanics' institute in 1831, which apparently did not survive the decade, and in the late 1840's or early 1850's organized still another, with a history equally obscure.[36]

Since mechanics' institutes, lyceums, apprentices' libraries, and other similar associations shared common goals—and in the same community overlapping membership—they merged easily from one institutional form to another, as local need dictated. Those sorts of permutations also make it difficult to describe a typical organization. Mechanics' institutes in the West and the South were not established until the 1840's and 1850's, and their emphasis tended to be upon exhibitions to encourage industry rather than on education. An announcement of the fourth exhibition of the Kentucky Mechanics' Institute in 1856 suggests that orientation:

Louisville is at this time more fully embued with the spirit of fostering and encouraging MANUFACTURERS AND MECHANICS than ever before. The action of the Chamber of Commerce to make Louisville the Manchester of the West, has met with the sanction and hearty cooperation of all classes of our

[33] Bailyn, *Education in the Forming of American Society*, p. 36.
[34] Bode, *The American Lyceum*, pp. 69–70, 71, 149.
[35] Charles P. Daly, *Origin and History of Institutions for the Promotion of Useful Arts* (Albany: American Institute, 1864), p. 26.
[36] Ibid., p. 30; Bode, *The American Lyceum*, p. 144.

citizens. The SPIRIT OF PROGRESS is aroused. The Manufacturer's, the Merchant's, the Mechanic's and the Artist's motto now is—ONWARD.[37]

Mechanics' institutes also changed over the years. The educational content in almost all of their programs declined seriously in time, just as in the lyceums. For example, the New York Society for Mechanics and Tradesmen, an early exponent of practical education, offered in its lecture series for 1850 talks on "Natural Relations between Animals," "Physiognomy: On the Signs of the Selfish and Social Faculties," "Holland: Its History, Trade, Character, etc.," and "The Constitution and Free Institutions of Our Country."[38] While some institutes were generalized out of existence by such pleasantly innocuous fare, others in time came to center on vocational training. The Ohio Mechanics' Institute, founded in 1828, conducted serious courses in science in its early years under the leadership of John Craig and John Locke, both men of learning. But changing tastes and the rise of public schools ultimately led the Ohio organization to specialize in evening courses toward certificates, among other subjects, in laundry engineering technology.[39]

In contrast with their British counterparts, American mechanics' institutes featured diversity. But all such organizations, certainly in the early years of the movement, were deeply committed to certain common objectives. Those shared aims connected them to powerful themes in American history and gave the institutes their vitality. At the center of all their hopes for the country's material progress and the ultimate proof of the democratic experiment was a new man, the "scientific," or "intelligent mechanic." He was called by those names in an explicit effort to denote a new type of person, and he had several distinguishing characteristics.

The scientific mechanic, in the first place, would be a skilled craftsman, practiced in his understanding of the properties of materials and the use of tools. He would also be an able draftsman—an important talent because drawing was the language of the mechanic arts. He would be inventive. He would possess a flexibility of mind uncharacteristic of a member of an old-world craft guild or of what Americans thought was guildhall thinking. His intellect would not be limited to

[37] *Circular, Fourth Exhibition of the Kentucky Mechanics' Institute, Louisville, September and October, 1856* (Louisville, 1856). By contrast, the Mechanics' Lyceum in Portland, Maine, made the temperance crusade one of its central objectives. "Portland Mechanics' Lyceum," *The Young Mechanic* 1 (September 1832): 137.

[38] Bode, *The American Lyceum*, p. 144.

[39] Edward N. Clopper, "The Ohio Mechanics' Institute: Its 125th Anniversary," *Bulletin of the Historical and Philosophical Society of Ohio* 11 (July 1953): 179–91.

the workshop; he would take part in community affairs, be able to turn
a direct and honest phrase, perhaps even to write a sturdy piece of poetry
now and then. Jefferson's idealized yeoman farmer—the repository of
virtue, fount of wisdom, and bulwark of democracy—had his counterpart in America's workshops in the form of the scientific mechanic.

Of all those qualities which would distinguish the intelligent
mechanic from the workman of the past, the most important was his
knowledge of science. More particularly, it was his understanding of the
scientific principles which lay behind his art. A thorough knowledge of
those basic and unchanging natural laws, when united with skillful
practice, would enable him to perceive new combinations of materials
and new uses for them. If the mechanic understood fundamental principles, he would also be able to recognize incorrect principle or faulty
design, and he would not waste his time and effort on things that would
not work. He would, in fact, be able to escape that cycle which had
limited craftsmen for centuries, that need to rediscover the same truths
every generation. Technical knowledge would become cumulative, and
that meant progress.

Even though a list of all the qualities an intelligent mechanic should
possess was never drawn up, most centers of technical activity had in
their populations men who approached the ideal. In Boston, in the
1820's, Timothy Claxton was one. Claxton was an Englishman who
emigrated to Boston in 1823 because, as he once wrote his brother-in-
law, "an industrious working mechanic need not be in want of the
necessaries of life, in any part of the United States."[40] But even at that
point in his life, Claxton was more than an industrious workman. During his apprenticeship as a whitesmith, and as a journeyman in a large
London machine shop, he had already displayed those qualities which
distinguished the intelligent mechanic. In his spare hours he studied
mathematics and drawing and improved both mind and hands in the
construction of various mechanical contrivances. Then in 1815, when
he was twenty-five, he attended a series of lectures on natural philosophy
and chemistry. That experience, he claimed, suddenly opened his eyes to
the delights of science and its value to the mechanic arts.

Claxton was so much impressed with the lectures that he wrote out
notes for all of them, read further in the subject, and made apparatus
at home so that he could repeat the experiments himself. He attended
other lectures and with the same zeal applied for membership in a
philosophical society. But like Samuel V. Merrick, Claxton was rejected,

---

[40] Claxton, *Memoir*, p. 166. Much of the biographical material was also printed
in another volume by Claxton, *Hints to Mechanics on Self-Education and Mutual
Instruction* (London: Taylor and Watton, 1839).

and he too decided to found an organization of his own. "I reasoned thus," Claxton said. "I am a mechanic; that is the difficulty. Well; suppose the mechanics should be invited to form themselves into a society for mutual improvement."[41] He set forth his ideas in a printed circular, which candidly presented the difficulties facing a workingman who sought additional learning:

We are well aware that there already exist many valuable Societies for the promotion of the Arts, but they do not seem to be adapted to the capacity of a Working Mechanic. We do not mean as to their terms of admission or subscription afterwards, but the recommendation they require seems to be the grand obstacle, combined with the very scientific style of language and the gentleman-like appearance of their Members; so that the class of people that compose those Societies, and the class of people that we should wish to see possessed of the leading principles of the various branches of science, do not seem to have any inclination to associate together. . . .[42]

What Claxton proposed was a society "a few degrees below those already in being," and in 1817 the Mechanical Institution was established in London to disseminate useful knowledge in science. The institution lasted until about 1820 and then faded from existence when Claxton contracted to go to Russia to work on the installation of a new gas lighting plant in St. Petersburg. But he remained convinced of the value of scientific principles for artisans and the need for organizations to provide that knowledge. He had some reason to believe that America would be more hospitable to those ideas, as well as to an ingenious mechanic seeking "the necessaries of life." Claxton did discover a comfortable reception for his altruism; but his career in this country also yields further information on the mechanics' institute movement and the American conception of the intelligent mechanic.

Claxton found employment first in the machine shop of a Metheun, Massachusetts, cotton factory. In his three-year stay at that place, he joined a local literary society and quickly infused it with a new vigor by redirecting its interests to science. When he moved to Boston in 1826, he pursued the same course. As soon as he learned that no mechanics' society existed there, he put articles in a local paper calling for a meeting on the subject, with the result that the Boston Mechanics' Institution was established that year. In the same fashion, Claxton was instrumental in the formation of the Boston Lyceum, when Josiah Holbrook brought his system for mutual instruction in the sciences to the city in

41 Claxton, *Memoir*, p. 34.
42 Ibid., p. 127.

1829, and again in 1831 when he and Holbrook organized the Boston Mechanics' Lyceum. Claxton served as president of the latter from its founding until 1835 and was actively involved in the publication of its magazine, *The Young Mechanic*.[43] Those kinds of community-spirited efforts gave Claxton a measure of public esteem, and certainly it was one of the aims of mechanics' institutes to raise the standing of artisans in society. In his case, the links to self-improvement associations also provided him with his most significant vocation.

By 1830 Claxton already had a reputation for his lectures in science, due in part to the fact that this self-taught mechanic had constructed the philosophical apparatus which he used in his demonstrations. Perhaps for those reasons, Josiah Holbrook visited Claxton in Boston around 1830 in search of simple and inexpensive instruments which could be used to teach science in schools and lyceums. In particular he was attracted to a small air pump and encouraged Claxton to manufacture them for sale. He did so, with a success that exceeded expectation and was soon launched as a manufacturer of a range of science-teaching devices. But the small air pump, which Claxton sold for thirty-seven dollars, remained his most popular item. He made it to fit in a portable case, with an explanatory pamphlet and a printed sheet of illustrations to show how the instrument could be used. It was devoid of ornamentation, uncomplicated, and cheap—an instrument of republican simplicity. Several hundred sets were sold in the United States, and some were also sent abroad.[44] It was the ideal tool for a democratic country where self-improvement in science was an important cultural value.

Claxton appreciated the connotations implicit in the popularity of his air pump, and his own explanation for his success defined perfectly the intelligent mechanic. In addition to the advantages of his position in Boston, he said, "the fact of my mind not having been biased, while young, to the regular routine of instrument makers, turned out to be a favorable circumstance. I had the theory, or principles of several sciences, and an extensive acquaintance with machinery, with something of an inventive mind."[45] Those were the qualities which led one of his admirers to say of Claxton that he was "undoubtedly entitled to the

[43] *The Young Mechanic* was published for two years, from 1832 to 1833, when it was replaced by *The Mechanic. A Journal of the Useful Arts and Sciences*, which survived another two years, until 1835.

[44] The Widener Library at Harvard University has bound into its copy of the *American Annals of Education and Instruction* 1 (May 1835) the illustrated *Catalogue of Philosophical Apparatus Manufactured and Sold by Claxton & Wightman, No. 33 Cornhill, Boston*. Claxton's pump is also described in the *Mechanics Magazine and Journal of Public Internal Improvement* (Boston), September 1830, p. 245.

[45] Claxton, *Memoir*, p. 67.

honor of being one of the most scientific and intelligent mechanics in the city of Boston."[46]

If Claxton was the exemplar of the scientific mechanic in Boston, he and a small group of friends also represent one end in the spectrum of the mechanics' institute movement in America. When Claxton and his associates in self-improvement organized the Boston Mechanics' Institution in 1826, their emphasis was particularly on fitting the instruction to the needs and abilities of workingmen.[47] Within four or five years, however, the institution was reduced to a single course of lectures and was then forced to suspend them when income from ticket sales failed to meet expenses. In Claxton's mind, the cause of the decline was the society's "unsocial character."[48] What he meant was that the managers of the institution were unable to appreciate the capacity of the "humbler classes" for knowledge and their desire for improvement.

Those circumstances led Claxton and a few friends to the conviction that mutual instruction was the workingman's best hope, and in 1831 they established the Boston Mechanics' Lyceum. Its major aim was to involve the mechanic himself in the educational process. Exercises conducted by the members were held every week to give instruction in scientific principles and training in composition, public speaking, and debate. The topic for each meeting was assigned in advance. For instance, in the first term of operation the discussion at one meeting centered on such classical mechanical topics as the lever and balance, wheel and axle, pulley, inclined plane, wedge, and screw. Following the discussion, a member read an essay on the "Rise and progress of Mechanics' Institutions."[49] Armed with the belief that workingmen had a right to broad knowledge, the Boston Mechanics' Lyceum designed an alternating program of technical and nontechnical exercises. The members were their own teachers in an enterprise which distilled mutual instruction to its purest form.

For a time Claxton and his colleagues represented one type of institution which emerged from the American mechanics' institute movement. And they defined for themselves the opposite end of the spectrum when they said: "We do not expect to be able to rival the Franklin Institute of Philadelphia."[50] The Franklin Institute had that kind of reputation very early in its history. Superficially there seemed little to distinguish it from other mechanics' institutes established at the same

46 Amasa Walker, as quoted in Claxton, *Memoir*, p. 102.
47 *American Journal of Education* 2 (January 1827): 58.
48 Claxton, *Memoir*, pp. 83–85.
49 *The Young Mechanic* 1 (August 1832): 124.
50 *Circular, Mechanic Fund Association* (Boston, 1834), p. 3.

time. Their objectives were basically the same, the means employed quite similar, and the rhetoric used to express their hopes almost identical. The Philadelphia organization was equally a product of that widespread interest in science current both in Europe and America, equally infused by the spirit of reform which stimulated other societies. It drew some inspiration from British example, although as with most other American institutions of the same sort, it rested on long-established native traditions and values. And yet, only two years after its founding, a knowledgeable observer claimed that it was "entitled to a distinguished place" among the mechanics' institutes of the country.[51] From the very beginning, the Franklin Institute seemed to be different.

[51] *American Journal of Education* 1 (December 1826): 758.

NOBLE AMBITIONS

In the minds of its founders, the Franklin Institute was built on noble ambitions. Consequently, when they gave their ideas visual form, they aimed at elevated expression. The neoclassical architecture of their hall was calculated to suggest strength and simplicity. Membership certificates were graced with sturdy cherubs demonstrating basic mechanical principles, or in a later design, with philosopher mechanics symbolically linking the wisdom of ages past to the art and industry of modern progress. And overlooking all the Institute's efforts was the benign spirit of Franklin.

If the designs spoke to the Institute's aspirations, they also reflected something of the men who employed them. The organization was established to provide education for artisans, but those who directed its programs were literate men of standing and reputation in the community. William H. Keating was an academic who had gone abroad for advanced training in science. Peter A. Browne was a prominent attorney, active in civic affairs. James Ronaldson was distinguished for his benevolences among the poor. Both Samuel V. Merrick and John C. Cresson enjoyed from birth the advantages of social position and financial security.

At least in visual form, the early symbols survived into the twentieth century. But by the 1920's its early leaders had themselves become part of an idealized backdrop.

Hall of the Franklin Institute, c. 1826.

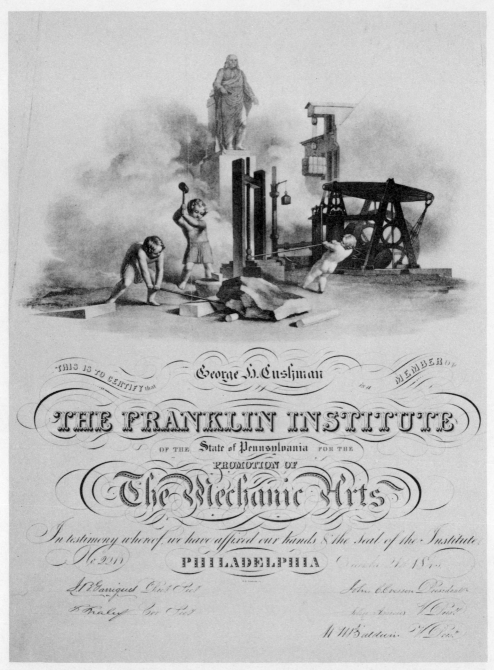

Membership certificate, 1845 (courtesy of the Franklin Institute).

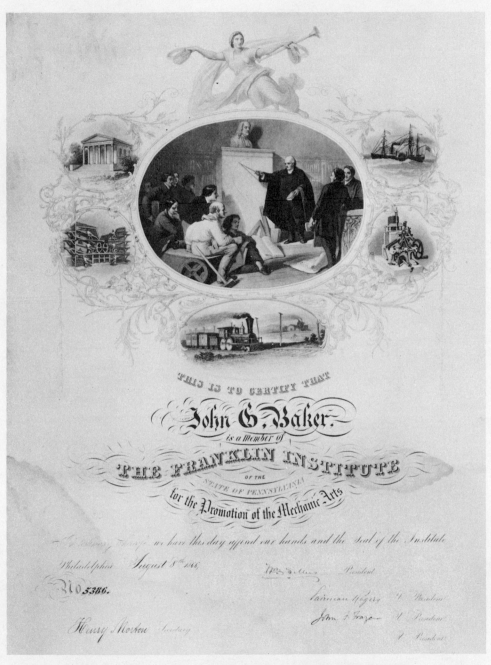

Membership certificate, 1866 (courtesy of the Franklin Institute).

Library of the Franklin Institute, Seventh Street building, c. 1920 (courtesy of the Franklin Institute).

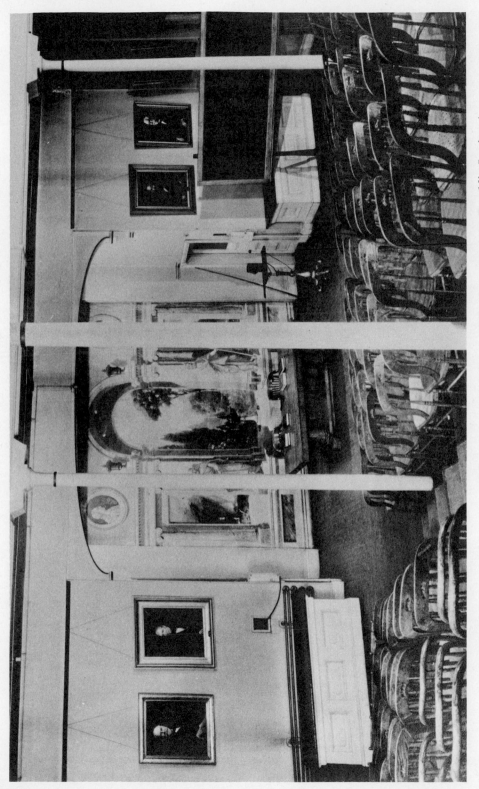

Lecture hall of the Franklin Institute, Seventh Street building, c. 1920 (courtesy of the Franklin Institute).

Top left, James Ronaldson, 1770–1841 (courtesy of the Free Library of Philadelphia); *right*, Peter A. Browne, 1782–1860 (courtesy of the Historical Society of Pennsylvania); *bottom*, Lecture admission tickets for 1826 and 1855–56, respectively (courtesy of the Franklin Institute).

Top left, Samuel V. Merrick, 1801–70 (courtesy of the Franklin Institute); *right*, John C. Cresson, 1806–76 (courtesy of the Free Library of Philadelphia); *bottom left*, William H. Keating, 1799–1840 (courtesy of the Franklin Institute); *right*, William Hamilton, actuary of the Institute 1828–71 (courtesy of the Franklin Institute).

II

"FOR THE PROMOTION OF THE MECHANIC ARTS": THE FOUNDING OF THE FRANKLIN INSTITUTE

Our community was ripe for this great undertaking.

Board of Managers, First Annual Report, 1825

It is often difficult to understand why some institutions succeed where others fail. The dynamics of voluntary organizations are complicated by timing, leadership, finance, and the degree to which public sympathy is stirred on their behalf. In the early nineteenth century, when Americans were so self-consciously looking for a formula to guide them to the realization of their ambitions, they named dozens of societies after Benjamin Franklin, hoping the magic of his name would prove their intentions worthy of support. But why did the mechanics' institute in Philadelphia, which honored Franklin, so suddenly enjoy prominence while those in other places languished?

One of the reasons might have been the city's mechanic community itself. From the time of Franklin and Rittenhouse, Philadelphia had been distinguished by its ingenious artisans. That reputation gained in lustre by the technical accomplishments of men like Oliver Evans and Jacob Perkins and by such engineering feats as the steam-powered waterworks. Descriptions of the city's mechanics portray them as an intelligent, amiable, and skillful group who relished the competitiveness of inquiry and experimented with enthusiasm. George Escol Sellers remembered vividly the excitement of his boyhood days in Philadelphia machine shops, the craftsmanship of Isaiah Lukens, William Mason, Matthias Baldwin, and Rufus Tyler, and the education open there to an inquisitive young man.[1]

[1] See Eugene S. Ferguson, ed., *Early Engineering Reminiscences [1815–40] of George Escol Sellers* (Washington, D.C.: Smithsonian Institution, 1965), for an excellent description of Philadelphia's mechanic community. An equally good picture of the city's ingenious men is given in Carl Bridenbaugh and Jessica Bridenbaugh, *Rebels and Gentlemen: Philadelphia in the Age of Franklin* (New York: Oxford University Press, 1965).

All of those men later played an active part in the affairs of the Franklin Institute, and one might expect they were instrumental in its beginnings. But they were not. In fact, the mechanic community was at first largely unmoved by the idea. Their indifference was revealed in a letter Samuel V. Merrick wrote describing his earliest efforts to establish the organization. In the fall of 1823, determined to begin an association of wider usefulness than the one which had rejected him, Merrick called a meeting at the hall of the American Philosophical Society of "some fifteen or twenty gentlemen" that he thought might be interested in a society of mutual improvement in science and the mechanic arts. None of them appeared on the night of the meeting; but after further conversation with some of them, Merrick scheduled another gathering, which met with the same lack of success. In still more discussion with William Kneass, a local engraver and die-sinker at the U.S. Mint, to whom he had confided his original plan, Merrick was acquainted with the earlier but similar efforts of William H. Keating, professor of mineralogy and chemistry at the University of Pennsylvania.

Reputedly "full of zeal for the diffusion of science applied to agriculture and the mechanic arts," Keating had been the secretary at several meetings held in 1822 to establish a school for scientific instruction. Keating's group had apparently tried to obtain a charity school bequest from the will of Christopher Ludwig, since the recent establishment of a public school system had obviated the need for charity schools. When that attempt failed, however, the movement died. It also appears that the first efforts of both Keating and Merrick suffered from local jealousies within the mechanic community. Two of the city's prominent architects were engaged in a personal feud, and any idea supported by the coterie of one drew the opposition of the other's friends.[2] That factionalism was apparently an inhibiting factor to the organization of any new society.

Once Keating and Merrick were united, however, their scheme gained shape and momentum. Merrick had family connections which

[2] *Commemorative Exercises at the Fiftieth Anniversary of the Franklin Institute of the State of Pennsylvania for the Promotion of the Mechanic Arts* (Philadelphia: The Franklin Institute, 1874), pp. 40–41. A somewhat different story is told in "Observations on the Rise and Progress of the Franklin Institute," *The Franklin Journal and American Mechanics' Magazine* 1 (February 1826): 66–71: In November 1822, Keating's group attempted to link their project with "a respectable institution, already in full operation in this city." Negotiations to that effect were conducted throughout the winter, but to no avail. "It was at last, found that no assistance could be expected from the old institution, many of whose members entertained serious doubts as to the legality, or even expediency, of any measures tending to change their accustomed objects of support."

were potentially valuable to their plan. One of his uncles, Benjamin Vaughan, was a man of historical importance.[3] He had studied with Joseph Priestley, was a close friend of Benjamin Franklin, and had played a major diplomatic role during the American Revolution. Another uncle, the London merchant Petty Vaughan, acted on behalf of the American Philosophical Society in that city and served as a valuable contact for many American men of science.[4] And in Philadelphia still another uncle, the wine merchant John Vaughan, was a central figure in the affairs of the American Philosophical Society and in the city's intellectual and cultural circles.[5]

If Merrick's family position gave their plans some possible standing, Keating brought focus to the alliance. He had studied chemistry at the University of Pennsylvania with Robert Hare and then spent three years in the technical schools of Great Britain and Europe studying chemistry, geology, mineralogy, and mining engineering. When he returned to Philadelphia in 1819, Keating had direct knowledge of European institutions teaching the practical applications of science. He was also familiar with Anderson's Institution in Glasgow and with the newly-formed New-York Mechanic and Scientific Institution.[6] Merrick and Keating met to discuss their mutual interests, and after some consideration of European precedents, they outlined a program for their proposed asso-

[3] *Dictionary of American Biography* (New York: Charles Scribner's Sons, 1943).

[4] Petty Vaughan acted as London agent for both the American Philosophical Society and the Franklin Institute. He collected foreign scientific and technical periodicals in exchange for the *Journal of the Franklin Institute*, bought books, forwarded parcels, and in a variety of other ways connected American institutions with their counterparts in Europe. For documentation of those activities, see the Petty Vaughan Letters, Franklin Institute Archives.

[5] John Vaughan, for years the secretary and librarian of the American Philosophical Society, was widely known for "his rare benevolence and kindness of heart." Daniel R. Goodwin, "Obituary Notice of Samuel Vaughan Merrick, Esq.," American Philosophical Society *Proceedings* 11 (1869–70): 586. Generosity may have been his undoing. Samuel Gross, who lived in the same boardinghouse, remembered him as "a broken-down merchant" as well as a kindly man. Samuel W. Gross and A. Haller Gross, eds., *Autobiography of Samuel D. Gross, M.D., with Reminiscences of his Times and Contemporaries*, 2 vols. (Philadelphia: W. B. Saunders, 1893), vol. 1, p. 44. See also Thomas Coulson, "Some Prominent Members of the Franklin Institute 1. Samuel Vaughan Merrick, 1801–1870," *Journal of the Franklin Institute* 258 (November 1954): 335–46.

[6] The *Charter, Constitution, and By-Laws of the New-York Mechanic and Scientific Institution* in the Franklin Institute's archives, for instance, was Keating's own copy. Keating's interest in the advancement of American technology is also suggested by a pamphlet he published, *Considerations upon the Art of Mining, to which are added, Reflections on its Actual State in Europe, and the Advantages which would result from an Introduction of this Art into the United States* (Philadelphia: M. Carey and Sons, 1821).

ciation, gave it a name, and scheduled a meeting to "give an official start to the machine."[7]

That meeting was held at the American Philosophical Society on December 9, 1823. According to the minutes, five men attended: Merrick; Thomas Fletcher, a silversmith and jeweler; Matthias W. Baldwin and David H. Mason, both of whom were partners in a firm which manufactured engravers' and bookbinders' tools; and Oren Colton, a local shuttlemaker. Fletcher was named chairmen of the meeting and Merrick secretary. Two resolutions were passed: first, to form a "Society for the Promotion of the Mechanic Arts"; and second, to appoint a committee to draft a constitution, call a subsequent meeting, and invite the attendance of those interested in the formation of such an institution.[8] Merrick, Keating, and Fletcher were appointed to the committee, along with M. R. Wickham, an arms manufacturer; Samuel R. Wood, a prominent Quaker tanner; James J. Rush, of Rush & Muhlenburg, successors of Oliver Evans's Mars Works, the home of high-pressure steam engines in America; and James Ronaldson, type-founder, cotton manufacturer, and a man already well known for his benefactions among the needy. Merrick and Wood were appointed a subcommittee to draw up a constitution, although Merrick recalled that he wrote it himself, since Wood was still convinced that the effort would not succeed.[9]

With that threat still over their heads, Merrick and his small group scheduled a public meeting for February 5, 1824, to test the city's response. At that point, some of the ingredients for success had already been incorporated into the plan. Perhaps most important was that the projectors themselves reflected a broad span of interests. Fletcher, Wood, and Ronaldson were well-established, substantial businessmen; Baldwin, Mason, and Rush were intelligent mechanics whose work was marked by technical sophistication; Keating and Merrick provided links to the University of Pennsylvania and the American Philosophical Society. Further to insure wide appeal and to avoid any imputation of faction or exclusiveness, the group printed over a thousand circulars to describe the purpose of the meeting, and they were given the widest possible distribution. Finally, their proposal was advertised in the city's newspapers:

[7] *Commemorative Exercises at the Fiftieth Anniversary of the Franklin Institute,* p. 41.

[8] Minutes of a meeting "held at the Philosophical Hall for the purpose of forming a Society for the promotion of the Mechanic Arts," Minutes of the Board of Managers, December 9, 1823, Franklin Institute Archives.

[9] *Commemorative Exercises at the Fiftieth Anniversary of the Franklin Institute,* p. 41.

A Meeting of Mechanics, Manufacturers, and persons friendly to the Mechanical Arts, will be held at the County Court House. . . . The object of the meeting is to consider the expediency of forming an Institute for the benefit of Mechanics, on the plan of similar institutions in all the manufacturing cities of Europe, and of that recently established in New York.[10]

Contrary to previous efforts and at least some expectations, the meeting was a grand success. By connecting their plans with well-accepted precedents and by a large-scale publicity campaign designed to promote a spirit of openness, Keating, Merrick, and their coworkers achieved the public support which they sought. Equally important for the health of their proposal, it came from some of the city's most prominent industrial and intellectual figures, as well as from her artisans. "The meeting," the *National Gazette* later announced, "was one of the most numerous and most respectable ever seen in this city."[11] James Ronaldson was elected chairman and Merrick secretary. Ronaldson apprised the meeting of the reasons it had been convened. He was followed by Peter A. Browne, a prominent member of the Philadelphia bar, who delivered "a short and eloquent address" in support of the association. If not already converted, Browne's speech apparently quelled any lingering doubts in his listeners, for the resolutions to establish a society were unanimously adopted.

The new institution's aims were simply stated. Its purpose was to promote the useful arts by diffusing a knowledge of mechanical science at little cost to the membership. That object would be carried out by a program of popular lectures, the formation of a cabinet of models and a library, and by the awarding of prizes for useful improvements in the arts.[12] In time both the Institute's goals and the means to achieve them would change, but at the beginning the program was simple and clear.

Merrick's constitution was presented and, in essence, adopted. With the nomination of another committee to prepare for an election of officers, and with membership provisions basically settled, the evening's business was completed. But in a sense these were details. The assembly was much more in the nature of a rally. All of the groundwork had been done beforehand; what was needed was a proper display of spirit,

10 *National Gazette and Literary Register*, February 2, 1824.

11 Ibid., February 6, 1824.

12 Minutes of the Board of Managers, February 5, 1824. Philadelphia newspaper editors cast the essential purpose of the organization with much the same directness: "A Society under the title of the Franklin Institute, has just been established in this city, which promises to be of considerable usefulness. Its object is to advance the general interests of Manufacturers and Mechanics, by extending a knowledge of mechanical sciences to its members, and others, at a cheap rate" (*The Saturday Evening Post*, February 14, 1824).

the right note for important beginnings. A letter from Nicholas Biddle, president of the United States Bank, set exactly the required tone: "I know of no enterprise, which promises more general utility than this effort to connect the theory with the exercise of these [mechanical] arts, and to blend science with practical skill."[13] There were countries, Biddle noted, in which knowledge was denied certain classes of citizens in order that a few might retain control of the many. But in America, through the availability of knowledge, "the avenues of power and distinction" were open to all. They stood in the shadow of Franklin, Biddle advised the founders of the new society, and they could have picked no better example. On that note, the Franklin Institute of the State of Pennsylvania, for the Promotion of the Mechanic Arts was launched.

There were still organizational details to be worked out. A membership campaign was begun, officers for the ensuing year were elected, regulations were adopted for the conduct of meetings of the Board of Managers, and a committee was appointed to draft a memorial to the state legislature for a corporate charter. Almost with each step, however, the scope of the Institute's interests broadened. As adopted on February 5, the constitution added the examination of new inventions as one of the Institute's main activities, along with lectures, collections, and prize awards. In its subsequent memorial to the legislature, natural history collections were added to those of books, models, and minerals, and the whole was called a museum. It was further suggested in the memorial that another of the organization's interests was the establishment of an "experimental Work-Shop and Laboratory," where direct experience would supplement the instruction of the lecture hall.[14] If the memorial represents a fair statement of the aspirations of the Institute's leadership, a subtle change was in process. The organization was already becoming something more than the plan originally sketched by Merrick and Keating.

Their initial aims had been twofold. The first was to provide instruction to workingmen in the principles of science. If that kind of knowledge were made easily available, artisans could rise to their proper place in a democratic society, and the second aim would be secured. As in Boston, that message was attractive to many Philadelphians. But if confined to those objectives, the program's primary appeal would have been limited to mechanics seeking self-improvement. Expansion of the program opened the way to wider interests. The plan for an experi-

13 Minutes of the Board of Managers, February 5, 1824.

14 The Memorial of the Officers and Board of Managers of the Franklin Institute of Pennsylvania for the Promotion of the Mechanic Arts, 26th February, 1824, Franklin Institute Archives.

mental workshop and laboratory, and for the investigation of new inventions, interjected the idea of "systematic investigation in science," a notion which implied the creation of knowledge, as well as its diffusion.[15] In their memorial to the legislature, the Institute's founders also argued that research would bring new applications of science and thus new wealth. That prospect linked the Institute to all those interested in Pennsylvania's progress and prosperity and in the larger issue of internal improvement.

Merrick and Keating had enlisted in their cause men whose interests went beyond the first ideas for the institution. It had originally been conceived as an aid to workingmen, but the public meeting was dominated by a banker and a lawyer. Nor would its first officers easily be described as artisans. James Ronaldson was chosen president. While he played a more modest role in the active direction of the Institute than subsequent presidents, Ronaldson was a man of wide concerns and strong conviction. A Scotsman who had made a comfortable fortune in manufacturing, he was a zealous advocate of education and of the idea that industrial advance was ultimately the best solution to poverty.[16] Matthew Carey, who was elected vice-president and served as chairman of the Board of Managers until 1826, had already made a national career of publicizing the advancement and the protection of American industry. He had been active in the formation of the National Institution for the Promotion of Industry in 1820, and he was one of the founders of the Pennsylvania Society for the Promotion of Internal Improvements in 1824.[17]

William Strickland, an architect and engineer, was elected recording secretary of the Institute and secretary of the Board of Managers. He was also closely connected with the Pennsylvania Society for the Promo-

---

[15] Ibid.

[16] James Ronaldson (1770–1841) was born near Edinburgh and emigrated to the United States in 1791. He established type-founding as an industry in America and engaged in other industrial activity as well. Like his friend and fellow Scotsman William Maclure, patron of the Academy of Natural Sciences in Philadelphia, Ronaldson used his wealth in a number of philanthropic enterprises on behalf of the poor, from soup kitchens to burial societies. The Vaux Papers and Poinsett Papers at the Historical Society of Pennsylvania contain Ronaldson letters which indicate the range of his social and political concerns. For biographical sketches, see Henry Simpson, *The Lives of Eminent Philadelphians, Now Deceased* (Philadelphia: William Brotherhead, 1859), p. 849; and Persifor Frazer, "The Franklin Institute: Its Services and Deserts," *Journal of the Franklin Institute* 165 (April, 1908): 251.

[17] Matthew Carey (1760–1839) emigrated to America from Ireland and established himself in Philadelphia as a publisher and editor. He was a persistent and zealous advocate of internal improvements and support for domestic manufactures. *Dictionary of American Biography*; Earl L. Bradsher, *Matthew Carey: Editor, Author and Publisher* (New York: Columbia University Press, 1912).

tion of Internal Improvements and was sent abroad by that group in
1826 to secure information on European technical advance.[18] Both
Carey and Strickland were on the committee assigned to draft the
memorial to the legislature.

The corresponding secretary, Peter A. Browne, would have to be
described as something more than a prominent local attorney. He was
avidly interested in geology and mineralogy, especially as an aid to the
exploitation of Pennsylvania's natural resources. He had as well an
amateur talent in science and some literary aspirations.[19] Browne was
an enthusiast of the kind that are attracted to new organizations, and
his zeal helped to shape the Institute's development. While the influence of men like Carey, Strickland, and Browne was more clearly
revealed in succeeding years, one already senses their touch in the
argument that an act of incorporation by the Commonwealth would
"give a greater development to the resources, powers, and skill of her
manufacturers and mechanics . . . and by thus leading to important
discoveries and improvements, augment the wealth and prosperity of
the State."[20] Almost from the outset, those men and their concerns
gave the Franklin Institute an ambitious character.

Organizations are also modified by the means they employ; and to
some extent the Institute's scope was widened simply by the steps taken
to implement its original goals. Concrete action gave the society a dimension which preliminary discussions lacked. By the end of February most
of the details to set the Institute in motion had been settled. Early in
March the first action on a program was taken. A Committee on Lectures, consisting of Browne, Carey, Strickland, and Merrick, was
appointed to develop a course of volunteer lectures. Browne was
appointed chairman, and on March 5, he wrote Robert M. Patterson,
professor of natural philosophy at the University of Pennsylvania: "The
managers of the Franklin Institute deem it essential to the prosperity of
the Society that lectures should, without delay, be delivered before the
Society." Lacking funds, however, the organization was forced to appeal
to the "patriotism and public spirit" of their members, and in that

18 The best source of biographical information on Strickland is Agnes Addison
Gilchrist, *William Strickland, Architect and Engineer, 1788–1854* (Philadelphia: University of Pennsylvania Press, 1950).

19 There is miscellaneous information on Browne in the Historical Society of
Pennsylvania and the Academy of Natural Sciences, as well as in the archives of the
Franklin Institute. Much of it has been ably summarized in William Stanton, *The
Leopard's Spots: Scientific Attitudes toward Race in America, 1815–59* (Chicago:
University of Chicago Press, 1966), pp. 149–54.

20 The Memorial of the Officers and Board of Managers of the Franklin Institute
. . . 26th February, 1824.

vein Browne asked if Patterson would give the introductory lecture "on some popular topic."[21]

Volunteer lectures on unconnected subjects continued throughout the spring of 1824. As designed, the lectures were varied in content; their function was to stimulate interest in the Institute. Keating's two lectures were entitled "Water" and "Time," titles well calculated to excite a sense of the sublime. Patterson spoke on perpetual motion, a favorite topic in mechanics' institutes because it so clearly juxtaposed chimera and science. Strickland, whose design for the second Bank of the United States had produced one of the city's most elegant neoclassic structures, gave a talk on architecture. Peter Browne provided a lecture on patent rights, another subject popular among mechanics with secret hopes for inventions of their own. And a lecture on bookkeeping by John Hamer, a local teacher, completed the series.[22] A conscious effort was also made to attract youth. On Browne's initiative, the committee distributed free tickets among the city's schools and urged the Board of Managers to allow members the privilege of bringing their sons, apprenices, or journeymen to the lectures.[23]

At the conclusion of the season, in June, the committee reported to the Board its observations and recommendations. In the committee's opinion, the lectures had been a great success and "completely answered" the Institute's objectives. In particular, they outlined three significant accomplishments: (1) the public's interest in the Institute had been increased, as evidenced by the number who joined the society after each lecture; (2) a "taste for scientific knowledge" had been stimulated in the mechanic community; and (3) the institution's strength, importance, and usefulness had developed to a point which "the most timid no longer pretend to deny."[24]

The first months were a time, as Peter Browne once said, of "testing the utility of the Institution."[25] It had to be determined whether the organization's aims and program would stimulate public interest. At issue were questions material and nonmaterial. Clearly the association needed financial support if it was to maintain operation. But the level of operation was determined in some measure by the extent to which the program received public approval. The series of volunteer lectures

[21] Report of the Committee on Lectures, [April 1824], Franklin Institute Archives. See the *Dictionary of American Biography* for a biographical sketch of Patterson.

[22] Report of the Committee on Lectures, June 3, 1824.

[23] Ibid.; Minutes of the Board of Managers, May 6, 1824.

[24] Report of the Committee on Lectures, June 3, 1824.

[25] *Letter from the Corresponding Secretary of the Franklin Institution of the State of Pennsylvania, for the Promotion of the Mechanic Arts*, Philadelphia, December 15, 1824.

provided both the enthusiasm and the funds needed. Crowds filled the hall each evening, and in increasing numbers they became members, paying three dollars a year in dues. The effect, as the Committee on Lectures noted, was enough to convince even the most sceptical of the organization's strength. As a result, a broader program of activities began to take shape by late spring 1824.

First to feel the change was the lecture system itself. Notwithstanding its popular success, the series of volunteer lectures was an educational program with distinct limitations. The committee had experienced considerable difficulty in finding speakers and in maintaining a schedule of lectures.[26] Furthermore, the series had a provisional quality. It was begun primarily to capitalize on the interest aroused by the Institute's inaugural meeting. If there were no more far-reaching considerations for a lecture program when the series was begun, there were by the time the committee made its report in June 1824. After the "most mature reflection" upon a matter of "superior moment," the committee recommended to the Board of Managers the development of a permanent course of lectures for the fall season. No less significantly, they proposed also that the Institute establish four professorships—in natural philosophy, in chemistry and mineralogy as connected with the arts and manufactures, in architecture and civil engineering, and in mechanics. In its report, the committee claimed that the appointments and regular lectures would "convince the world that we are serious and ardent in our endeavours."[27]

In very strong terms the Committee on Lectures also argued that a lecture series demanded suitable models as illustrative devices. It had been necessary to borrow apparatus to demonstrate Patterson's lecture on perpetual motion. A jurisdictional dispute with the Committee on Models further aggravated the problem. "Without models," the Committee reported, "it is impossible to get *some* gentlemen to lecture," and they made the acquisition of equipment for their use an absolute prerequisite for a regular system of lectures. The problem was that authority to purchase models rested with the Committee on Models, whereas it was the Committee on Lectures that needed them. On the strength of

---

[26] Report of the Committee on Lectures, June 3, 1824. Filling the schedule of volunteer lectures continued to be a problem. In the fall of 1824, the committee asked James Ronaldson to open the lecture season with a talk on "the rise, progress and future prospects" of the Institute. After a week's delay in responding, Ronaldson declined. Matthew Carey was then approached for the job. He accepted, and notice of the lecture was published in local newspapers. Then at the last moment, Carey informed the committee that he would be unable to deliver the lecture. Report of the Committee on Lectures, November 1824.

[27] Report of the Committee on Lectures, June 3, 1824.

their report, the Board appropriated three hundred dollars for that purpose. The Board also accepted the committee's proposal for a regular schedule of lectures, and the four recommended professorships were established. Robert M. Patterson was appointed professor of natural philosophy; Keating was named professor of chemistry and mineralogy; and Strickland was made professor of architecture.[28] The decision was critical for the Institute and sharply distinguished it from most other mechanics' societies. Regular lecture courses in those subjects closest to the mechanic arts would be taught by a paid faculty of academicians. Incidental lectures would still be offered for their popular appeal, but the courses in science were not left to chance. At a time when similar associations depended largely upon mutual instruction, Browne and his committee directed the Institute toward a formal approach to education, with more rigid control over both quality and content.

Once lecture courses were established, the Institute began a search for more permanent quarters. The University of Pennsylvania had allowed the Institute to use a room in the old Academy building on Fourth Street for its volunteer lectures; but the room, like the first lectures, was an interim solution. When the Board of Managers adopted the proposals of the Committee on Lectures, it also instructed the committee to apply to the city councils for a room in the State House. That appeal failed, however, and the committee was forced to look elsewhere. During the spring, the Board of Managers had regularly held their meetings in Carpenters' Hall, where both the Music Fund Society and the Apprentices' Library rented rooms. When the bid for space in the State House proved unsuccessful, the Board of Managers rather naturally settled on Carpenters' Hall as an alternative. The Committee on Lectures was authorized to conduct the negotiations and was given a free hand financially. In October they reported that the entire hall had been rented for five hundred dollars a year.[29] By continuing to sublet the second floor to its present occupants, the committee expected that the Institute's cost could be reduced by half, with the hope of a further reduction by other rentals. Work was then begun on the first floor to fit up a lecture hall and a room for meetings of the Board of Managers.

During that first year, when every step to implement the Institute's program seemed to generate new enthusiasm, the prospect of regular housing determined the Board of Managers to establish a mechanical drawing school under the Institute's auspices. Skill in drawing, as Timothy Claxton had pointed out, was a considerable asset to technical men; it was an aid to the powers of observation and a pleasant and

28 Ibid.
29 Minutes of the Board of Managers, October 21, 1825.

rational amusement.[30] But drafting also gave artisans the ability to express their ideas. In contrast to the image of the illiterate workman of the past, clarity and precision of expression was an important adjunct to rational technology and to the training of intelligent mechanics. The Committee on Lectures, with Peter Browne as chairman, was directed to work out the details for a school, and in October Browne presented a plan which the Board adopted. Open to members, their sons, and apprentices, the school would meet two evenings a week during the lecture season. Students would pay five dollars each, half of which would go to the professor and half to the Institute, which provided a classroom, heat, and lighting. Pupils of the school were entitled to attend the Institute's evening lectures at no extra charge. John Haviland, a local architect, was appointed professor of drawing, and the school was put into operation.[31]

Classes in the drawing school met two evenings a week. The school was an immediate success; by the end of the year upwards of fifty pupils were enrolled, and the Board of Managers could comfortably remark in its annual report:

The great importance of the art of Drawing to Mechanics and Artizans of all classes, is so generally felt, and has been so universally acknowledged, that your Board do not conceive it necessary to insist upon it here.[32]

Also in October, the Institute sponsored its first exhibition of products of American industry. The Institute's founders had always planned to offer awards for "useful improvements in the arts," perhaps in imitation of the New York Mechanic and Scientific Institution or the Society of Arts in England.[33] The New York association had hoped to hold

[30] Claxton, *Memoir of a Mechanic, Being a Sketch of the Life of Timothy Claxton, Written by Himself, Together with Miscellaneous Papers* (Boston: George W. Light, 1839), p. 26.

[31] Minutes of the Board of Managers, October 21, 1825.

[32] *First Annual Report of the Proceedings of the Franklin Institute of the State of Pennsylvania, for the Promotion of the Mechanic Arts* (Philadelphia: J. Harding, 1825), p. 52.

[33] The Society for the Encouragement of Arts, Manufactures, and Commerce, later called the Royal Society of Arts, was established in 1754, primarily to stimulate ingenuity through prize awards. For its history, see D. Hudson and K. W. Luckhurst, *The Royal Society of Arts 1754–1954* (London: Murray, 1954). Many subsequent organizations adopted the same idea. The founders of the New York Mechanic and Scientific Institution noted in a statement of their objectives: "The Managers also cherish the hope, that through the liberal support which this Institution will receive from an enlightened public, it will be in their power to afford a direct and positive encouragement to the arts, commerce and agriculture, by offering premiums for ingenious inventions, and by furnishing the means of periodical exhibitions of the finest productions of the workshop and manufactory. In this part of their duty it will

exhibitions of American industrial products, and the Board of the Franklin Institute began to think along those same lines in the spring of 1824. On April 1, a Committee on Premiums and Exhibitions was appointed, and the Board recommended "an Annual Exhibition for the products of National industry" to coincide with the quarterly meeting in October.[34]

Nothing was immediately done to implement the resolution. The committee reported in mid-April that it was inexpedient then to present any plan for awards or for an exhibition and that they would delay in doing so until "the circumstances of the Institute would warrant it."[35] By June, however, the same tide of optimism which moved the Board to establish permanent lectures also pushed them into a reconsideration of an exhibition. The Committee on Premiums and Exhibitions was requested to prepare an exhibition plan, which was presented and adopted late in June. Included in the committee's report were a schedule of premiums to be offered, an exhibition plan, and a circular addressed to manufacturers and mechanics throughout the union.[36] The affair was scheduled for fall, and as the date drew near, the Board advertised in the city's newspapers that their "first Annual Exhibition of the products of American Industry" would be held in Carpenters' Hall on October 18, 19, and 20.[37]

From the earliest consideration of the subject, the Institute's exhibition had a dual purpose. As with the volunteer lectures, it was designed to extend the society's reputation, increase the zeal of its members, and swell the membership roll.[38] The exhibition also aimed to encourage American manufactures. Prizes had the avowed function of stimulating a "justifiable rivalry" among manufacturers in the production of better goods at lower prices. But the exhibition also meant to encourage the consumption of domestic products. The Institute's purpose was to be that of middleman—to provide producers and consumers an opportunity "of becoming acquainted with one another."[39] The role was never seen in passive terms, however. The Institute's Board of Managers consciously sought "to excite a gratifying sense of pride in the

---

be their desire to imitate, with certain modifications, the societies of London and Paris for the encouragement of the arts . . ." (*Charter, Constitution, and By-Laws of the New-York Mechanic and Scientific Institution* [New York: New York Mechanic and Scientific Institution, 1822], pp. 4–5).

[34] Minutes of the Board of Managers, April 1, 1824.

[35] Ibid., April 15, 1824.

[36] Ibid., June 3, 1824.

[37] *National Gazette*, October 11, 1824.

[38] *First Annual Report of the Proceedings of the Franklin Institute*, p. 37.

[39] Ibid.

bosom of every well-wisher to the prosperity of our manufactures."[40] The effect they hoped for was embodied in the comment of a visitor to the exhibition:

We observed several pieces of broad-cloth, of different colours, equal, if not superior, in firmness and fineness of texture, to any we have seen from foreign manufactories, and to us it appears absolutely astonishing that men professing to be governed by patriotic motives, can, for an instant, prefer the products of importation to the more elegant, and, at the same time, less costly articles manufactured in American looms.[41]

Actually, the Institute's first exhibition was only a qualified success. There was not time for the publicity the Board hoped to give it, and as a result, the number of articles submitted and their geographic representation was limited. Nor was there sufficient time to strike the medals for those premiums awarded. But in the managers' minds, the defects in the exhibition stemmed from "inexperience, and from the hurry in which it was got up," not from the soundness of the idea.[42] Their immediate aims had been realized. The exhibition made the public more aware of domestic manufactures, brought in almost a hundred new members, and gained the Institute considerable publicity. "We hope," the *Evening Post* editorialized, "our citizens will do all in their power to further the object of this excellent institution, the benefits of which have already been so sensibly felt."[43] After the exhibition was over, a "splendid dinner" was held to celebrate the event, and before the year was out, plans were already being made for a second exhibition.[44]

40 Ibid.
41 *The Saturday Evening Post*, October 23, 1824.
42 *First Annual Report of the Proceedings of the Franklin Institute*, p. 46.
43 *The Saturday Evening Post*, October 23, 1824.
44 The dinner was reported in *Niles' Weekly Register*, October 30, 1824. Several toasts highlighted the affair. The first, naturally enough, was to the memory of Franklin, "*Drank standing and silent.*" Successive healths were offered to mechanics and manufacturers; to internal improvements—"the surest proofs of a wise government and a prosperous people"; and to the members of the Institute themselves in the form of an elaborate pun delivered by Peter A. Browne: "Our noble selves, viz: Type founders and printers, who are men of *letters*; architects who *build up* the country's fame; chemists who *retort* nothing but kindness; *lists* of taylors whose patriotism is without *measure*; saddlers who do good without *end*; coppersmiths, who are better *still*; engine makers, who erect a *horse power* for the public good; paper makers, who do more if re-*quired*; glaziers, whose *panes* are always to please; a *band* of hatters, who assist to *lower* a *crown*; bakers, the best *bred*, and who keep clear of John *Doe*; brick-makers of the old *stock*, made of *well tempered clay*; carpenters and masons, who have climbed *the ladders* of their professions; painters, who are sober, though *well primed*; coopers, who in new improvements *chime in*; gun-

A concern with the progress of domestic manufactures was less than abstract at the Institute. Many of the men on the Board of Managers were directly involved in industrial pursuits, and promoting the consumption of American manufactures was directly to their advantage. But there were more complex impulses behind the exhibition than self-interest. In part, the display was tied to the larger premise that material advance would justify the American political system. The exhibition also rested on the idea that a show of inventiveness would stimulate more inventiveness. One of the Institute's major goals was to encourage and reward ingenuity, and exhibitions served that purpose. Another means to the same end would be to establish impartial tribunals of technically knowledgeable men, whose function would be to examine all new inventions, to judge their value, and to diffuse that information. The public would thus be warned about worthless devices, or conversely, informed of inventions which showed beneficial promise. By early spring 1824, several such committees were already at work examining devices and improvements submitted to the Institute.[45]

Access to patents already granted was fundamental to committee investigations. The corresponding secretary therefore wrote William Thornton, superintendent of the Patent Office in Washington, requesting patent specifications to aid the examining committees in their work. "As our object is intimately connected with the public good," Browne noted, "we have flattered ourselves that our infant institution whose funds are yet low, will be liberally treated."[46] But that appeal for charity fell on deaf ears. Thornton replied that he felt "in honor bound to protect the Inventors" against possible secret use of their patents, and he refused to supply any specifications unless expired or unless the consent of the patentee had previously been obtained.[47] His refusal resulted in an argument between the Institute and the Patent Office which stretched over the next year and a half.

At least three issues were at stake. First, the availability of current patents was essential if the Institute was to function at all effectively in

---

makers, who at science *never go off half cocked*; joiners, who are *glued* to our cause; weavers, who in American manufactures *loom large*; smiths, whose forgeries would pass at the mint; dyers of all colours *alive* at their work; doctors, who *attend gratis* to their public duties; lawyers, who *try* to *suit* our *cause*; and *awl* the cordwainers, who come out best at the *last. Nine cheers.*"

[45] Investigations were conducted by ad hoc committees for the first year, but in June 1825, a Board of Examiners was made responsible for that task. Minutes of the Board of Managers, June 2, 1825.

[46] Peter A. Browne to William Thornton, March 6, 1824, Letterbook, Corresponding Secretary, 1824–1826, Franklin Institute Archives (cited hereafter simply as Letterbook).

[47] William Thornton to Peter A. Browne, March 10, 1824, Letterbook.

examining new inventions and diffusing the results of their investigations. Second, as an attorney, Browne was convinced that Thornton's stand was legally untenable. Finally, Thornton's position violated the principle that open channels of knowledge were vital to a democracy. But the desire "to avoid entangling the Institute in the first year of its existence, in a controversy with an officer of the federal government" led Browne and the Board to drop the issue temporarily.[48]

In June 1824, Browne obtained evidence that copies of patents had in fact been made available, both to private citizens and to the editor of a Washington journal. However, with the idea that Thornton might yet reconsider his position, the Institute still delayed taking any steps to secure patents. Then in January 1825, Browne wrote again, expressing the hope that "upon more mature reflection" Thornton might have taken up the question with the secretary of state and subsequently altered his position.[49] Thornton did not respond. Browne wrote again, angrily, asking if Thornton felt himself "under no honorary obligation not to answer a gentleman's communication." Thornton replied that he was "under an *honorary obligation* not to answer any Language that is calculated to insult," and he repeated that he would supply no patents which could "be practiced in secret."[50] The battle was now joined, and the Board of Managers directed Browne to apply to the proper authorities for redress.[51]

In this case the proper authority was the secretary of state, John Quincy Adams, since the Patent Office was then under his direction. Browne therefore directed his next letter to Adams, and he enclosed copies of his correspondence with Thornton, with the hope that Adams would view the law in a different light. Adams did not reply, and in February Browne wrote again.[52] By that time the cast of characters had altered: Adams was now president, and Henry Clay was secretary of state. Thus in March Browne set the Institute's case before Clay. Browne charged Thornton with "gross ignorance of the law," "gross partiality" in the exercise of his duty, and "gross inconsistency of official conduct," and he asked for an opportunity to substantiate the

48 Evelyn S. Paniagua, "American Inventors' Debt to the Institute," *Journal of the Franklin Institute* 247 (January 1949): 2.

49 Peter A. Browne to William Thornton, January 7, 1825, Letterbook.

50 Peter A. Browne to William Thornton, January 16, 1825; William Thornton to Peter A. Browne, January 29, 1825, Letterbook.

51 Minutes of the Board of Managers, January 17, 1825.

52 Peter A. Browne to the Honorable the Secretary of State of the United States, January 29, 1825; Peter A. Browne to the Hon. John Q. Adams, February 14, 1825, Letterbook.

charges. Receiving no answer, Browne wrote again.[53] By late March, having still received no response from Clay, Browne wrote the president, "with a view to bring this unpleasant business to a termination." Completely outlining the history of his efforts, Browne added the charge of extortion to those previously leveled against Thornton.[54] That letter brought results. Clay wrote Browne asking for the proofs of his allegations, and Browne set them out in a lengthy return letter.[55] Clay took no immediate notice of the charges of official misconduct; he rather devoted his attention to the legality of Thornton's position. William Wirt, the attorney general, was asked for an opinion, and he rendered an interpretation substantially the same as Thornton's.[56]

The Philadelphians were not without further resources. Horace Binney and John Sergeant, whom Browne called "two of the most eminent lawyers in the U.S.," were asked, on the Institute's behalf, for their interpretation of the patent law. They argued that neither the terms of the act nor its spirit specified that patents should be withheld from any person paying the stipulated fees. On the contrary, the inventor's rights were protected by damages on infringement and the public's rights were protected by publication. It was the intention of Congress not only to secure the rights of inventors but also to protect the public against patent frauds and to aid scientific improvement generally. Browne forwarded their opinion in another letter to Clay, with the suggestion that he might read it with interest.[57] Moved by the "high respect which I entertain for the judgments of those Gentlemen," Clay promised that he would reconsider the subject.[58]

In September 1825, Clay wrote Browne that he had examined the law and concluded that he was indeed authorized to furnish copies of patents upon application, with no condition other than payment of the

---

[53] Peter A. Browne to Henry Clay, March 5, 1825; Peter A. Browne to Henry Clay, March 15, 1825, Letterbook.

[54] Peter A. Browne to His Excellency John Q. Adams, March 23, 1825, Letterbook. The extortion, according to Browne, was committed when the Patent Office charged applicants extra sums for office services, over and above the fee for a patent.

[55] Henry Clay to Peter A. Browne, March 26, 1825; Peter A. Browne to Henry Clay, March 29, 1825, Letterbook.

[56] Henry Clay to Peter A. Browne, April 10, 1825, with enclosure, William Wirt to Henry Clay, Letterbook.

[57] Biographical sketches of both Binney and Sergeant are in the *Dictionary of American Biography*. Sidney George Fisher once wrote: "It is a saying that Philad. is celebrated for three things—The Fairmount Waterworks, The Wonderly Butter, and Mr. Binney. I hope his influence may long continue, for it is always exerted on the right side" (Nicholas B. Wainwright, ed., *A Philadelphia Perspective: The Diary of Sidney George Fisher, Covering the Years 1834–1871* [Philadelphia: Historical Society of Pennsylvania, 1967], p. 221).

[58] Henry Clay to Peter A. Browne, May 13, 1825, Letterbook.

set fees. Browne replied that the Institute had "never entertained a doubt" as to the legality of its position.[59] In quick exercise of that right, he sent a crisp note to Thornton requesting a patent and enclosed a five-dollar bill to cover copying costs. In a delightful anticlimax to the eighteen-month controversy, the Institute's money was returned by a Patent Office clerk, who claimed the bill was counterfeit.[60] It was duly certified by a Philadelphia bank, however, and the Institute received a copy of the patent.

The Institute's battle with Thornton was an important issue in the development of patent policy. It reflects the unspecific character of the 1793 act, which was merely one of patent registration. The legislation contained no provisions for novelty or patentability, and the whole question of validity was left for judicial settlement. Until the statute of 1836 completely reorganized Patent Office procedures, implementation of the law, to the frequent dismay of the mechanic community, was often on an ad hoc basis. In that respect, the conflict was of more point than a squabble between Browne and Thornton. Without explicit legislative guidance, the Patent Office was free to interpret policy as it saw fit in individual instances. Resolution of the Franklin Institute case provided some of the policy which legislation had omitted, and to that degree a wider interest was served.[61] Browne saw the whole affair in more simplistic terms; it had been a struggle between dark secrecy and the freedom of knowledge. In that vein, he reported to the Board of Managers: "Your Corresponding Secretary congratulates the Institute on this triumph of principle and Justice."[62]

But even before that sweet victory, the Institute's future looked bright. In a very short period of time many of its objectives had been successfully achieved. By the end of the first year of operation, the society numbered over six hundred members, "the greater part of whom

[59] Henry Clay to Peter A. Browne, September 12, 1825; Peter A. Browne to the Hon. Henry Clay, September 16, 1825, Letterbook.

[60] Peter A. Browne to Dr. William Thornton, September 26, 1825; William P. Elliot to Peter A. Browne, October 4, 1825; Peter A. Browne to William P. Eliot, October 6, 1825, Letterbook.

[61] The principal sources of discontent over the patent system were the flood of useless inventions and the litigation necessary to protect patent rights. The Institute's interest in examining new inventions stemmed partly from a desire to correct those weaknesses by noting significant advances and identifying their originators. For similar efforts to improve the patent process, see the call for a "National Academy on Patents," *The Mechanic. A Journal of the Useful Arts and Sciences* 3 (March 1834): 93; and the plan for a "Society for the Encouragement of Mechanical Genius," *The Young Mechanic* (Boston) 1 (January 1832): 12.

[62] Minutes of the Board of Managers, September 15, 1825.

will be found among the industrious part of the community."[63] The
Institute also enjoyed financial health. Even after the cost of outfitting
Carpenters' Hall, plus all other expenses, there was a treasury balance
of slightly over a thousand dollars. The drawing school had about
fifty pupils, and the lectures drew such attendance that the hall was
sometimes uncomfortably crowded. Since the organization had been
without a home until Carpenters' Hall was rented, little had been done
to organize a library or mineralogical collection. Lack of facilities had
limited book donations, and those which had been collected were temporarily housed with various members of the Library Committee. But
bookcases had been constructed, and if some financial help could be
found, it was anticipated that "a foundation can be laid for an extensive and valuable Library."[64] Similar hopes were entertained for the
mineralogical collections. In short, the popularity which had attended
all the Institute's activities convinced the managers "that our community was ripe for this great undertaking."[65] And as they looked to the
future, the managers could see the time when it might be necessary to
seek even larger quarters.

Carpenters' Hall met the organization's present needs, but "if the
increase of members should continue as we have a right to expect it
will," it was not a matter of "idle speculation" to consider the time
when a new hall would be required.[66] Some thought had clearly been
given to the subject. There was no hall in the city suited to the Institute's purposes, according to the Board; in their view a new building
would probably have to be constructed. Furthermore, they urged the
development of a permanent fund, which would supply the money when
the time for a new building came.

The time came sooner than the money. By early May 1825, just
over a year after the Institute's founding, preliminary plans for a new
building had already matured. At a meeting on May 5 the Board of
Managers decided to build a new hall. A lot was selected, and the architect John Haviland prepared plans for the structure. A building committee was authorized to perform the required contracts, and the finance
committee prepared a plan to obtain the necessary funds.[67] Construction was to be financed by a loan of thirty-four thousand dollars, issued

---

[63] "Fourth Quarterly Report, Made to the Institute, at a Meeting Held January
20, 1825," *First Annual Report of the Proceedings of the Franklin Institute*, p. 48.

[64] Ibid., p. 54.

[65] Ibid., p. 48.

[66] Ibid., p. 61.

[67] Minutes of the Board of Managers, May 5, 1825. Of the total amount of the
loan, $24,000 was allocated to construction and the remainder to purchase of the
land for the building and incidentals.

by the Institute in shares with a par value of fifty dollars, bearing five percent interest per annum, with dividends paid semiannually. The principal was irredeemable until 1840. Stock in the loan went on sale June 6, and by June 24, 545 shares—over three-fourths of the total—had been sold.[68]

The reason for the Institute's haste was opportunity. The Board learned that the U.S. circuit and district courts were seeking new quarters. The district marshal had been unable to find suitable housing, however, and he had no authority to construct a building. The managers of the Institute had the desire for a new building, but no funds. When the marshal offered a long-term rental agreement, the managers saw the income potential they sought, and a lease was agreed upon.[69] Since the courts needed space by January 1826, speed was essential, and construction started even before title to the property was conveyed.

Haviland, the building's architect, was an Englishman who emigrated to the United States in 1816, along with Hugh Bridport, his assistant in the Franklin Institute's drawing school. In Peter Browne's opinion, Haviland was a gentleman of "correct taste and profound knowledge."[70] His design for the building was in the neoclassic style then popular in Philadelphia. Its front elevation was closely patterned after the Choragic Monument of Thrasyllus, and initially there was some idea to surmount the structure with a statue of Benjamin Franklin.[71] The building, about sixty feet wide and one hundred feet deep,

68 Ibid., June 24, 1825.

69 The Eighth Quarterly Report of the Board of Managers, January 19, 1826, outlines the circumstances of the arrangement with the court. It was published in the *National Gazette*, January 26, 1826.

70 John Haviland (1792–1852) was associated with Browne in several architectural enterprises. The Philadelphia Arcade, in which Thomas P. Jones also had a financial interest, was one of their projects. The idea of skylighted avenues of shops under a single roof came from London, where the Burlington Arcade was then popular. The Philadelphia Arcade, designed by Haviland, was located on Chestnut Street, between Sixth and Seventh Streets. J. Thomas Scharf and Thompson Wescott, *History of Philadelphia, 1609–1884*, 3 vols. (Philadelphia: L. H. Everts & Co., 1884), vol. 1, pp. 617–18. Another Browne-Haviland enterprise was the Chinese Pagoda and Labyrinth Garden, located near Fairmount Park. It, too, was in imitation of European constructions, and, like the Arcade, it never realized the financial hopes of its projectors. Because of his connection to both these efforts, Browne earned the local nickname "Pagoda Arcade Browne." Information on Haviland, the Arcade, and the Chinese Pagoda is available in Hamlin Talbot, "Some Greek Revival Architects in Philadelphia," *Pennsylvania Magazine of History and Biography* 65 (April 1941): 121–44; and in Harold D. Eberlein and Cortland Van Dyke Hubbard, "The American 'Vauxhall' of the Federal Era," in ibid., 68 (1944): 150–74. The E. S. Burd Papers in the Historical Society of Pennsylvania also contain information on the Arcade.

71 The plan for the building was taken directly from James Stuart, *The Antiquities of Athens, measured and delineated by James Stuart and Nicholas Revett* (London: J. Haberkom, 1762), a favorite source for Philadelphia architects working in the

with three stories and a basement, was located on Seventh Street, between Market and Chestnut Streets, where it still stands.

Ceremonies to lay the cornerstone were held on June 8, 1825. The guests included Governor Geddes of South Carolina and Governor Clinton of New York.[72] Browne, who along with all his other Institute functions served as chairman of the building committee, delivered the principal address. The occasion which they had gathered to celebrate, Browne told his listeners, could hardly have come at a more appropriate time. Recent progress in science and the arts indicated that man stood at the threshold of a new age. The source of that advancement was education:

Knowledge ceases to be monopolized by few and is becoming the property of the many; theory and practice formerly disunited and unsocial, now walk hand in hand enlightening and correcting each other; the workman and the philosopher are united in the same person.[73]

In the Old World, when commoners aimed at the knowledge which had been a prerogative of upper-class position, governments trembled in "apprehension of the mischiefs of education among the working people." No such fears troubled America, where the rights of all were equal and where tyranny "flies before the piercing light of science." A free government and access to knowledge were the foundations of the nation's future, Browne concluded, and he urged his audience:

Americans, let us all unite in this determination, to encourage institutions *calculated to diffuse knowledge among* the people. Every nation ought to have a common standard round which it can rally, let *this* be ours, and we shall perpetuate our constitution. It will insure to us *religious, political and personal freedom*; and will, sooner or later, by our example lead to the emancipation of the world.[74]

---

neoclassic vogue, then so popular in the city. According to Browne, the structure would serve "as a specimen" of the taste of Philadelphia mechanics, and "like that highly useful class of the community, it should be distinguished not so much by ornament, as purity of design and solidity of construction" (*United States Gazette*, June 9, 1825).

[72] Geddes and Clinton, both strong supporters of internal improvements in the United States, were joined by city authorities and representatives from the Agricultural Society of Philadelphia, the Academy of Natural Sciences, and the American Philosophical Society. The cornerstone was laid in the Masonic ceremony and it contained the traditional capsule, with documents, medals, and coins. The parade and ceremony are described in the *United States Gazette*, June 8, 1825.

[73] *United States Gazette*, June 9, 1825.

[74] Ibid.

Men are beguiled by bricks and mortar. They think they have achieved more than a roof for their ambitions; construction seems to ratify the past and justify the future. Certainly, the Board of Managers was disposed to that attitude as it reflected on the short period of the Franklin Institute's life. At the end of two years, membership had doubled to over a thousand. The permanent fund was over three times as large as it had been a year earlier, amounting to almost two thousand dollars. The lease with the marshal of the district court provided a rental income of fifteen hundred dollars annually for ten years, and the managers expected an additional five hundred per year from the rental of office space.[75] While the Institute's means were far from lavish, they were sufficient for present needs. And what was most important, as the quick subscription of the building loan had demonstrated, the community appeared ready to support the organization.

Nothing in that year darkened the prospect. The second exhibition removed any lingering fears that the difficulties were greater than the rewards. Browne's quarrel with the Patent Office had ended in triumph. The lectures were firmly settled. Dr. Thomas P. Jones had been appointed to the professorship of mechanics, with the promise that he would conduct a periodical under the Institute's auspices. A chair in natural history had been established and a mathematical school begun. The Board could report that a society had been formed in Baltimore, "with similar objects, and with a similar plan," and that another had started in Boston, too. But best of all, a handsome new building offered visible proof of the organization's permanency and value. "Our success has been commensurate with our hopes," the Board modestly concluded in their second annual report.[76] The prosperity and usefulness of the Franklin Institute seemed a settled issue.

[75] The Eighth Quarterly Report of the Board of Managers.
[76] Ibid.

Professor John Griscom, a well-known lecturer and chemistry teacher, who had been instrumental in founding the society there.[2]

But there was still an undercurrent of interest in some kind of publishing activity, and it surfaced again in the fall under rather unusual circumstances. Early in October 1824, Samuel V. Merrick presented the Institute with several volumes of English technical journals. A committee of Browne, Merrick, and John Wetherill, a manufacturing chemist, was appointed to determine whether the Institute should subscribe to the works for its library.

The committee presented its report on October 21. After a few perfunctory remarks on the question of subscriptions, the committee turned to an admittedly different subject, which they claimed had naturally arisen in their discussions. What would be the point, they asked, of filling the shelves of a library with useful books if no one read them?

The keeping open of a room where any member of the Institute may pass a leisure hour in consulting the best authorities on the branch of business he pursues was a part of our original plan and will no doubt be of great utility, but the board must be sensible how few, comparatively, will come and among those few how small indeed will be the number who will be able to make a proper selection thus to read.[3]

Instead, it was argued that a committee should be appointed to make selections from foreign and domestic journals and publish them, together with the Institute's transactions, on a weekly basis in the city's newspapers. Such a predigestion would make available to Philadelphia's manufacturers and mechanics the most directly useful information. The scheme, according to the committee, "would also serve to feel the public pulse as to the publication hereafter of a separate sheet weekly devoted to this laudable object."[4] At the least, it is ironic that the committee should have argued a publication plan on the basis that workingmen could not read intelligently and would not use a library even if the Institute had one in operation. But at that moment the issue was in the hands of an attorney, not an artisan.

The Board of Managers tabled the report until November when Keating, Browne, and Carey were appointed a Committee of Publication, with Browne as chairman. They followed the plan suggested ear-

[2] The Griscom Collection at the New York Public Library contains fragments of information respecting the proposed journal. See, for example, Sam'l J. Smith to John Griscom, Burlington, [N.J.], April 12, 1824, in which mention is made of a "projected Mechanics & Manufacturers Mag."

[3] Reports of Special Committees, October 21, 1824, Franklin Institute Archives.

[4] Ibid.

lier, and in January 1825 they reported that they had made "copious extracts" from scientific and technical journals and published them weekly in local newspapers. But the real direction of the committee's thoughts is clear. Browne, a man with aspirations for scientific author-ship, suggested that members write original essays which could also be published—broadening the original plan—and he concluded: "Your committee look forward with pleasure to the time when the Institute will be able to support a periodical paper devoted entirely to scientific & Mechanical information."[5]

Perhaps to accelerate that day, the committee prepared a sample copy of a magazine "as an experiment" and presented it to the Board of Managers for their consideration. The Board took no immediate action, but the issue was far from dead. At the next meeting of the Board, Browne, as chairman of the Committee on Lectures, reported that Dr. Thomas P. Jones, of Oxford, North Carolina, had offered himself as a candidate for the Institute's unfilled professorship of mechanics. Browne urged the Board to engage Jones, "especially as in addition to his serv-ices as a Lecturer, the members of the Institute and the Mechanics of the City and County, would find Mr. Jones a valuable acquisition as the Editor of a Mechanics' journal which he has both the capacity and the desire to publish."[6] What Browne therefore proposed was that the Institute offer Jones the professorship of mechanics at an annual salary of four hundred dollars—one hundred dollars more than other faculty salaries—and that it provide a home for a mechanics' magazine, which Jones would publish. He did not suggest that the Institute pub-lish a journal, but rather that it give "countenance and approbation" to a venture which Jones would undertake. The Board of Managers favored that plan, and both of Browne's proposals were adopted. The Board was also willing to solicit subscribers for the journal if Jones would send a prospectus for their approval.[7]

While Browne seems to have been the moving force behind the push for a journal, circumstances aided his efforts. When the Board deferred earlier publication plans in favor of the proposed New York mechanics' magazine, they did so with the understanding that it would be edited by a man of scientific reputation whose views on education they would share. The New York journal was not published by the mechanics' institute there, however, and became instead a commercial

[5] Report of the Publishing Committee, January 6, 1825, Franklin Institute Archives.

[6] Report of the Committee on Lectures, February 17, 1825, Franklin Institute Archives.

[7] Minutes of the Board of Managers, March 3, 1825, Franklin Institute Archives.

venture titled the *American Mechanics' Magazine,* promoted by James Seaman, who did little more than copy the London *Mechanics' Magazine.*[8] Under those conditions, the Board felt no obligation to support the periodical, and the publication of a journal of its own, or some alternative plan, again became an open issue.

Browne seized upon the opportunity. When the Board adopted his proposals, he immediately opened a correspondence with Jones to induce him to take the faculty and editorial positions. Late in March 1825 Browne received Jones's acceptance, and he moved to secure public support for a journal by an open letter to the "Mechanics Artizans and Manufacturers of Pennsylvania," which he sent to the city's newspapers. Browne noted that physicians and lawyers had their own journals and merchants their own newspaper; the American Philosophical Society, the Academy of Natural Sciences, and the Agricultural Society also published their proceedings. Only mechanics and manufacturers lacked a voice—a remarkable fact in Philadelphia, he claimed, where one met "the moral and scientific artizan in the first circles."[9]

Browne and the Board of Managers had cause to believe that Jones was particularly suited to edit a journal for mechanics. No stranger to Philadelphia, he had a reputation both for intellectual attainments and practical knowledge. Jones was born in England in 1774 and trained there as a physician. He emigrated to the United States as a young man, perhaps in company with Joseph Priestley, the noted scientist and religious dissenter. Before the turn of the century he settled in Philadelphia, where he was a member of a small religious society formed in 1796 as a result of Priestley's lectures in the city.[10] Sometime afterwards he delivered scientific lectures in Albany, New York. By 1811 Jones was back in Philadelphia, where he offered a course of lectures on chemistry, optics, pneumatics, electricity, and galvanism. His lectures were well received, and in 1813 he added a course in science for boys and girls.[11]

In 1814 Jones was appointed professor of natural philosophy and

[8] The full title of Seaman's magazine, published on a weekly basis from February 1825 until February 1826, was *Mechanics' Magazine, Museum, Register, Journal and Gazette.*

[9] April 1, 1825, Letterbook, Corresponding Secretary, 1824–1826, Franklin Institute Archives (cited hereafter simply as Letterbook).

[10] Stauffer Collection, vol. 26, p. 2122, Historical Society of Pennsylvania. There are biographical sketches of Jones (1774–1848) in the *Dictionary of American Biography* (New York: Charles Scribner's Sons, 1943); and in Francis Fowler, "Memoir of Dr. Thomas P. Jones," *Journal of the Franklin Institute* 130 (July 1890): 1–7.

[11] In 1812 Jones wrote a friend that there were two other scientific lectures in the city, but "I had a class more numerous & respectable than either of them and have a brilliant prospect for the next season" (Thomas P. Jones to Ezra Ames, Philadelphia, April 12, 1812, Gratz Collection, Historical Society of Pennsylvania).

chemistry at the College of William and Mary, a position he held until
he returned to Philadelphia in 1818. He resumed his lecture course,
adding experiments on a working model of a steam engine.[12] At the
same time he joined Jacob Perkins in the manufacture of fire engines—a
partnership which was dissolved eight months later. It was that fire-
engine factory which Samuel V. Merrick ultimately took over, according to George Escol Sellers's reminiscences.[13]

Jones was an active member of Philadelphia's scientific and mechanic
community. In addition to his own courses, he gave popular experimental lectures at Peale's Museum. On those occasions, Sellers remembered, "I was always called on as Dr. Jones' assistant. I turned the
crank handle of the electrical machine, handed him magic lantern slides,
washed chemical bottles, and such like."[14] Jones was also on familiar
terms with Isaiah Lukens, Rufus Tyler, David Mason, and Matthias
Baldwin—mechanics and industrialists who later played an important
role in the Institute.[15] He left Philadelphia again to conduct a school
in Oxford, North Carolina, where he stayed until he returned to edit
the Institute's journal.

Academic commitments in North Carolina prevented Jones from
assuming his new position immediately, and he worked out the details
of the new journal with Browne by mail. Browne urged continual
haste in case the publication of a similar journal might spoil the market.

---

[12] Stauffer Collection, vol. 29, p. 2273.

[13] Eugene S. Ferguson, ed., *Early Engineering Reminiscences [1815-40] of George
Escol Sellers* (Washington, D.C.: Smithsonian Institution, 1965), p. 16.

[14] Ibid.

[15] Lukens and Baldwin, especially, were leading figures in the Institute. Lukens
(1779–1846) was a vice-president of the organization from its founding until his death,
except for a three-year period, from 1826 to 1829, during most of which he was
abroad. When the Committee on Science and the Arts replaced the Committee on
Inventions in 1834, Lukens immediately became its most active worker, and during the
next twelve years he participated in more of its investigations than any other member, then or since. For biographical information on Lukens, see "Obituary Notice of
the Late Isaiah Lukens," *Journal of the Franklin Institute* 42 (December 1846):
423–25; and Ferguson, *Early Engineering Reminiscences [1815-40] of George Escol
Sellers*, pp. 52–60.

Baldwin (1795–1866) became best known for developing the largest locomotive
works in America. His initial success as a machinist came from the manufacture, in
conjunction with his partner David Mason, of engraved rollers for textile printing, an
enterprise which stemmed from their production of bookbinders' tools. Baldwin apparently constructed a steam engine to provide power for the factory and from that
experience went into the business of making locomotives when railroads were introduced to Philadelphia. Malcolm C. Clark, "The Birth of an Enterprise: Baldwin
Locomotive, 1831–1842," *Pennsylvania Magazine of History and Biography* 90 (October 1966): 423–44. Baldwin served on the Institute's Board of Managers continuously
from 1827 to 1863. For details on his life, see Thomas Coulson, "Some Prominent
Members of the Franklin Institute 3. Matthias William Baldwin, 1795–1866," *Journal
of the Franklin Institute* 262 (September 1956): 171–84.

In May 1825, even before the format had been settled, a prospectus was published and then reissued in August. There was some question whether the journal would be in the form of a weekly newspaper, or a pamphlet to be published monthly. The newspaper style promised a potentially wider readership and income from advertisements, whereas a pamphlet seemed more "respectable and more permanent."[16] Remote from the Institute and from the opinion of his friends there, Jones was undecided as to format. It was his opinion, however, that the journal would ultimately take the form of a pamphlet. The Board of Managers concurred, and it was so described in a second prospectus.[17] Adoption of the more dignified format still left some feeling for a popular sheet, which might reach a larger audience. One of the ideas in that direction was to issue an almanac, along the lines of one published by the Pennsylvania Agricultural Society. It was decided that "such a publication might become very useful, by disseminating the knowledge of simple and useful improvements among many individuals who otherwise would have no opportunity of becoming acquainted with them." Perhaps not less important, an almanac seemed an easy and direct way to extend "a knowledge of the usefulness and objects of the Institute throughout the State."[18]

Uriah Hunt, a local bookseller and Institute member, offered to publish the almanac at his own risk, provided that he could title it "The Franklin Almanack, published under the patronage of the Franklin Institute of the State of Pennsylvania for the promotion of the Mechanic Arts." To confer a further aura of authenticity, Hunt proposed to use the head of Franklin as a frontispiece, perhaps with a facsimile of the Institute's seal. In exchange, he agreed to insert in the almanac any matter furnished him by the organization. Hunt's proposal was accepted, and in October the Board of Managers was informed that the almanac had been printed. Much to the Board's embarrassment, however, and contrary to their explicit instructions to him, Hunt had included in the almanac the traditional astrological device of a human figure, showing the influence of zodiacal signs. The design was a convention with almanacmakers, whatever their own personal beliefs, who had

16 Peter A. Browne to Dr. Thomas P. Jones, March 21, 1825, Letterbook. In the same letter, Browne remarked: "The publication of that [a mechanics' journal] must be *announced* immediately to prevent the members of the Institute from subscribing to a republication of the London Mechanics' Journal made in New York and for which a subscription paper is now handing about this City."

17 Thomas P. Jones to Peter A. Browne, April 3, 1825, Letterbook; Minutes of the Board of Managers, May 5, 1825.

18 Minutes of the Board of Managers, March 24, 1825; Miscellaneous Reports, September 1, 1825, Franklin Institute Archives.

long before learned that in the countryside its usage increased sales. But the figure was strongly offensive to the Institute's sense of scientific rationality, and Hunt was persuaded to reprint the almanac without the design. Further, the Committee on Publication was directed to advertise in the public press an Institute disclaimer of any responsibility or connection to it.[19]

Dr. Jones's journal presented no such problems. Although the magazine was to be entirely at his expense, Jones never saw it only as a profitmaking enterprise. In his mind, the project had some of the qualities of a crusade. "It shall be published," he once said, even if there were only a hundred subscribers, then "like the American Navy, let it fight its way into public favour by its intrinsic worth."[20] Peter Browne saw the journal with a missionary's eyes, too. He handled the details of printing and distribution for both issues of the prospectus, solicited subscriptions, and collected subject matter for future use. He told Jones that for the past year he had labored hard to develop a scientific correspondence, the fruits of which would also be placed at the editor's disposal. "I have several other projects in view," Browne wrote, "but they must lie by until the journal commences. *That is the grand lever with which we will raise everything.*"[21]

It was Browne's fervent hope that Jones would return to Philadelphia before the end of the summer, so that the first number could be published to coincide with the annual exhibition in the fall. But his affairs in North Carolina kept Jones there until December, and the journal was not begun until January 1826. It was not ready until February and had to be back-dated in order to maintain a complete series for the year.

Dr. Jones had originally proposed to publish material of interest to mechanics and manufacturers, as well as the transactions of the Institute. But before the first number was printed he bought Seaman's *American Mechanics' Magazine*, and when the periodical came out it carried the combined title *The Franklin Journal and American Mechanics' Magazine*. Acquisition of Seaman's journal gave Jones a broader subscription base and the impetus to expand on his original ideas. As he pointed out in an address to the public, "a mere book of recipes and notices" would neither satisfy his aims nor "supply the wants of the intelligent artisans and manufacturers of our country."[22]

---

[19] Minutes of the Board of Managers, September 1, November 26, 1825.

[20] Thomas P. Jones to Peter A. Browne, June 2, 1825, Letterbook.

[21] Peter A. Browne to Thomas P. Jones, August 22, 1825, Letterbook.

[22] As quoted from an address by Jones, published in the last issue of Seaman's *American Mechanics' Magazine*, February 11, 1826.

In an appeal to that larger audience, Jones listed seventeen categories of information in which the journal would publish, encompassing subjects as disparate as architecture and botany, mathematics and agriculture, American manufactures and mechanical jurisprudence. But the most important element was that *The Franklin Journal and American Mechanics' Magazine* was begun with the idea that it would be addressed to issues more than local and would appeal to more than a local circulation.

It was tacitly assumed that Jones and the Institute were copartners in an enterprise which rested on shared values and shared aims. But as the magazine took shape, clearly it was less oriented toward ordinary workingmen than might have been expected of a mechanics' magazine. An inexpensive newspaper format, which might have enjoyed greater circulation among artisans, was rejected in favor of a more "respectable" style of publication. As the journal developed, in Peter Browne's mind, it came to have the character of the periodicals of such institutions as the American Philosophical Society and the Academy of Natural Sciences in Philadelphia.[23] In that sense, it would be a serious scientific and technical journal rather than a popular sheet for the instruction of workingmen.

That idea undoubtedly had personal appeal to Browne. And other members of the Institute shared the notion that the *Journal* might become the authoritative voice in America on matters technical, especially since absorption of Seaman's magazine had removed the only competitor for that role. But there was another side to the interest in a journal of more than local consequence. For Browne, Jones, and others in the Institute, science and its applications led directly to a concern with the exploitation of Pennsylvania's natural resources, the progress of American manufactures, and all manner of internal improvements. Browne had already suggested his view of that relationship when he called upon those liberal and enlightened mechanics who supported canals, turnpikes, and literary and charitable institutions also to lend their aid to the *Journal*.[24] His plea was not directed toward sweaty Philadelphia laborers; nor did the journal reflect their interests. But for others the connection had distinct appeal.

For example, when Matthew Carey formed the Pennsylvania Society for the Promotion of Internal Improvements in 1824, it enjoyed immedi-

23 "To the Mechanics Artizans and Manufacturers of Pennsylvania," April 1, 1825, Letterbook.
24 Ibid.

ate Institute support.[25] Two-thirds of the Society's acting committee were also members of the Institute. And in the summer of 1825, before the exact nature of the *Journal* had been settled, Browne tried to join the Institute's publication plans with those of the Pennsylvania Society. While nothing came of that particular scheme, the journal did become an important vehicle for propagandizing the aims of the Society. "The object of this association," Jones noted in the first issue of his periodical, "is so intimately connected with the general prosperity of the state, as to address itself, most powerfully, to the interest, and to the patriotism, of every class in the community."[26] Seldom had a more disinterested effort been made on the Commonwealth's behalf, the editor claimed, and he freely opened the columns of his journal to the Society's transactions.

The Pennsylvania Society for the Promotion of Internal Improvements had been established primarily to lobby for a transportation link to the West, since New York's Erie Canal threatened to cut the state off from that market. But the type of transportation system best suited to connect Philadelphia and Pittsburgh was a question whose answer required technical knowledge. Therefore, early in 1825, the Society decided to send an agent to Europe "to collect information of all the valuable improvements in the construction of Canals, Roads, Railways, Bridges, Steam Engines, and all other information calculated to promote the objects of the Society."[27] That effort provided an additional bond to the Franklin Institute, since William Strickland was selected as the Society's agent. Furthermore, Strickland was to be accompanied by Samuel Kneass, the son of another of the Institute's founders, who had acted as an assistant to the secretary and the treasurer at the Institute.[28]

This early relationship between the Pennsylvania Society and the Institute is historically instructive; it tells something of the manner in

[25] For information on the Society, see Richard J. Shelling, "Philadelphia and the Agitation in 1825 for the Pennsylvania Canal," *Pennsylvania Magazine of History and Biography* 62 (April 1938): 175–204.

[26] Peter A. Browne to Thomas P. Jones, August 22, 1825, Letterbook; "Pennsylvania Society for the Promotion of Internal Improvements in the Commonwealth," *The Franklin Journal and American Mechanics' Magazine* 1 (January 1826): 10–11.

[27] "Pennsylvania Society for the Promotion of Internal Improvements in the Commonwealth," p. 12. Strickland published the results of his trip in an illustrated work entitled *Reports on Canals, Railways, Roads, and other Subjects, made to the Pennsylvania Society for the Promotion of Internal Improvement* (Philadelphia: Carey and Lea, 1826).

[28] Samuel Honeyman Kneass (1806–1858) was a student in Strickland's office and later went on to an active career in canal and railroad construction. Biographical sketches of Samuel, his younger brother Strickland, and of his father William Kneass are in the *Dictionary of American Biography*.

which certain members of the Institute interpreted its own aims. Strickland's instructions, for instance, reveal a range of interests beyond transportation systems. He was given a hundred pounds sterling to obtain information on iron smelting and an equal sum to buy "memoirs, publications, models and drawings of useful machines, and authentic information on all subjects, a knowledge of which, in this country, he might deem important."[29] But he was cautioned not to waste his time on theory. The point of his tour, he was advised, was to bring back information in "such minute and particular" form that similar works could be established in Pennsylvania, without the need for "superior skill and science."[30] It never occurred to Jones, who enthusiastically publicized the Society's affairs, that those instructions were contrary to the essential spirit of the Franklin Institute, which was precisely to stimulate theory and practice.[31] Nor was it a contradiction to Browne. He himself had once described the primary function of scientific education:

Believe me, this subject is intimately connected with the great plans of internal improvement, which are now justly occupying the public mind. Nothing in my apprehension can so effectually dissipate the narrow prejudices that are said to exist against a liberal policy of state improvements than intellectual advancement.[32]

Browne was a man of grand projects, and his formulation of the purpose of education was consistent with other of his ideas. But he did voice a growing sense, shared by many in the Institute, that the organization might well be directed toward advancing technical skill and industrial power on a national scale. The *Journal* caught some of that feeling, and so did the plan to examine and report on new inventions. Unlike the journal, which owed its origins as much to Browne's ambitions as to the Institute's first hopes, judgment on the worth of new inventions was an early and explicit aim. Diffusion of knowledge was usually claimed as the central purpose of that activity, but actually there were several aims involved. The most obvious was to save Americans from having to reinvent machines and processes already known to Europe. Then, too, examinations could reveal worthless inventions and lines of mechanical investigation without value. Reporting on new discoveries was also a means of insuring that American inventors would

[29] *The Franklin Journal and American Mechanics' Magazine* 1 (January 1826): 12.
[30] Ibid., 1 (February 1826): 73.
[31] Jones advertised the publication of Strickland's reports in vol. 1 of the *Journal*, pp. 64 (January 1826), 128 (February 1826).
[32] Browne's remark was made in a pamphlet entitled *To the Freemen of Philadelphia* (Philadelphia, June 2, 1825).

receive proper credit for their ideas, a function which appealed to
national pride as well as to visions of commercial profit.

Those ideas were put into practice simply and directly. When an
invention was submitted for examination, a committee of men with
talents and experience relevant to the issue was selected. The first report
made illustrates both the plan of practice and its potential importance
to national concerns. Joshua Shaw had requested an investigation of
percussion caps he had developed for firing rifles and cannons. A committee was established which included two men of known mechanical
talents, David H. Mason and Isaiah Lukens, and a local sugar refiner,
John S. Phillips, who had knowledge of chemistry. A series of tests was
performed at the nearby Frankford arsenal, the detonating materials
were analyzed, and the whole report was published. The committee was
enthusiastic in its praise and urged wide adoption of the devices, not
only because of the effectiveness of the caps but also "for the honor of
our country, as well as for the reputation of our inventive genius."[33]
Conducting the tests at a federal arsenal only reinforced the sense of
importance attached to the Institute's purposes. And even though the
committee's relationship with arsenal officials was an informal one, the
tests suggested a precedent for future uses of the Institute's experts.

Even with such an auspicious beginning, work went slowly the first
year. The Board of Managers blamed it on the conflict with Thornton
and the Patent Office, but it also took some time for inventors to learn
of the service. By the fall of 1824, committees had reported on several
inventions, including a steam engine invented by Robert Mills, a South
Carolina engineer of some reputation.[34] Then in the spring of 1825, the
examination of new inventions suddenly became a focal point of attention, due again to the ubiquitous Peter A. Browne. On May 5, the
Board of Managers was apprised that the corresponding secretary had
been accused in the public press of having stolen and patented someone
else's invention. Browne requested that a committee be formed to investigate the charge, and he notified the Board at its next meeting that he
would call for the appointment of a formal Board of Examiners for all
new inventions.[35]

[33] National Gazette, July 9, 1824.

[34] For biographical information on Mills (1781–1835), including his autobiographical sketch, see Helen M. Gallagher, Robert Mills, Architect of the Washington Monument (New York: Columbia University Press, 1935). The committee to examine Mills's
engine was made up of Robert M. Patterson, of the University of Pennsylvania; Isaiah
Lukens; Frederick Graff, engineer of the Fairmount Water Works; James J. Rush, of
Rush and Muhlenberg, Oliver Evans's successors; and Rufus Tyler, another of that
remarkable group of Philadelphia machinists. Minutes of the Board of Managers,
October 27, 1824.

[35] Minutes of the Board of Managers, May 5, June 2, 1825.

The contested discovery was a piston for pumps and steam engines which incorporated an improvement in stuffing material to secure a better seal in the cylinder. From the report made by the Franklin Institute's committee (James Ronaldson, William Keating, and Samuel R. Wood), it appears that Browne and John Barton of London had both developed similar devices at about the same time. Browne went to England to patent and market his device and there met Barton. The two entered into what was actually a sales agreement, namely, that each would patent and sell his invention in his own country. In exchange for an exclusive American market, Browne agreed to divide equally with Barton all net profits arising from the invention's use in the United States. The committee did not inquire into the question of whether Browne modified his invention after learning of Barton's, but in any event the real issue seems to have been that Barton had received no return from the agreement. Evidently, he believed that Browne had been profiting secretly from the patent and consequently complained to Thomas Gill, editor of *Gill's Technical Repository*, who published the charge of fraud.[36]

For the Institute, it was a serious charge, not only because of Browne's relation to the organization but also because America's technical reputation was in question. Witnesses were called and depositions sworn to before the presiding judge of the district court. The investigating committee was made up of men distinguished for probity as well as expertise. Their report, which exonerated Browne from any wrongdoing, was given full publicity.

That same seriousness of purpose infused the administrative procedures which the Institute then adopted to regularize the examination of new inventions. As he had promised, Browne introduced a series of resolutions to establish a Board of Examiners. The new standing committee would consist of five Institute members, with power to call on other members for additional knowledge when necessary. When relevant, the Board would attempt to secure models and drawings of inventions submitted. The Board would also keep its own minutes, report to the Board of Managers at their stated meetings, and make their records available for publication in the *Journal*.[37]

From the outset, it was clear that the Board of Examiners would be one of the Institute's more important committees. Those named to it

[36] The committee's report, with supporting documents, was incorporated in the Minutes of the Board of Managers, July 7, 1825. Philadelphia newspapers picked up Gill's charge from the London periodical and reprinted it.

[37] Terms of reference for the Board of Examiners were outlined in the Minutes of the Board of Managers, June 2, 1825.

were among the most prominent of the Institute's members—James
Ronaldson, the organization's president; William H. Keating; Samuel
R. Wood; Samuel V. Merrick; and Robert M. Patterson, professor of
natural philosophy and mathematics and vice-provost of the University
of Pennsylvania, who was named chairman. The Board was given further power at a meeting of the Board of Managers on July 14, 1825,
when it was authorized to conduct its investigations without any prior
consultation with the Board of Managers. At the same time, it became
the Committee on Inventions.[38] A circular letter announcing the formation of the new committee, printed in September, promised that investigations would be conducted "with ability and impartiality." The circular was given national distribution by Browne, in his capacity as
corresponding secretary, and he advised its recipients that he would
communicate the results of investigations in a manner "best calculated
to serve the interest of our country."[39]

In an organizational structure which already made committees
powerful, the Committee on Inventions enjoyed almost complete
autonomy. Some independence was necessary for the confidentiality and
impartiality which investigations demanded; but it also made the committee susceptible to domination by those who might have their own
interpretation of its purposes and of the best interest of the country. In
1826, for instance, the committee became especially concerned with
technical advances in internal improvements. Major Stephen H. Long,
of the Topographical Engineers, submitted for examination plans and
specifications for improvements in steam locomotives and the method of
transferring loaded railway carriages from one level to another.[40]
Long's ideas received particular attention from the committee, and
when he presented the Institute a model of his invention, he was voted
a life membership. Improvements in marine railways, canal locks, and
inclined planes where canals were not feasible also received more than
usual consideration, both from the committee and in the pages of the
Journal.[41] Some of the committee's interest in those subjects stemmed

38 Minutes of the Board of Managers, July 14, 1825.

39 *Circular Letter from the Corresponding Secretary to the Franklin Institute,
Philadelphia, September 6, 1825,* Franklin Institute Archives.

40 S. H. Long, "Specification of certain improvements in the locomotive Engine,
and in the mode of transferring loaded carriages from one level to another, in their
passage upon rail-ways," *The Franklin Journal and American Mechanics' Magazine*
2 (September 1826): 129–39.

41 Minutes of the Board of Managers, January 6, 1825. For a sample of the Institute's interest see the report of a special committee—made up of two engineers, John
Wilson, a civil engineer from South Carolina, and Hartman Bache, of the U.S. Topographical Engineers, and two Institute members, George W. Smith, an attorney, and
Gerard Ralston, a merchant active in the Pennsylvania Society for the Promotion of

directly from their relevance for the Pennsylvania canal system, where
an inclined railroad proposed to cross the Alleghenies, with the necessity for cargo transfer at the incline. But the committee was also tempted
by the lure of grand-scale projects—a very different goal from the
original one to aid creative young mechanics.

An example of that divergence from the original aims is the reaction
to a newly invented dry dock by Commodore James Barron of the U.S.
Navy. In 1826, Barron submitted his design to the Committee on Inventions. After a preliminary investigation, the committee discovered that
the ship-repair facilities of this country were really quite limited. Larger
vessels were especially affected, and when major repairs were necessary,
owners normally sent those ships to Europe. The committee decided to
appoint a select committee of naval officers, civil and military engineers,
and local shipwrights to consider the entire question of American ship-
repair facilities, costs, and methods of construction and operation with
reference to their importance to both commerce and national defense.[42]

The select committee made its report, Jones published it in the
Journal, and its findings were particularly recommended to the merchants of Philadelphia.[43] In terms of local interests, there was a point to
the committee's efforts; if Philadelphia had extensive dry-dock facilities,
the commerce she had lost to the port of New York might be regained.
But in straining to seize upon issues of great immediacy and import,
the Institute went beyond administrative logic. Select committees made
up of men who were not members of the Institute were entirely outside
its control, and there was no compelling reason for a connection between
the two. The lesson was not lost on the Institute managers. It never
again conducted that form of investigation, and at least for a time, the
Committee on Inventions settled down to more prosaic tasks.

It was a matter of discovering limits. The Institute's leaders were
men with ambitions for the society, and in a very short period of time

---

Internal Improvements—formed to examine Professor James Renwick's inclined plane,
"in order to insure that attentive consideration, which was demanded by the importance of the subject" ("Report of the Committee of the Franklin Institute, on the
Inclined Plane of Professor James Renwick," *The Franklin Journal and American
Mechanics' Magazine* 2 [November 1826]: 257–63; [December 1826]: 321–32).

42 The committee included J. Humphreys, Charles Stewart, and A. J. Dallas, all
of the U.S. Navy; Hartman Bache, John Wilson, John Randel, a civil engineer involved in the construction of the Chesapeake and Delaware Canal, and George W.
Smith.

43 The report on Barron's dry dock, and on a similar plan submitted by Captain
Thomas Caldwell, was published in the *Franklin Journal and American Mechanics'
Magazine* 3 (January 1827): 3–10. For additional comment, see ibid., 3 (February 1827):
87–91. Details of Barron's life are in Paul Barron Watson, *The Tragic Career of
Commodore James Barron, U.S. Navy (1769–1851)* (New York: Coward-McCann, 1942).

they had made it into something quite different from most mechanics' institutes. But each undertaking had to be measured against the society's ability to carry it out, and frequently that knowledge came only with experience. Not all projects were subjected to that kind of test, however. The competition between ideas within meetings of the Board of Managers offered another opportunity for making choices. And since that group included individuals of strong opinion and diverse personality, debate led easily to conflict. That is what happened when the Institute decided to expand its educational program in 1826. Once more, Peter A. Browne was at the center of the controversy.

Early in 1826, it became apparent to some members of the Board that the evening lecture courses did not entirely meet the Institute's educational goals. The lectures were too abstruse for those without any background in science, and yet it did not seem appropriate to reduce their content to a beginner's level. A mathematics school which had begun under the Board's auspices the previous year had only a few students. And so the Committee on Instruction, which replaced the Committee on Lectures, was charged to consider a plan for extending the Institute's schools "to embrace the different branches of an elementary education." A sense of the discontent that moved the Board is reflected in the committee's comment: "It has been the opinion of many that the Institution has not fulfilled all the objects for which it is intended & not produced all the effect which was expected."[44]

To remedy the defect, the committee proposed that schooling be directed particularly to the "rising generation." Starting with a fresh slate, the society should provide a step-by-step education in mathematics, "the groundwork in all useful & scientific education," and also in reading, writing, and geography. When students reached more advanced standing, they should receive instruction in mechanics, natural philosophy, chemistry, and drawing. The committee recommended that these courses be taught by the Institute's existing faculty, with a principal hired to superintend the whole system.[45] The point of the report was to suggest a general plan for extending the present facilities; details were left for further consideration.

But something was in the air even before the Committee on Instruction made its report. At the same meeting in which the committee was first directed to look into the question, Peter A. Browne already had a proposal of his own for a school of arts and sciences with the

44 The mathematics school is discussed in chapter 5. Minutes of the Board of Managers, February 2, 1826; Report of the Committee on Instruction, March 1, 1826, Franklin Institute Archives.
45 Report of the Committee on Instruction, March 1, 1826.

grand title, "The Franklin College, attached to the Franklin Institute
of the State of Pennsylvania, for the Promotion of the Mechanic Arts."
Browne's argument was that education should have direct practical
utility. Knowledge of the sciences was most useful, but it was only
available in colleges and universities where one needed Latin and Greek
to gain entrance. Since the "operative members of society," the working
classes, could not spare the time to learn those languages, "the system
tends to shut the door to science against a numerous class of the most
useful citizens."[46] The classics were surely a waste of time for artisans,
according to Browne, and he suggested that universities gave them too
much time as well. There ought to be in the city, he claimed, one
"seminary of learning" without such impediments, and he urged the
Board to establish a school which would teach all subjects, except Greek
and Latin, necessary to create the "Scientific Mechanic or Manufacturer," at a cost within the reach of the most humble artisan.[47] While
he called it a college, Browne was actually suggesting a vocationally-
oriented secondary school.

Browne's plan and the initial report from the Committee on Instruction were both tabled in order to give the Board of Managers an
opportunity to consider them. But factions very quickly formed.
Browne's college, his assault on the classics, and the specter of class
exclusiveness all constituted an attack on the University of Pennsylvania,
wittingly or no. If nothing else, that provided a basis for opposition,
certainly for those in the Institute with links to the University. Thus,
when the Committee on Instruction offered a plan alternative to
Browne's, Robert M. Patterson, professor and vice-provost of the University, spoke for the committee instead of its chairman, who would
normally have presented the report. It must have seemed like a storm to
Browne, who remembered later: "when the project was submitted to the
Board of the Institute, nearly all the leading members were opposed to
it, on the ground of its incompatibility with the duties of the board."[48]

Actually, the function of the Institute's educational program was at
issue. Was it to provide practical training for mechanics, that is, directly
useful information, or was it to offer an academic kind of education,
more abstract in its utility? Was it to be a genuine educational opportunity for the workingclass poor or did it speak to other ambitions?

---

[46] Apparently Browne's resolutions were originally presented to the Board at its
meeting of February 2, 1826. They appear in the minutes for March 2, 1826, but with
a motion by Jones that the minutes of the prior meeting be corrected to include them.
[47] Minutes of the Board of Managers, March 2, 1826.
[48] Papers respecting the Conference between the Franklin Institute and the
projected New College, Committee on Instruction, Franklin Institute Archives.

Debate on these questions rapidly spread from Board meetings to the public press, and as positions hardened, to a pamphlet warfare.[49] Browne, supported mainly by Matthew Carey, Dr. Jones, and the architect John Haviland, stood on one side. On the other side was the Institute's Committee on Instruction, whose spokesmen were Patterson and Samuel V. Merrick. Browne's original proposal to the Board had been printed in pamphlet form, and a board of trustees for the college had been named, to give substance to the idea and, hopefully, to generate enough public support to induce the Institute to support the plan.

The Committee on Instruction, however, argued for a different type of school. Merrick best expressed what its purpose should be when he argued that elimination of the ancient languages would bar admission to any who might wish to attend university. Many artisans felt the same, he claimed:

Amongst enlighten'd Mechanics I find this sort of feeling existing with respect to Browne's college: "Let them establish a college in which we can have the option of learning the languages if we please, but do not set up the doctrine that we have no right to the opportunity, we will admit of no such invidious distinction."[50]

The Franklin Institute's school, according to Merrick, should provide a thorough training for the young man who would be a mechanic, but it should also give him the opportunity for "the higher branches of education, which are only attainable in the colleges."[51]

What the Committee on Instruction then proposed was a high school department in the Institute to teach a mixture of science and liberal arts courses, Latin and Greek, and perhaps some of the modern languages. Where Browne saw the need for a radical educational departure—a separate and distinct scientific and technical school—the Committee on Instruction envisioned a high school that would be a direct link between the city's common schools and the University of Pennsylvania, as an integral part of Philadelphia's educational establishment. To make that connection even stronger, merit scholarships to

[49] Matthew Carey defended the college in his *Reflexions on the Proposed Plan for Establishing a College in Philadelphia* (Philadelphia: Carey & Lea, 1826). John Sanderson, a local teacher of Greek and Latin, took the opposite side in *Remarks on the Plan of a College (About to be established in this City)* (Philadelphia: J. Maxwell, 1826).

[50] S. V. M. to [?], March 16, 1826, High School File, Franklin Institute Archives.

[51] Ibid. The same sentiments were incorporated in an *Address of the Committee of Instruction of the Franklin Institute of Pennsylvania, on the Subject of the High School Department attached to that Institution* (Philadelphia: The Franklin Institute, 1826).

the University were proposed for the best of the high school's students. But Merrick was aware of sympathy in the Board of Managers for directly practical knowledge, and to meet it, he suggested clouding the issue. As he pointed out in a private communication, "the uselessness of the dead languages to operatives is a popular theme in our board at present," and he counseled keeping "the main object in the Back ground," emphasizing instead "the necessity of a mechanical education to meet the demands of the age."[52] The classics could be slipped in through the back door later.

The Board of Managers, faced with growing hostility between these rival factions in its membership, sought some resolution of the problem. A meeting was arranged between Browne and Carey, representing the trustees of the college, and Merrick and Patterson, for the Committee on Instruction. Browne and Carey wanted to share faculty and laboratory apparatus with the Institute; in exchange, they were willing to admit the classical languages into the college on an optional basis. Some kind of compromise might also have been acceptable to Merrick and Patterson, but only on the condition that the Institute control the educational program. Those terms were totally unacceptable to the representatives of the proposed college, and the meeting ended badly. In a bitter report, Browne claimed that the "sickly state" of their own schools should have made the Institute's managers more eager to join their efforts with the new college, instead of opposing it. Since they were not interested in cooperative action, however, Browne recommended an end to any ideas of union.[53]

Under the new title, "The Polytechnic and Scientific College," Browne and his fellow trustees attempted to secure public support for their project. In the fashion traditional for such enterprises, an advertised meeting was held in the city, with speeches and resolutions. Jones noted the effort in his pages, with the opinion that it incorporated neither class bias nor hostility to the University. But public support in any tangible form never came, and Browne's college idea failed for the funds to give it life.[54] The Institute's Board of Managers, in the meantime, adopted a series of resolutions offered by Merrick, for the Committee on Instruction. They proposed expansion in two directions. First, the evening program should be extended to include instruction

52 Ibid.

53 Papers respecting the Conference between the Franklin Institute and the projected New College, Committee on Instruction.

54 The public meeting was reported in the United States Gazette, March 27, 1826. See also "Proposed Polytechnic and Scientific College, in Philadelphia," Franklin Journal and American Mechanics' Magazine 1 (March 1826): 189–91.

in mathematics, natural philosophy, literature, and moral and political science. Those subjects would be taught by the methods "usually practised in schools and colleges" but would be aimed toward apprentices and would have no language requirements for admission. Second, a high school should be established, teaching all the normal academic subjects, including the classics. It would be conducted during the day, and its students would presumably include some who would go on to the University.[55] The committee's resolutions were adopted by the Board without opposition, although at a subsequent meeting Browne and his faction unsuccessfully attempted to block use of Institute facilities for the high school.

The high school, as well as the other schools conducted by the Institute, will be given further attention in a subsequent chapter. At this point, however, some of the effects of the controversy should be noted. The quarrel was the first serious disruption in the Institute's affairs, marking an end to the early, balmy days of uncritical optimism. It was inevitable. Putting ideas into action naturally brought differences of opinion, and while those tensions were creative and vital to organizational health, they were nonetheless tensions. Implementation and expansion of objectives had also increasingly complicated the Institute's administrative affairs. There was a building to be maintained, lectures to be organized, and schools to be run. The work of ten standing committees required coordination. There were meetings to arrange, and a mounting pile of details needed attention. The standing committees nominally handled those varied activities and their financing, but the administrative structure was one that depended mainly on voluntary labor, and by 1826, cracks were beginning to appear.

The most obvious solution was to hire administrative help. At first, Samuel Kneass, a young man of technical interests, was employed to aid various officers when the pressure of their duties became too great.[56] But the need for a more mature agent soon became apparent, and in August 1825 John R. Warder was appointed clerk at a salary of one hundred dollars a year. Warder's job was to act as secretary to the Board of Managers and assistant to the treasurer.[57] But a part-time administrator was still not a solution. The management of the Institute's finances, especially the daily collection and disbursement of funds, lacked continuity. The Committee on Models complained that expensive architectural and mechanical models were falling apart for

---

[55] Minutes of the Board of Managers, April 6, 1826.
[56] Ibid., June 10, 1824. Kneass's salary was not to exceed one dollar per meeting.
[57] Ibid., July 14, August 4, 1825.

lack of care. Members of standing committees found it more difficult to carry out their duties, and the managers fell to quarreling with the janitor.

The need for a full-time officer to manage the Institute's affairs had become apparent. Less obvious was where his salary would come from. But in the summer of 1827, Samuel V. Merrick proposed an attractive solution. Merrick had been elected treasurer in July to fill the vacancy created by John Richardson's resignation. But the demands of his own business pressed on Merrick, too, and at a special meeting in August he made a multi-faceted proposition. The Institute would take over financial responsibility for the *Journal*. Dr. Jones would be named editor, and also treasurer, and his compensation would come from a percentage of publication receipts and of membership dues. That plan would provide and pay for an administrator; and, as an extra advantage, the Institute could exchange copies of the *Journal* for other periodicals and thus enlarge the library.[58]

Merrick's idea was an interesting balance of need and opportunity, and a committee was formed to consider it and report back to the Board. Three days later the committee presented a slightly modified scheme. They recommended first that the Institute assume control of the *Journal* and that it be managed by the Library Committee, since periodical exchanges would provide an important means of increasing the size and usefulness of the library. An editor, to be appointed by the Board—Jones was elected—would receive seventy-five cents per journal subscription as compensation. Jones was also elected treasurer and librarian, and for those services he would receive ten percent of all membership dues collected and ten percent of all *Journal* receipts, plus his collection expenses in both cases.[59]

The committee's recommendations were adopted by the Board, the magazine was renamed the *Journal of the Franklin Institute*, and January 1828 was set as the time they should be put into effect. But even before the deadline arrived, the situation changed. Jones had been offered a teaching position at the University of Virginia, and the possibility of his acceptance forced the Board of Managers to separate the editorship from the other offices Jones had been expected to perform. In a new proposal, Jones was offered lifetime tenure as editor, at an annual salary of nine hundred dollars if he remained in Philadelphia, or seven hundred and fifty dollars yearly if he lived elsewhere. That latter amount was to be reduced by a hundred dollars if income

58 Ibid., August 8, 1827.
59 Ibid., August 11, 1827.

from the *Journal* did not cover expenditures. The offices of treasurer, librarian, and clerk of the Board of Managers were combined as before, with a slightly more attractive compensation.[60] Jones undoubtedly could have filled all those positions, but in May 1828 he left to accept the superintendency of the Patent Office. He continued as editor of the *Journal*, but his departure made it all the more imperative that a full-time administrator for the Institute be found.

Aware that Jones was considering a move of one kind or another, the Board had formed a committee to reconsider the question of organization. Their report perfectly outlined the Institute's state. All institutions enjoy, gratuitously, an abundance of zeal when they are first established, the report noted. There are many eager hands to perform the labor necessary to set the society in motion:

But when once firmly established and pursuing its course with steadiness, the performance of the numerous details required have no charm of Novelty to sustain its early friends or induce those who succeed them to go thro' the Labors of their predecessors, and in addition, the changes constantly taking place deprive it of the support of its original members and the institution gradually falls into decay.[61]

To prevent the Franklin Institute from following the same declining path, the committee urgently called for the appointment of an officer who would be treasurer, secretary to the Board of Managers and to all standing committees, and librarian. No less important now, since Jones was moving, was an agent for the *Journal*, acting both to protect the Institute's financial interest and to provide liaison between Jones and a Committee on Publication. Finally, some one person was needed to assume responsibility for all the Institute's property. The committee's report was accepted by the Board, and on March 13, 1828, William Hamilton was appointed actuary of the Franklin Institute.[62] He was an unknown, with little to recommend him except a willingness to work long hours for little pay. He did that for forty-three years and gave the society the administrative continuity it needed, as well as a model for loyalty to be copied by other men in other times.

When Browne described the *Journal* as a "grand lever," he had no

60 Ibid., January 16, February 7, 1828.
61 Report of the committee "To enquire into the expediency of appointing an officer with a salary to perform the duty of Treasurer, Sec'y &c.," February 7, 1828, Actuary file, Franklin Institute Archives.
62 Minutes of the Board of Managers, March 13, 1828.

idea that it would raise up a long-lived and dedicated functionary for the Institute. But it is characteristic of those early years that some things happened by indirection. The original desire for a publication, for instance, came out of a question of library acquisitions. And when the Board of Managers determined to assume control of the periodical, it was not out of any explicit ideas for the *Journal* but from a need to fund the services of an administrator, with the additional benefits to the library, again as frosting on the cake. Indirection, the force of personality, and the particular requirement of the moment—these ingredients were just as potent for the shape and momentum of the Franklin Institute as high-sounding ideals. There were ideals, of course, and idealists. Merrick's advice to disguise the real purpose of the high school was not a piece of unmitigated cynicism; he deeply believed that education should open doors of opportunity rather than fix class lines by occupation. But the organization had become a complex and potentially powerful institution, controlled by men prominent as attorneys, industrialists, and academicians. They seemed to recognize, intuitively, that the Institute's vigor depended on connecting it with the vital issues of the day. That meant experimentation and change. It also meant that the society was vulnerable to the exercise of particular kinds of interests.

A COMMUNITY OF CRAFTSMEN

Philadelphia's mechanic community was an important ingredient in the Institute's vitality. Benjamin Franklin may have been the most famous of the city's ingenious artisans, but there were many others during his time and afterwards who also gave Philadelphia its name for skilled craftsmanship. Building fire engines was one of the community's mechanical specialties, and when Samuel V. Merrick took over the management of a firm which manufactured them, he joined the company of men whose reputation for skill stretched back into the eighteenth century.

The talents required to make fire engines rather naturally led Philadelphia mechanics in two related directions—the production of steam engines and of machine tools. Dr. Jones, who had also once engaged in the manufacture of fire engines, carried advertisements in his *Journal* which called attention to their increasing versatility. Artful and gregarious, already disposed to the sociable interchange of technical information, men like Isaiah Lukens, William and David Mason, Benjamin Reeves, Rufus Tyler, and Thomas Fletcher provided much of the mechanical knowledge upon which the Institute's success rested. Their skills gave substance to the examination of new inventions and contributed directly to the construction of apparatus for experimental investigations.

THE

FRANKLIN JOURNAL,

AND

American Mechanics' Magazine;

DEVOTED TO THE

USEFUL ARTS, INTERNAL IMPROVEMENTS, & GENERAL SCIENCE.

UNDER THE PATRONAGE OF THE

FRANKLIN INSTITUTE

OF THE

STATE OF PENNSYLVANIA

EDITED BY DR. THOMAS P. JONES,

PROFESSOR OF MECHANICS, IN THE INSTITUTE.

VOL. IV.—No. 3.—SEPTEMBER, 1827.

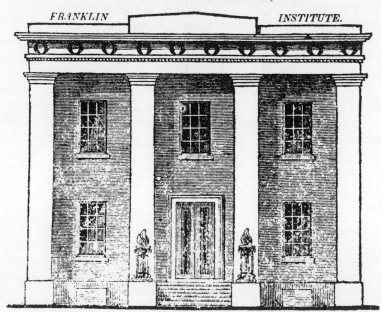

FRANKLIN   INSTITUTE.

PHILADELPHIA:

PUBLISHED BY JUDAH DOBSON, AGENT, 108 CHESNUT STREET:

AND SOLD BY J. M. CAMPBELL, No. 9, ARCADE, NEW-YORK.

Jesper Harding, Printer, 36 Carter's Alley.

::::::::::::::

1827.

Front page from the *Franklin Journal and American Mechanics' Magazine* 4 (September 1827).

LOCOMOTIVE ENGINES.

EASTWICK & HARRISON,

Locomotive and Stationary Engine Makers,

AND

General Machinists,

North-west corner of James and Twelfth streets,

ON THE WILLOW STREET RAIL ROAD, PHILADELPHIA.

Are prepared to receive orders for Machinery in their line, which they will engage to execute with promptness, and in a workmanlike manner.

They would particularly call the attention of Rail Road Companies to the improvements they have made in Locomotives, by which either anthracite coal or wood can be used, with perfect facility, in boilers of the ordinary horizontal form. Also, to their eight-wheel engines, which are admirably adapted to roads having high grades to overcome, and are capable of drawing heavier loads (with less injury to rail-roads) than any other description of engine of the same weight used in this country.

Satisfactory references can be given as to the power and workmanship of their Engines by those who have used them.

A. M. EASTWICK.   JOSEPH HARRISON, Jr.

Cover advertisement, *Journal of the Franklin Institute* 28 (October 1839).

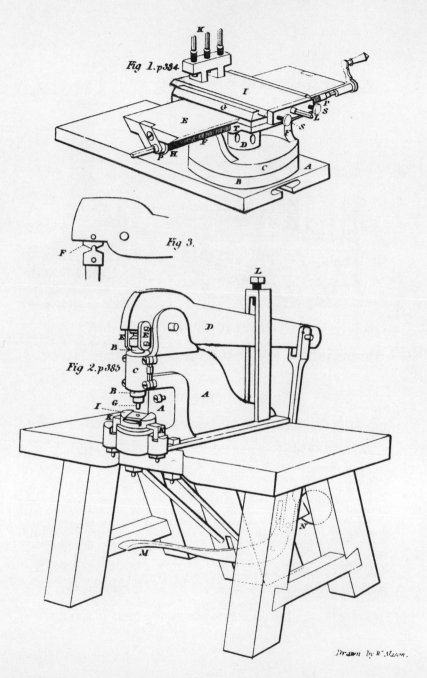

Improved slide rest and press from Mason & Tyler, in the *Franklin Journal and American Mechanics' Magazine* 2 (August 1826).

RUSH & MUHLENBERG'S

IMPROVED

HIGH-PRESSURE STEAM ENGINE.

MARS WORKS.
Steam Engine Manufactory and Iron Foundry.

The Subscribers continue to make Steam Engines on the high or low-pressure principle, of any power required, a number of which are to be seen in the city and its vicinity in steam-boats and manufactories, performing to the entire satisfaction of their proprietors.

They also furnish Pumps for raising water; Sugar Mills of the latest and most approved plan, with boilers and all the machinery appertaining thereto; Drudging Machines for Canals; Rolling Mills; Forge Hammers and Anvils; Gudgeons; and other Castings of every description and weight, are now made at their works, by experienced workmen, clear of sand, and in the most perfect manner, entirely from English and American Pig Iron.

Machinery of every description made and repaired.

From the long experience they have had, (a period of 20 years) they flatter themselves that they can furnish articles in the above lines at such prices as will be satisfactory to their friends and the public generally. Orders received at their counting-house, corner of Ninth and Vine Streets, or at the establishment, Bush Hill, in the vicinity of Philadelphia.

RUSH & MUHLENBERG,
Successors of Oliver Evans.

☞ Fire Brick of the best quality always on hand.

Cover advertisement, *Journal of the Franklin Institute* 20 (July 1835).

Cover advertisement, *Journal of the Franklin Institute* 20 (July 1835).

Fire engine from S. V. Merrick & Co., in *A Description of the Patent Improved Fire Engines, and other Hydraulic Machines, Invented by Jacob Perkins, and Manufactured by S. V. Merrick & Co.* (courtesy of the Library Company of Philadelphia).

Top left, Matthias W. Baldwin, 1795–1866 (courtesy of the Free Library of Philadelphia); *right*, Isaiah Lukens, 1779–1846 (courtesy of the Franklin Institute); *bottom*, Thomas P. Jones, 1774–1848 (courtesy of the Franklin Institute).

MATTHIAS W. BALDWIN,
Machinist and Engraver,

Has removed from 14 Minor Street to Lodge Alley, in the rear of the Masonic Hall, Philadelphia,

Where he has considerably enlarged his establishment, and is now prepared to execute at the shortest notice, orders for

STEAM ENGINES, LOCOMOTIVE OR STATIONARY, of any power, specimens of which may be seen in operation.

Wrought or Cast Iron Screws, of superior workmanship, suitable for al kinds of heavy pressing.

Hydrostatic, Drop, Piercing, and Seal Presses; Dividing Engines; Turning Lathes of various descriptions; Slide Rests, &c.

Calico Printing Machines for one or more colours; Surface, Padding, and Drying Machines; Calenders for Silk, Cotton, or paper.

Cylinders for Calico Printing; from long experience he is enabled to furnish engravings suitable for the quality of goods manufactured in this country.

Book-binders' Ornaments of all the various patterns are constantly kept on hand.

FIRE ENGINE MANUFACTORY,
No. 340 Vine Street, Philadelphia.

JOHN AGNEW,

FORMERLY OF THE FIRM OF MERRICK & AGNEW,

Continues the business of manufacturing Fire Engines of every description ndvariety, and all other articles connected therewith, at the old established and as above.

Top, Cover advertisement, *Journal of the Franklin Institute* 20 (July 1835); *bottom,* Cover advertisement, *Journal of the Franklin Institute* 42 (July 1846).

IV

A PROGRAM FOR ECONOMIC DEVELOPMENT

To the person who shall have manufactured in
Pennsylvania, the greatest quantity of Iron from
the ore, using no other fuel but anthracite. . . .
A Gold Medal.

Committee on Premiums and Exhibitions, 1825

One of the most pressing issues of the early decades of the nineteenth century for all Americans was the nation's economic health. Material development was an important part of the democratic ideology and of ideas about national destiny, but there were many unresolved problems. The Revolutionary War had powerfully demonstrated the country's dependence on foreign supplies for all manner of goods. During the War of 1812, factories had sprung up in many parts of the country to supply wartime needs. But in the years immediately following, British products flooded U.S. markets, and most of the enterprises which had seemed to promise economic independence wilted under the competitive pressure of cheaper and better made imports.[1] Payments to overseas suppliers drained badly needed development capital, but equally troublesome, imports raised the question of whether Americans had the technical skills to compete with European workmanship, or for that matter, to build the transportation systems necessary to create an internal market.

Americans were clearly an enterprising people. Indeed, getting on in the world seemed to be their consuming passion, according to European commentators, who always stood somewhat amazed at the single-

[1] Some Americans were convinced that there was an active British campaign to destroy America's industrial ability, by espionage and sabotage, as well as by ruinous competition. Their fears were not allayed by Henry Brougham's statement to Parliament in 1816 that it would be well "to stifle, in the cradle, those rising manufactures in the United States, which the war has forced into existence, contrary to the natural course of things" (Victor S. Clark, *History of Manufactures in the United States*, 2 vols. [Washington, D.C.: Carnegie Institution, 1928], vol. 1, p. 240).

mindedness with which Yankees pursued wealth.[2] The problems, however, were not soluble simply by individual efforts, even steadfastly applied, and many turned to the collective power of government. When constitutional strictures prohibited federal funds and organization for roads, canals, and railways—or for any other form of economic development—the several states proved willing to use their authority for those purposes.[3] And emerging lines of economic activity made that approach relatively easy, for the nature of American economic activity in the early nineteenth century was essentially regional.

All along the Atlantic seaboard there developed an intense competition among major urban centers for the trade and markets of land west of the Appalachians. Nor was the struggle confined only to large cities. The citizens of smaller towns were equally concerned with sustaining economic vitality in the face of changing patterns of agriculture, commerce, and manufacturing. Anyone might have echoed the complaint of a Wilmington, Delaware, editor:

Every citizen of discernment must be sensible of the absence of everything like prosperous commerce in Wilmington. Our trade is cut off on the north by Philadelphia, and on the south by Baltimore. The trade of the Susquehanna, which at one time contributed considerably to the prosperity of our city, now goes to one or the other of the above places.[4]

Under those circumstances, Americans thought naturally of association along regional lines in order to deal with common problems. The most obvious source of collective strength was political, and Americans employed various combinations of public and private enterprise to provide the capital and direction for internal improvements. Economic historians differ in opinion about the effectiveness of state governments in planning or funding the development of their regions, but most of them agree that because of the vacuum created by federal hesitancy, economic advancement during the second quarter of the nineteenth century was largely pushed forward by the states.[5]

An important factor has been left out of that equation, however. In many areas of the country there existed independent voluntary socie-

[2] The best single collection of European attitudes on this theme is presented in Marvin Fisher, *Workshops in the Wilderness: The European Response to American Industrialization, 1830–1860* (New York: Oxford University Press, 1967).

[3] For a study of the economic activities of Pennsylvania's state government, see Louis Hartz, *Economic Policy and Democratic Thought: Pennsylvania, 1776–1860* (Cambridge, Mass.: Harvard University Press, 1948).

[4] *Delaware Gazette*, October 8, 1833.

[5] Robert A. Lively, "The American System: A Review Article," *Business History Review* 29 (1955): 81–96.

ties, functioning in the gap between private individuals and government, which played an important role in defining economic objectives and providing means to reach them. The Pennsylvania Society for the Promotion of Internal Improvements was such an organization. It saw the Commonwealth's central economic objective as the creation of a transportation system which would link the Eastern seaboard to the Ohio Valley and create a large internal market for domestic manufactures. To realize that goal, it sent William Strickland to Europe to bring back the necessary technical knowledge. But the Franklin Institute is an even better example of that kind of intermediary organization which played a significant, though unrecognized, part in the remarkable advance of the American economy.

Philadelphia felt the same economic pressures as other regions, and the Franklin Institute's response was most immediately to local conditions. All during the 1820's and 1830's, the city was engaged in bitter economic rivalry, with both New York and Baltimore, for commercial supremacy of the mid-Atlantic area.[6] By 1825, New York's recently completed Erie Canal threatened to draw off Pennsylvania's entire Western trade. When it came to freight costs, Conestoga wagons were no match for canal boats, and what the New Yorkers failed to capture seemed likely to float out of grasp down the Susquehanna to Baltimore. Pennsylvanians, especially those in the east, felt caught in giant economic pincers, and they struggled for some way out. The rapid construction of a transportation link to the West offered one escape; making Philadelphia the country's premier manufacturing center and developing the state's mineral resources were others.

The Institute was an appropriate vehicle for those ambitions, perhaps especially because of its status as a disinterested, nonpolitical, educational institution. The *Journal* offered the means for transmitting European experience in manufacturing and internal improvements and for diffusing knowledge of American innovations; the Institute's schools and lectures promised a supply of intelligent, scientifically trained mechanics; constructive criticism to inform and stimulate American technical progress was available from the Committee on Inventions; and, finally, there were the organization's annual exhibitions of the products of American industry, where skill and ingenuity would reap their just rewards. All of those activities were

---

[6] James W. Livingood, *The Philadelphia-Baltimore Trade Rivalry, 1780–1860* (Harrisburg: The Pennsylvania Historical and Museum Commission, 1947), describes some elements of that competition. See also Carter Goodrich, ed., *Canals and American Economic Development* (New York: Columbia University Press, 1961), pp. 96–97.

potentially serviceable to the region's economic needs, and perhaps in time, to national concerns as well.

But the Institute, through its Board of Managers, needed first to develop a sense of its own usefulness. Part of that awareness came directly out of the experience of the initial exhibition of domestic manufactures in 1824. The use of industrial exhibitions to stimulate manufactures was familiar, both in America and abroad. Napoleon had established periodic exhibitions as part of his campaign to advance French industry, and agricultural fairs in Great Britain and the United States for years included categories and prizes for manufactured items. Mechanics' institutes in Britain gave awards for technical improvements, after the manner of the Society of Arts, a practice also adopted in America.[7] Out of that amalgam of precedent, the Institute fashioned its first exhibition. But unlike in any previous display, at least in this country, the managers circulated in advance a list of the premiums to be awarded, both to excite competition and to call special attention to those categories of industry "worthy of encouragement." It was one of the first industrial exhibitions held in America, but more important, it became the model for similar efforts in Baltimore, New York, and Boston, throughout the Midwest, and in the Far West when mechanics' institutes were established there.

In terms of their own hopes, the managers did not feel entirely comfortable about the Institute's first exhibition, as earlier suggested. They had planned the affair in some haste, the number of articles received for display was less than hoped for, and the award medals were not ready in time. But in fact, cotton and woolen textiles came from Massachusetts, Rhode Island, and Ohio, as well as from Pennsylvania and nearby Delaware. The Committee on Premiums and Exhibitions selected the judges with care, and they made awards to several items of more than passing interest. Joseph Saxton, an ingenious Pennsylvanian who, like Jacob Perkins before him, left Philadelphia for London, was awarded a silver medal for a new type of clock of unusual workmanship. The firm of David H. Mason and Matthias Baldwin won honorable mention for their engraved copper cylinder for calico printing. S. V. Merrick and Company made the cylinder, and Baldwin and Mason, previously known for their bookbinders' tools,

---

[7] There were a variety of organizations, other than agricultural societies or mechanics' institutes, which also employed premium awards or related schemes to promote industrial development. Some of them are described in Samuel Rezneck, "The Rise and Early Development of Industrial Consciousness in the United States, 1760–1830," *Journal of Economic and Business History* 4 (August 1932): 784–811.

engraved it for printing with such skill as to remove the "one great obstacle" to successful competition with imported goods.[8]

But the display which best realized the ambitions of the exhibition was the sample of wood screws from the factory of Phillips and Company in Phillipsburg, Pennsylvania. The committee picked out the company's produce for special notice because the screws were "made at one operation, by a *machine of American invention*, from Iron of their own manufacture."[9] That was the ideal: mechanical ingenuity and self-sufficiency joined in the production of an article "superior to the best imported." The value to the Commonwealth of that sort of enterprise was clear, and it dawned on the Board of Managers that future exhibitions might be utilized to define more sharply those mechanical and industrial pursuits whose advancement would be most advantageous to Pennsylvanians.

The second exhibition was held the following year, in October 1825, and with it the Franklin Institute began a remarkable program which aimed at nothing less than the rational economic development of the region and the nation. "Under proper regulations," as the Board of Managers expressed it, "we shall soon discover what manufactures flourish in the country,—what objects are successfully prepared by our mechanics,—and in what respects they are deficient."[10] By identifying those industries and techniques most in need of attention, priorities of development could be set. The next stage would be to define the proper market, both in terms of product and geography. Finally, some attempt would be made to set standards of quality. The key to those objectives was proper regulation, and that concept led to an unusual, coordinated effort to identify the major elements of economic advance and to organize them for maximum result.

Exhibition policy was especially directed toward the exploitation of Pennsylvania's natural resources and toward the application of machinery in the production of low-cost items for a mass market. And the Board of Managers was explicit about its objectives: "Among the subjects upon which the board have thought it necessary to lay most stress, are the manufactories of iron and steel in all their branches," as well as the cotton and woolen textile industries.[11] But coal in particular deserved "the greatest attention." Simply for its own value, its promotion by Pennsylvanians was clearly a matter of interest; but the

[8] *First Annual Report of the Proceedings of the Franklin Institute of the State of Pennsylvania, for the Promotion of the Mechanic Arts* (Philadelphia: J. Harding, 1825), p. 74.

[9] Ibid., p. 68.

[10] Ibid., p. 37.

[11] Ibid., p. 56.

Board was also concerned about the relationship between the coal and iron industries. As they noted in their fourth quarterly report:

The manufacture of iron, which may be considered as one of the staple products of Pennsylvania, cannot, under existing circumstances, be carried to a much greater extent than it is at present, from the increasing scarcity and price of wood. If coal cannot be resorted to, the quantity of iron manufactured a few years hence, far from keeping pace with the general increase in our manufactures, will be completely checked by want of fuel.[12]

The schedule of premium awards for the second exhibition, which was printed and distributed throughout the country in January 1825, emphasized the same priorities. There were eighty-three prizes, consisting of medals of gold, silver, and bronze. All the gold medals were reserved for improvements in the utilization of Pennsylvania's two great natural resources—coal and iron. One of the gold medals was for the production, within the state, of the greatest amount of iron in a blast furnace fired only with anthracite. Similarly, there was a gold medal to be awarded to the person smelting the most iron using bituminous coal or coke. Another gold medal awaited the Pennsylvanian who produced the most cast iron from that ore known in the state as "argillaceous carbonate of iron." Finally, if anyone in the country could produce a sample of blister steel "superior to any imported," the Institute stood ready to award him a gold medal.

The second level of premium awards, the silver medals, was not so egregiously centered on the needs of the Commonwealth. Out of a total of sixty-three silver awards announced, slightly less than a quarter of them were restricted to Pennsylvanians, mainly for improvements in iron and steel production, the manufacture of chemicals and dyestuffs, and two or three other miscellaneous categories. Most of the other silver medals were for textiles, copper and brass manufacture, and improvements in ship construction. In practically all cases, the standard against which any item was to be measured was its imported counterpart. In that respect, also, most of the awards were for manufactured goods, and the idea, simply enough, was to encourage successful American production of those things. But a few of the silver medals were to stimulate the solution of particular technical problems. For example, a medal would be given to the author of "the best treatise" on the construction of water wheels, which would describe how to achieve maximum efficiency, but in language "intelligible to common workmen."[13] Another prize was set for the best analysis of the causes

12 Ibid.
13 Ibid., p. 105.

of steam-boiler explosions. The author had to base his investigation on experiments and provide more information than what was already publically available.

If the Committee on Premiums and Exhibitions had done nothing more than indicate those areas of industrial activity which most needed improvement in order to compete successfully with imported goods, or those technical problems most in need of solution, their efforts would have been noteworthy. But the Institute was more ambitious than that, and the second schedule of prizes also defined markets and standards of production. Many textile mills, for instance, attempted to compete with Great Britain or Europe in the production of high-quality fabrics and fine yarns, the very level at which experience counted most and mechanization least. To counteract that tendency, prizes were offered for coarse types of fabric, and it was made a condition of the award that a large amount be available at a given price. The medal for "Negro cloth," a rough fabric then emerging as a trade staple for the Southern states, the Caribbean, and Latin America, would be awarded on the basis of cheapness and only with the assurance that 2,000 yards would be available at the exhibited price. A constant theme in the exhibitions was that goods for display should be "such as are of universal consumption, and as are manufactured in large quantities."[14]

The Institute's aim was to improve quality as well as quantity. One of the silver medals was for the best bar iron made in Pennsylvania suitable for conversion into steel. But the committee, in its "Proposals for the Exhibition of 1825, Addressed to the Manufacturers and Mechanics of the United States," pointed out:

The Institute having observed with regret, that a practice prevails among iron masters, to leave a portion of crude metal at the end of their bars, forming what is termed a *fag*, the competitors for this premium are informed that the neatness of the bars will be considered, and that no bars presenting a fag end will be received for competition.[15]

By those sorts of prohibitions, or encouragements, the Institute meant to define the markets in which American manufacturers were best suited to compete and the kind of goods they should produce for those markets.

[14] Ibid., p. 101; *Address To the Manufacturers of the United States*, Philadelphia, 1828, p. 4; *Address of the Committee on Premiums and Exhibitions of the Franklin Institute of the State of Pennsylvania, for the Promotion of the Mechanic Arts: with a List of the Premiums offered to Competitors at the Eighth Exhibition to be Held in October, 1833* (Philadelphia: T. W. Ustick, 1833), p. 3.
[15] *First Annual Report of the Proceedings of the Franklin Institute*, p. 99.

In their eagerness to award progress, especially in selected industries, the managers were also sometimes willing to bend the rules. At the second exhibition, for instance, William Coleman and Company, of Lancaster County, sent samples of bar iron too late to be tested by conversion into steel. But a silver medal was awarded despite that fact, both because of the firm's established reputation and "on account of the importance of this manufacture (which is all essential to Pennsylvania)."[16] Flexibility in the award system was also achieved by empowering the Committee on Premiums and Exhibitions to give prizes for entries not included in the advance schedule of premiums but which struck them as particularly deserving of mention. And by a variety of other means, prominence could be given items of special concern. "With a view to elucidate the subject of rail roads," as the committee put it, "a very beautiful imported model of a locomotive engine was also exhibited."[17] The model, of a Stephenson engine, had been sent by William Strickland while on his tour for the Pennsylvania Society for the Promotion of Internal Improvements. Also to emphasize steam power, a high-pressure stationary engine made by Rush and Muhlenberg was kept in operation throughout the exhibition.

But whatever the means, the central and conscious concern of the Franklin Institute's exhibitions from 1824 to 1838 was to advance the technical level of manufacturing skills, to increase the use of mechanical power, and to develop mineral resources. The *Journal* was heavily used in the campaign. Dr. Jones published a steady stream of articles on iron manufacturing and the coal industry. When an English patent promised an improved method of combining anthracite with bituminous coal, Jones called the attention of his readers to its "very great interest, not only to Pennsylvania, but also to various other parts of the United States."[18] Two issues of the *Journal* were almost wholly devoted to a series of anthracite experiments conducted by Marcus Bull, president of the North American Coal Company and a man of scientific disposition.[19]

16 *Report of the Second Annual Exhibition of the Franklin Institute of the State of Pennsylvania for the Promotion of the Mechanic Arts* (Philadelphia: The Franklin Institute, 1825), p. 15.

17 Ibid., p. 27.

18 "English Patents," *The Franklin Journal and American Mechanics' Magazine* 1 (February 1826): 89.

19 Bull was said to have been once associated in London with Jacob Perkins and with Murray, Draper, Fairman & Company. He was described as "a gentleman, well educated, of a philosophical turn, prepossessing appearance and great suavity of manners" ("Recollections of a Cinquegenarian," *Philadelphia Sunday Dispatch*, March 27, 1859). Bull first presented the results of his research in a paper read before the American Philosophical Society. Jones published the paper in the May 1826 issue of

Of course, Bull probably had some personal stake in the promotion of coal consumption, but the managers of the Franklin Institute saw themselves as engaged in a large-scale cooperative effort on behalf of Commonwealth and country. An individualistic, secretive technology smacked of old-world ways in their minds, and they sought to make the Institute a focal point and clearing house for information of all kinds on coal and iron production. Their efforts brought results. Edward Sims wrote from Virginia:

I have a redundancy of water power and wish to erect a plain simple forge for beating out bar iron from the Pig. I shall use bituminous coal—the Richmond Coal. I should take it as a favor if you would give me any information upon the subject. I am a complete novice in the business. I should like to get someone to come here and undertake the matter. Perhaps you can name someone. . . .[20]

Most queries were more explicit, however, and were for information on furnace dimensions or layout, blowing equipment, mine ventilation, and related issues. The successful use of heated air in blast furnaces created considerable interest in that process. One correspondent noted:

Having lately noticed in Several publications that Mr. Grubb of Lancaster County Pa. has adopted the hot air Blast in his Furnace for Smelting Iron with great Success I think you could not render the country a greater service than to obtain from him the particulars attending his experiment and publishing them in your very useful Journal.[21]

Other correspondents provided information for the Institute to disseminate. Joshua Malin, of the Delaware County Rolling Mill, for instance,

---

his *Journal*. He subsequently argued, without success, that Bull's research should have been awarded the Rumford prize, held in trust by the American Academy of Arts and Sciences for the most important discoveries on heat or light. "Notice of Mr. Bull's 'Defence of the Experiments to determine the comparative value of the principal varieties of fuel, used in the United States,' &c.—Philadelphia, Judah Dobson, Chestnut Street," *The Franklin Journal and American Mechanics' Magazine* 5 (April 1828): 273.

[20] Edward Sims to William Hamilton, Virginia Mills, Virginia, January 30, 1836, Incoming Correspondence, Franklin Institute Archives.

[21] D. Graham to the Editor of the *Journal of the Franklin Institute*, Drapers Valley, Virginia, August 17, 1837, Incoming Correspondence. Various members of the Grubb family were actively involved in iron manufacturing in Lancaster County at that time. See James M. Swank, *History of the Manufacture of Iron in All Ages* (Philadelphia: The American Iron and Steel Association, 1892), pp. 182ff.

sent for publication in the *Journal* a description of his blast furnace, in which anthracite had been employed.[22]

The interchange the society sought was best typified in a letter from Hardeman Phillips, who forwarded coke and iron specimens from his works, with the comment:

My principal object in submitting these specimens to the public inspection is to invite the manufacturers of Philadelphia to the study of the resources of their own state, so well calculated, if duly fostered, to render the country independent of foreign supplies.[23]

Phillips's letter touched two sensitive chords. The Institute's ambitions to serve the economic development of the state found a rewarding acceptance. Industrial advancement depended on technical knowledge, and until some more organized fashion of diffusing information was found, the clearinghouse concept filled an important need. But it also became obvious that Pennsylvania was not the only area with such concerns. Letters came from New Jersey and Virginia as well, and all looked to the Institute as a source of expertise. That response was rewarding, too, and played upon a feeling already extant that the institution might serve equally well the technical requirements of the nation. In any event, when letters arrived, such as the one from General William Ashley, of St. Louis, with specimens of Missouri iron to be tested "by the scientific gentlemen of the Franklin Institute," it appeared that national prominence had come, whether or not consciously sought.[24]

A program to encourage manufacturing and stimulate industrial advance might easily have led to political action. The American Institute of New York, founded in 1828, conducted industrial fairs along lines similar to the Franklin Institute's exhibitions and from the outset determined "by every legitimate means in their power" to secure a protective tariff.[25] Publicists of like mind were immediately attracted by the Philadelphia exhibitions. Hezekiah Niles, a zealous propagandist for domestic manufactures, reported that the Franklin Institute

[22] Joshua Malin, "Description of a furnace for smelting Iron, by means of Anthracite," *The Franklin Journal and American Mechanics' Magazine* 4 (October 1827): 217–19.

[23] Minutes of Meetings of the Franklin Institute, August 25, 1831, Franklin Institute Archives.

[24] General William H. Ashley to William Hamilton, St. Louis, September 4, 1832, Incoming Correspondence.

[25] Charles P. Daly, *Origins and History of Institutions for the Promotion of Useful Arts* (Albany: American Institute, 1864), p. 29.

had been established "to make a market" for the products of American industry and to promote their consumption. At the conclusion of the second exhibition, Niles claimed that even the stoutest of opponents to the "abominable tariff" could hardly fail to be moved by "the beauty, extent and perfection" of American manufactures displayed there and by the necessity for their protection.[26] That kind of thinking led several members of the Institute, under the leadership of Matthew Carey, to form a society whose purpose was to establish a warehouse for "the reception and sale of American manufactures" and to hold a national exhibition of domestic industry in Washington, D.C.[27]

In that expansive mood, it was not always a simple matter to remain objective about the tariff issue. The Institute's leadership denied any concern with politics. As Dr. Jones claimed, "The Franklin Institute interferes not in the great question of protecting duties; it has no political object in view." But in practically the same breath, he announced that the function of exhibitions was to induce the unprejudiced citizen to buy American-made products, "to the exclusion of foreign artists."[28] The same kind of ambivalence can be seen in a special report made by the Committee on Inventions relative to Isaac Macauley's carpeting factory. Macauley's products had received favorable notice at the first exhibition and prize awards at the second. But in 1829, he came before the Board of Managers, requesting an examination of his product because, he suggested, "unfair comparisons between it and the foreign fabric" had been made by local dealers in imported goods in an attempt to influence public opinion.[29] In its report, the committee noted that they would not normally interfere in a dispute between rival domestic manufacturers but that it was entirely within their proper sphere to allay "any prejudice that exists against our own products when the foreigner comes into competition, whenever the former is worthy of protection."[30] Under those circumstances, the committee made a complete tour of Macauley's factory and reported their entire satisfaction with his product and methods of manufacture.

26 *Niles' Weekly Register,* October 30, 1824; October 15, 1825.

27 The idea was apparently an outgrowth of the Institute's first exhibition. The Philadelphia group, which included Ronaldson and Merrick, proposed a national exhibition and, in cooperation with committees from New York and Baltimore, staged the display in Washington in February 1825. *Niles' Weekly Register,* December 18, 1824; Samuel Rezneck, "The Rise and Early Development of Industrial Consciousness in the United States, 1760–1830," p. 805.

28 "Observations on the Rise and Progress of the Franklin Institute," *The Franklin Journal and American Mechanics' Magazine* 1 (March 1826): 130.

29 Report of the committee appointed to visit Mr. Macauley's Floor Cloth Manufactory, February 10, 1829, Committee on Inventions, Franklin Institute Archives.

30 Ibid.

Not only was the fabric durable, but by the introduction of machinery, its price had been reduced.

The Macauley episode was an isolated instance, however, and the Institute never came closer to the question of protecting American industry. The organization's faith was an optimistic one. Given the proper encouragement, the Board of Managers felt that American productions would equal those of Europe, and as a general rule they preferred positive rather than negative measures, stimulation rather than restriction. And that attitude was echoed by the subcommittee of the Committee on Premiums and Exhibitions in charge of woolen goods, the group potentially most concerned about tariff protection. In an advance circular to exhibitors, the subcommittee advised:

The undersigned are deeply impressed with the conviction that the success of those engaged in manufacturing in this country, depends more upon a general and zealous competition for preeminence among themselves, than upon any other cause. Progressive improvement is the surest and best resource on which the Manufacturer can rely. It is this that will eventually achieve, by individual exertion, that true protective policy which, whilst it discharges the obligation incurred for legislative patronage, will secure the home-market to our own Manufacturers, and enrich the country with the fruits of their labors.[31]

The Franklin Institute aimed to stimulate American industrial development, and by almost any measure it succeeded. The exhibits themselves became a great popular attraction in Philadelphia, as they later did in other cities. The Institute pioneered in a number of the crowd-pleasing displays that were to become standard techniques for expositions by the end of the century. Moving machinery was first used to dramatize a particular technology. The Board soon realized that there was a popular appeal in operating mechanisms. "Experience has shown the interest which the public take in them," prospective exhibitors were advised, and the committee promised to provide a "competent superintendent."[32] During the 1828 exhibition, one of the machines in operation was a portable press on which an ode to celebrate the occasion was printed and distributed to visitors. A stanza may be worth quotation, if only to suggest the spirit:

> Genius of Art! What achievements are thine?—
>   To delight and astonish the mind
> The efforts of knowledge and fancy combine;
>   But the triumph to thee is assigned.

[31] *Address of the Committee on Premiums and Exhibitions*, 1833.
[32] Ibid., p. 5.

How high swell the bosoms of patriots with pride,
To behold the rich treasures which here are supplied;
  While Invention's bright wand
  In the artizan's hand,
Points to glory the freemen of Freedom's own land.[33]

As crowds increased, the Institute imposed a small admission charge and moved its fairs to larger quarters. The first took place in Carpenters' Hall, but subsequent exhibitions were held in Masonic Hall. It was estimated that at least fifteen to twenty thousand people visited the second exhibition in 1825, and double that number in the following year.[34] But more often than attendance figures, newspapers and committee reports spoke simply of vast crowds. To accommodate them, the three-day exhibition was lengthened to four days in 1827; by 1831 it lasted five days; and in 1838 it became of a week's duration. Also by 1838, exhibits spilled over from the large "saloon" of Masonic Hall into several other rooms, each allotted to specific types of items. A single steam engine was used to power all working machinery, and an additional building was constructed in front of the hall for testing all stoves, grates, and kitchen ranges "by actual service."[35]

Since one of the primary aims of the exhibitions was to join producer and consumer in an atmosphere congenial to American manufactures, popular approval was an important yardstick of success. The award of premiums, on the other hand, was meant to excite genius. There was no better way to spend money, Jones argued in the *Journal*, than to reward "merit and skill in the arts."[36] Basic rules were established for awarding prizes. No member of the Board of Managers, or of any committee, was eligible for any kind of award. Proof of origin was required for all articles submitted for competition, and no item which had previously received a premium, at any exhibition anywhere, was eligible for an award. The premium system worked well and attracted outside sponsorship for special awards.

For the seventh exhibition, in 1831, the coal mine owners of the Pottsville district subscribed one hundred dollars as a prize to be

---

[33] James M'Henry, *An Ode, Written by Request, On the Opening of the Exhibition at the Franklin Institute of Philadelphia, October, 1828* (Philadelphia, 1828).

[34] The editor of the *National Gazette* argued that the Institute's exhibitions provided a far better means of publicity than expensive advertising campaigns: "The productions of art are exhibited to the eyes of at least fifteen or twenty thousand spectators" (*National Gazette*, September 23, 1826).

[35] *Circular letter from the Committee on Arrangements*, October 1, 1838, Committee on Premiums and Exhibitions, Franklin Institute Archives.

[36] *The Franklin Journal and American Mechanics' Magazine* 1 (March 1826): 132–33.

awarded by the Committee on Premiums and Exhibitions for the cooking stove which most successfully used anthracite as a fuel. The Mine operators on the Schuylkill and Lehigh added to the fund in 1833, and in the exhibition for that year, an award of a silver medal and twenty dollars was scheduled for the best coal-burning domestic cooking stove, "the price not to exceed ten dollars."[37] The system served government as well as private enterprise. In 1833, the city of Philadelphia gave the Institute $100 to be used as an additional stimulus to the invention of the best lamp for lighting city streets. And in the same year, the New Castle and Frenchtown Turnpike and Railroad Company provided the sum of $200 to be awarded for the best plan for preventing the escape of sparks from locomotive smokestacks.[38] Both the street lamp and spark arrestor prizes, to which the Institute added silver medals, were incentives to the solution of particular technical problems. Craft skill was also awarded in the exhibition of 1835, when the Stone Cutters Company of Philadelphia provided the funds for a series of cash prizes to apprentices for excellence of workmanship.[39]

One of the most dramatic efforts to advance technology through cash and prize awards was to encourage production of Russian sheet iron. Rolled iron, in imitation of the Russian product, was used chiefly in the manufacture of stove pipe, and it was a branch of the iron industry, as one authority put it, "full of difficulties and peculiarities."[40] Its production depended traditionally on charcoal fuel, a good source of iron, and ample power. Since Pennsylvania had all three ingredients, the industry was an obvious candidate for transplantation. But first, the techniques had to be acquired.

The first notice of interest in the subject at the Institute came in the advance list of premiums for the exhibition of 1828, when a silver

[37] *Address of the Committee on Premiums and Exhibitions*, 1833, p. 2. For a discussion of the domestic use of coal, see Frederick M. Binder, "Anthracite Enters the American Home," *Pennsylvania Magazine of History and Biography* 82 (January 1958): 82–99.

[38] The conditions for both awards were described in the *Address of the Committee on Premiums and Exhibitions* for the exhibition of 1833. The spark-arrestor prize attracted special notice because of its value. See the *National Gazette*, September 10, 1833; and the *Journal of the Franklin Institute* 16 (September 1833): 158.

[39] The Stone Cutters Company had responded to a public appeal from the Board of Managers for a conference with local trade organizations, to determine premiums for the 1835 exhibition. Minutes of the Board of Managers, March 18, 1835, Franklin Institute Archives. The premiums are described in the *Address of the Committee on Premiums and Exhibitions of the Franklin Institute of the State of Pennsylvania, for the Promotion of the Mechanic Arts: with a List of the Premiums offered to Competitors at the Ninth Exhibition, to be Held in October, 1835* (Philadelphia: T. W. Ustick, 1835), pp. 15–16.

[40] John Percy, *The Manufacture of Russian Sheet-Iron* (Philadelphia: Henry Carey Baird, 1871), p. 21.

medal was offered for six sheets of rolled iron equal to the imported kind. By 1833, it was decided that a silver medal was not a sufficient attraction, and the Board of Managers, through a special committee, approached the iron manufacturers of the country with an appeal for donations to a prize fund.[41] In a circular drawn up for that purpose, the committee argued that "the beauty and superiority of the article named is so well known; and the producing it in the United States is so generally admitted to be a great desideratum that its importance will be self evident." The problem, however, was to find "some practicable method of inducing the ingenious to make experiments."[42] The Institute's solution was a monetary prize to compensate for the expense of experimentation, and it suggested a fund of from one to two thousand dollars. Any successful claimant would divulge his process to the Institute, which would then spread the knowledge freely "for the benefit of the public."

The Board of Managers also decided, perhaps in case cash or native ingenuity failed, on a somewhat more devious stratagem. It authorized the chairman of the Board to write the secretary of state, suggesting that he might direct the U.S. minister to the Russian court "to use his influence in order to ascertain the process of manufacturing sheet iron in that country."[43] The State Department was apparently not warm to that approach, and the idea seems to have been dropped. Nor is there any evidence that the iron industry provided funds for a large cash award. But the Institute maintained its own interest in encouraging the manufacture and in the awards for the exhibition of 1835 offered a gold medal for 100 sheets, of a quality comparable to Russian iron.

Monetary awards, offered in conjunction with medals, provided additional interest for the Institute's periodic exhibitions. They also served to reinforce the idea that the organization was the logical resort for technical information. Outside support for premiums was an early, if somewhat naive, form of industrial research. In the case of the prize offered by the New Castle and Frenchtown Railroad for a spark arrestor, the firm had in mind a device to prevent the escape of sparks, but the solution was not simply one of putting a cap on a smokestack. Maintenance of a proper draft and levels of fuel consumption were important elements of the problem, and the railroad meant to encourage

[41] Minutes of the Board of Managers, March 14, 1833.

[42] Manuscript of a circular to Iron Masters on Russia Sheet Iron, April 1833, Incoming Correspondence.

[43] Minutes of the Board of Managers, April 11, 1833.

experimentation, not tinkering.[44] At a time when neither industry nor government had significant facilities to solve problems of a technical nature, and before engineering schools or other agencies existed to provide organized knowledge, the Institute's role as a center of expertise was of considerable importance. That reputation, in turn, added value to the premium awards.

Manufacturers came quickly to realize that display of their wares offered a potential competitive advantage, especially if medals were won. James Chappell, for instance, entered a transfer system for textile printing with the hasty note, "It was late in time of exhibition before I deposited, and should have not done so at this time had not others— Competitors been seen there." Chappell was particularly anxious to display his system at the exhibition because he planned to market it in Europe, where "Your favourable notice would be of service to me."[45] In very much the same fashion, the Poughkeepsie Screw Company used the Institute's exhibition to introduce its product into the Philadelphia area. After winning a silver medal for the best small machinery castings, Jonathan Bonney of Wilmington, Delaware, assured his customers that "all work undertaken by him, . . . shall be of the same character as that which secured the approbation of the above named institution."[46]

The market value of the Institute's seal of approval led naturally to controversies with disappointed entrants. The Fairbanks scales company was concerned that their competitors had sent scales especially prepared for the exhibition and queried William Hamilton whether items submitted should not be *a fair sample of those kept in the market.*[47] Local representatives of the Middlesex Manufacturing Company at Lowell, Massachusetts, were upset over the failure of their product in winning a medal. They had entered nine pieces of cassimere for the silver medal offered for that type of fabric. The goods had been awarded a certificate of merit; but on the grounds that theirs was the

[44] The railroad had conducted some experiments of its own, the results of which it offered freely to share with contestants for the prize; and several other railroad companies subsequently made equipment available to those who wished to conduct trials of spark arrestor designs. The correspondence pertaining to the subject is contained in the Locomotive Spark Arrestor file in the Franklin Institute Archives. For a discussion of the technical problems involved, see John H. White, Jr., *American Locomotives: An Engineering History, 1830–1880* (Baltimore: The Johns Hopkins Press, 1968), p. 114.

[45] James H. Chappell to the Committee of the Franklin Institute Fair, Philadelphia, November 14, 1833, Incoming Correspondence.

[46] Thomas W. Harvey to William Hamilton, Poughkeepsie, N.Y., September 4, 1837, and newspaper clipping from the *Delaware Free Press*, 1833, both in the Franklin Institute Archives.

[47] E. & J. Fairbanks & Co. to William Hamilton, St. Johnsburg, Vt., August 10, 1835, Incoming Correspondence.

only cassimere exhibited, and the best made in America, they argued that the premium should have been awarded them.[48]

Such complaints were the natural outcome of a successful program. If the Institute's exhibitions had failed to create interest in the manufacturing community, or if the prizes had had little value, there would have been no quarrel. As it was, the exhibitions attracted hundreds of entrants from all over the country, and competition for premium awards was keen. It was impossible to avoid occasional controversy, and as Dr. Jones philosophically noted:

Some are offended, and refuse again to enter the lists, new combatants appear, and supply their places, whilst time and reflection suffice, in general, to subdue that momentary irritation which disappointed hope is so apt to produce.[49]

For the Institute, however, the exhibitions answered most of the hopes of those in the organization who sought to use it as a positive force in the progress of American industry.

With the passage of time, those in charge of planning exhibitions could afford to look back at the earliest efforts with a comfortable sense of accomplishment. The announcement for the eleventh exhibition was cast in that vein:

It is within the recollection of many who are yet actively engaged in business pursuits that the artizans and manufacturers of our country were to be found labouring in their useful avocations, without the stimulus of a public acknowledgement of their importance as a class of citizens, without any concert of action or interchange of experience; a knowledge of the skill and peculiar productions of each individual not extending beyond the limited sphere of his own personal influence; a jealousy and dread of the rivalry of fellow craftsmen, producing cautious secrecy of supposed improvements, and as a natural consequence, the prolonged and feeble infancy of American manufacturers.[50]

All that had been changed, however, and there were those, the announcement claimed, "among our wealthy and influential citizens" who could trace their own progress in the Institute's exhibitions.

Perhaps it is not surprising that the Committee on Premiums and Exhibitions should have felt its efforts had been valuable. But whether

[48] Brown & Hanson to the Board of Managers of the Franklin Institute of Pennsylvania, Philadelphia, December 14, 1833, Incoming Correspondence.

[49] "Fifteenth Quarterly Report of the Board of Managers of the Franklin Institute of the State of Pennsylvania," *The Franklin Journal and American Mechanics' Magazine* 4 (November 1827): 330.

[50] *Address of the Committee on Premiums and Exhibitions*, Philadelphia, 1840, p. 2.

the Franklin Institute's attempts to program the advance of American industry had had all the effect desired is another question. Those who answered in the affirmative were not always explicit. For example, Solomon W. Roberts, a man who had gained distinction as a civil engineer, once said, "It is impossible to estimate correctly the benefits that have been conferred by the Institute upon the City of Philadelphia, and the State of Pennsylvania, and upon the mechanic arts of the country at large."[51] Roberts meant that in a positive way, of course, but his words suggest the difficulty in framing an answer. In some cases the response was, not as much as hoped. Despite gold medals, advice from the committee on inventions, and information in the *Journal*, ironmasters in Pennsylvania and elsewhere were slow to adopt anthracite as a fuel. Similarly, the Institute was not as successful as it had hoped to be in organizing a large-scale assault on the duplication of Russian sheet iron. And yet, there is at least circumstantial evidence that its efforts in that direction were not without effect. When the society began its campaign to encourage the production of sheet iron, that industry was scarcely extant in America. But in 1871, the English metallurgist John Percy claimed that its manufacture had been "carried to a higher state of advancement in the United States than anywhere in the world save Russia."[52] Even more remarkable was the fact that American sheet-iron production was almost completely localized in Philadelphia or in nearby establishments controlled by Philadelphians.

The leaders of the Franklin Institute could see that kind of progress, and they visualized their exhibitions, together with all other activities related to the same purposes, as a struggle to lift American manufactures from languor and technical backwardness to efficiency and prosperity. By the 1830's it seemed as if the distance to that goal had been substantially reduced. Exhibits had reached a variety and level of perfection unknown in earlier days. The public thronged in ever larger numbers—over 40,000 attended the 1838 exhibition. Of equal satisfaction was the knowledge that the Institute's example had furnished the pattern for industrial fairs in most major cities throughout the nation. Indeed, attending such events became a great American pastime.

---

[51] Solomon W. Roberts, *An Address, Delivered at the Close of the Sixteenth Exhibition of American Manufactures, held in Philadelphia, by the Franklin Institute of the State of Pennsylvania* (Philadelphia: John C. Clark, 1846), p. 21. Local newspapers usually responded in a similar vein. At the close of the third exhibition, for instance, it was reported that "the Franklin Institute is justly regarded as a *national* institution" (*National Gazette*, October 10, 1826). A decade later, it was argued that the Institute was "not exceeded in reputation by any other institution in the United States" (*The Saturday Evening Post*, October 10, 1835).

[52] Percy, *The Manufacture of Russian Sheet-Iron*, p. 21.

Since they have never received detailed study, it is difficult to assess the general importance of exhibitions in stimulating economic advance in the pre-Civil War era. Historians have often suggested that American industrial development depended on systems of interchangeable-parts manufacture, developed in New England arms factories and textile mills, and that their display at the 1851 Crystal Palace Exhibition in London marked the country's emergence as a serious competitor to the industrial nations of the world.[53] But by that time, Americans had a quarter-century of experience with industrial exhibitions. While Europeans might not have been aware of it, Americans had been competing with them for years. The constant theme of the Institute's exhibitions was to encourage manufactures "equal to or superior" to the imported article. Nor was that objective limited simply to the domestic marketplace. Exhibitions annually gave Americans the opportunity to reaffirm their faith in industrial progress and technological advancement. For almost three decades before the Crystal Palace Exhibition, industrial fairs were an important vehicle for the inculcation of those values and for emphasizing resource development, mechanization, and inventiveness. The ingenuity which surprised visitors to London in 1851 was something Americans were accustomed to seeing.

Partly out of a sense that industry had achieved a healthy adolescence, the Board of Managers felt able to move on to other objectives. In their annual report in January 1838, the Board explained the shift in policy. When the Institute was begun, American manufactures "were in a condition of weak and destitute infancy." Exhibitions had been established to alter that state of affairs, both by stimulation of the artisan's talents and by the consumer's willingness to buy his products. At least partly as a result of that program, the managers claimed, domestic industry had grown to such strength and maturity that it no longer required aid. Furthermore, frequent displays cost a great deal of labor, and "the energies of the Institute have become too valuable to be expended in getting up a mere idle pageant."[54]

Exhibitions did demand a considerable amount of work, and all of it, except for that of the actuary, William Hamilton, was voluntary. In 1831, for instance, the premium list enumerated eighty-nine awards. They had to be determined in advance, and the list had to be printed early in the year and then distributed over the country. The nine men

[53] The best recent study to incorporate that view is Nathan Rosenberg, ed., *The American System of Manufactures. The Report of the Committee on the Machinery of the United States 1855 and the Special Reports of George Wallis and Joseph Whitworth 1854* (Edinburgh: The University Press, 1969).

[54] Fourteenth Annual Report of the Board of Managers, January 1838, Franklin Institute Archives.

on the Committee on Premiums and Exhibitions were responsible for the general oversight of the exhibition. The twenty-nine committees of judges required the participation of sixty-five additional members. The displays were open to the public for five days, during which time about 10,000 paid admissions were collected and at least double that number admitted free. The entries had been collected at the Institute's hall and then required transportation (at no cost to the exhibitors) to Masonic Hall, where they were arranged by the committee and set up for display. Records were kept for all articles entered so that they could be returned in good order after the exhibition was over. Judges made their choices, and the committee had then to secure the medals and see that they were properly engraved. The culmination of the whole affair was an award ceremony, open to the public and distinguished by a speaker of some note. And in 1831, as if their labors had not been enough to tax the dedication of the most zealous, the committee was forced dolefully to report that the speaker had declined to deliver his address.[55] Exhibitions could sometimes be a chore.

Still, there were other factors behind the reassessment of exhibition policy, and they were in motion as early as 1828. In his report as chairman of the Committee on Premiums and Exhibitions, Samuel V. Merrick called for a review of the program: "Five Exhibitions having been held by this Institute, a tolerably just opinion may now be entertained with respect to their utility."[56] Exhibitors received a notoriety which was directly to their personal benefit. The public at large had been made aware of the extent and quality of American manufactures, and in those respects the exhibitions had proved equal to expectations. But annual repetition had dulled the interest of both producer and consumer, according to Merrick, who claimed, "In a word, the exhibitions have been overdone." Biennial or triennial displays would have been a better idea from the beginning, he said, but by holding them annually, the Institute was committed to the public. The question, as Merrick saw it, was "how to discontinue them with credit?"[57]

During the fall of 1828, there had been unofficial conversations between the Committee on Premiums and Exhibitions and officers of the Maryland Institute in Baltimore toward the idea of joint exhibitions, which Merrick offered as a diplomatic solution to the problem. Since the Maryland Institute also sponsored exhibitions, joint commit-

[55] *Report of the Seventh Annual Exhibition of the Franklin Institute of the State of Pennsylvania for the Promotion of the Mechanic Arts* (Philadelphia: J. Harding, 1831).
[56] Report of the Committee on Premiums and Exhibitions, January 5, 1829, Franklin Institute Archives.
[57] Ibid.

tees from each society could be appointed, the work load shared, and
the fairs held in each city in alternate years. The president of the Baltimore organization had responded favorably to the idea, Merrick said,
and as a result, the Board of Managers approved his proposal.[58] No
exhibit would be held in 1829, and the committee was directed to
draft a plan of joint action to the Maryland Institute. For unknown
reasons, nothing came of the idea of cooperation, but Merrick's report
signaled the beginning of a movement within the Institute opposed to
annual exhibitions. A sense of decorum pervades the official records, and
conflicting positions are not always clear. But it was not simply a matter
of scheduling. The issue was larger, having to do with major policy. To
maintain annual exhibitions would demand a large share of the Institute's energy and resources; it would become a full-time job, in effect,
and there were those who disagreed strongly with that view of the
organization's mission.

In line with Merrick's earlier recommendation, no exhibition was
held in 1829. Plans for one the following year were accepted without
controversy, and it was held as scheduled. By 1831, however, when
William H. Keating proposed at a meeting of the Board of Managers
that an exhibition be held that year, the subject clearly had become a
matter of dispute. Keating put his motion forward in a tentative fashion,
to bring the matter before the Board, as he said, perhaps for their action
at the next meeting. But sterner spirits prevailed; it was moved to consider the question immediately, and the issue was joined. An attempt to
amend Keating's resolution—to have the exhibition in 1832 instead of
1831—was defeated, after "a full discussion," thirteen to eight. The
preliminary vote settled the outcome for 1831, and the managers decided
to hold the exhibition. It had been a serious division, despite the
laconic quality of the minutes of that meeting, with the threat of Merrick's resignation hanging in the air.[59] Of the eight voting for biennial
exhibitions, the most conspicuous were Merrick and a newcomer to the
Board, Alexander Dallas Bache. Their opposition was led by Ronaldson,
Keating, Matthias Baldwin, and Frederick Fraley. When the Committee
on Premiums and Exhibitions was appointed for 1832, it was made up
entirely of those who supported the idea of annual exhibitions, and
essentially the same group controlled the committee for the next two
years. Actually, there was no exhibition in 1832, but it had nothing to
do with the controversy. The cholera epidemic of that year and "the

58 Ibid.; Minutes of the Board of Managers, January 5, 1829.
59 Minutes of the Board of Managers, January 24, 1831. See also the minutes for
the meeting of January 19, 1831.

unsettled state of the public mind" induced the managers to postpone the event.[60]

In 1834, the appointment of Merrick as chairman of the Committee on Premiums and Exhibitions suggested a change in policy. At the first meeting of the Board that year, Alexander Dallas Bache moved that the committee should report whether "in their opinion it would be advisable to hold the next exhibition."[61] The report was never made, and the Board was conspicuously silent on the subject until its quarterly report in April, when it revealed that "after mature deliberation" the decision was made in the negative. In that quiet fashion, the Institute moved into a biennial system of exhibitions. Time ratified the action, and even though no formal vote on the subject was ever recorded, by 1836 the Board could report that the plan was "in conformity with a regulation adopted some years back."[62]

Change came easily for several reasons. By 1834 the Institute had available other mechanisms to reward ingenuity and display industrial advance. Exhibitions had shown the society to be a logical and convenient repository for prizes to stimulate inventiveness. Industry had used it in that manner, and so had the city of Philadelphia when it wanted new ideas for street lighting. Those were occasional situations, however, when outside funds came to the Institute to be directed toward specific objectives. But in 1834, the Select and Common Councils of the city gave the Institute control over the Scott Legacy, a permanent fund designed to reward technical creativity. John Scott was an Edinburgh chemist who at his death bequeathed $4,000 to the city "to be distributed among ingenious men and women, who make useful inventions." The premiums would be a copper medal with the inscription, "To the most deserving," and a cash award not to exceed twenty dollars.[63] The Scott Legacy premiums gave the Institute an important tool which could be utilized outside the framework of exhibitions.

An alternative mechanism had also been developed for the display of American manufactures. It came, curiously enough, out of an attempt to reform the monthly membership meetings of the Institute. In 1829, procedural rules for the conduct of meetings were adopted, both to give formal order to the meetings and to increase their educational quality.[64]

60 *National Gazette*, September 15, 1832.
61 Minutes of the Board of Managers, January 25, 1834.
62 Thirteenth Annual Report of the Board of Managers, January 18, 1837, Franklin Institute Archives.
63 Minutes of the Board of Managers, April 3, 1834. The terms of the award were regularly published in the *Journal* from 1834 onwards.
64 Minutes of Meetings of the Franklin Institute, April 16, 1829.

The rules included a plan for the self-instruction of members. Topics of discussion, selected by a committee, would be taken up after routine business was finished.

The idea was a failure, almost from the beginning. The topics first selected for consideration were self-consciously abstruse. At one of the early meetings, for instance, among the proposed topics was the query, "Does a body descending on an inclin'd plane, with an accelerated motion, press the plane with the same force, through every portion of its length?" Discussion, in such circumstances, amounted to little more than "a few desultory remarks."[65] In an attempt to structure a better response, members who volunteered for the task were assigned to open the discussion, either by presentation of a paper or by some form of prepared comment. That change tended to improve the quality of meetings somewhat, although the system still depended on the effort members displayed in collecting and presenting sufficient information to create a viable discussion. Monthly meetings limped along in that style for the next three years. When the subject matter was clearly defined and bore some relation to the talents and experience of the membership, discussions were fruitful. But all too often, the topics were speculative or assignments were not well carried out, and by 1832 the Committee on Instruction was constrained to report that "few of the Monthly meetings have been such as to interest the members of the Institute."[66]

In 1832 Alexander Dallas Bache became chairman of the Committee on Instruction. To remedy the defects his committee found in the organization of monthly meetings, Bache proposed that they be replaced by monthly conversational meetings, the *conversazione* long popular with learned scientific societies. The regularly scheduled quarterly meetings were sufficient for the transaction of Institute business, Bache argued, and he recommended that the reading room be open one evening a month for "conversation & the exhibition of new or interesting machines & inventions."[67] The plan proved an immediate success. By 1837 conversation meetings were so widely used as a showcase for new or unusual products that the Committee on Premiums and Exhibitions suggested a display at those gatherings rather than an exhibition that year.

Conversational meetings and the Scott Legacy premiums gave the Franklin Institute other means by which it could achieve objectives similar to those of the exhibitions. But new tools alone do not explain

65 Ibid., May 28, 1829.
66 Report of the Committee on Instruction, December 1832, Franklin Institute Archives.
67 Ibid.

major policy changes; there has to be a disposition to use them. By 1830 a new set of leaders was emerging, with different interests and different views of the most effective way for the organization to use its resources.

It is important to realize that reassessment of the Institute's policy on exhibitions or procedural changes in the conduct of meetings were not issues of relevance to the society only. The questions raised were at the heart of American industrial development. The Board of Managers realized this, and they showed an extraordinary understanding of the ways in which the Institute and organizations like it could relate to concerns of national consequence.

In 1824, the most critical need in a thoroughly agricultural country was for an industrial consciousness: to reduce the predilection Americans had for imported goods, which reached back into the colonial era; to give domestic manufacturers the confidence and the market they wanted for their own development; and to stimulate the improvement in techniques which would raise their productions to a competitive, if not dominant, position at home and abroad. The industrial exhibitions which the Institute inaugurated in America were highly successful in those respects and widely imitated. The exhibitions, as well as all those other attempts to direct the course of economic development, brought some valuable insights to the Board of Managers and to those who were emerging as its leading spokesmen. Their clearest perceptions were that resource development and industrial production offered great wealth and that lack of organized technical knowledge was the principal impediment to achieving it.

Samuel V. Merrick and Alexander Dallas Bache were the outstanding personalities of the new leadership. Merrick, of course, had been influential in the organization's founding and had gained a reputation within the society for his informed judgment.[68] In the early years, however, he was somewhat overshadowed by older and more prominent men like Browne and Carey. Bache, who did not join the Institute until 1829, shortly after his appointment to the faculty of the University of Pennsylvania, was elected to the Board of Managers the following year. By that time, the two had already taken the place of earlier leaders. Browne's membership on the Board ended in 1827, and he was never again close to power in the institution. Matthew Carey left the Board in 1828; and William Strickland became involved in other

---

[68] The best single source of biographical information on Merrick is Thomas Coulson, "Some Prominent Members of the Franklin Institute 1. Samuel Vaughan Merrick, 1801–1870," *Journal of the Franklin Institute* 258 (November 1954): 335–46.

enterprises after his return from Europe. Those men had given the Franklin Institute immediate prominence by their affiliation and had shaped it to match their own attitudes and interests.

With Bache and Merrick, the current turned in a different direction, and they led the Institute to an increasing concern with science, technical research, and education. Bache was especially equipped to direct the society into new channels. The great-grandson of Benjamin Franklin, his Philadelphia credentials were impeccable. He was a superb organizer, with excellent scientific training and an acute political sensitivity. Bache later became head of the U.S. Coast Survey, first president of the National Academy of Sciences, and an outstanding figure in American science.[69] The Institute, a young organization in a state of transition, gave him an early opportunity to exercise his talents, and his efforts there are a microcosm of his later career.

Together with like-minded members of the Board of Managers, Bache and Merrick brought about substantial changes in the Institute. The *Journal* was transformed from a mechanics' magazine to a learned scientific and technical periodical. Conversational meetings became a means of introducing scientific discoveries, as well as new products. Sophisticated research projects were undertaken, with important industrial applications, but also for the sake of knowledge. It was a fundamentally different direction than the Institute's original course. James Ronaldson, the organization's president and an exemplar of the early viewpoint, once summed up his concept of the Institute's function:

The objects of the Franklin Institute are to develop the resources of our country; to throw all the light, possible, on the processes of industry, and to make the bringing of the products into the market as simple as the nature of the case will admit; to cultivate whatever is calculated to make a demand for labour, and the employment of all; according to their respective capacities and means, to the end that there should be none who shall not be in the enjoyment of the necessaries and comforts of life.[70]

Ronaldson's pleasantly vague idealism could hardly have been farther removed from the ideas of the new men. They shifted the organization's emphasis and reformed its operating procedures. Advance pre-

[69] Merle M. Odgers, *Alexander Dallas Bache: Scientist and Educator, 1806–1867* (Philadelphia: University of Pennsylvania Press, 1947), is the most available biographical study, but Nathan Reingold, *Science in Nineteenth-Century America: A Documentary History* (New York: Hill and Wang, 1964), adds valuable interpretive insights into Bache's career.

[70] "Proposed methods for facilitating the Extraction of Oil from Cotton Seed," *Journal of the Franklin Institute* 16 (November 1833): 289.

mium lists for exhibitions were terminated. Members who failed to pay their dues were stricken from the rolls. The conduct of meetings was reorganized, and no one was admitted to lectures without first showing his ticket. And there were complaints. Not everyone was pleased with the new regime, and one of the letters William Hamilton received in 1833 came from "A Member for Years," who swore he would "never again visit the hall while the Institution is under such Aristocratical regulations."[71]

71 "A Member for Years" to the Curators of the Franklin Institute of Pennsylvania, February 12, 1833, Incoming Correspondence.

V

EDUCATION
AT THE INSTITUTE

For whom are lectures on Technology designed?

James C. Booth to Frederick Fraley,
May 23, 1836

The mechanics' institute movement was the first concerted effort in America to provide technical training for a large class of the citizenry.[1] It started out as a democratic reform—all mechanics' institutes, including the one in Philadelphia, were primarily founded to diffuse knowledge among those who had been denied much schooling, either by economic or occupational circumstance. Charged with a missionary zeal, the movement carried hopes of social improvement. But there were other considerations, too. The publicly supported school system, even where well developed, was limited to elementary education. Mechanics' institutes aimed to give additional instruction, especially in the principles of science. The Franklin Institute's initial intent was to fill an important educational gap, thereby opening avenues of opportunity, while at the same time providing a better basis for technical advance.

The task proved more complicated than it had originally seemed. Precisely who was to be educated—workingmen, apprentices, or bright young men with a talent for science? How was the educational process to take place—through evening lectures or night schools, or were there other alternatives? Where would the financing come from, what would the content be, and how would it relate to the existing educational system? These issues raised serious tensions and discontinuities within the Board of Managers. But they were issues which had to be resolved

---

[1] From its founding in 1802, the U.S. Military Academy at West Point trained engineers whose education fitted them for civil as well as military pursuits. And after a reorganization in 1818, it provided unquestionably the best technical education available in the country. But it never aimed at any large-scale educational reforms, and in fact it was used as a point of contrast by educators who sought to provide practical training to larger masses of people. For a discussion of the role of West Point in providing technical education, see Daniel H. Calhoun, *The American Civil Engineer: Origins and Conflict* (Cambridge, Mass.: The M.I.T. Press, 1960).

before technical education, generally, could be established on a sound footing in this country.

The most obvious solution was evening lectures in science and its applications; and it had several advantages. It was sanctioned by time and experience. Both in America and abroad, popular lectures on science and technology had been a staple technique for diffusing knowledge since the eighteenth century. For the individual workingman, as Timothy Claxton had discovered, it was a cheap and convenient mode of self-improvement. And if hired lecturers were employed, the economics were clear and clean; ticket sales were a precise barometer of public interest, paid the speaker's fee, and provided a source of revenue if income exceeded expenses. Whether instruction for artisans should be conveyed in an academic style was sometimes a matter of dispute, but the majority of institutes used lectures as the most expeditious means of providing knowledge. The Franklin Institute began its educational program in that fashion, with a series of voluntary lectures in the spring of 1824. The success of those lectures, coupled with an urge to legitimize the instructional process, led to the establishment of a faculty of academicians in the summer.

The decision to employ as a faculty at the Institute men well trained in science and its applications immediately set the organization apart from most other efforts of informal education. Mechanics' institutes, lyceums, and other types of self-improvement societies generally emphasized a participatory kind of learning, in which the ideal lecture was one delivered by an ordinary workingman, in plain speech and from the truth of his own experience.[2] The Franklin Institute chose the more traditional pedagogical mode and placed the dissemination of knowledge in the hands of professional teachers. Dr. Robert M. Patterson, professor of natural philosophy at the University of Pennsylvania, was appointed to the same chair at the Institute. William H. Keating was named professor of chemistry and mineralogy, which was his position at the University. And William Strickland, who was made professor of architecture, took architectural and engineering students into his office as a regular part of his professional practice. Lectures were organized,

---

[2] Timothy Claxton argued that mutual instruction was "far more productive of solid improvement, than the mere attendance upon popular lectures." Most of the audience, he claimed, "are too apt to go away with the impression that, because the lecturer's duty is performed, their own task is certainly completed" (Timothy Claxton, *Memoir of a Mechanic, Being a Sketch of the Life of Timothy Claxton, Written by Himself, Together with Miscellaneous Papers* [Boston: George W. Light, 1839], p. 137). See also Carl Bode, *The American Lyceum: Town Meeting of the Mind* (New York: Oxford University Press, 1956), p. 67, for a comparison between the Institute's professorships and the means employed by most other societies.

academic fashion, in courses which met regularly for a ten-week term in the winter and then again for the same period of time in the spring. During the first year, Patterson and Strickland alternated their lectures on Monday evenings, and Keating delivered his every Saturday evening. Each was paid fifteen dollars per lecture. From the beginning, the Institute tied its educational program to the concept of an academic faculty, composed of distinguished scientists and engineers. It was not a program designed by workingmen struggling to educate themselves.

Volunteer lectures might have been utilized as an opportunity for artisans to try their skill at public speaking, but even that series was dominated by men of professional standing, or by those with the hope of future prominence. For example, James P. Espy, a mathematics teacher in one of the city's private schools who had aspirations for a scientific career in meteorology, gave two of the first year's volunteer lectures on that subject. Dr. John Godman, a young man on the threshold of promising studies in natural history, also used the lectures as a platform for his interests. The series served young members of the medical profession with similar career ambitions. In his autobiography, Samuel Gross remembered his anatomy lecture at the Institute in terms of his hopes "of earning a little reputation."[3] Lectures on anatomy were a continual favorite, as were lectures on the diseases especially incident to the working classes. Established scientists also gave voluntary lectures—Robert Hare delivered several on electricity in 1825—and Peter A. Browne was always willing to speak, but the series was particularly used by young men in search of position and professional esteem. There were topics of practical utility interspersed among scientific, medical, and legal subjects, but even in those cases they were never contributed by men directly engaged in the mechanic arts.

While organized along systematic lines of instruction, the aim of the first regular series of lectures was described simply as the diffusion of knowledge. By the summer of 1825, however, when the second season was being planned, the Committee on Instruction had begun to think also in terms of a lecture's potential popularity. In the fall Strickland would be out of the country, leaving only two courses of lectures for the season. To fill the gap, the committee recommended to the Board that a professorship of natural history be established. In their report, the committee admitted that the subject was not as closely related to the Institute's interest as lectures in mechanics or chemistry, but they argued that in "the whole range of the sciences there is none more

    [3] Samuel W. Gross and A. Haller Gross, eds., *Autobiography of Samuel D. Gross, M.D., with Reminiscences of his Times and Contemporaries*, 2 vols. (Philadelphia: W. B. Saunders, 1893), vol. 1, p. 157.

pleasing in the investigation."[4] The Board adopted the committee's recommendation, and John Godman was appointed to the position. Lectures on natural history were continued until the summer of 1826, when Godman resigned at the end of the year to accept the chair in anatomy at Rutgers Medical College. He was replaced by Constantine Rafinesque, a Sicilian naturalist of wandering disposition and colorful character, who gave lectures on botany and natural history, as well as volunteer talks on the "Ancient history & monuments of North America."[5]

The educational program for the year 1825–1826 was remarkable, for both its variety and its vitality. Patterson and Godman alternated lectures in their subjects on Tuesday evenings. Keating, as in the previous year, gave his lectures each Saturday night. Thomas P. Jones had assumed the professorship of mechanics, and he met his class every Wednesday evening. Volunteer lectures were on Thursday evenings, and during the year they included Hare on electricity, Browne on the laws of apprenticeship, Dr. William Darrach on the human frame, and Dr. Robert Griffith on diseases in the mechanic community. Classes in the drawing school met on Tuesday and Friday evenings and those of the mathematics school on Monday, Wednesday, Thursday, and Saturday evenings. Members who had paid their annual dues of three dollars were admitted to all lectures free of charge. Additional tickets for all lectures were available to members for their minor sons or apprentices at one dollar each. The schools had their own tuition fees, but they included admission to the lectures at no further charge. For those disposed toward self-improvement, it was a rich offering. There are no records to show lecture attendance; the managers spoke rather of the hall as "inconveniently crowded." But in addition to whatever portion of the 1,000 members of the Institute who came to hear the lectures, there were 135 more tickets sold for the admission of minors that year, plus 91 tickets for Dr. Godman's lectures alone.[6]

The wide popularity of natural history lectures established a pattern for the future. Pushed perhaps by the need to pay for the Institute's new building, Committees on Instruction in succeeding years generally included popular lectures on science to stimulate attendance. Browne delivered a course of lectures on geology; others were given on astron-

[4] Report of the Committee on Instruction, September 1, 1825, Franklin Institute Archives.

[5] C. S. Rafinesque to Thomas Fletcher, Philadelphia, August 24, 1826, Committee on Instruction, Franklin Institute Archives. For details of Rafinesque's life, see the *Dictionary of American Biography* (New York: Charles Scribner's Sons, 1943).

[6] The Eighth Quarterly Report of the Board of Managers, January 19, 1826, published in *National Gazette,* January 26, 1826.

omy, meteorology, zoology, and subjects no more related to the mechanic arts than natural history. Lectures on natural history set another precedent at the Institute. The series had been initiated for its general interest, and for one dollar members were allowed to introduce ladies to them. Much to the Board's surprise, nearly a hundred women attended the lectures. The Committee on Instruction was not slow to see the financial potential and recommended a raise in the price of ladies' tickets.[7] By the fall of 1827, the idea of female attendance was so well accepted that the Board admitted them to any of the Institute's lectures. While the managers spoke of the value of "rational amusement" for ladies and of the "order and decorum" which their presence would bring to the lectures, the action suggests also an attempt to capitalize on a wide interest in popular scientific lectures.[8]

To some, the fashion was a puzzling phenomenon. The Philadelphia diarist Sidney George Fisher attended one of Robert Patterson's Athenian Institute lectures on astronomy, "a dry uninteresting subject" to his own taste, and discovered to his surprise:

I did not hear a word of it, as I arrived late, & the crowd was so large that I could not get within earshot. Was indeed quite astonished to see such a multitude assembled, to listen to a discussion on such a subject. One third of the audience were women, and many of our most fashionable ladies were present.[9]

The Institute's managers were at first no less astonished, but they soon acted to offer lectures which might be entertaining as well as instructive, to attract adults of both sexes as well as young apprentices.

The Board of Managers was moved by financial considerations as much as any other. The lectures, excepting those delivered by volun-

[7] Report of the Sub-Committee on Instruction, February 28, 1826, Franklin Institute Archives. As it was pointed out in an early account of the Institute: "About the middle of November last, a third course of instruction was commenced, which included, besides the regular lectures of the preceding winter, a course of Practical Mechanics, and one of Natural History. To the latter, the members were allowed to introduce ladies; it had been believed that few would avail themselves of the privilege, and it was therefore with surprize, as well as pleasure, that the Board found the class included nearly one hundred ladies" ("Observations on the Rise and Progress of the Franklin Institute," *The Franklin Journal and American Mechanics' Magazine* 1 [March 1826]: 131).

[8] The move was also justified on the grounds that it was the practice of the London and Glasgow mechanics' institutes to admit women to lectures. "Fifteenth Quarterly Report of the Board of Managers of the Franklin Institute of the State of Pennsylvania," *The Franklin Journal and American Mechanics' Magazine* 4 (November 1827): 331.

[9] Nicholas B. Wainwright, ed., *A Philadelphia Perspective: The Diary of Sidney George Fisher, Covering the Years 1834–1871* (Philadelphia: Historical Society of Pennsylvania, 1967), p. 27.

teers, were a direct expense to the Institute. Depending on the number of lectures delivered, professors were paid from 150 to 400 dollars annually. Their salaries constituted the largest single operating expense aside from the cost of repaying the building loan. On the other hand, lectures provided the greatest attraction to membership, the Institute's primary source of revenue. The organization was therefore faced with the dilemma which troubled all similar associations. They could increase attendance by broadening the popular content of lectures, but that would mean aiming at an audience composed of more than simply mechanics and their apprentices.

The result was that some mechanics' institutes drifted away from their original objectives and became lost in the general stream of lecture societies. Others, such as the Franklin Institute, more nearly resembled England's Royal Institution in the effort to develop a program which satisfied objectives and yet also provided the necessary financial support. The Institute sought to maintain attendance by offering lectures whose content had a more general intellectual appeal than the direct practical application of science to the mechanic arts. The effect, as with the London lectures, was to attract a society audience, too.[10] While there was no Philadelphia counterpart to the popular success of the Royal Institution's Michael Faraday, a conscious effort was made to secure the speaking talents of well-known local scientific figures, whose reputations would insure the attendance of all ranks of society.

An example of how the Institute's program differed from that of similar organizations can be seen in a comparison of two lecture courses on chemistry. At the Providence, Rhode Island Mechanics' Institute, lectures on "Chemistry Applied to the Mechanic Arts" included information on the composition of building materials, the construction of chimneys and furnaces, and animal and vegetable substances used in textile manufacturing.[11] By contrast, Dr. John K. Mitchell's introductory lecture on applied chemistry at the Franklin Institute was entitled "The Wisdom and Goodness of God as evinced in the Natural History of Water." Mitchell's own "genius and science" made the lecture "a most delightful entertainment" to the "crowded and respectable audience" which flocked to hear him.[12] Introductory lectures were specifically designed to attract membership subscriptions. They were open freely to the public and purposely popular in nature. They were also slanted to attract for the remainder of the series the "respectable" audience which Mitchell's lecture drew. Mitchell himself

10 L. Pearce Williams, *Michael Faraday* (New York: Basic Books, 1965), p. 320.
11 Bode, *The American Lyceum*, p. 137.
12 *National Gazette*, October 31, 1833.

was a physician of some standing with a reputation for research and publication, but in Philadelphia he was also known for his literary and speaking abilities.[13]

Part of the Institute's early success with its lecture program came from the same general popularity of science lectures which stimulated mechanics' societies and lyceums all over America. Part of it came from the enthusiasm within the Institute for diffusing knowledge and from the careful selection of speakers who could accomplish that aim in a pleasing and instructive fashion. The results were a crowded lecture hall, new members, income for the treasury, and a growing local reputation. At the commencement of the 1829 season, a local newspaper editor called the attention of his readers to the lectures:

The increase of knowledge upon scientific and mechanical subjects, among a large class of the people, which has grown out of this excellent institution, is a matter of experience to those who have watched its progress. . . . But the benefits of the Institute are by no means confined in their operations to mechanics. All classes may derive useful information; and to youths intended for every occupation, the lectures offer many facilities of improvement. The style adopted by the professors is easy and familiar, and the demonstrations are so conducted as to be intelligible to all.[14]

But even at that point in time, the lectures were changing in content and style and were losing interest within the Board of Managers.

Establishment of the Institute's high school diverted concern in a new direction, and as had been the case with industrial exhibitions, time served to dull the Board's zeal for the efforts required to produce a full series of lectures. Until 1831, volunteer lectures were continued on a weekly basis. For two seasons Peter Browne delivered a series of ten lectures on geology, and additional volunteers discoursed on miscellaneous subjects. During the same period, however, the formal lecture courses were reduced by half. The professorship in natural history was discontinued after Rafinesque's series of lectures, Jones's departure for Washington left the Institute without a course in practical

---

[13] "Dr. John K. Mitchell," it was reported in the biography of his son, S. Weir Mitchell, "began as all physicians did in those days, by teaching." One of his first posts was as professor of chemistry at the Franklin Institute. He later filled the chair of medicine at Jefferson Medical College and was visiting physician to the Pennsylvania Hospital. In addition to his literary abilities, Mitchell published widely in medicine, particularly on spinal diseases and epidemic fever. Anna Robeson Burr, *Weir Mitchell: His Life and Letters* (New York: Duffield & Company, 1930), p. 18. Additional details are available in the *Dictionary of American Biography*.

[14] *The Saturday Evening Post*, October 24, 1829.

mechanics, and William Strickland never resumed his lectures on architecture. Even the success of volunteer lectures was more apparent
than real. It depended on the indefatigable Peter Browne, who carried
half of the load for two years. Committees on Instruction actually
experienced increasing difficulty in securing a sufficient number of
volunteer lecturers.

The Institute's lecture program was also considerably altered by a
changing sense of mission. In 1831 Alexander Dallas Bache was
appointed chairman of the Committee on Instruction. His election
signaled the beginning of a campaign to elevate the content of both the
formal and volunteer lectures, which were also altered by Bache's
interest in the physical sciences. One of his earliest moves was to
recommend that the course of lectures in natural philosophy and
mechanics be divided. The two had been treated separately when Patterson lectured on natural philosophy and Dr. Jones taught the class
in practical mechanics, but when Jones left they were joined as one
course. Natural philosophy, Bache argued, was "the very element of all
the subjects taught in the Institute's lecture room" and should therefore receive separate consideration.[15] When Walter Johnson, principal
of the high school, replaced Jones, he was requested to revise the
course, giving "particular attention" to physics and its application.[16]
The plan suited Johnson's ideas. In his mind the Institute's courses of
scientific instruction constituted its "chief usefulness," and he prefaced
the outline of his lectures with the remark: "I have endeavoured so to
exhibit theory that practice should not be forgotten, & so to illustrate
practice that theory should not be dishonoured."[17]

In a series of twenty-one lectures, Johnson presented a straightforward course in physics, including the principles of hydrostatics and
hydraulics, the properties of air and light, elastic bodies, and heat, and
six lectures on electricity, galvanism, magnetism, electro-magnetism,
and thermo-electricity. His concluding lecture consisted of a summary
statement of the known relations between imponderable agents.[18] To
complete the rearrangement of the lecture courses, Franklin Peale was
appointed professor of mechanics, a position he filled from 1831 to
1833. Son of the painter Charles Willson Peale, he was a man of con-

[15] Eighth Annual Report of the Board of Managers, January 18, 1832, Franklin
Institute Archives.

[16] Minutes of the Committee on Instruction, October 11, 1831, Franklin Institute
Archives.

[17] W. R. Johnson to Messrs. Samuel J. Robbins & Frederick Fraley, July 3, 1833,
Committee on Instruction.

[18] Ibid. Johnson's lecture notes—or those of any other lecturer—have not survived in the Institute's archives.

siderable inventive talent and was later responsible for several notable technical improvements at the U.S. Mint in Philadelphia.[19] With Peale's appointment and Johnson's course revisions, the relationship between theory and practice was once again clearly established.

Bache and his committee also changed the content of volunteer lectures. Their previously miscellaneous character was eliminated. No longer were lectures presented on anatomy or bookkeeping; the emphasis was placed instead on the physical sciences. In 1833 and 1834, Dr. Gouverneur Emerson delivered two series of lectures on meteorology, a subject in which he was actively involved both at the Institute and at the American Philosophical Society. John Millington, previously on the faculty at London's Royal Institution, lectured on astronomy.[20] James P. Espy, who had by then begun his researches on the subject, also delivered a lecture course on meteorology. When lectures were given in natural history, they were in those branches which had more relevance to the Institute's purposes. In 1834, for example, the Committee on Instruction gave Henry Darwin Rogers the use of its lecture room for a lecture course of his own on geology, in exchange for reduced admission rates for Institute members. Rogers returned the favor the following year by offering the same course as a series of volunteer lectures. The culmination of the trend Bache had begun came in 1836, when volunteer lectures were suspended entirely. In their place, the Institute hired James C. Booth to deliver a series of lectures on industrial chemistry which outlined the latest European advances in that field.

Rogers and Booth typify the changes which Bache had inaugurated and the spreading influence within the Franklin Institute of a small group dedicated to professional science. The third of four brothers famous for their scientific accomplishments, Rogers taught chemistry and natural philosophy at Dickinson College for a brief period before traveling to London. While there, he was active in the London Geological Society and became acquainted with Lyell and other prominent

[19] The best source of information is Robert Patterson, "An Obituary Notice of Franklin Peale," American Philosophical Society Proceedings 11 (1869–70): 597–604.

[20] Emerson, "one of the busiest and most successful Philadelphia physicians," was a man of varied interests in the sciences and in scientific agriculture. Dictionary of American Biography. Millington also gave lectures on science at the London Mechanics' Institute, of which he was a vice-president, and was secretary of the Astronomical Society of London. In 1823 he published his lectures under the title, An Epitome of the Elementary Principles of Natural and Experimental Philosophy (London: privately printed, 1823). Millington emigrated to the United States and apparently moved from Philadelphia to Virginia, where he published a book, Elements of Civil Engineering (Philadelphia: J. Dobson, 1839); and an article, "Address on Civil Engineering," Southern Literary Messenger 5 (1839): 592–95.

English geologists.[21] When Rogers returned to lecture on geology at the Institute, he was thoroughly conversant with current European theory and practice. The contrast between Rogers and Peter A. Browne, who had earlier given volunteer talks on geology, illustrates the extent to which the new professionalism dominated the Institute's lectures. Browne was an amateur enthusiast with varied interests, including geology. He was a man of many parts, but science was his avocation, and there was no room for him in the new program. Rogers, on the other hand, was committed to a life of science. He was professor of geology and mineralogy at the University of Pennsylvania and was named to head the geological surveys of both Pennsylvania and New Jersey. His connection to Pennsylvania's geological survey was also important to Bache's group in other ways. The state survey provided funds for a program of meteorological research at the Institute and assistant geologist posts for Booth and John F. Frazer, a Bache protégé from the University of Pennsylvania.

James Curtis Booth was also a thoroughly trained professional. He had studied chemistry with Hare and Keating at the University of Pennsylvania. In 1831 he went to Germany, where he studied analytical chemistry with Wöhler and Magnus, attended lectures in Vienna, and toured the industrial chemical firms of Europe before his return to Philadelphia.[22] In addition to his lectures at the Institute and the University of Pennsylvania, Booth conducted a laboratory of industrial chemistry, where several distinguished chemists were trained. Dr. John K. Mitchell, professor of chemistry at the Institute from 1832 to 1838, sent his son S. Weir Mitchell to Booth for the additional training useful in a medical career. "My father," the son later recalled, "was twice as wise as regards a part of my education. He insisted that I should spend part of the spring and summer of two years in a laboratory of analysis; and this I did with Booth, and the lesson in accuracy was just what I needed."[23] Booth published widely in his field and served twice as president of the American Chemical Society. His clear professional standing, like that of Rogers, marked the change in the Institute's lecture program.

The shift in emphasis did not come without attendant problems, however. The lectures, both formal and volunteer, had declined in importance at the Institute, and other interests had assumed a com-

[21] *Dictionary of American Biography.*

[22] Booth's European trip is described by Wyndham D. Miles in "With James Curtis Booth in Europe, 1834," *Chymia* 11 (1966): 139–49.

[23] Burr, *Weir Mitchell*, p. 47. For a brief sketch of Booth's career, see Edgar F. Smith, *James Curtis Booth, Chemist, 1810–1888* (Philadelphia: privately printed, 1922).

manding share of the leadership's concern. Thus, at the same time
that efforts were under way to alter the content and quality of instruction, the Institute was also moving to reduce its obligations to a hard
core of lectures which could be maintained with the least effort. The
result was an unavoidable tension, some of which was apparent as
early as 1828. When William Keating left for a mining venture in
Mexico in 1826, Franklin Bache, Alexander Dallas Bache's first cousin,
was appointed professor of chemistry, and he occupied that chair
until 1832. He was a conscientious and careful man, and in order to
carry out his duties effectively, he appealed to the Committee on
Instruction for a complete overhaul of the Institute's chemistry
facilities.[24]

The apparatus was located in the basement, where dampness rusted
iron implements, covered bottle labels with mould, and rendered chemical salts useless. Extremes in temperature had also opened all the
joints in the pneumatic cistern. Experiments on gases, which constituted "the most striking and interesting" phase of the course and that
"most likely to interest a popular class," were therefore difficult to
carry out.[25] Bache suggested that proper instruction and research
could only be conducted with proper facilities, and he proposed to the
committee that one of the first-floor rooms be appropriated for the use
of the professor of chemistry. No action was taken on his request, and the
following year Bache appealed directly to the Board of Managers to
devote a suitable room, properly equipped, for his exclusive use.[26]
That appeal met the same fate.

Walter R. Johnson, who lectured in natural philosophy at the Institute from 1828 to 1837, also urged the Board to make a better accom-
modation for the lectures by establishing separate rooms for the professors of chemistry and natural philosophy. The Board referred his
request to the Committee on Instruction, and their response reveals one
of the factors which inhibited an extension of the lecture program.
The committee admitted the desirability of better facilities but presented two arguments in opposition. First, to appropriate the only
room available, the library and reading room, would deprive members
of "privileges which they enjoy & hold in high esteem." The other
alternative was to use rooms currently rented, which would cost the
Institute revenues that were necessary in order to repay the building

24 Information on Bache is available in Edgar F. Smith, *Franklin Bache, 1792–
1864, Chemist* (Philadelphia: privately printed, 1922).

25 Franklin Bache to the Committee on Instruction of the Franklin Institute,
July 22, 1828, Committee on Instruction.

26 Minutes of the Board of Managers, June 11, 1829, Franklin Institute Archives.

fund debt. In the face of those objections, the committee recommended against any change in accommodations.[27]

Alexander Dallas Bache, who was chairman of the committee that year, was committed to the idea of conversation meetings, which were held in the library and reading room. Furthermore, the conversation meetings were dominated by the Institute's scientific clique, who used the occasions for discussion and experiments in subjects of their current interest. Improvement in the lecture facilities was sacrificed to the aims of a relatively small group within the organization. Bache's second argument, that the Institute could not afford to lose any rentals, is also interesting in that such a decision more properly belonged to the Board of Managers than to the chairman of the Committee on Instruction. But the committee was one of the centers of power within the Institute, normally controlled by the current leadership, and Bache's decision was accepted.

The Institute's efforts at education through evening lectures were thus considerably altered during the first decade of operation. A program originally designed to provide mechanics and their apprentices with a practical understanding of the scientific principles behind their arts was soon transformed into general science lectures for both sexes and all classes of society. In one respect, the transformation was highly successful. Lectures continued to attract large audiences, even after Bache's reforms; astronomy, meteorology, and geology proved to be just as interesting to mixed audiences as anatomy and natural history had been.[28] But in other respects, uncomfortable issues were raised. Contrary to one of the organization's prime goals, the lectures served an adult rather than a youthful audience. And even with speakers of professional competence, there was a growing concern that effective technical education required a more formal organization of knowledge. James C. Booth inadvertently exposed one facet of the problem in a letter to Frederick Fraley, who was chairman of the Committee on Instruction in 1834. At the head of an outline entitled "For whom are lectures on Technology designed?" Booth suggested that there were four constituent classes in the audience: (1) artisans, (2) those interested in the advancement of manufacturing, (3) those

[27] Report of the Committee on Instruction, June 14, 1832.
[28] The Institute's lecture hall was crowded for practically all lectures. Since the actual seating capacity in the early years is not known, the best indication of numbers comes from annual reports of the Board of Managers. In 1839, for example, 295 tickets for minors, 75 for women, and 17 for strangers were sold during the season. Those admissions were in addition to whatever portion of the Institute's 2,500 members attended. Fifteenth Annual Report of the Board of Managers, January 16, 1839, Franklin Institute Archives.

concerned with knowledge for its own sake, and (4) "a set of inoffensive individuals, attending lectures only for the purpose of staring at brilliant experiments, and capable of doing neither benefit nor injury."[29] In terms of a serious desire to elevate technical practice, lectures had their limitations, and the Institute was left with an unsettled tension between objectives and implementation.

The Institute experienced similar difficulties with the schools it established. With one exception, the organization's schools suffered from internal conflict and lack of financial support. And like the lecture program, the schools were altered by shifting emphasis as the Institute's leadership changed. Ironically, the drawing school, the most successful of the Institute's educational endeavors, was begun with the least idealism. The idea came as a result of negotiations for the rental of Carpenters' Hall in the summer of 1824. In a report to the Board of Managers, the Committee on Lectures called attention to the fact that there was no school for architectural drawing in the city. However, there was substantial demand for one, the committee claimed, and they expressed no doubt that such a school would be "a Considerable source of profit and popularity."[30] Their assessment proved entirely correct. The drawing school enjoyed an immediate popularity, which was sustained throughout the nineteenth century.

The drawing school was organized along lines which would become characteristic of the Institute's other schools. The society provided space, heating, and lighting, set tuition fees and terms of admission, appointed the professors, and handled administrative details. But the faculty received its salary from a portion of the tuition fees, not directly from the Institute's treasury. That device shifted a burden of risk onto the professors, but it protected the organization against undue expense if the school failed to attract students. The drawing school opened in the fall of 1824. It met twice weekly for a ten-week season coinciding with the lecture term. John Haviland was appointed professor of drawing, and Hugh Bridport was his assistant. The Board of Managers fixed tuition at five dollars per season, the receipts to be divided equally between teachers and the Institute. Initially, admission was restricted to members, their sons, and apprentices. In December, however, the Board relaxed those limitations somewhat to allow members to send one minor person outside of his family or workforce, and the faculty's income was increased to two-thirds of tuition fees.[31]

29 James C. Booth to Frederick Fraley, May 23, 1836, Committee on Instruction.
30 Report of the Committee on Lectures, August 4, 1824, Franklin Institute Archives.
31 Minutes of the Board of Managers, October 27, December 2, 1824.

If the Board of Managers had any fears for the experiment, these were soon stilled—almost fifty students enrolled for the first season. The school supplied directly usable knowledge, and there appeared to be a clear market for that kind of education. There were several programs of study within the school—architectural drawing, mechanical drafting, lettering, and landscape and ornamental drawing. In each case the emphasis was on practical instruction. Mechanical drafting, obviously practical, involved learning to draw patterns and machine parts to size and to scale. Architectural drawing embraced the principles of carpentry, as well as a study of classical orders. And even ornamental drawing was taught in terms of its applicability to textile printing and to other forms of industrial design.[32]

Demand for instruction in drawing increased over the years. The school met an obvious need, and the Institute responded by reducing tuition and enlarging its facilities. The school also enjoyed the services of talented teachers. When the pressures of his own successful architectural practice forced Haviland to resign, his place was taken for a time by George Strickland, William Strickland's brother. Hugh Bridport resigned to seek a post teaching drawing at West Point, and in 1834 the school came under the direction of William Mason, a skillful craftsman who taught mechanical drawing to a generation of Philadelphia engineers.[33] By 1839, over a hundred pupils were enrolled in the school, and its reputation had transcended the boundaries of the city and state.[34] There was no conflict of means or objectives with the drawing school. It was the most vocation-oriented of the Institute's educational endeavors, and the most successful.

The mathematics school never enjoyed the same prosperity. From the beginning, it failed to attract sufficient students to make it financially interesting, despite the efforts of three successive teachers. Begun in April 1825, under Levi Fletcher, its general objective was the same

[32] "On the Importance of Drawing, to Mechanics," *The Franklin Journal and American Mechanics' Magazine* 2 (September 1826): 190.

[33] Mason was remembered as "a gentleman of fine taste" who helped to usher in "a new era in the history of wood engraving in this country" ("Recollections of a Cinquegenarian," *Philadelphia Sunday Dispatch*, March 13, 1859). For additional information on Mason, see Eugene S. Ferguson, ed., *Early Engineering Reminiscences [1815–40] of George Escol Sellers* (Washington, D.C.: Smithsonian Institution, 1965).

[34] Statement of cash received from Pupils in the Drawing School, Drawing School Records, Franklin Institute Archives. In 1835, for instance, F. J. Davis wrote from Virginia to inquire into the tuition for "those branches of drawing which embrace Building, Machinery and Engineering," how long it might take a young man to become proficient in those subjects, and what one might expect to pay in Philadelphia for a "genteel boarding house." F. J. Davis to William Hamilton, Petersburg, Virginia, February 27, 1835, Drawing School Records.

as the drawing school's, namely, to increase educational opportunities for the working class at a cost they could afford. Tuition was set at four dollars, three of which the instructor retained. The Institute's dollar was to be used to purchase books for those students who otherwise could not afford them.[35] The school taught arithmetic, algebra, geometry, the applications of mensuration, navigation, and surveying —subjects of practical utility to artisans and their apprentices. Tuition was reduced from four dollars to three in the fall term to stimulate enrollment, but without success. James P. Espy, who had a considerable local reputation as a mathematics teacher, took over the school, and he also failed to increase the number of pupils. In the fall of 1827, when the Committee on Instruction made its report for the coming season, they included the recommendation "that the Mathematical School, which has always failed to receive the attention of the public and consequently to accomplish the wishes of the Board be postponed at least for the present."[36] But a fallow season did little to alter the basic problem. Sears C. Walker, later to achieve fame as an astronomer, was appointed teacher, with the same unhappy consequence as before. The managers tried again in 1829, reappointing Levi Fletcher to take Walker's place. Fletcher fell ill, and the school had to be closed once more. But the Committee on Instruction persisted in the face of that incredible array of omens, and in the fall of 1830 reported —"with much pleasure"—that the school had been completely reorganized to "adapt it entirely to the wants of the youth connected with the Institute"; and it was opened again under Fletcher.[37] When the mathematics school went down for the fifth time, the committee was finally forced to admit that it did not "supply the wants of the portion of the community who were expected to have been interested in it."[38]

The Board of Managers did not struggle to maintain the mathematics school simply out of stubbornness. They sensed a vacuum in the city's educational structure, especially with respect to technical training, and they sought to fill it. Philadelphia's schools fell into two categories. Tax-supported elementary schools had been established in the city since 1818. But they still carried some of the stigma of charity schools for the poor, and in any case, instruction was limited simply to reading, writing, and arithmetic.[39] A more extensive education was

[35] Minutes of the Board of Managers, March 3, 1825.
[36] Report of the Committee on Instruction, October 2, 1827.
[37] Ibid., October [13?], 1830.
[38] Ibid., March 10, 1831.
[39] J. Thomas Scharf and Thomas Wescott, *History of Philadelphia, 1609–1884*, 3 vols. (Philadelphia: L. H. Everts & Co., 1884), vol. 3, pp. 1926ff. In defining the

available in the city's private schools. There were many of them, and
some, such as the Friends' Academy or the Germantown Academy, had
excellent reputations. But they emphasized a classical education, and
they cost money. The Board of Managers saw a need for some kind of
instruction beyond the public schools, less expensive than private education, and which included training in science and its uses. Moreover,
they soon recognized that the Institute's lecture courses would not
provide that kind of instruction. The Board of Managers was correct
in its perception of the problem: some system of technical education
was needed, and not just for Philadelphia. Its miscalculation was in
limiting the mathematical school's scope and thus its potential as a
mechanism for social mobility.

Social mobility was the issue behind the quarrel between the Institute and Peter A. Browne. The conflict flared up out of an inquiry into
ways of extending the Institute's educational effectiveness. The Committee of Instruction, directed mainly by Samuel V. Merrick and
Robert M. Patterson, proposed a high school to bridge the gap between
public schools and the University of Pennsylvania. Since it was meant
as a link to the University, whose entrance requirements included a
knowledge of Latin and Greek, the high school would teach the ancient
languages. But Peter A. Browne, supported by Matthew Carey, argued
that classical study was a waste of time for boys who at the age of
fourteen or fifteen would be apprenticed to trades and crafts. In the
period after completion of study in the city's common schools, which
they generally left around the age of ten, and before the beginning of
apprenticeship, there was not time enough to learn the languages well;
nor was there any use to the knowledge they did gain. And it was
ridiculous, Browne said, to claim that the University of Pennsylvania's science courses were easily available for those who wished additional knowledge—out of a city population of 130,000, the University's
enrollment was 64 students. The only answer to such exclusiveness
was a scientific and technical school which would "embrace every
branch of instruction required for the agriculturist, the mechanic or
manufacturer, the architect, the civil engineer, the merchant, and
other man of business."[40]

---

audience for whom the Institute's schools were designed, it was pointed out: "There
are in the city, and among the members of the Institute, many persons whose circumstances in life, are such as not to make it necessary for them to depend on public
schools for the instruction of their children; but, to whom, the prices paid at most
private schools, would be inconveniently high" ("Observations on the Rise and
Progress of the Franklin Institute," *The Franklin Journal and American Mechanics'
Magazine* 1 [March 1826]: 132).

[40] *To the Citizens of the City and County of Philadelphia* (Philadelphia, 1826).

The Institute's Committee on Instruction never argued, as Browne did, that the high school was to provide education for those who had been denied it. They proposed instead to give those of moderate means the educational opportunities which had previously been the choice of the wealthy. It was more democratic, the committee claimed, to keep the avenues of social and economic advancement open than to fix class lines by separate educational systems. In fact, the committee even rejected the use of terms which suggested social distinctions "inconsistent with the spirit of our republican institutions." In America, they claimed, "it is impossible to tell, from the situation of the parents, what may be the destiny of the child."[41] And even if he were to be a mechanic, the student's future life should not be bounded only by workshop walls. To deny anyone the advantages of a liberal education was to deny the possibility of professional distinction, social esteem, or political preferment—the ambitions to be served by the high school. When the Board of Managers adopted the committee's plan, they rejected the idea that secondary education should be vocational or terminal. Knowledge should be the vehicle for social advancement, as well as a useful occupational tool.

The Institute's high school was filled almost to capacity when it opened on September 4, 1826. Out of a total of 304 places in the school, 252 were taken. The school was an immediate success for several reasons. Perhaps the first was its low cost—seven dollars per quarter, or twenty-eight dollars for forty-eight weeks of instruction. The major deterrent to a scientific education had been expense. But according to the Committee on Instruction, "modern improvements in education" allowed for a substantial reduction in tuition fees. The school was established on the monitorial plan, a system introduced to America by Joseph Lancaster, who had championed his ideas throughout the country in the preceding decade. The city's common schools were Lancastrian in organization, primarily because of the economies of the system.[42] Monitorial instruction involved the use of student monitors and tutors, as well as teachers, with an elaborate division of labor between the three levels. In a series of articles in the *Journal of the Franklin Institute*, Walter R. Johnson, principal of the high school, explained:

---

41 Report of the Committee on Instruction, March 30, 1826.
42 *Address of the Committee of Instruction of the Franklin Institute of Pennsylvania, on the Subject of the High School Department attached to that Institution* (Philadelphia: The Franklin Institute, 1826).

The duties of teachers consist in instructing the tutors and monitors in their respective branches, and all the other members of their classes in those parts of the subject which require a master's talents.[43]

Monitors heard recitations within divisions of each class, and tutors oversaw the performance of monitors. The essence of the monitorial system was to employ more advanced students to carry out the details of instruction, plus most of the paperwork, thus allowing for a smaller faculty and reducing the cost of education.

Another factor in the high school's popularity was the appeal it had to what might be described as middle-class ambitions. The school was aimed not at those who needed charity but rather at those in moderate circumstances, whether or not engaged in trade and manufactures, who wanted the educational advantages of the wealthy. In operation, the Franklin Institute's high school mirrored the aspirations which had given it life. As one student later recalled, it was "well patronized by the best families of the city."[44] The course of studies included those subjects the committee said would be "universally selected by the enlightened parent." If the student attended the full three-year course, he took Greek and Latin every year, three years of mathematics and French, two years of Spanish and drawing, plus courses in history, geography, political economy, astronomy, natural philosophy, natural history, chemistry, bookkeeping, and stenography. Additional training in science was to be provided by the Institute's regular evening lectures.[45] It was exactly the curriculum needed for the young man who might go on to the university, or more likely, into the family's business or manufacturing establishment. The fact that it was conducted during the day made its facilities unavailable to apprentices.

Finally, some of the high school's success came from the reputation of the faculty and from endorsement by leading men in the community. Roberts Vaux, Daniel B. Smith, Dr. John K. Mitchell, and Henry Troth were added to the Committee on Instruction, to give it "the experience of gentlemen well acquainted with the system of monitorial instruction." But the appointments of Vaux and Smith, especially, also gave a mark of approval to the enterprise. Smith was one of the directors of the city's schools, and Vaux was president of the Controllers of

43 W. R. Johnson, "On the Combination of a Practical with a Liberal course of Education," *Journal of the Franklin Institute* 6 (November 1828): 354.

44 Elizabeth B. Pharo, *Reminiscences of William Hazell Wilson, 1811–1912* (Philadelphia, 1937), p. 40.

45 *Address of the Committee of Instruction . . . on the Subject of the High School Department. . . .*

the Public Schools, who had the entire responsibility for the public schools.[46] All four were members of the Institute, but it was their connection to education which helped elevate the high school in the public consciousness. The appointment of Walter Rogers Johnson as principal produced a similar effect. Johnson was born in Massachusetts in 1794 and graduated from Harvard in the class of 1819. He taught in Massachusetts for two years, and then in 1821 he came to Philadelphia as principal of the Germantown Academy. Johnson soon became vitally interested in the cause of public education and wrote widely on the subject. His standing among educators and within the city predetermined a measure of acceptance for the high school, even before it opened, and Johnson could later report that "the names of many of our most wealthy and respectable citizens" could be found on the school's register.[47]

A man of considerable learning, Johnson taught Latin and Greek, as well as the science courses, in the high school. The Committee on Instruction also employed four other teachers. Antoine Bolmar, who reputedly had served as one of Napoleon's officers, was appointed to teach French, and by 1828, the French class was using Bolmar's edition of Telemachus for its text. German was taught by Siegfried Walter. He was not popular with his students, who called him "the Dutchman." And when Walter apparently absconded with some school funds, the boys posted a couplet on the classroom door: "Siegfried Walter ran away / on the fourteenth day of May." The other teachers were Eli Griffith, who taught mathematics, and Felix Merino, named "the happy sheep" by his students, who taught Spanish.[48] By 1828, when a primary division was added to the school, the faculty had increased to eight. Griffith was shifted to the primary division, and Sears C. Walker was appointed as mathematics teacher. William Adams and William Mason, who gave the drawing lessons, were the

[46] Board of Managers, Tenth Quarterly Report, July 20, 1826, Franklin Institute Archives. See also Joseph J. McCadden, Education in Pennsylvania, 1801–1835, and its Debt to Roberts Vaux (Philadelphia: University of Pennsylvania Press, 1937).

[47] George Pettengill, "Walter Rogers Johnson," Journal of the Franklin Institute 250 (August 1950): 93–113; Walter R. Johnson, "On the Combination of a Practical with a Liberal course of Education," Journal of the Franklin Institute 6 (August 1828): 110.

[48] Bolmar's full name was Jean Claude Antoine Brunin de Bolmar, but he shortened it in America. His text was entitled Key to the first eight books of the adventures of Telemachus, the son of Ulysses (Philadelphia: P. M. Lafourcade, 1828). Bolmar also published a conversational French text, which after the first printing went through dozens of editions: A Collection of colloquial phrases, on every topic necessary to maintain conversation (Philadelphia: Carey & Lea, 1830). The other information on the school is from Pharo, Reminiscences of William Hazell Wilson, pp. 39–40.

other members of the staff. There were four twelve-week quarters in the school year. Classes were generally held for three hours in the morning and three hours in the afternoon. Johnson described the complete curriculum, together with the texts utilized, in one of his articles for the *Journal of the Franklin Institute*.[49]

At a time when high schools in America were a distinct novelty, the Institute's effort was naturally of interest to educators elsewhere. The editor of the *American Journal of Education* observed:

Among establishments devoted to scientific improvement in connection with preparation for the duties of an active life, the Franklin Institute of Philadelphia is entitled to a distinguished place. Its Magazine for mechanics, and its High School for a superior style of practical education among youth destined for active pursuits, furnish advantages of a character hitherto new in this country; and which will, in all probability, exert a highly favorable influence on institutions that may spring up in other places, for the advancement of similar objects.[50]

The Committee on Instruction regularly visited the school to observe and report on its work, and they extolled its virtues, too:

For the very small sum of $28 per annum, pupils may be taught six languages, together with the various other branches of knowledge that are required to fit them either to enter the colleges advantageously, or engage at once in the active duties and callings of life. The man in moderate circumstances, therefore, who wishes to place his son on a footing, in respect of moral and intellectual worth, with the offspring of his wealthier fellow citizen, finds in this truly republican institution every facility for the gratification of so laudable an ambition.[51]

And yet, before the school was three years old, its connection with the Franklin Institute was terminated.

The difficulties which led to the withdrawal of Institute patronage were primarily financial, but with overtones of a personality clash. In an effort to encourage the undertaking, the Committee on Instruction had originally offered Johnson quite liberal terms. Their agreement with him specified free space for a year but then a rent of two dollars per pupil annually if the enrollment afterwards exceeded one hundred

---

49 Walter R. Johnson, "On the Combination of a Practical with a Liberal course of Education," *Journal of the Franklin Institute* 6 (August 1828): 111–13.

50 *American Journal of Education* 1 (December 1826): 757–58.

51 "Franklin Institute. Report of the Committee of Instruction. March 12, 1828," *The Register of Pennsylvania* 1 (March 15, 1828): 175.

and fifty. They also promised to furnish desks, maps, globes, and scientific apparatus. By the end of the sessions in June 1828, Johnson and the Board of Managers had begun to quarrel over whether he owed the Institute money.[52] An attempt to renegotiate the original agreement failed when Johnson refused to accept the terms. By September, a temporary peace had been arranged, and the school was conducted normally for the following year. But the Board had the whole subject under reconsideration, and when the quarter ended in June 1829, the Institute concluded its sponsorship.

As might be expected, both parties were disenchanted, even before the end. The Board of Managers had lost interest in the school. One of the special committees appointed to negotiate with Johnson in the summer of 1828 reluctantly reported that "there has been a lukewarmness & indifference displayed by the managers of the Institute" toward the school.[53] For his part, Johnson argued that educational institutions were not something to be "meddled with," especially by those who did not share the same financial stake he had in the high school.[54] And more than his salary was at issue; the principal had been forced to spend almost $3,000 of his own money when the Institute failed to provide teaching aids and the apparatus for science teaching. Johnson's was a prickly personality, and on more than one occasion he had defended his right to the entire management of the school. But by 1829, the Institute was beginning to feel financially pinched. Contributions which the Board of Managers had hoped to raise for furnishing the high school had not been half realized, and the Institute, too, was out of pocket on the school's behalf. The *Journal* was running an annual deficit, members were slow in paying their dues, and a new technical research project threatened additional expense. Revenues had not kept pace with increasing expenses, and with some relief the Committee on Instruction rented the schoolrooms back to Johnson for $500 per annum. For the next three years he conducted his own school, called the Philadelphia High School, independent of Institute patronage but within the society's building. Then, in 1832, Johnson moved to quarters on St. James Street, near Seventh, where he conducted his school for another three or four years.[55]

When the original understanding with Johnson was terminated in

52 Minutes of the Board of Managers, August 28, 1828.

53 Report of the Special Committee appointed to make an arrangement with the principal of the High School, September 8, 1828, High School File, Franklin Institute Archives.

54 W. R. Johnson to Dr. Isaac Hays, S. V. Merrick & Thos. Fletcher, Esqrs., [October 1828?], High School File.

55 Pettengill, "Walter Rogers Johnson," p. 97.

June 1829, the Franklin Institute was once again without any program of formal education, except the drawing and mathematics schools. But there was still sentiment in the Board of Managers for a venture which would provide instruction of general utility, beyond an elementary level. The attempt to reorganize the mathematics school in 1830 sprang from that desire, and Alexander Dallas Bache seems to have been the force behind it. He was chairman of the Committee on Instruction, and in the following year when the mathematics school was closed for the last time, Bache argued that its failure was due to "a radical defect in the plan" rather than to its teachers.[56] He reported to the Board that his committee was therefore working on an alternative idea, and they presented it in the fall of 1831. On that occasion, Bache repeated his claim that the mathematics school had failed because of its "nature," and he notified the Board that the committee intended "to substitute an English school in its place, where the branches of a common English education may be received."[57] Seth Smith, a local teacher, was placed in charge, and by November the school was in operation.

The English school shared with the high school the same basic purpose. Like Benjamin Franklin's plan for an English school, both embodied the concept that education should not train for limited goals. The schools incorporated a broad vision of the utility of knowledge. By calling it an English school, the Committee on Instruction meant to distinguish it from a classical school. The emphasis was on the training a young man would need for the active pursuits of life, which was not provided in the public schools. At the Institute that viewpoint also carried the idea that a thorough scientific education required more advanced and more rigorous schooling, a concept for which Bache was responsible. The Institute's new school, however, differed from the earlier high school in that it aimed at a different audience. The English school was directed specifically toward apprentices, and it was conducted in the evenings. In urging support of the school, the Board of Managers called attention to the fact that a master was required by law to provide his apprentice with a given amount of education during his period of service, and they recommended the English school for that purpose.[58] The Institute's records do not reveal much about the school. It began with twenty-three students and never seems to have had a great many more. In 1833, Bache reported that "the English school has received this year an increased patronage but one which

56 Report of the Committee on Instruction, March 10, 1931.
57 Ibid., October 13, 1831.
58 Eighth Annual Report of the Board of Managers, January 18, 1832.

falls much short of its merits & of the supposed ability of the Institute to encourage such an establishment."[59] Over the ensuing years, successive Committees on Instruction repeatedly urged its support, but by 1837 the school ceased and slipped quietly from the Institute's attention.

On balance, with the exception of the drawing school, the Institute's efforts at formal classroom instruction were not very successful. The organization's leaders never correctly assessed the response which the mathematics and English schools might receive. The Board of Managers assumed that workingmen generally shared their own ambitions and perceptions of the best vehicle for advancement, but they were wrong. To the degree that Philadelphia workingmen organized themselves at all on these issues, they called for free public education rather than for more private schools—even those directed by the best of motives.[60] The Institute's high school enjoyed its brief success because it was never aimed at the lowest social classes. Excluding again the drawing school, the method of organization was also a source of trouble. Lacking the funds to support schools themselves, the Board employed a system of sponsorship which entailed certain defects. The method tended to fragment interest. Shifting a large part of the economic burden to the teachers made it convenient to neglect the schools, especially as newer projects were inaugurated. Lack of a clearly defined financial commitment ultimately meant lack of support from the management.

But the Franklin Institute's school experiments were highly significant in another respect. They were an essential part of the larger process whereby Americans worked out their ideas about technical education. Philadelphians were not unique, either in their efforts or their aims. The New York Mechanic and Scientific Institution, mainly through the energies of John Griscom, opened a science-oriented high school in the city in 1825. During its short life, it also drew students from "the best families" and provided the same kinds of courses as the Philadelphia school, for the same reasons.[61] And in Troy, New York, Stephen Van Rensselaer and Amos Eaton started the Rensselaer school as a reform experiment in teaching "the application of science to the common pur-

[59] Report of the Committee on Instruction, January 10, 1833.

[60] The education workingmen wanted is discussed in Edward Pessen, "The Workingmen's Movement of the Jacksonian Era," *Mississippi Valley Historical Review* 43 (December 1956): 428–43.

[61] John Griscom, *Monitorial Instruction. An Address, Pronounced at the Opening of the New-York High-School* (New York: Mahlon Day, 1825), p. 213.

poses of life."[62] These were the new kinds of schools the governor of
Connecticut had in mind when he addressed the state legislature in
1825:

By the common progress of science in our country, institutions are gradually
forming, which are designed to promote every branch of useful knowledge, with
appropriate applications to the minds of young men of the principles of mathematics, chemistry, geology, mineralogy, botany, zoology, and natural philosophy.
By a knowledge of these sciences, they become intelligent agriculturists, machinists, manufacturers, architects, and civil and military engineers.[63]

The Franklin Institute's schools, and others like them, established
some important precedents for America. Philadelphia's quarrel over
Latin and Greek was part of a larger process of determining what
technical education would be, where it would be taught, and who would
be instructed. Despite their disagreements, Browne and the Institute
shared certain implicit assumptions. The first of them was that present
generations were too wedded to existing techniques to be aided significantly by organized technical instruction, and they fastened their hopes
on "the rising generation." Technical education would not take the
form of adult education; it contained no concept of retraining or skill
improvement. The two sides also shared the belief that the kind of
instruction they had in mind necessitated special educational structures.
Existing institutions did not answer the need. When the Institute's
Board of Managers rejected Peter Browne's plan, they rejected also the
idea that a high school should be vocationally oriented. It would teach
those sciences upon which engineering skills might be based, but not
the kind of knowledge apprentices would employ as they went to their
trades. Without the support of Philadelphia's industrial community, or
at least its leadership, Browne's idea quickly died. With it died as well
any viable link between reform zeal and technical education. The
Franklin Institute's high school did not alter the educational circumstances of the workingclass poor, nor did New York's.

The advent of tax-supported high schools did not change anything.
They tended to be patterned after private schools and were frequently
directed by the same people. Public funds only made it easier to realize
the same objectives. When the Pennsylvania legislature provided support for high schools in 1836, those who had ordered the Institute's

62 Samuel Rezneck, *Education for a Technological Society: A Sesquicentennial
History of Rensselaer Polytechnic Institute* (Troy, N.Y.: Rensselaer Polytechnic Institute, 1968), p. 3.
63 Griscom, *Monitorial Instruction*, p. 26.

educational program played a major role in shaping the city's new Central High School. Alexander Dallas Bache was appointed Central High's first principal in 1839. With his educational background at West Point, his experience as chairman of the Institute's Committee on Instruction, and a faculty partially comprised of Institute professors, Bache fashioned a school which blended excellence in the sciences, their industrial applications, and the studies traditional for college entrance.[64] His approach was perfectly tailored to the needs of the school's constituency. Urban centers, the locus of the most active support for public education, were just beginning to react to the emergence of industrial capitalism. And as Michael Katz has pointed out in his study of education in Massachusetts, high schools found their champions not from the ranks of the city's poor but among those ambitious members of society who could see the shape of the future.[65]

What they saw was the need for knowledge of increasing sophistication in order to exploit most rationally America's economic potential. The nation's material advance was always part of the litany which linked democratic ideology and useful education. But the sharp sectional competition in the decades before the Civil War stimulated the belief that specialized skills were the best guarantee for economic survival. Railroad commissioners might damn a highly trained West Point engineer for his intellectual snobbery, but the technical schools of the time— real or hoped for—tried to imitate his standards.[66] Americans talked practicality, but they institutionalized theoretically.

Once high schools were fitted into the educational establishment, with an academic rather than a vocational mission, it meant that sophisticated technical instruction would find its home in the university, or in university-level institutes. In Philadelphia, the second tendency followed directly on the heels of the first. The same year Central High opened, Philadelphians petitioned the legislature for the funds to establish a state technical university. Entitled the School of Arts, it was to be attached to the Franklin Institute, but in every other respect it was

[64] For a study of the school, see Franklin Spencer Edmonds, *History of the Central High School of Philadelphia* (Philadelphia: J. B. Lippincott, 1902).

[65] Michael B. Katz, *The Irony of Early School Reform: Educational Innovation in Mid-Nineteenth Century Massachusetts* (Cambridge, Mass.: Harvard University Press, 1969).

[66] Calhoun, *The American Civil Engineer*, p. 137. At the University of Michigan, for example, Henry Tappan claimed: "we followed as a model the military academy at West Point, and succeeded, after much effort, in securing two professors educated there to conduct it. Our aim was to organize a scientific school of the highest character" (Henry P. Tappan, *Review by Rev. H. P. Tappan of his connection with the University of Michigan* [Detroit, 1864]). I am grateful to my colleague M. P. Winsor for this note.

analogous to the agricultural and mechanical colleges called into existence by the Morrill Act of 1863.

The principal objective of the proposed school—"one vast *University*" its promoters called it—was to unite science and practice in a new combination. Previous efforts to teach the artisan those scientific principles which underlay his craft had generally been limited to demonstrating the action of simple mechanical powers and the chemistry involved in elementary industrial processes. Or at least it seemed the artisan had not absorbed much more than that. One always hoped that the first taste of science would lead to another, but the school's advocates suggested there was no longer leisure for hoping. In the iron industry, for example, they claimed Pennsylvania was economically threatened by technological advances in New York and New Jersey. Science alone could replace outmoded practices and secure a trade which the Commonwealth should "have monopolized."[67] Similarly, the coal-mining industry, if the state properly supported the School of Arts, could be made the great staple for Pennsylvania which cotton was for the South. What was needed was a technical school which would incorporate an experimental farm, operational workshops, and an analytical laboratory. It was in these adjuncts to the classroom that theory could be applied directly to industrial production, resource development, and agricultural improvement.

Instruction in the school was organized into departments corresponding to civil, mining, mechanical, and chemical engineering, mathematics, and agriculture. Within the departments, teaching, laboratory training, and field experience were all directed so that the best technological solutions were defined as those most economically feasible. The student in the mining course, for instance, would take lessons in the field employing the science of geology to locate and assess mineral resources. He would also learn the techniques of mine construction, extraction processes, ore dressing and handling, and the surveying and plotting of mine fields. Geology and mineralogy would form the theoretical base of his instruction; the practical side would include all the techniques necessary for converting a natural resource into a commercial product. Rational technology was the key to obtaining the earth's wealth, "abundantly and at least expense."[68]

[67] *Memorial of a Committee appointed at the town meeting of the citizens of the City and County of Philadelphia, Held January 4, 1838, Praying for the Establishment of a School of Arts* (Harrisburg: Packer, Barbette and Parke, 1838), p. 6.

[68] *For the Establishment of a School of Arts. Memorial of the Franklin Institute, of the State of Pennsylvania, for the Promotion of the Mechanic Arts, to the Legislature of Pennsylvania* (Philadelphia: J. Crissy, 1837), p. 8.

In such a single-minded educational plan, there was neither time nor point to the traditional liberal studies. But because theoretical science played a key role in their proposal, the Philadelphians conceived a school intellectually more sophisticated than a vocational institution. Its graduates, therefore, deserved some special place in the community, notwithstanding any lack of the social polish that might normally come from a higher education. The answer was one that has been attractive to engineers ever since. It was to be a "professional education," specialized in the same way that the education of university-trained attorneys and physicians was specialized.[69] Since it was an equivalent education, the graduates would also enjoy the same social esteem as those in the other learned professions.

But 1838 was fiscally a bad year for Pennsylvania; the legislature was unsympathetic to any further drain on its funds, and the idea was never carried into effect. Even stillborn, the proposal reflects another important plateau for American technical education. For the remainder of the century, when they talked about technical education, Americans meant advanced education. That restricted definition always surprised Europeans, who took the term to encompass a wide variety of schooling, from purely vocational instruction at an elementary level to highly theoretical study at a university. Because Americans came to think of technical education as higher education, in time they also came to think of it in terms of specific occupational groups with specialized curricula. In 1838, however, those attitudes were relatively novel. Greater public consciousness had to come before financing followed.

It was at least another decade before any institutions like the School of Arts were established in America. The particular insight that technological advance demanded specialization, and specialists, came early to Philadelphians for two reasons. First, by a trial-and-error process of educational experimentation, they learned how much or how little science could be conveyed in courses of general education. Second, the Franklin Institute had become deeply involved in scientific and technical research and had learned first-hand the value of expertise. Even more to the point, the Institute's educational program during the 1830's was controlled by the same men who directed its research activities. They were professionals themselves, and they stimulated in the organization an unusual awareness of the nation's technological requirements.

[69] Ibid., p. 11. See also the *American Railroad Journal and Advocate of Internal Improvements* 6 (January 14, 1837): 4.

VI

RESEARCH, KINDRED SPIRITS, AND THE RISE OF SCIENCE

> Kindred spirits, ready to discuss the principles or
> the applications of science, and prepared to
> extend their views over the whole horizon of
> physical and mechanical research.
>
> Alexander Dallas Bache

It is difficult to know precisely why the Franklin Institute engaged in large-scale, complicated research projects. No other American mechanics' institutes did. Nor did any of the other organizations founded in the 1820's to diffuse scientific knowledge conceive that an important part of their function might also be to add to the stock of man's knowledge. Obviously, a large part of the difference had to do with the men who directed the Philadelphia institution. They were not ordinary working-men, even though some of them worked with their hands. Most of the Institute's leading figures—Merrick, Keating, William Strickland, Matthias Baldwin, Matthew Carey, Isaiah Lukens, Thomas P. Jones, and Alexander Dallas Bache—either were or soon became members of the American Philosophical Society, the nation's premier scientific society. The Institute's faculty, with few exceptions, were also members of the Philosophical Society, as well as faculty members at the University of Pennsylvania. Franklin Bache, Robert Patterson, Keating, and James C. Booth were professors of their respective subjects both at the Institute and at the University. Other men provided other links. Dr. John K. Mitchell was on the faculty of Jefferson Medical College; Keating, Lukens, Peter A. Browne, and Walter R. Johnson were active members of the Academy of Natural Sciences. They were, all of them, the prominent men in Philadelphia's learned institutions, and they lifted the Franklin Institute to an equivalent position.

But mechanics' institutes elsewhere enjoyed the concern of scientific men. Locke and Craig in Cincinnati were both men of learning. The institute in Baltimore employed professors from the University of Maryland to deliver its lecture courses. And in New York, John Griscom was a chemist of distinction. Clearly, the Institute had other causes to be different. One of them was that the organization reflected the intellectual quality of the community. Philadelphia was still the scientific capital of the country when the Franklin Institute was founded, and it remained so for another decade and a half. Learned societies, the University, museums, libraries, hospitals, and a strong medical profession insured the city's preeminence as an intellectual center. Moreover, it was an urbane intellectualism. Wistar parties, convivial monthly evenings for men of science and letters, were a Philadelphia institution. Begun in the eighteenth century by Dr. Caspar Wistar, they were continued into the next century as a social adjunct to the American Philosophical Society.[1]

Science was a matter of interest in Philadelphia. Joseph Henry sensed that quality, and in a letter to his friend Alexander Dallas Bache, he described his feelings about the difference between New York and the Quaker city:

I almost always return from New York dispirited in the way of science. I am there thrown among, it appears to me, all the Quacks and Jimcrackers of the land. I am disgusted with their pretensions and annoyed with their communications. How different is my feeling on a return from the [city] of Brotherly love!! There is there jealousy and rivalry, but also science and intelligence, and trade and money not the only things which occupy the mind.[2]

The city had other advantages, too. In the 1820's Philadelphia was the nation's banking and publishing center. It still enjoyed, despite New York's dominance, a prosperous foreign trade. And of special importance for a mechanics' institute, the city was the hub of a rising industrialism.

---

[1] Joseph Henry described to his wife his own introduction to Wistar parties: "Last evening after my letter to you I called at Dr. Hare's but did not find him in, on my way however down Chestnut Street I accidentally met with old Mr. Vaun [John Vaughan] who insisted on my accompanying him to a party given by Matthew Carey to Mr. Lesley the painter, on account of his return to America. I was very politely received and introduced to most of the company which consisted of the principal & most celebrated *savants* of the city. Among the number were Dr. Hare Prof. Bache Dr. Hase [Isaac Hays?] Dr. Chapman. It consisted entirely of men and was one of the kind called Whistar Parties." Joseph Henry to Harriet Henry, Philadelphia, November 1, 1833, Joseph Henry Private Papers, Smithsonian Institution Archives. For further information on Wistar, see Carl Bridenbaugh and Jessica Bridenbaugh, *Rebels and Gentlemen: Philadelphia in the Age of Franklin* (New York: Oxford University Press, 1965).

[2] Joseph Henry to A. D. Bache, Princeton, October 25, 1839, Joseph Henry Private Papers.

Because of all of these factors, as Whitfield Bell has pointed out, "any Philadelphia institution found itself marked for special opportunity and influence."[3]

In an urban and urbane context, scientific research was not a strange notion. Perhaps more easily than others, the Franklin Institute's managers could imagine that the organization might engage in original investigations. But as with so many Institute activities, the conception was initially surrounded with ideological implications. Useful research, as opposed to pedantic theorizing, depended upon a new and dynamic combination of science and craft skill. In somewhat the same way that alchemists once dreamed of a "philosopher's stone" which would turn base metals to gold, the image of theory and practice fused in productive union had an almost magical quality for the men of the Franklin Institute. At one level, their vision had strong symbolic elements. In the leaden times of the past, science was the intellectual luxury of a privileged few and limited by the speculations of idle philosophers. Craftsmen had no access to the principles of science. And without "the piercing ray" of its light, as Peter A. Browne had argued, the productive classes of society were condemned to a dark subjugation which was social, political, and economic in its consequences.[4]

Browne's formulation was one which had wide popularity in early nineteenth-century America, and it tended to elicit two categories of response. On the one hand, knowledge gave a new dignity to pursuits once ignominious:

There is a philosophy in the mechanic arts. The mechanic who brings to his occupation an inventive, enlightened, and inquiring mind, who is master of his craft, in theory as well as practice, has more of real philosophy in him than twenty of those minute philosophers, who spend their lives in puzzling the world with empty metaphysical speculations.[5]

That reaction had a defensive quality to it, however, not echoed by those who saw in the unity of science and practice an escape from name-calling among the social classes. Their idea, on the other hand,

[3] Whitfield J. Bell, Jr., "The American Philosophical Society as a National Academy of Sciences, 1780–1846," *Ithaca* 9 (1962): 167.

[4] Exactly the same ideas were expressed by T. B. Wakeman in a lecture at the American Institute in New York: "They were for ages excluded from the benefits of science, the great vivifier of the arts. The laboratory was kept far off from the workshop; and the fabricators of our comforts were suffered to grope in ignorance and darkness" ("Introductory Lecture delivered before the American Institute of the City of New York, the second Thursday in January, 1835," *Mechanics' Magazine and Register of Inventions and Improvements* 5 [February 1835]: 80).

[5] "Dignity of the Mechanic Arts," *The Mechanics' Register; or, Journal of the Useful Arts, Trades, Manufactures, Science, &c., &c.* 1 (February 1837): 3.

was that the skillful use of scientific knowledge was the way to eliminate artificial social distinctions. Practice improved by theory led to freedom, America's special gift to the world.

Besides its value as a democratic symbol, the image of a new combination of theory and practice also had direct point. Technical progress demanded more than traditional craftsmanship. If skilled mechanics understood scientific laws, the laborious process of experimentation by trial and error would be unnecessary. The application of principles would direct ingenuity into fruitful channels of endeavor, at a savings of time and money. Moreover, those results would have a cumulative quality; industry advanced by knowledge would stimulate more inventiveness and more industrial progress. All of the Franklin Institute's activities were potentially serviceable to that goal. Education provided knowledge to rising generations. Exhibitions offered the stimulus of competition. And both the *Journal* and the work of the Committee on Inventions diffused technical information in the mechanic community. But these were all more or less indirect links between theory and practice. There was another possibility which promised more immediate results: the Institute could itself engage in research. The idea had a powerful attraction. The membership included men of great practical skill and academicians thoroughly versed in scientific theory. Joined together in a research program, the Institute could immediately achieve the great *desideratum*.

There was ample precedent for the idea. Societies at home and abroad had pursued original research. The American Philosophical Society had in fact established its scientific reputation on its observations of the 1760 transit of Venus. And with Michael Faraday's chemical analyses for industry, London's Royal Institution provided the perfect model of an organization which simultaneously incorporated popular lectures and serious research in science.[6] The laboratory was clearly a natural and fruitful meeting ground for theory and practice, and one of the Institute's earliest ambitions was to establish some kind of a research facility. The value of original investigations found expression in the petition to the state legislature for a corporate charter and in early reports from the Board of Managers. In their first report, for instance, the Board made "the establishment of an Experimental Workshop and Laboratory" an object of first priority. In addition to its

---

[6] For a discussion of the early years of the American Philosophical Society, see Brooke Hindle's *The Pursuit of Science in Revolutionary America* (Chapel Hill: University of North Carolina Press, 1956), pp. 127ff. L. Pearce Williams has described research at the Royal Institution in his study, *Michael Faraday* (New York: Basic Books, 1965).

teaching function, one of the principal purposes of the facility would
be "to promote the improvement of the arts, by testing by a series of
experiments, the merit of every new process or invention, and by analyz-
ing, free of charge, all the products that may be sent to it from different
parts of the state."[7]

The conception was grand enough—an industrial research laboratory at the service of the entire state—but funds were never found to
match it. As a result, the Institute was left with the hope that prize
awards might stimulate a future solution to particularly baffling technical problems. The investigations of the Committee on Inventions
were otherwise the closest they came to research. The committee went
at its work with a self-conscious will to bring practical experience and
the principles of science to its investigations. Some inventions did not
require much of either for a report on their usefulness. For example,
when Samuel Lehman of Philadelphia submitted his improvement in
fire ladders for the committee's inspection in 1826, the examiners found
"considerable ingenuity" in his device. But since the supporting
apparatus for the ladders required a "house nearly thirty feet in length,
about eight in width, and ten in height," they perceived an "insuperable
objection" to its wide employment.[8] In a similar fashion, committees
could easily report to inventors of washing machines and other commonplace devices that their efforts had been anticipated. The Committee
on Inventions was composed of men with considerable training and
experience, and they recognized that technical advance was a matter of
many small accretions to knowledge. In that vein, they were careful
to point out improvements which promised useful applications. But a
large majority of the devices sent in for consideration were lacking either
in novelty, practicality, or in correctness of conception. Some ideas
arrived "in so loose a form as to render the draughting of a Report on
their merits scarcely possible."[9] American inventors, Dr. Jones suggested in his *Journal*, displayed in about equal parts great ingenuity
and great ignorance.[10] They would save considerable time, money, and

[7] Board of Managers, First Quarterly Report, April 15, 1824; Fourth Quarterly
Report, January 20, 1825. Both are published in *First Annual Report of the Proceed-
ings of the Franklin Institute of the State of Pennsylvania, for the Promotion of the
Mechanic Arts* (Philadelphia: J. Harding, 1825).

[8] "Report of the Committee of Inventions, on an improvement in the Fire-Ladder,
for which improvement a patent has been obtained by Samuel Lehman, of the city of
Philadelphia," *The Franklin Journal and American Mechanics' Magazine* 2 (September 1826): 145–46.

[9] Report of the Committee on Inventions, January 5, 1826, Franklin Institute
Archives.

[10] "New Steam Engine," *The Franklin Journal and American Mechanics' Magazine* 2 (September 1826): 187.

embarrassment, he advised, by availing themselves of the facilities of the Franklin Institute.

Despite the defects in many of the improvements submitted, the Committee on Inventions performed an important function, particularly during that period before Patent Office procedures were reorganized in 1836. Since the element of novelty was not a consideration in the granting of patent rights prior to that time, the system produced a considerable amount of confusion. One mechanic wrote in desperation: "Who is the judge of the usefulness and practicality of inventions to be patented? Is it left to the judgment of the patentee or his friends whom he may consult?"[11] In that apparent chaos of uncertainty, the committee's investigations protected the public against claims of originality where, in reality, none existed. Committee reports also served consumers by pointing out which invention in any given category best performed the job for which it was designed. Finally, publication of the reports diffused knowledge which might serve the cumulative process of technical advancement. In those respects, the examination of new inventions was an important task. Committee reports were widely republished, and mechanics' societies in other cities set up groups of their own for the same purpose.

Yet, at the same time, the work of the Committee on Inventions did not provide the opportunity for an organized, concerted assault on recognizable technical problems. Nor did special investigations which grew out of the committee's labors, such as the one on American dry-dock capabilities, seem the most effective answer. Without the funds for a laboratory or experimental workshop, and faced with the random variety of improvements sent in for examination, the Institute was frustrated in its desire to bring science and practice directly to the solution of pressing technical questions. There was recurrent talk about a research activity, but the lack of finance remained a persistent obstacle. Then, in 1829, perhaps out of a sense of the organization's growing reputation in the industrial community, the Board of Managers hit upon an idea. The Institute would conduct an investigation into the most efficient means of using water power, if industry would support the costs of experimentation. It was a bold scheme; industrial research was unheard of in America, as were technical experiments on the scale proposed.

Institutional records often reveal what has already been decided rather than the decisionmaking process itself; and such was the case

11 "National Academy on Patents," *The Mechanic. A Journal of the Useful Arts and Sciences* 3 (March 1834): 93.

with the water-power experiments. At a meeting of the Board of Managers on March 12, 1829, Samuel V. Merrick presented a formal preamble and a series of resolutions relative to the proposed research. With no recorded discussion, they were unanimously adopted. The central reason for the project, according to Merrick's preamble, was that the value of water as a prime mover and its effect on different kinds of water wheels "has never been fix'd by actual experiment on a scale of sufficient magnitude to settle principles upon which it is to be calculated."[12] He proposed a "course of experiments" and the appointment of a committee to solicit funds and to apply to city authorities for the use of facilities at the Fairmount Water Works. Actually, Merrick had already approached Frederick Graff, engineer at the city's waterworks, and he read Graff's reply at the meeting. There was ample space for a variety of experimental wheels at Fairmount, Graff said, and he was certain the city would allow the Institute to use it: "The results would be of the utmost importance to every person interested in the internal improvements now making in every section of the U. States."[13]

The idea that experimental research into water power was linked to the progress of American internal improvements was in the Board's mind, too, and it shaped their appeal to industry for the money to carry it out. A circular letter, describing the objective of the research and calling for the suggestions of men of experience as well as for their money, was printed for distribution throughout the country. The committee—Samuel V. Merrick, Benjamin Reeves, Isaiah Lukens, Rufus Tyler, and Andrew Young—estimated the cost of experimentation at $2,000. It was expected that the project would be carried out at the Fairmount Water Works, "on water wheels of all constructions, where every facility of conducting them, under a head and fall of eight feet, will be at their disposal, with means of accurately measuring the water expended, and ascertaining its effect." If the experiments could be conducted "on a sufficient scale, and unfettered for want of pecuniary means," their importance and value "must come home to every gentleman engaged in operations connected with water power, and every well wisher in the scientific reputation of our country."[14]

---

12 Minutes of the Board of Managers, March 12, 1829, Franklin Institute Archives.
13 Ibid. Eugene S. Ferguson gives some information on Graff in *Early Engineering Reminiscences [1815–40] of George Escol Sellers* (Washington, D.C.: Smithsonian Institution, 1965). A good brief description of the Fairmount Water Works is provided in Carroll W. Pursell, Jr., *Early Stationary Steam Engines in America* (Washington, D.C.: Smithsonian Institution, 1969), pp. 31ff. There is also a Frederick Graff Collection in the Franklin Institute Archives.
14 Circular Letter, March 16, 1829, Committee on Water Wheels, Franklin Institute Archives.

Nothing better illustrates the demand in America for technical information than the response to the Institute's circular. Water power still provided the motive force for most of the nation's industry. But mill owners were forced to depend on tradition or rule-of-thumb methods for efficient use of their water power, and they eagerly sought a more rational procedure. Within a matter of months, the committee received letters from New England, the Middle Atlantic States, and even a scattered few from west of the Appalachians. They came from mill-wrights, engineers, and prominent manufacturers, but best of all, they included practical suggestions and the promise of financial aid. The most immediate response came from manufacturers on the Brandywine, in Delaware, where the river's power had been used for a wide variety of mills since colonial times. Their initial reaction was that the eight-foot fall at Fairmount would not answer the purposes for which the experiments were intended. "It would seem to me," Caleb Kirk wrote from Barleyville, on the Brandywine, "that you expected to require a *heavy power.*"[15] James Siddall, of the Rokeby Cotton Works, seconded the argument: "It is certainly a matter of vast importance and interesting to all in any way connected with waterpower, but I would respectfully suggest to the committee, the impossibility of testing the matter fairly with so little fall, as the Fairmount dam can give." He suggested instead that there was a vacant mill on Squirrel Run, a small stream feeding into the Brandywine, and that its fall of twenty-five or thirty feet would "give a much fairer test."[16]

Warren Colburn, engineer for the Locks and Canal Company at Lowell, Massachusetts, leveled the same objection in his reply to the committee's circular, and he also proposed shifting the site of the inquiry:

If the Institute would consent to perform their experiments here, we would afford them every facility, and render them all the assistance in our power— and bear a proportional part of the expense. We would put up such buildings as would be necessary. I do not believe, considering our facilities and our means of rendering assistance, that a place can be found in the United States equal to this.[17]

The committee never entertained any ideas of moving the project away from the Institute. Colburn's response, and that of the Brandywine

---

[15] Caleb Kirk to the Committee on Water Wheels, Barleyville Brandywine, April 20, 1829, Franklin Institute Archives.

[16] James Siddall to the Committee of Enquiry, Brandywine, May 12, 1829.

[17] Warren Colburn to the Committee of Enquiry, Lowell, April 25, 1829.

millers, only reinforced the conviction that the experiments had great value. Even crusty old Caleb Kirk, who out of his fifty years of experience mistrusted books, millwrights schooled in them, and sometimes the best of "our self-taught men," promised his aid.

Money was all that was needed, and it came from all quarters. One of the earliest to reply was Anthony Earle, from Pemberton in the Moyamensing district of the city, who wrote, "You may put me down for Ten Dollars, and if Twenty should be my fare proportion on the Accomplishment of the Object, I will Chearfully pay it to your Order."[18] R. H. Gardiner, of Gardiner, Maine, sent twenty-five dollars and promised a cast-iron reaction wheel for the experiments. Daniel Livermore forwarded five dollars from Summit Bridge, on the Chesapeake and Delaware Canal; and Benjamin Webb wrote from nearby Wilmington: "Notwithstanding I am not so much interested as some others, I am willing to throw in my mite in the encouragement of any usefull enterprise."[19] The Brandywine millers did not contribute as much to the fund as might have been expected—Oliver Evans had earlier experienced their conservatism—and James Canby wrote to Merrick:

I immediately sent the subscription Paper to E. I. du Pont and it was only returned to me yesterday—there is but 80 Drs suscrib'd & it will not be increased much—I only wait a check from E. I. du Pont for the amo't suscribed in his neighborhood to forward the whole.[20]

But larger contributions came from other sources, and in a way which helped to dramatize the importance of the research. John Colt, agent of the Society for Establishing Useful Manufactures, founded by Alexander Hamilton as part of a grand scheme for an industrial community at the falls of the Passaic at Paterson, New Jersey, contributed $100 for the experiments.[21] The most impressive donation, however, came from the New England Society for the Promotion of Manufactures and the Mechanic Arts, an organization which represented powerful Boston textile interests. The Locks and Canal Company at Lowell was

---

[18] Anthony Earle to Benjamin Reeves, Pemberton, April 17, 1829.

[19] R. H. Gardiner to Samuel V. Merrick, Gardiner, Maine, June 29, 1829; Daniel Livermore to William Hamilton, Summit Bridge, June 20, 1829; Benjamin Webb to the Committee of Enquiry, Wilmington, April 24, 1829.

[20] James Canby to S. V. Merrick, Brandywine, July 7, 1829. Evans's efforts to interest mill owners in his new automated flour milling improvements are described in Greville Bathe and Dorothy Bathe, *Oliver Evans: A Chronicle of Early American Engineering* (Philadelphia: Historical Society of Pennsylvania, 1935).

[21] John Colt to Samuel V. Merrick, Paterson, July 9, 1829.

controlled by the same firms, and in his first letter to the committee, Warren Colburn said a pledge would undoubtedly be made toward the costs of experimentation. Colburn talked with Nathan Appleton about the project in the fall of 1829, after Appleton returned from a trip to Philadelphia, and he was assured that "something would be done by the companies here, or by the gentlemen in Boston concerned in Manufactories."[22] Apparently it seemed best to use the New England society as an agency for the contribution, and a committee of Patrick Tracy Jackson and Henry A. Dearborn was appointed by the society to consider the issue. One of them visited Philadelphia to see the project, and in May 1830 the society sent a check for $300 together with a testimonial from their inspection visit:

We are happy to assure you, of our entire confidence, in the abilities of the gentlemen charged with this highly interesting and important inquiry, and of our satisfaction, as to the manner in which it is prosecuted. The results cannot fail to be of great public utility, and to do honor to the institution which caused them to be attained.[23]

But even before the contribution from Boston, almost $1,500 had been suscribed for research, and the committee decided to go ahead with the project.[24] On the advice of its correspondents, the committee abandoned the idea of conducting the experiments at Fairmount. Instead a test facility was constructed on a vacant lot at the corner of Ninth and Vine Streets, donated for that purpose by Rush and Muhlenberg—a convincing display of generosity, given their commitment to steam engines. To help plan and carry out the experiments, James P. Espy, Matthias Baldwin, John Levering, John Agnew, Samuel Haines, Graff, Keating, and James Rush were added to the committee. A shed was built on the lot, large enough—twenty-four feet wide, ninety feet long, and thirty-three feet high—to house apparatus and to provide working

[22] Warren Colburn to Samuel V. Merrick, Lowell, November 18, 1829. Colburn also told Merrick: "when I first saw your proposals for making experiments, it occurred to me, that a more perfect mode of measuring power applied to moving machines was a desideratum." He then built a dynamometer "which operates very perfectly" and offered drawings of it for the experiments. He described the machine, and in a letter to Merrick on December 16, 1829, made some additional suggestions for its improvement.

[23] P. T. Jackson and H. A. Dearborn to Samuel V. Merrick, Boston, May 6, 1830. Some additional information on the New England society is available in Justin Winsor, ed., *The Memorial History of Boston*, 4 vols. (Boston: Ticknor and Company, 1880).

[24] Minutes of the Committee on Water Wheels, July 25, 1829. To make up the difference between subscriptions and anticipated cost, each member of the committee personally pledged himself to an apportioned amount, should further contributions not be found.

space. Water was supplied to the installation by the city at no charge.

The main components of the apparatus consisted of a forebay, or reservoir, for the water; the supporting structure for the wheel; an afterbay, for collecting and measuring the water used; the water wheel itself; and the constuction used to measure the effect produced, which would be determined by the time it took a measured amount of water to raise a given weight to a given height. A variety of additional devices were incorporated for accuracy of timing and weight measurements. Both reservoirs were fitted with indicators to show water level. For the afterbay, where weight measurement was critical, the gauge showed the amount to within five pounds of water. A valve was employed in the tailrace so that only the water actually used in the experiment would be collected in the afterbay. That valve was connected to both a bell and a timing device which indicated how long it took to raise a given weight to a given height. The bell rang when the valve was closed, signaling the beginning of an experiment; when the valve was opened, the bell rang again, signaling the end of the experiment. "A very accurate time-piece," with its dial graduated in half-second intervals, showed the lapse between bells. The whole apparatus, of course, was basic to all the experiments; but to give a full range of results, four different sizes of wheels were used. The largest was twenty feet in diameter, the smallest six feet, with intermediate wheels of fifteen and ten feet. In addition, different bucket constructions were employed, along with seven different chutes to apply the water at various points on the periphery of the wheels. It was an imaginative and sophisticated facility, carefully devised to test all possible variables under conditions of the strictest accuracy.[25]

The primary purpose of the research, simply stated, was to determine "the mode of applying any given head of water, so as to produce the greatest ratio of effect to power expended."[26] In practice, however, that was a complicated problem, involving experimental variations in the head of water, wheel size and type, size of the aperture which let water to the wheel and the form of the gate employed in the chute, the number of buckets on a wheel, their shape and position, and finally, the velocity of the wheel. The effect of friction and inertia for each wheel combination had to be determined, and in the interest of further accuracy, each experiment for each variation of each variable

[25] In the records of the Committee on Water Wheels, there are two committee reports which give some information on the test facility. But the best source is the Committee's first published report, in the *Journal of the Franklin Institute* 11 (March 1831): 145–54.

[26] Ibid., 12 (August 1831): 80.

was run twice, or more if necessary. The apparatus was ready by the spring of 1830, and most of the experiments were performed from then until late in December. Three men were needed to carry out an experiment. One man opened the forebay gates to apply water to the wheel until a basket of weights was raised to a point at which measurement began. At exactly that instant, a second man closed the tailrace valve; the bell rang, and the third man noted the time. The first man maintained a constant water level in the forebay, and at the moment an indicator signaled that the weights had been lifted to a predetermined height, the tailrace valve was opened, ringing the signal to mark the time and stop the water onto the wheel. By means of a frictional brake, the weights were lowered back into position, the amount of water in the afterbay was noted, and the experimenters were ready for another trial. They recorded 1,381 experiments in their reports, meaning, of course, that they went through the procedure twice that many times.[27] The labor was voluntary, done by men who were regularly occupied at their normal pursuits.

When the results of the water-power research were made available —the first report was published in the *Journal* in March 1831—they provided exactly the information the committee had set out to discover.[28] By recourse to the tabular data of the reports, millwrights could determine the limits of efficiency in whatever combination of elements they had at their command. They could discover how to combine the elements of a water power to achieve maximum efficiency. The research did not produce radically new ideas; no one expected that it would. It did extend existing knowledge. When the committee talked about the project's magnitude, they were talking—undramatically— about experiments extensive enough to cover all conceiveable cases. John Smeaton's well-known experiments in the late eighteenth century, for instance, had been made with models, and the difference in scale rendered his results often difficult to apply in practice. Subsequent research, even when performed with full-size apparatus, tended to be

[27] In preparing the reports for publication, the committee decided that it would be simple and less confusing to list all trials of any given combination as a single experiment. For purposes of reference, the experiments were then numbered in the reports.

[28] Under the title "Report of the Committee of the Franklin Institute of Pennsylvania, Appointed May, 1829, to ascertain by experiment the value of Water as a Moving Power," the reports were published in the *Journal of the Franklin Institute* in succeeding numbers throughout 1831 and 1832. There were plans to publish an abstracted version to point out general conclusions, but it did not appear in the *Journal* until the number of March 1841 and in the four following numbers. A further idea, to publish a shortened version particularly for practical use, was apparently never realized.

restricted to a single type of wheel.[29] And in any event, as Oliver Evans had discovered thirty-five years earlier when preparing *The Young Miller and Millwright's Guide,* the theorists disagreed among themselves.[30] Magnitude and accuracy sufficient to produce sound general conclusions were the important contributions made by the Franklin Institute's water-power research. George Rennie, described by Alexander Dallas Bache as the greatest living authority on the subject, presented a paper before the British Association for the Advancement of Science in 1832 entitled "Report on the Progress and Present State of our Knowledge of Hydraulics as a Branch of Engineering." In his paper, Rennie noted that he himself had "made a great many experiments on the maximum effect of water wheels; but the recent experiments of the Franklin Institute, made on a more magnificent scale . . . eclipse everything that has yet been effected on this subject."[31]

The only sour note in the whole enterprise was that it cost about $500 more than the amount received in contributions. But in every other respect, it was a remarkable success. Nothing of its kind had ever been accomplished in America or Europe. For the Franklin Institute, the research held profound implications. At the most immediate level, one of the best rewards was the complimentary notice which the effort received. Local newspapers proudly reprinted the remarks of the editor of the London *Mechanics' Magazine*:

We should be doing a great injustice to our American brethren, were we to omit mentioning, with the praise it deserves . . . the extensive experiments recently instituted at Philadelphia, by means of public subscription, promoted by the Franklin Institute, to ascertain the value of water as a moving power.

The Franklin Institute have done, in this particular instance, exactly what we apprehend it will be one business of the 'British Association' to do in similar cases of deficient information.[32]

The London editor republished the committee's first report as an example of "organized and co-operative" research. The Institute's

[29] "Report of the Committee of the Franklin Institute of Pennsylvania, Appointed May, 1829, to ascertain by experiment the value of Water as a Moving Power," *Journal of the Franklin Institute* 11 (March 1831): 146.

[30] Bathe and Bathe, *Oliver Evans,* p. 45.

[31] A. D. Bache, *Anniversary Address before the American Institute, of the City of New York* (New York: Pudney & Russell, 1857), p. 28. The first part of Rennie's report was published in the *Journal of the Franklin Institute* 19 (January 1835): 57–64; (February 1835): 125–35.

[32] *National Gazette,* July 7, 1832.

investigation, he concluded, *"constitutes another of its exclusive claims to the favor of the scientific public."*[33]

A Boston book firm, operating perhaps on the presumption that what was current in London was currency in America, bought 350 copies of the English journal for its New England customers. When the Institute's Committee on Publication learned of the action, they immediately protested, on the grounds that sales of the journal constituted a violation of their own copyrights to the research report. The Bostonians argued, in turn, that cutting the article out would make their copies rather difficult to sell. They also suggested, with what must have been more telling effect:

If the article has to be cut out, it will probably excite the same feelings in England, as would be experienced here, if we should hear that 350 copies of the Franklin Institute Journal, sent to London, were mutilated because they contained an article, with a complimentary acknowledgement, extracted from an English Journal.[34]

Legally, the Institute's position might have been difficult to sustain; editors at that time freely copied from each other, with or without acknowledgment. In any event, that was not the real issue. Sales of the London magazine cut into Institute hopes to recoup some of its loss on the experiments through its own publication of the reports. In that spirit, the committee gave the Boston firm permission to sell existing stocks only and suggested that if it wished the *Journal* for future sales, a large order would bring it, "upon very favourable terms."[35]

The episode was momentarily troublesome for an organization where ambitions often outran income, but in other respects the water-power experiments had great significance for the Franklin Institute, and for the development of American technology. Foreign comment illuminated one important characteristic of the research, namely, that major technical problems were best solved by "organized and co-operative" investigation. Individual discoveries might be made all along the technological frontier, but the most dramatic advances came through combined efforts. Organization meant assembling the requisite talent, and it meant funding beyond the abilities of single individuals. When the editor of the *Mechanics' Magazine* compared the water-power

33 Ibid.
34 Isaac Hays to Gray and Bowen, February 29, 1832; Gray and Bowen to Isaac Hays, Boston, March 5, 1832, Committee on Water Wheels.
35 Isaac Hays to Gray and Bowen, March 12, 1832, Committee on Water Wheels.

research with the work expected of the newly formed British Association for the Advancement of Science, it was implicitly suggested that organization also meant high standards of intellectual activity. The conclusions were inescapable. Research in technology, just as in science, was defined in terms of intellectual standards, the cooperative effort of its practitioners, and outside funding.

At the Franklin Institute, the water-power inquiry had other important effects. The project gave direct experience in establishing a research facility, devising test apparatus, and in planning and conducting a course of experiments. And even if costs exceeded available financing, the investigation provided an example of how the society could indulge its taste for research. Viewed simply as a starting point, the inquiry clearly led to a variety of subsequent research projects. But there was another, even more crucial result. The water-power investigation provided one more plank in the platform Alexander Dallas Bache and a small circle of men were erecting at the Institute. They dedicated their program to experimental research, the professionalization of science and technology, and the elevation of America's scientific and technical reputation. In carrying out their platform, they transformed the Franklin Institute.

More than any other single person, Alexander Dallas Bache was responsible for the change. Just twenty-three years old when he joined the Institute, Bache was already heading toward a brilliant future.[36] He had entered West Point at a time when the Academy was the country's outstanding school for a scientific and technical education, and he graduated with highest honors. He served on the faculty there for a year and then spent two years as a lieutenant in the Army's elite scientific corps, the Topographical Engineers.[37] In 1828, however, Bache left the army and returned to Philadelphia to accept the professorship of natural philosophy and chemistry at the University of Pennsylvania. He was elected to the Institute in 1829, and in the years

[36] See Merle M. Odgers, *Alexander Dallas Bache: Scientist and Educator, 1806–1867* (Philadelphia: University of Pennsylvania Press, 1947); and Nathan Reingold, *Science in Nineteenth-Century America: A Documentary History* (New York: Hill and Wang, 1964). In addition, an excellent biographical sketch on Bache is by Joseph Henry, "Eulogy on Prof. Alexander Dallas Bache, Late Superintendent of the United States Coast Survey," *Annual Report of the Board of Regents of the Smithsonian Institution, Showing the Operations, Expenditures, and Condition of the Institution for the Year 1870* (Washington, D.C.: Government Printing Office, 1872), pp. 91–116.

[37] Some aspects of the Topographical Engineers Corps are described in Forest G. Hill, *Roads, Rails & Waterways: The Army Engineers and Early Transportation* (Norman: University of Oklahoma Press, 1957).

which followed he profoundly influenced the development of the organization which had been named in honor of his great-grandfather.

Bache was immediately projected into the Institute's inner councils.
Little more than a year after his admission to membership, he was
elected to fill a vacancy on the Board of Managers, a position he held
without interruption until 1837 and then again from 1839 until his
departure for Washington in 1843. Bache was also influential on some
of the Institute's most important committees. He served on the Committee on Inventions for three years, and for the three years after that
he was chairman of the Committee on Science and Arts, when that
group took over the responsibility for examining new inventions. For
seven years Bache was chairman of the Committee on Instruction, and
for four of the eleven years of his appointment to the Committee on
Publication he was also its chairman. He was the first chairman of
monthly conversational meetings and for five more years served as
chairman or a member of the committee which arranged them. During
the years from 1839 until 1844, he acted also as the Institute's corresponding secretary.[38] In addition, Bache was prominent in the
Institute's special investigations. Shortly after his election to membership, he was added to the committee conducting experiments on
water power and was responsible, along with Espy and Reeves, for
publication of its reports. In the following year he was appointed a
member, then chairman, of a special inquiry into the causes of steamboat boiler explosions. Bache also headed the committee formed to
establish a standard system of weights and measures for the state of
Pennsylvania. It was on his suggestion that the Institute first began
meteorological observations, and he was responsible for linking the
Institute's research with similar efforts at the American Philosophical
Society. In any of the Institute's activities which had scientific implications, Bache was clearly the dominant figure.

His influence in shaping the Institute is discernible in other ways.
There was always a latent interest in natural history in the organization, but Bache recognized the dangers inherent in a diffusion of the
Institute's energies. When the organization acquired the collections
of the Maclurean Lyceum, a short-lived natural history society named
after William Maclure, Bache argued that natural history specimens
and books should be sold or exchanged to support the Institute's pri-

[38] A brief account of Bache's influence at the Institute is given in Henry Butler
Allen, "Alexander Dallas Bache and his Connection with the Franklin Institute of the
State of Pennsylvania," American Philosophical Society *Proceedings* 84 (May 1941):
145–49.

mary objectives.[39] In much the same way, he voted against the establishment of a professorship of geology and against Institute participation in a national convention of lyceums. He was also responsible for significant internal modifications. Conversational meetings were the result of Bache's instigation, and they were almost completely controlled by the scientifically-oriented members of the Institute. An even more important procedural reorganization came in 1834, when Merrick and Bache proposed that the Committee on Inventions be replaced by a Committee on Science and the Arts.

In his draft of the Board's annual report, Bache suggested the reason for the change. The Institute's fiscal organization and its economy as "a body politic" probably could not be improved, Bache claimed. However, he noted, "your Board are of opinion that such is not the case with arrangements for the scientific labours of the institution," and the Committee on Science and the Arts was proposed to remedy the deficiency.[40] The Board of Managers adopted a series of resolutions to put the new committee into operation. Two of the resolutions were particularly important. One gave the committee greater autonomy than that enjoyed by any other committee at the Institute; the other invested the committee with the primary responsibility for the organization's scientific labors. The Committee on Science and the Arts still retained the responsibility for the examination of new inventions; but it was also made the society's scientific arm, with power to initiate whatever investigations it chose, and was charged in its efforts to sustain "the scientific character of the Institute."[41] Bache was elected the committee's chairman, and he held the position until his departure for Europe in 1836.

Undoubtedly, Bache's Philadelphia connections aided his rise to power at the Institute—he and Frederick Fraley had been boyhood friends, and Merrick proposed him for membership—but Bache was also a man of great abilities and personal charm. All of the qualities ascribed to him in later life—superb intellectual endowment, administrative genius, scientific talent, and magnetic personality—found full expression at the Franklin Institute. In after years, as head of the U.S. Coast Survey and as first president of the National Academy of

[39] "Quarterly Report of the Board of Managers," *Journal of the Franklin Institute* 16 (September 1833): 159. Some account of the society is available in *Contributions of the Maclurean lyceum to the arts and sciences* (Philadelphia: J. Dobson, 1827–29). See also Minutes of the Board of Managers, March 14, April 11, May 9, and June 13, 1833.

[40] Tenth Annual Report of the Board of Managers, January 1834; Minutes of the Board of Managers, January 9, 1834, Franklin Institute Archives.

[41] Tenth Annual Report of the Board of Managers.

Sciences, his friends and admirers called Bache "The Chief."[42] He had enjoyed the same esteem earlier in Philadelphia, and it was there that the force of his personality was first employed in a crusade to advance the cause of science in America.

In a nation which had not yet provided much tangible support for science, the main concerns of Bache's crusade were employment, research facilities and funding, and a greater public estimation for men of science. But tied to all those needs was the strong desire to make the intellectual standing of science in America equal to the standing it had in the Old World. The Franklin Institute was well suited to Bache's ideas. Lectures yielded a modest income at a time when employment in science was difficult to find. Probably more important, they offered public exposure, the chance for other lecture opportunities, and a measure of distinction. Teaching in the Institute's schools had the same advantages. But for aspiring scientists research and publication were the main avenues to reputation. In that respect, the Institute's experimental projects and its *Journal* were vitally important to men of ambition. Bache gained his earliest scientific reknown in the organization's research, as did James P. Espy and Walter R. Johnson. Because of his participation in the water-power and steam-boiler investigations, city authorities sent Samuel V. Merrick to England to study gas lighting when its use was being considered for Philadelphia. And Sears C. Walker first exercised his astronomical interests at the Institute. "Kindred spirits," Bache called the Institute's scientific circle, "ready to discuss the principles or the applications of science, and prepared to extend their views over the whole horizon of physical and mechanical research."[43]

It was a tight-knit group, and they cooperated closely. Like Benjamin Franklin, Merrick made meteorological observations on his voyage to London in 1834 and sent the results back to Bache and Espy. Espy called Johnson's attention to an article on hydraulics in the *Revue Encyclopédique*. He and Johnson repeated the experiments at one of the Institute's conversation meetings, and Johnson published the results in Benjamin Silliman's *American Journal of Science*.[44] When

[42] Nathan Reingold, in *Science in Nineteenth-Century America*, reprints a delightful series of letters to Bache which reveal the admiration of his friends.

[43] The remark was made in Bache's eulogy of James P. Espy, in the *Annual Report of the Board of Regents of the Smithsonian Institution, showing the Operations, Expenditures, and Condition of the Institution for the Year 1859* (Washington, D.C.: Thomas Ford, 1860), p. 109.

[44] S. V. Merrick to William Hamilton, Liverpool, May 7, 1834, Incoming Correspondence, Franklin Institute Archives; Walter R. Johnson, "On the apparent anomaly observed in the rotation of liquids of different specific gravities when placed upon each other," *American Journal of Science* 27 (January 1835): 84–88.

Bache became involved in a controversy with Professor Denison Olmstead of Yale over the analysis of a meteoric shower, Espy joined the
fray in an article for the Institute's *Journal*, basing his evidence on
the reports from his corps of weather observers.[45] In a similar fashion, Bache and other members of the Philadelphia coterie sided with
Espy in his long dispute with William C. Redfield over a true theory
for the action of storms.

These men not only worked together; they sought as well to advance
the state of science through publication of their results. Primarily
through the efforts of Merrick and Bache, but with aid from their
colleagues, they transformed the *Journal* from a mechanics' magazine
into a prominent scientific publication. Scientific experiments and discussions in the monthly conversation meetings also served to publicize
the group's findings. For example, Joseph Saxton, a self-trained Pennsylvania instrumentmaker living in London, sent plans for a variety
of electromagnetic machines to his friend Isaiah Lukens. Lukens,
another Philadelphia-spawned mechanical genius, constructed the
machines, and they were displayed and operated at conversational
meetings and then made the subject of *Journal* articles.[46] Both
Johnson and Bache also published articles stemming from Institute
research in the *American Journal of Science*, and the Committee on
Publications freely exchanged articles and woodcuts for supporting
illustrations with Silliman.[47]

In addition to their professional associations, these men were linked
socially as well. Bache was the center of the circle. Years before he,
Louis Agassiz, Joseph Henry, and others would form an elite group to
control the standards and practice of American science—they mock-
ingly called themselves the Lazzaroni, after the street beggars of
Italy—Bache established its predecessor in Philadelphia.[48] There was

45 James P. Espy, "Remarks on Professor Olmstead's Theory of the Meteoric
Phenomenon of November 12th, 1833, denominated Shooting Stars, with some other
Queries towards forming a just Theory," *Journal of the Franklin Institute* 19 (Janu-
ary 1835): 9–10.

46 *Journal of the Franklin Institute* 17 (March 1834): 159; (April 1834): 224–25.

47 For examples, see Walter R. Johnson, "Remarks on the Strength of Cylindri-
cal Steam Boilers," *American Journal of Science* 22 (January 1833): 68–75; and
Alexander Dallas Bache, "Safety Apparatus for Steam Boats," *American Journal of
Science* 20 (July 1831): 317–22, both of which were the subjects of conversation meetings at the Institute and first published in its *Journal*.

48 For brief accounts of the Lazzaroni, see A. Hunter Dupree, *Science in the Federal Government: A History of Policies and Activities to 1940* (Cambridge, Mass.:
Harvard University Press, 1957); Reingold, *Science in Nineteenth-Century America*;
and Edward Lurie, *Louis Agassiz, A Life in Science* (Chicago: University of Chicago
Press, 1960).

no name for the earlier group except "the club." Apparently organized
shortly after Joseph Henry came to Princeton in 1832, it was composed
of men primarily interested in the physical sciences—Bache, Henry,
Espy, Henry D. Rogers, and Sears C. Walker. According to Bache, the
club was formed "for promoting research, and especially for scrutiniz-
ing the labor of its members."[49] Its purpose was to raise standards, as
well as to conduct experiments, and its membership emphasized a
full-time, professional commitment to science. Bache had apparently
argued the need for such groups to Joseph Henry, who later wrote
him:

Still I am now more than ever of your opinion that the real working men in
the way of science in this country should make common cause and endeavour
by every proper means unitedly to raise their own scientific character. To make
science more respected at home to increase the facilities of scientific investigations and the inducements to scientific labours.[50]

The club went into decline around 1837, with both Henry and Bache
abroad, but some of its purposes were served by the United Bowmen's
Company of Philadelphia, an archery group to which several of the
Institute's scientific circle belonged.[51]

American scientists were struggling for a professional life with
status, standards, and support. Bache, Henry, Espy, Walker, Johnson,
and men like them were the first generation of Americans who sought
to make science a full-time occupation. Convivial social clubs provided
some comfort, but employment and the chance to do research were the
critical needs. In a context of limited opportunities the Franklin Institute played an important role. James P. Espy, for example, found in
the Institute critical early support for his career in meteorology, a
subject itself in the process of becoming a science.

Espy was educated at Transylvania University in the brilliant

49 *Annual Report of the Board of Regents of the Smithsonian Institution . . . for
the Year 1859*, p. 109.
50 Reingold, *Science in Nineteenth-Century America*, p. 85.
51 The United Bowmen were a group of young men of "social disposition and
scientific proclivities." The membership included Titian and Franklin Peale, James C.
Booth, John F. Frazer, Samuel S. Haldeman, and Charles B. Trego. See Jessie Poesch,
Titian Ramsay Peale, 1799–1885, And His Journals of the Wilkes Expedition (Philadelphia: American Philosophical Society, 1961), for an account of the society. The
Frazer Papers at the American Philosophical Society also contain information on the
"Toxies," as they liked to call themselves. See, for example, Haldeman to Frazer,
December 31, 1839.

early years of its history.[52] His interests had a scientific bent, but
like Johnson and Walker, Espy taught school in order to earn a living. By the early 1820's he had an established reputation in Philadelphia as a teacher of mathematics and the classics. By that time Espy
had also become increasingly attracted to the study of meteorology.
Around 1830 he gave up his school to devote full time to the subject,
hoping to earn enough from lectures to support his research. Two
activities in particular occupied Espy's time. He sought to stimulate
interest in meteorology, and he worked to develop a network of observers who would provide him with the data for the formulation of a
theory to account for weather phenomena. In both cases the Institute
provided Espy with a framework for his efforts.

The Institute's lecture hall and its *Journal* provided Espy with a
forum for his views. While he had delivered a series of volunteer lectures on meteorology in the Institute's first year of operation, it was
not until the early 1830's that Espy began seriously to use the organization as a vehicle for his interests. Early in 1831, on Bache's
motion, a committee was appointed to keep a meteorological register,
to be published monthly in the *Journal*.[53] Espy was a member of the
committee, which was authorized later in the year to purchase the
instruments necessary for their labors. Membership in the Institute's
Committee on Meteorology, of which he was later chairman, gave Espy
a further opportunity to pursue his interests, and he began shortly to
publish articles in the *Journal*.[54]

To develop any kind of a meaningful theoretical structure, however,
Espy needed additional data. He had already developed an informal
network of weather observers simply by soliciting information from
individuals interested in the subject.[55] But an organized system which
would provide him with simultaneous observations from a variety of
locations was what Espy wanted, and in a series of resolutions before
the Committee on Science and the Arts in 1834 he urged a grand
scheme to that end. Meteorology, he claimed, was on the verge of a

[52] Brief biographical information on Espy is in the *Dictionary of American
Biography* (New York: Charles Scribner's Sons, 1943); L. Morehead, *A Few Incidents
in the Life of Prof. James P. Espy* (Cincinnati: R. Clarke & Company, 1888); and
"Sketch of James Pollard Espy," *The Popular Science Monthly* 34 (April 1889): 834–40.

[53] Minutes of Meetings of the Franklin Institute, January 27, 1831, Franklin Institute Archives.

[54] James P. Espy, "On the Importance of Hygrometric Observations in Meteorology, and the means of making them with accuracy," *Journal of the Franklin Institute*
11 (April 1831): 221–29.

[55] James P. Espy, "Meteorological Remarks," *Journal of the Franklin Institute*
16 (November 1833): 295.

"glorious revolution." The dew-point hygrometer promised to be for meteorology what the telescope had been for astronomy, according to Espy, and he urged its exploitation. Congress should be petitioned for the funds to establish ten observatories, under the Institute's control and directed by a full-time meteorologist, to provide combined observation of meteorological phenomenon. Espy suggested that the petition to Congress should enumerate the practical benefits which would flow from his scheme in order to make it more attractive to the legislators. But he saw the plan as essentially scientific and one which would link all the colleges and learned societies in the country.[56]

When Espy's proposals were presented to the Committee on Science and the Arts, Alexander Dallas Bache, the committee's chairman, pointed out that the American Philosophical Society was also considering the establishment of a network of weather observers. Espy and Bache therefore proposed cooperation, and a subcommittee, which included Bache, Espy, Henry D. Rogers, and Sears C. Walker, was appointed to confer with the Philosophical Society's meteorological committee. A cooperative plan was developed, and a joint committee, headed by Espy, printed and distributed circulars calling for volunteer observers. During the course of the next three years the committee developed a correspondence with observers from widely scattered points of the country, collated the information, and printed three reports on meteorology.[57] Nothing had come of Espy's call for federal funds, however, and he still sought a more comprehensive network of observers, in a system which would also give him full-time employment.

Partial realization of Espy's aims came in 1837, when the Pennsylvania legislature appropriated $4,000 for a state-wide meteorological research program. The funds were placed at the disposal of the Franklin Institute, which then formed a joint committee with the American Philosophical Society to carry out the investigation. Standardized reporting forms were printed, and each official county observer was provided with a barometer, thermometers, and a rain guage.[58] Espy was appointed meteorologist, yielding the chairmanship of the joint committee to Dr. Robley Dunglinson, president of the American Philosophical Society. In a pamphlet entitled *Hints to*

---

[56] Minutes of the Committee on Science and the Arts, June 12, 1834, Franklin Institute Archives.

[57] Ibid., November 13, 1834; December 10, 1835; November 10, 1836. See also Armand N. Spitz, "Meteorology in the Franklin Institute," *Journal of the Franklin Institute* 237 (May 1944): 286.

[58] Minutes of the Board of Managers, April 19, 1837; Minutes of the Committee on Science and the Arts, April 18, 1837.

Observers on Meteorology, Espy suggested that the primary aim of the committee was *"to find out the course that storms take over the surface of the earth in all the different seasons of the year."*[59] Espy was at that time engaged in sharp conflict with William C. Redfield over a true theory for the action and shape of storms, and he used the Institute's meteorological program to support his own views.

But the joint committee's work had limitations for Espy's ultimate goal; he wanted nothing less than a national system of observers. In his pamphlet, which was issued under state support, he actually directed his remarks as much to out-of-state observers as to those connected with the project, outlining the kinds of information which could be obtained without instruments. He again urged the Institute to seek federal support, with the result that the Board of Managers authorized the joint committee "to memorialize Congress for the purpose of obtaining national aid."[60] In a letter to Senator James Buchanan, Espy outlined his ideas: "This state you know, has given $4000 for the advancement of Meteorology, but this is altogether inadequate to the mighty purpose." Instead he proposed that the federal government establish 300 stations under the direction of a skilled meteorologist. At the same time, Espy lectured before the New York State legislature, seeking aid there for an extension of his research.[61]

Espy continued as meteorologist at the Institute until April 1839, when he left for Washington in hope of federal financing. By that time he had already developed an international reputation. The American Philosophical Society had awarded him its Magellanic Premium in 1836 for his storm theory, which he was later invited to explain before the British Association for the Advancement of Science and the French Academy of Sciences. He published his major work, *The Philosophy of Storms,* in 1841 and was appointed meteorologist to the War Department the following year.[62] Espy was wrong in his dispute with Redfield about the elliptical shape of storms but correct in his theories of heat effects. That and his efforts to promote the systematic collection of data through large networks of observers were his significant contributions to meteorology. He was a persuasive speaker, and he used that skill to promote weather observation

[59] James P. Espy, *Hints to Observers on Meteorology* (Philadelphia: The Franklin Institute, 1837), p. 1.

[60] Minutes of the Board of Managers, July 19, 1837.

[61] James P. Espy to James Buchanan, Philadelphia, June 19, 1837, Buchanan Papers, Historical Society of Pennsylvania; Reingold, *Science in Nineteenth-Century America,* pp. 95–96.

[62] James P. Espy, *The Philosophy of Storms* (Boston: Little and Brown, 1841).

throughout the United States. After Espy made a Southern lecture tour, one of his listeners wrote:

Professor Espy left us last Sunday, after having afforded the Citizens of Mobile the gratification of hearing him lecture upon the Science of Meteorology, & has excited a degree of interests, among the few who devote themselves to scientific subjects I little expected previous to his visit.[63]

Espy remained in Washington for the remainder of his scientific career. Through the intercession of political friends, he was able to secure positions with a variety of governmental agencies.[64] But he never found the support he sought for a federally-financed national system of observers, with himself as the government's chief meteorologist. The network he had developed at the Institute, augmented by the volunteers he solicited while at the War Department, was absorbed by the Smithsonian when Joseph Henry made meteorology one of his chief concerns.[65] Espy was also the victim of his own efforts to promote meteorology. During the course of his lifetime, the subject became a study of increasing sophistication, and the science was taken over by younger men more competent theoretically than Espy. As early as 1839, Bache expressed private reservations about some of Espy's work, and Joseph Henry later urged him to reexamine his theoretical speculations in order to present more matured views.[66]

Despite the fact that Espy's contributions to meteorology were outstripped in his own lifetime, he earned a scientific reputation both in America and abroad. The Franklin Institute provided him with the means for that professional development. In that respect, Espy's career paralleled those of the other members of the Institute's scientific circle. Leadership in the organization passed to Bache and his "kindred spirits" after 1830, and they used it to advance their own scientific interests. The association gave them an opportunity, at an early stage of their development, to practice the skills upon which later prominence depended. At the same time, their labors gave the Institute

[63] J. B. North to W. Hamilton, Mobile, March 22, 1840, Incoming Correspondence.

[64] See, for instance, Espy's letter to Senator Truman Smith, Washington, January 16, 1842, soliciting a position as meteorologist at the Smithsonian. Gratz Collection, Historical Society of Pennsylvania.

[65] Bruce Sinclair, "Gustavus A. Hyde, Professor Espy's Volunteers, and the Development of Systematic Weather Observation," *Bulletin of the American Meteorological Society* 46 (December 1965): 779–84.

[66] A. D. Bache to Prof. Lloyd, Philadelphia, May 4, 1839, Joseph Henry Private Papers; *Annual Report of the Board of Regents of the Smithsonian Institution . . . for the Year 1859*, p. 110.

new fame. Experimental research, begun with the water-power investigation, made the organization the nation's most logical resort for informed judgment on problems requiring specialized expertise. Reputation brought new members, support for more research, and new confidence in the rewards which flowed from the union of theory and practice. What the Institute's leaders were perhaps less conscious of was that the nature of the union had been altered by their own research activities.

THE SCIENCE OF TECHNOLOGY

It is often argued that American technology, especially in the period before the Civil War, was largely a mixture of cut-and-try methods and Yankee ingenuity. However, the experimental equipment employed at the Franklin Institute in the water-power and steam-boiler investigations reveals a much more sophisticated approach to technical problems. In both cases, the apparatus was thoughtfully designed to produce a high degree of accuracy and a broadly useful range of results. The water-power experiments were carried out with full-scale wheels, for example, while in his strength-of-materials research, W. R. Johnson devised a novel technique for measuring temperatures beyond the limits of mercury thermometers.

The Institute's experimental style of technical research reflected the energies and interests of a remarkable group of young scientists. James P. Espy later gained a wide reputation in meteorology, as did James C. Booth in industrial chemistry. Walter R. Johnson also used his Institute experience as the springboard to a research career. Alexander Dallas Bache was the dominating spirit, and he subsequently gave momentum to a national scientific community. His protégé, John F. Frazer, took Bache's place at the University of Pennsylvania and for over fifteen years served as editor of the *Journal of the Franklin Institute*.

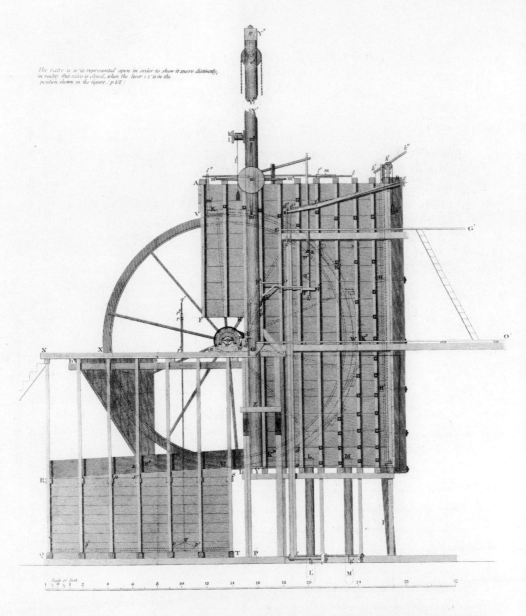

Front view of the experimental equipment designed by the Franklin Institute in 1830 to conduct tests on water-power efficiency. It is shown with the twenty-foot wheel in place. Levers at the top regulated water flow, and a series of valves insured accurate measurement of the water employed.

Rear view of the water-power test installation. The forebay structure, *upper left*, fed by pipes from the city's water system, contained the water used in the tests. The afterbay, *lower right*, collected for measurement the water required to raise a given weight to a given height.

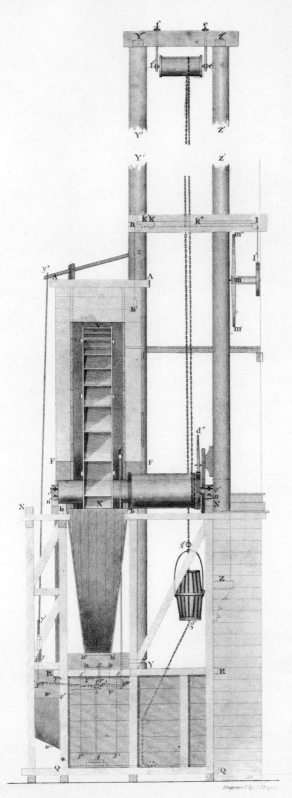

End view of the water-power apparatus, showing the basket of weights and associated mechanisms to measure the effect of a given amount of water.

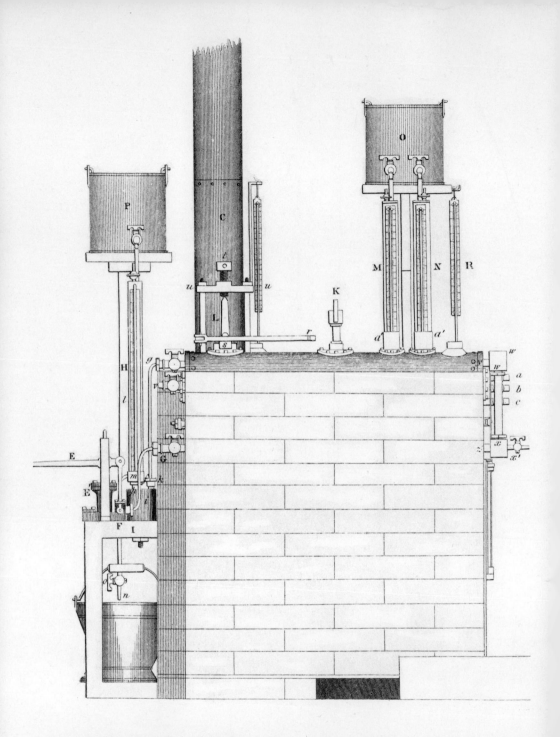

Side view of the experimental boiler used from 1830 to 1835 by the Institute committee investigating the causes of steam-boiler explosions. It was fitted with a variety of gauges and thermometers in order to measure water level and the temperature of steam and water within the boiler.

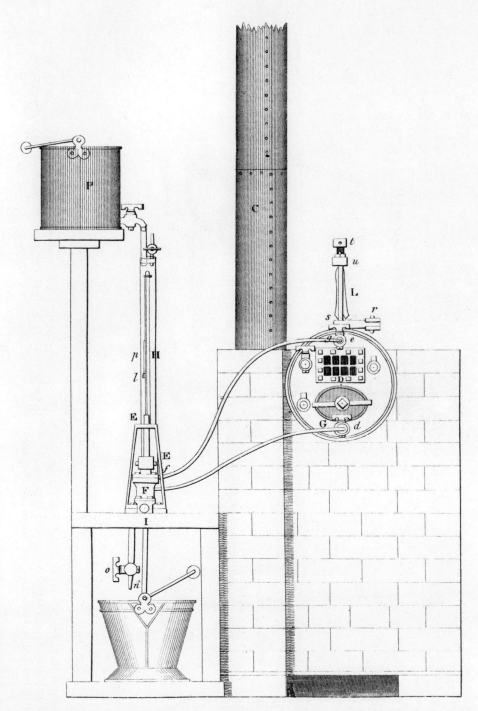

End view of the experimental boiler, showing the glass plate through which the effects of the foaming action of water could be observed and the pump which supplied the boiler with water.

MACHINE FOR PROVING TENACITY.

Testing machine employed by Walter R. Johnson's committee for its strength-of-materials experiments from 1831 to 1836 and later by Joseph Henry's committee investigating the cannon explosion on the *U.S.S. Princeton* in 1844. The machine measured the amount of longitudinal stress required to fracture a sample of the material being tested.

Apparatus for testing the strength of materials at high temperatures. Samples of boiler material were immersed in a bath of oil or molten metal to test the effects of varying temperature on tensile strength.

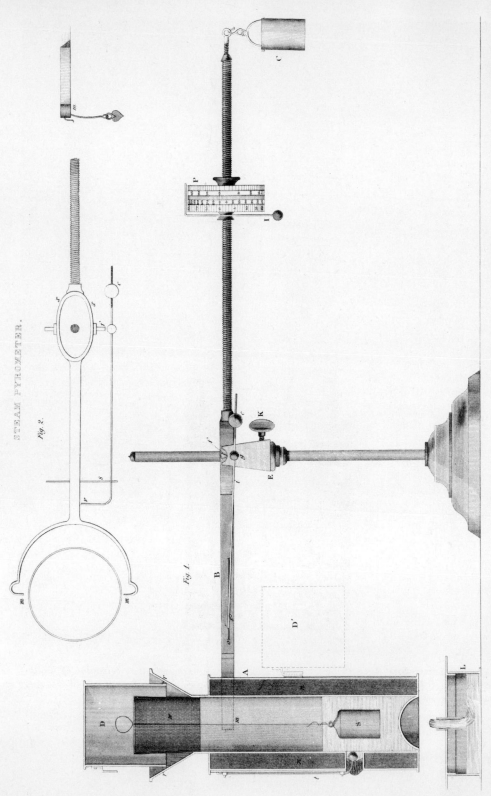

STEAM PYROMETER.

Fig. 2.

Fig. 1.

The steam pyrometer, devised by Walter R. Johnson for the Institute's strength-of-materials experiments. It was used to measure temperatures above the range of the mercury thermometer.

Top left, James P. Espy, 1785–1860 (courtesy of the National Portrait Gallery, Smithsonian Institution); *right,* Walter R. Johnson, 1794–1852 (courtesy of the Free Library of Philadelphia); *bottom left,* John F. Frazer, 1812–72 (courtesy of the University of Pennsylvania Archives); *middle,* Alexander Dallas Bache, 1806–67 (courtesy of the University of Pennsylvania Archives); *right,* James C. Booth, 1810–88 (courtesy of the Free Library of Philadelphia).

VII

GOVERNMENT, SCIENCE, AND THE INSTITUTE

The Treasury has at its disposal a fund applicable to such objects, and it has occurred to me that it might be usefully applied in making some experiments. . . .

Samuel D. Ingham to William Hamilton, August 15, 1830

Nineteenth-century Americans fervently believed that technological advancement came with a knowledge of science. The conception that craftsmen armed with the principles of science would bring "a new era in productive labor," a new chapter in "the proud dominion of mind over matter," was an unchallenged article of faith.[1] It was echoed in the pages of every mechanics' magazine and in countless addresses at industrial exhibitions, and it was the staple ingredient of lectures in mechanics' institutes and lyceums throughout the country. And yet, in the Franklin Institute's educational activities the Board of Managers, and successive Committees on Instruction, discovered that evening lectures on science did not provide knowledge which artisans could assimilate easily or apply directly on the job. The Committee on Inventions also learned that their reports, however well calculated to impress upon inventors the value of sound principles, did not alter the frequent submission of ideas faulty in theory and unworkable in practice.

The problem was that the fundamental and unchanging laws of nature had little immediate relevance to the mechanic arts.[2] Mill-

[1] Thaddeus B. Wakeman, "Introductory Lecture delivered before the American Institute of the City of New York, the second Thursday in January, 1835," *Mechanics Magazine and Register of Inventions and Improvements* 5 (February 1835): 80. For the same sentiments, see "Science and Art," *The Young Mechanic* 2 (January 1833): 5–7.

[2] For an acute analysis of the relation between science and technology, see Edwin T. Layton, "Mirror Image Twins: The Communities of Science and Technology in Nineteenth-Century America," *Technology and Culture* 12 (October 1971): 562–80.

wrights needed principles of engineering design, not principles of science. Rather than a knowledge of the actions of atoms and molecules, they needed to know, in terms of cost, how to achieve maximum efficiency with any given set of parameters. In short, Americans had to realize that technology was pointed toward different goals than science, that it required its own kind of education, and ultimately, its own specialized practitioners. The Franklin Institute came to that realization as a result of its research projects. Experimentation was the key; technology progressed not through the content of science but by the use of its methods. The water-power investigation had indicated the effectiveness of planned experimentation in testing the facts which lay between hypothesis and conclusion. Instead of a deeper understanding of nature, however, the conclusions led rather to the solution of man-made problems.

Even before their first research project was concluded, the Institute's experimentalists turned their attention to one of the nation's most dramatic man-made problems. If the hydraulics investigation had suggested the value of experimentation, the Institute's inquiry into the causes of steamboat explosions proved it beyond all doubt. By 1830, when the Franklin Institute began its inquiry, the hazards of steamboat navigation were already a matter of great concern. Almost sixty boats had blown up in the United States since Fulton's voyage on the *Clermont*, and by 1830 over three hundred lives had been lost in those disasters. Although the steam engine ultimately became a great source of industrial power, its introduction to America came first as a boon to transportation.[3] The internal migration and burgeoning trade of a vast territorial expanse required fast and cheap transportation. The economic vitality of the Ohio and Mississippi River Valleys, in particular, depended on the steamboat, and its use in those areas had increased very rapidly since the first ship successfully steamed from New Orleans to Pittsburgh in 1815.[4] In America, where more steamboats were in service and more high-pressure engines were employed to propel them, explosions were particularly acute, in terms of loss of life and as a threat to progress.

Nineteenth-century Americans were aware that technology had a

[3] See Carroll W. Pursell, Jr., *Early Stationary Steam Engines in America* (Washington, D.C.: Smithsonian Institution, 1969), for an account of the introduction of the stationary steam engine in America and its application to a wide variety of industrial purposes.

[4] The best study of steamboats on the great rivers of America is Louis C. Hunter, *Steamboats on the Western Rivers: An Economic and Technological History* (Cambridge, Mass.: Harvard University Press, 1949).

dark as well as a bright side. Both those aspects found play in the steamboat. Romantic illustrations portrayed moonlight races on the Mississippi, with all their excitement. And other prints illustrated the great material prosperity inherent in the scene of a steamer loading hundreds of cotton bales for the textile mills of the North. The dark side had its own artistic mode. Steamboat disasters created a new literary genre, which soon encompassed railroad collisions, bridge collapses, and other particularly affecting calamities.[5] There seemed to be something especially poignant about death coming as the result of a technology which had otherwise such great promise for mankind. But the ambivalence Americans felt towards the steamboat had another facet. The technology was still new in 1830. No governmental traditions existed to control its misuse; indeed, it was an unsettled question whether government should even attempt control. Nor were there any guidelines if the industry wanted to regulate itself, should such a disposition have existed. In either case, regulation depended upon a sure knowledge of the causes of steamboat boiler explosions, and neither industry nor government had that kind of expertise at its command.

There had been attempts to understand the reasons for boiler explosions. One of the earliest in the United States took place in Philadelphia in 1817, when the city councils appointed a committee to consider appropriate regulations for the use of steam.[6] A panel of some of the city's prominent scientists and engineers, "disinterested persons, of unquestionable scientific knowledge," was formed to aid the committee's deliberations. The panel—Dr. Thomas Cooper, Joseph Cloud, Jacob Perkins, and Frederick Graff—came to no conclusions with respect to the causes of boiler explosions, but they presented three recommendations to lessen their effect. They suggested that two safety valves be employed, one of which should be kept locked in order to

---

[5] A good example is *Steamboat Disasters and Railroad Accidents in the United States* (Worcester, Mass.: Warren Lazell, 1846), which includes dramatic eye-witness accounts, names and ages of those killed or wounded, and where particularly touching, the reaction of survivors when the deceased were interred. For a similar example, see James T. Lloyd, *Lloyd's Steamboat Directory and Disasters on the Western Waters* (Cincinnati: J. T. Lloyd, 1856).

[6] A pamphlet describing the committee and its report was reprinted in *Communications Received by the Committee of the Franklin Institute on the Explosion of Steam Boilers* (Philadelphia: The Franklin Institute, 1832). The latter report was published in the *Journal of the Franklin Institute* 12 (October 1831): 234–47, (November 1831): 306–15, (December 1831): 374–88; 13 (January 1832): 12–30, (February 1832): 89–101. Subsequent communications to the committee were also published in the *Journal*, in vols. 13 (June 1832): 362–69; 14 (July 1832): 1–9, (October 1832): 226–32; and 15 (January 1833): 15–18.

prevent tampering. Next, they advised a system of testing boilers along the same lines as gun barrels were proved. Finally, the committee proposed shipbuilding techniques similar to those used by gunpowder manufacturers, who channeled the force of accidental explosions through a weakly constructed wall or roof. The analogy was hardly one to inspire confidence, but the report raised a more troublesome issue. If the recently introduced high-pressure steam engine came into wide usage, the results of explosions must be even more disastrous. At that point city authorities decided the problem demanded state action, and they forwarded the papers from their investigation to the legislature, with a call for the collection of further data and "such legal restraints as the object manifestly requires."[7] The state, however, failed to take any corrective measures.

Subsequent calamities repeatedly focused attention on the problem, if only temporarily. An explosion on the high-pressure steamboat *Aetna*, in 1824, brought a Congressional investigation, but it was also inconclusive in nature and resulted in no legislation. One of the difficulties which faced those who tried to discover causes from the testimony of witnesses was that it was notoriously unreliable. If engine operators survived a blast, their minds "received a bias" which colored their views. The conflicting opinions of other survivors was equally unenlightening, and as Alexander Dallas Bache later observed:

An appearance of mystery is thrown around the whole matter, calculated to baffle research, and to alarm the community, who are exposed to a recurrence of the same dangers. Thus it happens that of the numerous explosions on record, few are made to subserve the cause of humanity, by a knowledge of their proximate causes.[8]

If the American public was to be protected from a continuation of steamboat disasters, the first and most important step was to discover why boilers exploded. Next it was necessary for the government to define its position in the potential conflict between public safety and private interest.

Nowhere are the issues and their potential resolution more clearly stated than in the discussion which led the Franklin Institute to undertake an investigation into the causes of steam-boiler explosions. William Keating raised the question in a meeting of the Board of Managers on May 13, 1830. "Numerous accidents have occurred of late in Steam

---

[7] *Communications Received by the Committee of the Franklin Institute*, p. 3.

[8] *General Report on the Explosions of Steam-Boilers, by a Committee of the Franklin Institute of the State of Pennsylvania for the Promotion of the Mechanic Arts* (Philadelphia: C. Sherman, 1836), p. 4.

Boats," Keating noted, "the effect of which is to impair the confidence of the public in the merit of an invention which has shed vast honor on the American name and which has essentially contributed to the prosperity of this country." Since, he pointed out, the Franklin Institute had been founded "to promote the success of the mechanic arts by all the means within their power," a committee should be appointed to consider an investigation into the problem.[9] Keating, George Fox, Isaiah Lukens, Matthias Baldwin, and Samuel V. Merrick were appointed, and they reported back to the Board on June 10th. Their report opened with two irrefutable points:

The application of steam to navigation has been attended with such unforeseen advantages to the world at large and to our country in particular, that no series of accidents in Steam Boats however frequent their recurrence, or fatal in their consequences could probably deter the public from the use of them.[10]

If, however, boats continued to operate "unrestrained by any regulation whatsoever," even greater loss of life and property was easily predictable. The central elements of the problem, according to the committee, were clear. Accidents were avoidable; and "that there must be a power lodged in the community somewhere to protect the people at large against any evil of serious & frequent occurence is self evident." It was equally certain that to frame any regulations required a knowledge of "the true cause of these accidents."

The committee's report also revealed an acute recognition of the difficulties confronting legislative action. If the problem could receive a thorough governmental investigation, the committee argued, consideration by the Institute would be unnecessary.

But it is well known that from the many subjects which press upon the attention of Congress, & from the indisposition to follow the British precedent of instituting enquiries founded upon the evidences of practical and expert men, it becomes a difficult task for a committee of their body to possess themselves of a knowledge of the facts that have been developed during an experience of twenty years over a country so extensive as ours.[11]

Given their analysis of the problem, the committee's conclusion was obvious. In their opinion, a "public body whose views are so well known & appreciated by the community as to place their motives beyond suspicion," could most suitably conduct the investigation. "That our

[9] Minutes of the Board of Managers, May 13, 1830, Franklin Institute Archives.

[10] Ibid., June 10, 1830. Both committee reports were also published in the *Journal of the Franklin Institute* 10 (July 1830): 33–35. George Fox was a local attorney. The other committee members have been identified above.

[11] Ibid.

society constitutes such a body," they claimed, "no one will doubt." The Board of Managers therefore appointed a seventeen-man committee "to examine into the causes of the explosions of the Boilers used on Board Steam Boats and to devise the most effectual means of preventing the accidents or to diminish the extent of their injurious influence."

The committee was an equal blend of skillful mechanics and men of science. Keating was named chairman. The other members included Dr. Robert Hare, Samuel V. Merrick, Alexander Dallas Bache, James Rush, James Ronaldson, Frederick Graff, Dr. Robert Patterson, Dr. John K. Mitchell, Benjamin Reeves, George Fox, Dr. Thomas P. Jones, Walter R. Johnson, Matthias Baldwin, James P. Espy, and George Merrick.[12] The investigation which the committee proposed was not intended to be an experimental inquiry. Like previous investigations in Philadelphia and by the federal government, it was to be a fact-finding project. The Institute had once considered a fairly extensive series of experiments on the nature and properties of steam, but they had been postponed because of expenses incurred in the water-power investigation.[13] The function of the Committee on Steam Boilers was to collect data, sift the evidence, and if an identifiable pattern emerged, to determine the causes and means of preventing explosions. To accomplish those objectives, the committee sent a circular to all who might be acquainted with the subject.[14]

---

[12] James Rush was associated with David Muhlenberg in the manufacture of high-pressure steam engines. Both married daughters of Oliver Evans and after his death continued the operation of his Mars Works. Greville Bathe and Dorothy Bathe, *Oliver Evans: A Chronicle of Early American Engineering* (Philadelphia: Historical Society of Pennsylvania, 1935), pp. 170–71. Bache once described Benjamin Reeves, an iron manufacturer, as "acute and laborious . . . equally able in devising experiments and mechanism, and in using them" (A. D. Bache, *Anniversary Address before the American Institute, of the City of New York* [New York: Pudney & Russell, 1857], p. 29). In the Institute's membership records, George Merrick is listed as a civil engineer.

[13] Boiler explosions, like the efficiency of water wheels, were among the Institute's early interests. Prize awards were offered at the second exhibition for treatises which would bring important new information on either subject. At a meeting of the Board of Managers on June 24, 1825, Keating, Patterson, and Merrick were appointed a committee "to investigate the probable causes of the accidents which happen to steam engines and consider the measures which would be most effectual in preventing them," but no further action was taken. In a letter to Samuel Ingham on August 31, 1830, Merrick said the Institute had thought of an experimental inquiry into the nature and properties of steam. It had been postponed, however, because "the contributions they have levied on the liberality of the public in the prosecution of their enquiries relative to water power, have been so great that they were apprehensive a sufficient fund could not be obtain'd immediately from the same source" (Minutes of the Committee on Steam Boilers, August 28, 1830, Franklin Institute Archives).

[14] The circular was reprinted in the *Journal of the Franklin Institute* 10 (July 1830): 35–37.

At the same time, Congress was once again prompted to action by an explosion on board the steamboat *Helen McGregor* at Memphis, Tennessee, in which about fifty lives were lost.[15] A resolution in the House of Representatives on May 4, 1830, directed the secretary of the treasury to report on the means of protecting against such accidents and placed funds at his disposal for carrying out the project. The secretary, Samuel D. Ingham, and the Institute's committee proceeded along exactly parallel lines. Both printed circulars to be distributed widely among steam-engine manufacturers, boat operators, and others who might contribute useful information. Both depended on special observers for more detailed knowledge—Thomas W. Bakewell, an engine-builder at Cincinnati, Ohio, served as the western correspondent for both investigations; Professor James Renwick, of Columbia College (now Columbia University) in New York, was apparently the secretary's Atlantic coast observer.[16] The Institute's ultimate objective also pointed toward federal legislation as the solution to the problem. Although Ingham was a Pennsylvanian from Bucks County, neither party learned of the other's efforts until early August, when the secretary read in a newspaper of the Institute's inquiry. On August 15th, he wrote a letter to William Hamilton, the actuary, suggesting cooperative action, and noted that the appropriation at his command "might usefully be applied in making some experiments."[17]

Ingham's proposal suddenly and dramatically changed the nature of the Institute's investigation. At a special meeting of the committee, Bache, Keating, S. V. Merrick, Espy, Matthias Baldwin, and Benjamin Reeves were appointed to draw up a plan of experiments; and in a letter to Ingham, agreeing that "many valuable and important facts may be ascertain'd by a course of experiments on the nature & properties of steam," Merrick offered the Institute's services "in the prosecution of any experimental inquiries that may be deemed judicious."[18] Ingham

[15] For an account of the explosion, see *Steamboat Disasters*, pp. 127–32.

[16] U.S. Congress, House, *Letter from the Secretary of the Treasury, Transmitting a report on the subject of steam boilers, March 3, 1831*, 21st Cong., 2d sess., doc. no. 131. Renwick edited several American editions of Dionysius Lardner's *Treatise on Steam Engines* and corresponded with Ingham on a variety of subjects relating to steam engines at the time Ingham began his inquiry. For biographical details on Bakewell, see Bruce Sinclair, "Thomas Woodhouse Bakewell's Autobiographical Sketch and its Relation to Early Steamboat Engineering on the Ohio," *The Filson Club History Quarterly* 40 (July 1966): 235–48.

[17] S. D. Ingham to William Hamilton, Washington, August 15, 1830, Steam Boiler Committee, Franklin Institute Archives. Correspondence between the Treasury Department and the Institute on the subject of the investigation is also preserved in Record Group 56, National Archives, Washington, D.C.

[18] S. V. Merrick to the Hon. Samuel D. Ingham, August 31, 1830, Minutes of the Committee on Steam Boilers, August 28, 1830.

responded by asking for information on the proposed experiments and their probable expense. Bache submitted a set of experiments, estimated to cost $1,500, which was forwarded to the secretary.[19] While waiting for his reply, the committee hired David H. Mason, William Mason's brother and Matthias Baldwin's partner, to superintend the experiments. In October 1830, Ingham wrote expressing his support and promising the necessary financial assistance.[20] With backing from the secretary of the treasury and supported by federal funds, the Franklin Institute's investigation into the causes of steam-boiler explosions was begun. The inquiry was the first ever conducted in this country on an experimental basis and an important step toward a science of steam engineering.

The set of experiments which Bache submitted for Ingham's approval is noteworthy on several counts, not the least of which is its grasp of the essential questions which required examination and the most effective means of finding the answers.[21] The investigation was divided into two main categories: (1) experiments to discover the causes which produced steam to critical pressures and (2) experiments to discover the causes resulting from faulty indication of water level, imperfect operation of safety devices, defects in the manufacture of boiler materials, or build-up of incrustation within the boiler. There were two experiments which fit neither category, designed especially to deal with theories having popular currency but known to be incorrect. Bache's eleven "subjects of investigation" became with only slight modification the experimental plan which the Committee on the Explosion of Steam Boilers followed. His original concept of the research also served as a basis for subdividing experimental labors and indicated the nature of the test apparatus which would be required.

When federal funds became available for the project, Bache, Reeves, Keating, Baldwin, Lukens, and S. V. Merrick were appointed a subcommittee to conduct the boiler-explosion experiments. Merrick and Reeves were assigned the task of finding a suitable place for the research, and a house for that purpose was shortly constructed on a lot donated

[19] William H. Keating to the Hon. Samuel D. Ingham, September 30, 1830, Minutes of the Committee on Steam Boilers, September 28, 1830.

[20] S. D. Ingham to William H. Keating, October 21, 1830, Record Group 59, National Archives.

[21] The experiments are best described in *Report of the Committee of the Franklin Institute of the State of Pennsylvania, for the Promotion of the Mechanic Arts, on the Explosions of Steam Boilers. Part I, Containing the first Report of Experiments made by the Committee, for the Treasury Department of the U. States* (Philadelphia: John C. Clark, 1836), pp. 9–10. The plan is also given in the *Journal of the Franklin Institute* 21 (January 1836): 7–8.

by the firm of Merrick & Agnew, at Twelfth and Vine Streets.[22] The committee used two types of boilers for most of its experiments. One was a glass cylinder, fourteen inches long and eight inches in diameter, fitted with brass heads at each end. Thermometers were employed to measure both steam and water temperatures. A gauge to show water level and any discrepancies between indicated and true level was also fitted to the boiler, as was a half-inch common safety valve.[23] The other boiler was arranged with similar equipment, but on a larger scale. It was made of iron, twelve inches in diameter and almost three feet long, and enclosed in a brickwork furnace. In addition to a glass water gauge, three gauge cocks, spaced at vertical intervals on the head of the boiler in the manner of their arrangement on steamboats, were also used to test water level. A glass plate was installed in one end to provide direct visual observations, and finally, a steam gauge was employed to indicate boiler pressure. Much of the committee's labor during the fall of 1830 was directed towards accurate calibration of all the instruments. Since the apparatus was on a smaller scale than that normally used in practice, accuracy was particularly important, and elaborate measures were taken to eliminate instrumental error.[24]

By early 1831, the research facility for those experiments related to boiler explosions was completed. At that point, the investigation was divided into two parts. Experiments to test the strength of boiler materials of different thicknesses at different temperatures had been included in Bache's original plan. Exactly who was responsible for the idea was later to become a matter of controversy, but in any event, Walter R. Johnson displayed an interest in the subject during the early meetings of the committee, and he was appointed chairman of a subcommittee, additionally composed of Bache and Reeves, to conduct those experiments.[25] It took Johnson's committee almost a year to design and have fabricated their own test apparatus, but by the spring of 1832 he reported that the machinery had been set up in the Institute and that experiments were under way.

Meanwhile, Bache's subcommittee, had begun its work. Existing theories about boiler explosions were tangled together in an intricate

[22] Minutes of the Committee on Steam Boilers, November 4, 1830. No details were given of the dimensions of the experiment house.

[23] Ibid., November 3, 1830. The glass boiler was apparently used only for the first experiment, to determine the effect of foaming within a boiler as it related to both accurate measurement of water level and the degree to which water was splashed on the sides of the boiler.

[24] The experimental apparatus, as well as the calculations necessary to calibrate thermometers and to arrange the equipment for use, is described both in *Report of the Committee . . . Part I*, pp. 1–8, and in the *Journal* 21 (January 1836): 2–6.

[25] Minutes of the Committee on Steam Boilers, January 4, 1831.

mass of truths, half-truths, and error.[26] The experimental plan was carefully devised to deal with each in an interrelated set of tests. That an inadequate supply of water in the boiler was the origin of most accidents was a widely held idea, but there were a variety of explanations for what subsequently happened to produce the explosion. Under normal operating circumstances, all parts of a boiler in direct contact with fire were covered on the other side by water, and the boiler plate thus maintained the same temperature as the water. If, for whatever reason, the water level was lowered, however, the uncovered part of the boiler was subject to undue heating. In some minds, that excessive heat was sufficient by itself to bring disaster, through weakening of the metal. Unduly heated metal provided the basis for other theories, some contradictory, some wildly erroneous. One of the most persistent notions was that if water were suddenly supplied to an overheated boiler, it decomposed on striking the hot metal, and the resultant hydrogen produced the explosion. Other ideas were not as easily dealt with. Jacob Perkins had claimed that when metal was overheated, steam in the boiler became so saturated with heat that any added water was transformed into highly expansive steam. Both because of his own reputation in steam engineering and because of the complexity of the subject, the most detailed and elaborate experiments were concerned with discovering what happened when water came into contact with heated metal.[27] That led to a consideration of rates of evaporation at varying temperatures and surface conditions. The question was never, Can highly heated metal produce highly expansive steam? Obviously it could. The issue was rather to discover the conditions under which water vaporized most rapidly, and with respect to the operation of steamboats, what conditions would lead to that result.

In contrast to the subtlety of some experiments, others were quite straightforward. For instance, ever since the British Parliamentary investigations into boiler accidents in 1817, informed men knew that a gradual increase in pressure could sunder a boiler just as effectively as the sudden production of steam. Yet on the western waters of the United States, many steamboat operators held firmly the opinion that a sufficient water supply was the best possible guarantee against an explo-

[26] The best single collection of ideas on the cause of explosions is in *Communications Received by the Committee of the Franklin Institute.*

[27] One of the most important things that happened, as the experiments conclusively demonstrated, was that steam pressure was reduced and "*the greater the quantity of water thus introduced, the more considerable was the diminution in the elasticity of the steam*" (*Report of the Committee . . . Part I*, p. 21).

sion.[28] It was only when water was low, they reasoned, that steam could be produced in dangerous quantities. The committee therefore conducted two experiments in a deserted quarry on the banks of the Pennypack River, where copper and iron boilers well-supplied with water, and leaks, too, in one case, were purposely exploded to prove the point. With each, steam pressure was gradually increased until it exploded, throwing parts in all directions, and the committee concluded: *"All the circumstances attending the most violent explosions may occur without a sudden increase of pressure within a boiler."*[29]

By its very nature, the research was dangerous, and some experiments were "violently" terminated. "No small amount of personal courage," as Joseph Henry put it, was required from the investigators. Something of the same, mixed perhaps with patience, was needful for those living in the vicinity when "explosions were produced which alarmed the neighborhood."[30] As the experimenters discovered, explosions were often produced because safety devices were misused or failed to work properly.[31] In some cases, steam was so suddenly produced, and in such volume, that safety valves were inadequate to their task. The committee gave considerable attention to valve design, and Bache himself developed safety devices which acted on both steam pressure and heat to signal an alarm.[32]

One of the more creative accomplishments of the investigation was the determination that fusible alloys, used either as a plate in the boiler or as the link in a safety mechanism, were subject to the effect of pressure as well as of heat. The alloy's function was to melt at a given temperature, triggering an alarm or opening a hole in the boiler. Partly as the result of the investigation of members of its Academy of Sciences, the French government had required their use on all French steam-

---

[28] The popular expression among Western riverboat engineers was that "a boiler cannot burst with 'fair play,' " that is, with an adequate supply of water. *Communications Received by the Committee of the Franklin Institute*, p. 35.

[29] *Report of the Committee . . . Part I*, p. 69.

[30] Joseph Henry, "Eulogy on Prof. Alexander Dallas Bache, Late Superintendent of the United States Coast Survey," *Annual Report of the Board of Regents of the Smithsonian Institution . . . for the Year 1870* (Washington, D.C.: U.S. Government Printing Office, 1872), pp. 94–95.

[31] One of the frequent causes of steamboat disasters was purposeful loading of the safety valve, usually to achieve faster speed. The practice, and its consequences, were well known: "This insane policy, this poor ambition of proprietors and captains, has almost inevitably tended to the same melancholy results" (*Steamboat Disasters*, p. 134).

[32] A. D. Bache, "Safety Apparatus for Steam Boats, being a combination of the Fusible Metal Disk with the Common Safety Valve," *Journal of the Franklin Institute* 11 (April 1831): 217–21; idem, "Alarm to be applied to the interior Flues of Steam Boilers," *Journal of the Franklin Institute* 14 (October 1832): 217–23.

boats. Bache's subcommittee discovered, however, that steam pressure within the boiler could force out of the alloy those elements with lower melting points, thus altering the compound and consequently its effectiveness as a safety mechanism. With a nice understanding of heat transfer, Bache proposed enclosing fusible materials subject to pressure within a hollow metal tube or case so that they would react to temperature but not to pressure.[33]

The research took much longer than anyone anticipated. Bache's subcommittee finished its experiments first, and they presented their report to the general committee in June 1835. It was accepted, and Levi Woodbury, the third secretary of the treasury since the investigation had begun, authorized the publication of 500 copies. Difficulties with the printer delayed the report, however. Woodbury was eager to submit the report to Congress, and twice he pressed Bache, who had taken over direction of the entire project in 1832, for the committee's report. Harassed by the printer and obligated both to the University and the Institute to the extent that he had given up his private research, Bache was nettled by the secretary's insistence. The Paris Academy had taken four years to complete their experiments on the elasticity of steam, Bache noted, and he asked the secretary:

If the paid labours of French scavans whose *business* it was thus to labour, required so much time, surely the Committee of the Franklin Institute who have in the midst of other business undertaken gratuitous labours of not less than seven fold amount, & incomparably more dangerous in their nature, will not be thought to have exceeded the time which would reasonably have been allotted to them.[34]

Within the next few days, however, the printer finished his work, and the report was issued. It was also published serially in the *Journal of the Franklin Institute* from January to May 1836.

When Bache's subcommittee completed its work, it became important to conclude the strength-of-materials experiments and to prepare the report of that subcommittee. Logically, the reports of the subcommittees, containing details of the experiments and their results, would then be followed by the general report of the whole committee, summarizing the investigation and concluding with recommendations based on the research. However, Johnson's report was late in coming, the normal plan of presentation was spoiled, and the result was an unfortunate controversy.

[33] *Report of the Committee . . . Part I*, p. 33.
[34] A. D. Bache to the Hon. Levi Woodbury, Philadelphia, January 29, 1836, Record Group 59, National Archives.

When Bache wrote Woodbury originally to make arrangements for printing the report of his subcommittee, he suggested that the strength-of-materials report would shortly be completed. Johnson took exception to what he considered an interference in the affairs of his committee and a threat to the careful execution of experiments which still were to be performed. He wrote the secretary that Bache's remark was "entirely unauthorized," that the experiments should be pursued to a full conclusion, and implied at the same time that he had originated the research.[35] It was an ill-considered reaction, since Bache, as general chairman of the investigation, was entirely within the bounds of his authority to discuss any part of the research. Woodbury responded as the protocol of the situation would normally have dictated. He sent a copy of Johnson's letter to Bache asking for an explanation.[36] Bache's answer was succinct. He quoted two resolutions passed by the general committee. First, all of the chairman's correspondence had the committee's sanction, whereas Johnson's letter was unofficial. Second, while the Institute was responsible for initiating the strength-of-materials research, it was not "indissoluably connected with the main questions to be solved," and no delay need result in publishing the first report. In the interest of decorum, Johnson wrote a letter of apology to Woodbury, but his heart wasn't in it. He still wanted more time for his experiments.[37]

When the report of Bache's subcommittee was published, Johnson's report was still unwritten. By April 1836, the general committee was instructed "to report forthwith" to the Board of Managers the results of the strength-of-materials experiments.[38] Bache advised the Board that Johnson's absence from the city prevented any action. He was still out of town by the July Board meeting, and Bache was again compelled to report that his committee had been unable to comply with their instructions and that, as Johnson had all the papers in his possession, no one else could write the report.[39] Johnson, in Washington at the time, was involved in the preparations for the U.S. Exploring Expedition, for which he was to perform research in the physical sciences. The demands of that enterprise may well have made it difficult for him to resolve his other obligations. Bache, however, was in a difficult position. His depar-

[35] Walter R. Johnson to the Hon. Levi Woodbury, Philadelphia, June 5, 1835, ibid.

[36] Levi Woodbury to Professor Alexander Dallas Bache, June 8, 1835, ibid.

[37] Alexander Dallas Bache to the Hon. Levi Woodbury, Philadelphia, June 11, 1835; Walter R. Johnson to the Hon. Levi Woodbury, Philadelphia, June 11, 1835, ibid.

[38] Minutes of the Board of Managers, April 20, 1836.

[39] Ibid., June 15, July 20, 1836.

ture for Europe was imminent. Under the circumstances, there seemed little reason to delay preparation of the general report of the investigation, and by September it was sent to the printer. By the end of 1836, Johnson was given an ultimatum. The Board of Managers requested Bache to write Johnson requiring him either to make his report or to turn the minutes of the experiments over to the Institute.[40] Three weeks later the report was presented to the Board, and the secretary of the treasury instructed the committee to print 350 copies at the Treasury Department's expense.

The controversy notwithstanding, Johnson's report was a remarkable piece of work. Research into the strength of materials, one of the engineering sciences which grew out of the application of scientific methods to technological problems, was a new endeavor in the United States, and Johnson's experiments made an important contribution to its beginning. The apparatus which his committee designed was the first of its kind in America, and it included sophisticated devices to apply and measure high temperatures to the specimens being tested. "The machinery," according to one mechanics' magazine, "is said to be better than any ever tried in Europe, and is so contrived as to be used at any temperature of the metals, from 0 to 500 degrees Fahrenheit."[41] In his eagerness to trumpet American advances, the editor erred on both counts. Significant advances in testing machinery had taken place in Europe, and Johnson was aware of them. Furthermore, the noteworthy feature of the apparatus was its ability to go beyond the range of a mercury thermometer. By an ingenious use of molten tin, temperatures over 1300° F were reached, and equally skillful devices were employed to record them.[42]

The experiments aroused considerable public interest, since they promised the first significant analysis of American iron, and it was variously suggested that Johnson had been "appointed by a vote of Congress" or that he was in charge of the whole steam-boiler investigation.[43] For his own part, Johnson dropped none too subtle hints that if the other subcommittee's experiments had not taken so much of the

[40] Ibid., December 21, 1836.
[41] "Steamboat Safety Apparatus," *Mechanics' Magazine and Register of Inventions and Improvements* 2 (July 1833): 30–31.
[42] Chester H. Gibbons, *Materials Testing Machines* (Pittsburgh: Instruments Publishing Company, 1935), pp. 16–17.
[43] *Mechanics' Magazine and Register of Inventions and Improvements* 2 (July 1833): 30–31, (August 1833): 67, (October 1833): 225. Some indication of popular interest is suggested by the fact that the editor reprinted notices of the research which had appeared in the *Pennsylvanian*, the Baltimore *American*, and the Albany *Daily Advertiser*.

appropriation, his research would have included "other points of great practical and scientific importance."[44] Nonetheless, his experiments revealed an important relationship between temperature and the tensile strength of boiler materials. The tensile strength of copper decreased steadily and markedly with an increase in temperature. Iron, conversely, actually increased in strength when subjected to temperatures up to about 600°. Beyond that point its strength decreased significantly. Johnson examined a large number of foreign and domestic iron samples, and his tests showed not only that quality varied widely but also that the method of manufacture was crucial to tensile strength. The experiments revealed that boiler-construction techniques, especially with regard to riveted joints, were an equally critical issue in the safety of steam boilers.[45]

The strength-of-materials investigation determined the course of Johnson's future career. In his mind, the subject was one of great importance, and he once remarked on the curious fact that while many steamboat inquiries had looked for the cause of danger, "so little should have been attempted in regard to the most direct and obvious means of security." Apparently to that end, he had himself been collecting specimens of metal "for a private course of investigations on several scientific and practical points, relating to tenacity."[46] Federal funds gave Johnson the opportunity to pursue his research interests, and he used it very successfully. He wrote a large number of articles for scientific journals, many based on the strength-of-materials experiments and others on related subjects, in which the testing machine was applied.[47] Those researches gave Johnson a considerable reputation, and in 1836 he applied for a position in the scientific corps being assembled for the U.S. Exploring Expedition. Benjamin Silliman, Joseph Henry, and others wrote in support of Johnson's application. Henry described him as "one of the most industrious & successful experimental Philosophers

[44] "Report of the Committee of the Franklin Institute of the State of Pennsylvania on the Explosions of Steam Boilers, of Experiments made at the request of the Treasury Department of the United States. Part II. Containing the report of the subcommittee to whom was referred the examination of the strength of the materials employed in the construction of Steam Boilers," *Journal of the Franklin Institute* 23 (February 1837): 75. Johnson's report was published in book form by Merrihew and Gunn in Philadelphia under the same title in 1837.

[45] Johnson's experiments were reported serially in the *Journal of the Franklin Institute* in volume 23, from January to June 1837, and in volume 24, July and August 1837.

[46] "Report of the Committee . . . Part II," *Journal of the Franklin Institute* 23 (January 1837): 73, 82.

[47] The best sketch of Johnson's research and publication is George Pettengill, "Walter Rogers Johnson," *Journal of the Franklin Institute* 250 (August 1950): 93–113.

of our Country." Dr. John K. Mitchell added something of the physician's touch in his appraisal:

In industry, perserverence, invention and felicitous discovery, Prof. J. has few equals and no superiours in our country, & as he is possessed of a Herculean constitution which is in the very prime of life, those who are here best acquainted with him anticipate many splendid achievements of his future progression.[48]

Johnson was appointed to the expedition, in charge of the physical research, but he never sailed. A factional dispute over the role to be played by civilian scientists and naval officers soon developed, and other administrative problems delayed departure for two years. When research in the physical sciences was finally given to naval officers, Johnson was rather summarily left behind.[49] But he continued to see the federal government as the primary source of research support, and in 1838 he published a memorial to Congress, calling for the establishment of a national institution to finance experimental work in science. After a brief stint at college teaching, Johnson returned to experimentation and was employed by the Navy Department to make an extensive series of tests on the properties of American coal. In 1842 he conducted tests for the Navy on the sheathing copper used on its ships and was later one of a commission to report on floating dry docks. In 1844, along with Dr. Jones, editor of the Institute's *Journal*, Johnson carried out a series of investigations of inventions designed to prevent boiler explosions in Navy ships.[50] He never succeeded in persuading the government to appropriate funds for further research on the properties of copper, iron, and coal, but his experiments at the Institute and his study of coal gave Johnson an international reputation. The steam-boiler research did the same for Bache.

Publication of the Institute's investigation immediately brought foreign notice and a transatlantic quarrel when the reports were mis-

[48] The original letters are in the manuscript collections of the American Philosophical Society, and copies are available in U.S. Exploring Expedition, MSS Collection 39, Academy of Natural Sciences, Philadelphia.

[49] Nathan Reingold, *Science in Nineteenth-Century America: A Documentary History* (New York: Hill and Wang, 1964), pp. 109ff, describes the incident. For a full account of the expedition, see David B. Tyler, *The Wilkes Expedition* (Philadelphia: American Philosophical Society, 1968).

[50] Walter R. Johnson, "Institution for experiments in physical sciences. Memorial praying for the establishment of a National Institution for the prosecution of experiments and researches in those physical sciences which are required by the public service and for the general welfare of the country," in *The Smithsonian Institution: Documents Relative to its Origin and History*, edited by W. J. Rhees (Washington, D.C.: Smithsonian Institution, 1879), pp. 172–86.

treated in an English periodical. The *Magazine of Popular Science,*
issued in London by J. W. Parker, published an abstract version of the
report of Bache's subcommittee on boiler explosions when it first came
out. In his account of the research, Parker interlarded the report with
sarcastic comments on the timidity of the experimenters for not pressing
more hazardous trials, for the lack of detail in some subjects, and in
other cases, for the forwardness with which Americans challenged
received opinion. But Parker's most egregious criticism related to the
section dealing with the decomposition under pressure of fusible alloys.
Bache and his committee understood the nature of heat transfer. Parker
did not, and he derided the idea of enclosing alloy in a protective tube:

We cannot help thinking that the following parallel case of a 'true remedy'
would be prescribed by this sub-committee, if the question were presented to
them. Suppose a man has a box which can only be opened by a certain crooked
sixpence; what is the best way of being sure to have the sixpence always at hand
when wanted? Answer: shut it up in the box!—*Enclose the metal in a case!*[51]

"There must be a district in Pennsylvania," Parker suggested, "where
the shamrock is worn!"

Parker's magazine reached Philadelphia as the Committee on Publication was reading proof for another installment of the steam-boiler
report. Ignoring Parker's other remarks, they addressed themselves to the
alloy issue. Parker should read the report again, they recommended, or
failing that, seek the aid "of some *intelligent* friend." There were no
shamrocks in Pennsylvania, Parker was advised, "though we have
thistles and thorns aplenty."[52] If the affair had ended at that point, it
would have been simply a momentary irritation, of no great consequence to anyone. But in the following year, Parker began work on an
abstract of Bache's *General Report.* He had the October 1836 number of
the Institute's *Journal,* containing the first installment of the report, but
bad weather had apparently delayed shipment of those numbers which
contained the remaining parts. However, Joseph Henry was then in
London, and Parker prevailed upon him for help. As Parker put it,
"The offer of a friendly *Savan,* who has recently landed in this country

[51] "Prevention of Explosion in Steam-Boilers. Analysis and Cursory Examination
of a Report, Made in Consequence of an Inquiry into the Causes and Means of Prevention of the Explosions of Steam-boilers; Recently Transmitted to the Government
of the United States, by the Franklin Institute of Pennsylvania," *Magazine of Popular
Science and Journal of the Useful Arts* 3 (1836): 119.

[52] "Report of the Committee of the Franklin Institute of the State of Pennsyl-
vania for the Promotion of the Mechanic Arts, on the Explosions of Steam Boilers.
Part II., containing the General Report of the Committee," *Journal of the Franklin
Institute* 22 (November 1836): 305-6.

from the United States, relieved us from this state of suspense. Thoroughly acquainted, before he left America, with all the proceedings of this important inquiry, he has been kind enough to place at our disposal an analysis for the General Report."[53] Actually, Parker put a good face on a different set of circumstances. Henry and Bache crossed paths in London, and Bache warned him of Parker's earlier treatment of the subcommittee report.[54] Henry therefore exacted a promise from Parker that the analysis should be printed as written, or else returned. The work had already cost Henry "several days of assiduous labor." He had written to his wife that he "was very much engaged in preparing an analysis of the experiments and reports of the Franklin Institute of Phila. on the bursting of steam boilers to be published in one of the Scientific Journals of this city."[55] When Parker agreed to the terms set, Henry turned the manuscript over to him.

But Parker lived up to all of Bache's fears. He published Henry's paper in a badly abridged form, with all the footnotes cut out. Even worse, Parker claimed in his own introductory remarks that he had eliminated only those passages which Henry had inserted in a "naif" attempt "to make us *eat our own words!*" He meant nothing but friendly criticism, Parker said, and the only issue was the "morbidly exquisite" sensitivity of Americans to foreign comment.[56] The Americans, obviously enough, felt differently. Henry had left London for Paris before the magazine was printed. Bache was still in the city, however, and he wrote Henry:

Instead of returning to me your paper according to your direction to him he has published it in a mutilated form, cutting out the pungent part, reflecting in a balderdash way upon brother Jonathan's thin-skinnedness, etc., etc.[57]

In an effort to save Henry's paper, Bache persuaded Sir Charles Wheatstone, the eminent English scientist, to call upon Parker for a retraction. But the editor declined, and Bache wrote to William Hamilton at the Institute, "The journal is below contempt & has done itself no good by this affair."[58]

[53] "Prevention of Explosion in Steam-Boilers . . . ," *Magazine of Popular Science and Journal of the Useful Arts* 3 (1837): 321–22.
[54] A. D. Bache to William Hamilton, London, June 26, 1937, Incoming Correspondence, Franklin Institute Archives.
[55] Joseph Henry to Harriet Henry, London, May 9, 1837, Joseph Henry Private Papers, Smithsonian Institution Archives.
[56] "Prevention of Explosion in Steam-Boilers . . . ," *Magazine of Popular Science and Journal of the Useful Arts* 3 (1837): 322.
[57] A. D. Bache to Joseph Henry, London, June 7, 1837, Joseph Henry Papers.
[58] A. D. Bache to William Hamilton, London, June 26, 1837, Incoming Correspondence.

Bache and Henry were both in Europe for the first time. They were committed to a life of science, and their individual aspirations were interchangeable with their ambitions for the reputation of American science. Self-conscious in both those respects, Parker's gratuitous slurs touched sensitive nerves. He was not himself a figure of great importance, but Henry and Bache were vitally concerned that American research be fairly reviewed. Actually, publication of the reports had already insured a favorable reception for Bache, as Henry later reported:

No American ever visited Europe under more favorable circumstances for becoming intimately acquainted with its scientific and literary institutions. His published researches had given him a European reputation, and afforded him that ready access to the intelligent and influential classes of society which is denied the traveller whose only recommendation is the possession of wealth.[59]

Henry himself had aided that welcome. Before Bache left, he wrote to Professor James Forbes at the University of Edinburgh, sending reprints of the steam-boiler reports with the note: "They are published under the direction of a committee, but the experiments were entirely made by Prof. Bache."[60]

Bache was more generous in his own estimation of his coexperimenters, but he was clearly the dominant figure in the enterprise. His hand is also unmistakably evident in the form and content of the *General Report on the Explosion of Steam Boilers.*

The *General Report* had a different function from that of the subcommittee reports. As chairman of the investigation, it was Bache's responsibility to state the nature of the inquiry, to summarize the experimental data, and to make the recommendations necessary for legislative action. His report was meant to survey the problem and to provide definitive answers. The report outlined, in a crisp, methodical fashion, the major causes of boiler explosions. Equally important, in Bache's mind, was to show "what are certainly not causes," and one of his main objects was to settle conclusively the variety of popular notions which existed on the subject. Catastrophic theories fitted the instantaneous nature of explosions and seemed appropriate to their disastrous consequences. But explosions were not beyond science, Bache argued, and once facts had been applied to prevent the danger, there would be ample time to look for "occult" causes.[61] The report included an

59 Henry, "Eulogy on Prof. Alexander Dallas Bache," p. 97.
60 Joseph Henry to Prof. James Forbes, Princeton, September 19, 1836, Joseph Henry Private Papers.
61 *General Report on the Explosions of Steam-Boilers,* pp. 4–5.

analysis of various safety devices, advice on the design, materials, and construction of steam boilers, and information for proper maintenance and safety-checking procedures. It was a model presentation of the current state of a problem which had engaged scientific men throughout the world.

From the beginning of the investigation, the committee had entertained no doubts of the necessity for regulation in the interest of public safety or of the power of Congress to pass appropriate legislation. If anything, that view was strengthened during the course of the investigation. Bache's *General Report* was cast in near perfect form to secure legislative action. The report was complete and thorough. The problem and its solutions were clearly outlined and firmly supported. It was an authoritative document and self-contained, even to the point of including at the end a bill which would provide the necessary regulation. Experimental results were translated into three proposed categories of regulation: the establishment of an inspection and certification system for steam boilers; minimum standards for safety devices, operating procedures, and personnel qualification; and penalties for improper operation or noncompliance. Bache's report incorporated all the work of a legislative staff committee. In order to be effective, the Institute's labors had to be cast in a form which Congress could most easily digest. Bache understood the role of science administrator long before he was appointed to head the U.S. Coast Survey.

When the Franklin Institute's investigations into the causes of steamboat boiler explosions was concluded, the federal government was provided with the information it needed to legislate preventions against such disasters. In addition to experimental data, the reports contained the observations of men long connected with the steamboat industry, eyewitness accounts of explosions, and the theoretical judgments of science. The bill appended to Bache's report also provided the government with a concisely stated set of measures for enactment. Congressional action was slow in coming, however, and then it was ineffectual.[62] The Institute's reports were available to Congress early in 1837, as were the findings of a committee of the House of Representatives appointed the previous year. But no action was taken, and the explosions continued. One of them, late in 1837, caused President Van Buren to urge legislative action. The Senate reported a regulatory bill out of committee, and it was passed in January 1838. In the House, however, the

[62] The story of the government's gradual acceptance of the idea that regulation was necessary is ably told in John G. Burke, "Bursting Boilers and the Federal Power," *Technology and Culture* 7 (Winter 1966): 1–23. I am indebted to Professor Burke's article for compilations of disaster losses.

bill was stalled until the spring, when the crack new steamer *Moselle* exploded at Cincinnati, with the loss of over 150 lives.[63] That tragedy stirred the House to action, and a bill was finally passed in July 1838.

The new legislation incorporated several sections of Bache's proposed bill, but the most crucial regulatory provisions had been cut out. Congress had yet to accept the principle that public safety demanded constraints on private industry. The inspection system Bache had provided for was emasculated, and the requirement that steamboat engineers possess minimum qualifications was eliminated. Even the penalties against racing were struck out. The bill did provide that a boiler explosion was prima facie evidence of negligence, in the event of damage suits, but that section simply reflected Congressional opinion that the best regulation would come from industry itself.

With an ineffectual law, however, industrial enlightenment never materialized. Instead, deaths from steamboat explosions steadily multiplied over the years. By 1848, when Edmund Burke, the Commissioner of Patents, investigated the subject, 233 steamboats had exploded in America, at a cost of more than 2,500 lives and property loss estimated at over $3 million. Burke had been asked by the Senate whether a revision in the patent laws might aid in the prevention of explosions. He replied that the only answer to the cause of boiler explosions was to be found "in the researches of men of true science, conducted by the order of the government and at its expense." And that, Burke told the Senators, had already been done:

The most valuable contributions to our knowledge of the causes of explosions have been made by scientific labors of the committee of the Franklin Institute, undertaken at the request and prosecuted at the expense, so far as the apparatus was concerned, of the Treasury Department in 1831.[64]

Two decades later, in 1852, Congress was finally able to accept the implications of regulation, and it passed legislation effective enough to bring about a substantial reduction in steam-boiler explosions.

The investigation was the most ambitious and most successful research performed by the Franklin Institute in its early history. It established beyond any reasonable doubt the major causes of boiler explosions. By various means, the three reports enjoyed an extensive circulation. They were published serially in the *Journal of the Franklin*

---

[63] For an account of the *Moselle* explosion see, again, *Steamboat Disasters*, pp. 134ff.

[64] U.S. Congress, Senate, *Report of the Commissioner of Patents, to the Senate of the United States, on the subject of steam boiler explosions*, 30th Cong., 2d sess., 1848, doc. no. 18.

Institute, and at the cost of the Treasury Department, printed separately as pamphlets. They were reprinted in the London *Mechanics' Magazine* and abstracted in Parker's journal.[65] Abstracts were also published in Burke's 1848 report, of which the Senate ordered 10,000 copies reprinted. For years afterwards, the reports served as the standard text on the subject, and they were widely cited, both in America and abroad. It always pleased Americans that one of their own institutions had accomplished the work. In 1872, for instance, the secretary of war reported:

It is gratifying to know that the experiments which have led to the most reliable information hitherto possessed by the scientific world on this difficult subject were instituted and conducted by an American institution (the Franklin Institute of Pennsylvania), under the patronage of our government, over thirty years ago.[66]

From the beginning, one other aspect of the research also captured the public imagination: namely, that the experiments were supported by an appropriation from the federal government. That fact alone gave novelty to the inquiry. The government was not in the habit of underwriting the research projects of private societies. Federal funding also conveyed the stamp of authority. Tax dollars seemed to legitimize the Institute's national standing, and many assumed that the organization had been especially selected to perform the research.

At the Institute itself, the investigation had a profound effect. Public distinction swelled the membership rolls, and by 1837 there were 2,004 society members. The inquiry also strengthened the power of Bache, Merrick, and the Institute's scientific circle. To them, government support opened new vistas of research opportunity. The prospect of shaping government policy in matters scientific and technical was equally stimulating. Those two factors marked the future course of research at the Institute, but they suggested as well other important benefits to the organization. It seems clear that Bache and his circle recognized, if only intuitively, that the Institute needed a clientele for its services. Research for the government offered the promise of funds for experimental costs, not incidental to a society which always had to struggle for its financial life. Better still, public support gave the Institute a sense of mission and organizational vitality. Out of that perception the Institute's leaders worked to establish a posture of objective expertise readily available to all levels of government for the solution of scientific and technical problems.

65 In the London *Mechanics' Magazine,* the reports were published serially in volumes 25 (May 1836) through 27 (February 1837).

66 Quoted in Thomas Coulson, "The First Hundred Years of Research at the Franklin Institute," *Journal of the Franklin Institute* 256 (July 1953): 9.

One of the Institute's later investigations, a study of weights and measures, illustrates how the organization's managers wanted to function and what was embodied in the clientele concept. In 1833, the Pennsylvania House of Representatives completed a bill for the establishment of a system of weights and measures for the Commonwealth. Before the legislation was taken further, however, the bill was directed to the Institute with the request that a report be made on it. For that purpose, the Board of Managers appointed a nineteen-man committee, headed by Bache and including Merrick, Keating, Rufus Tyler, Baldwin, Patterson, Sears C. Walker, Reeves, and Frederick Fraley.[67] Instead of considering the bill submitted to them—acting in a secondary advisory capacity—Bache's committee undertook a thorough review of the entire question. The systems of Britain, France, and America were studied, as were the methods employed in Philadelphia markets. In addition to units of measurement, the committee also studied the manufacture, testing, and maintenance of permanent standards.

Two other considerations came to the committee in their investigation. While individual states might establish their own systems, the reality of commerce more often connected cities of adjacent states rather than the extremes of a given state. Furthermore, the federal government would someday get around to a national standard for weights and measures, and in that eventuality, Pennsylvania's system would have to be changed. The most crucial issue, therefore, was uniformity:

So impressed are the Committee with this view, that they would express it as their decided opinion that the most imperfect system of weights and measures which has ever been framed, would if applied in all the states of our union, be preferable to the most perfect system which should be adopted by any one commonwealth singly.[68]

The Constitution gave Congress the authority to set a national standard, but notwithstanding the efforts of Thomas Jefferson and John Quincy Adams, little had been done. Since it appeared there was no immediate likelihood of federal standards, the Institute's committee prepared an entirely new bill for the Commonwealth, which they submitted with a proviso. They argued the great need for a uniform system and urged the state first to use its political influence in an attempt to secure Congressional action. Moreover, they suggested, their own pro-

67 The pertinent documents, together with the managers' action in appointing the committee, were published in the *Journal of the Franklin Institute* 16 (November 1833): 304-9.

68 "Report in Relation to Weights and Measures in the Commonwealth of Pennsylvania," *Journal of the Franklin Institute* 18 (July 1834): 13.

posal cast the subject "in a form so conveniently adapted to their legislation upon it" that Congress could quickly act on the matter.[69] If, however, national legislation was not forthcoming, they recommended their own bill for the state's use.

A national system did not come, and in 1834 Pennsylvania enacted its own standards for weights and measures. "This Act of Assembly," the Board of Managers was advised by James Findlay, secretary of the Commonwealth, "was passed in conformity to the Report of the Institute to whom the subject was referred by the House of Representatives."[70] The "cheerfulness" with which the Institute had responded led the governor to make another request, according to Findlay. The new bill made the governor responsible for obtaining the positive standards and for testing them against certain physical constants, and he wondered if the Institute "would consent to become his agent in procuring the standards."[71] In that fashion, the Commonwealth became one of the Institute's clients. The state provided no funds for the organization's operating costs—the relationship was more subtle—but there were benefits. The state provided the money for printing the committee's report and for obtaining permanent standards. For Bache, it opened a line of investigation which was to last for the remainder of his life. The Institute reaped the prestige of serving as technical advisor to the state, and in 1837, when state funds were allocated for meteorological research, they were given to the Institute.

The federal government was also an obvious client, especially after the successful conclusion of the steam-boiler investigation, and its subsequent appeals for the Institute's expertise reinforced that idea. For example, in 1837, while the Delaware breakwater was still under construction, the secretary of war requested the organization to conduct a study of building stone from Pennsylvania and Delaware quarries for use in the construction of breakwaters and other public works.[72] In the same year, the secretary of the treasury asked for information about overland telegraphic communication by semaphore. The response to his request reflects the eagerness of the Institute's leadership to act as federal advisor. Within five days of the secretary's letter, the Committee on Science and the Arts prepared and submitted a complete report on a

69 Ibid., p. 14.
70 James Findlay to William Hamilton, Harrisburg, November 17, 1835, Committee on Weights and Measures, Franklin Institute Archives.
71 Ibid.
72 Minutes of the Committee on Science and the Arts, June 5, 1837, Franklin Institute Archives. A. Hunter Dupree has described the evolution of science in the government in his study, Science in the Federal Government: A History of Policies and Activities to 1940 (Cambridge, Mass.: Harvard University Press, 1957).

recommended telegraphic system, setting forth transmission times, the manpower required to staff it, details of tower and signal construction, and cost.[73]

In these investigations and others like them in the years that followed, the Institute functioned as a technical consultant to the government, even if unofficially. At whatever level, governments were not obligated to employ outside talents. The cohesiveness of the clientele situation depended on their need for expertise and the Institute's willingness to supply it. The water-power experiments had demonstrated that industry was a logical recipient for the organization's services. But research costs had not been adequately met, and when an investigation into steam-boiler explosions first occurred to the Board, they dismissed private sources of support as too limited. In 1830, even given the contributions received for the water wheel trials, industry was not sufficiently organized to support the costs of experimental research. Government was, and it had public funds at its disposal. The steam-boiler investigation brought that reality home to the Institute's Board of Managers.

There were other important consequences from the research. The experiments conclusively illustrated how major technical problems were to be solved. Primarily through Bache and Johnson, the methods of science were brought to technology. Johnson found his career in that combination and spent the remainder of his life in engineering science. Technical research also gave the Institute a clear sense of mission as its initial objectives declined in importance. Finally, it brought fame. Through its water-power investigation, the weights-and-measures study, and the steam-boiler experiments, the Board of Managers could confidently speak of "the high estimation in which the disinterested labours of the Institution are held, as well at home as abroad, throughout our own State and by our Countrymen."[74] Such pride spoke directly to the aspirations of the Institute's scientific coterie. They were ambitious young men, and they saw in the Institute's success a springboard to their own careers. At the same time, they transformed the organization, shaping its direction for years to come.

[73] Minutes of the Committee on Science and the Arts, April 13, 18, 1837.
[74] Board of Managers, Quarterly Report, April 1834.

VIII

THE GRAND LEVER: THE JOURNAL OF THE FRANKLIN INSTITUTE

> The honorable standing which this journal has attained, is attested by the copious extracts from it constantly found on the pages of the foreign journals.
>
> Committee on Publications, April 1835

To Bache and his circle at the Institute research always implied publication. Publishing was infused with the same values, the same ambitions, as original investigation in science. Publication was the way to reputation for men with career aspirations. But it was also the yardstick of a man's talents, because it revealed whether or not he had the ability to frame important questions and to provide conclusive results. For those who were eager, as Joseph Henry once put it to Bache, to root out the "charlatanism of our country," publication was the most positive means of erecting standards for the form and content of science.[1] In the same way as research, publication also mixed individual ambition with the hopes Americans had for the reputation of the nation's science. One way for Americans to secure proper credit for their discoveries and inventions in the often crucial race for priority was by publication in journals of their own, of sufficient standing to command European notice and respect. The *Journal of the Franklin Institute* was a natural field for the exercise of those interests and ideals. But as in so many other Institute activities, an existing set of ideological convictions had first to be dispensed with.

When Dr. Thomas P. Jones began his magazine in 1826, it was one element in a larger crusade to make knowledge open to all classes of society. "The age of secrets in arts and trades," Dr. Jones advised readers in an "Address" prefixed to the first number of the journal,

---

[1] Joseph Henry to Alexander Dallas Bache, Princeton, August 9, 1838, Joseph Henry Private Papers, Smithsonian Institution Archives.

"has nearly passed away."[2] The periodical was to serve the same egalitarian objectives as the Institute's other programs—the diffusion of scientific knowledge "among the operative classes, to whom it is calculated to be eminently useful; and thus to aid in elevating them to that station, which, from their numbers, the value of their services, and the genius of our institutions, they ought to occupy."[3] The best way, in Jones's opinion, to make science useful was by plain language. Workingmen needed information cast in "a style as familiar, and as little technical, as the nature of the subject will admit."[4] From the outset, Jones specifically disclaimed any efforts at originality. The primary aim of the *Journal* was to diffuse knowledge, not to advance it. The editor's function was to make a "judicious selection" of articles from foreign periodicals which had special interest to American readers and to introduce them with explanatory comment when they employed phraseology which might not be understood by ordinary workingmen. Jones encouraged queries and communications from practical men, but they were subject to the same selection process, and in the conviction that long pieces frightened readers away, strictly limited in length.[5]

In a situation parallel to that which confronted the Institute's lecturers, Jones soon discovered that it was a difficult business to strip technical language of its confusing terminology and at the same time convey meaning with precision. His first thought was to include a vocabulary with each number of the journal, but that idea quickly proved unsatisfactory, and he shifted instead to a series of special features entitled "The Artisan." The series had something of the quality of an elementary lecture on science, and in the first article, published in the November 1826 issue of the *Journal*, Jones reiterated the main object:

These papers are not meant as contributions to the stock of knowledge possessed by those who are habituated to the pursuits of science, but are intended to diffuse some acquaintance with its principles and processes, among practical men, to who it may prove a valuable auxiliary, in their respective occupations.[6]

2 "Address," *The Franklin Journal and American Mechanics' Magazine* 1 (January 1826): 2.

3 "Preface," *The Franklin Journal and American Mechanics' Magazine* 2 (July 1826): iii–iv.

4 "Address," p. 2.

5 Ibid. As Dr. Jones pointed out in the first number of the *Journal*: "Originality is not so much our object, as the diffusion of that knowledge among the great body of workmen, which is now confined to a comparatively small number." (1 [January 1826]: 47–48).

6 *The Franklin Journal and American Mechanics' Magazine* 2 (November 1826): 353.

The series opened with a simple discussion of specific gravity, illustrated with observations by Robert Hare on devices to measure it. Subsequent papers dealt with the difference between chemistry and the other branches of natural philosophy; an explanation of basic chemical terms; and the essential theory and facts of hydraulic pumps.[7]

"The Artisan" was well suited to Jones's talents. His reputation as a popular lecturer rested on his ability to explain easily the principles of science. Having also been a manufacturer, he was familiar with those commonplace productions and processes which could be used to demonstrate scientific theory. The series exemplified his conception of technical journalism. In his opinion, most of the books designed to give artisans an understanding of science failed in their purpose because their authors recognized neither the needs nor the comprehension of the audience. "To practical men," Jones claimed, "theoretical discussions are, in general, unintelligible."[8] "To pretend that artisans will, or can, become men of general science" was a "ridiculous" notion. Jones had no doubts about the value of science to working men; he was convinced also that the form of its presentation determined its utility. The *Journal*'s task was therefore to diffuse the principles of science in such a clear and straightforward fashion that they had a direct bearing on the improvement of mechanics and manufacturers, "a class of our fellow-citizens whose importance we are only beginning to appreciate correctly."[9]

The Patent Office seemed to offer even greater scope to Jones's

[7] Ibid., 3 (January 1827): 41–47, (May 1827): 345–48; 4 (December 1827): 416–20.

[8] Ibid., 4 (December 1827): 380. To Jones, experience was the best antidote to theory. He commented on the work of one author: "his theoretical views appear to us to be, sometimes, not merely gratuitous but absurd; he however, it seems, is young, and this should be deemed a sufficient apology for that fondness of theory, which time and experience will undoubtedly chasten and regulate" (Ibid., 4 [December 1827]: 380–81). The editor's penchant for plain and practical expression made him a popular teacher. In addition to his Institute commitments, he continued the same kind of science lectures which had given him earlier renown in Philadelphia. For one of them, on the steam engine, he advertised: "A perfect working model will be exhibited, and such other experimental illustrations given, as will render its structure, and mode of operation, clear to every person" (*U.S. Gazette*, June 12, 1827). See also Greville Bathe and Dorothy Bathe, *Jacob Perkins* (Philadelphia: Historical Society of Pennsylvania, 1943), p. 134; and idem, *Oliver Evans: A Chronical of Early American Engineering* (Philadelphia: Historical Society of Pennsylvania, 1935), pp. 264–65. For a time, he was also associated with the Philadelphia Institution for Correcting Impediments of Speech, which advertised the success of its methods on the back cover of *The Franklin Journal and American Mechanics' Magazine* 2 (October 1826).

[9] *The Franklin Journal and American Mechanics' Magazine* 3 (January 1827): 42; 5 (January 1828): iii.

talents, and when he was appointed superintendent in 1828, he confidently predicted:

It has already become known to the patrons of the work, that the direction of the National Patent Office has been committed to the Editor. . . . Whilst this station will enlarge the sphere of his usefulness, by putting into frequent requisition, that information upon the practical application of mechanical and chemical science, which it has been the labour of his life to obtain, it will also enable him, through the medium of the Journal, to lay open those stores of the genius and skill of our countrymen, which, although existing in the Patent Office, have hitherto been but very partially known.[10]

The transfer to Washington also freed Jones from all except editorial concerns. The Institute had taken over ownership and management of the *Journal*, according to a plan which had been developed earlier to pay the actuary's salary. The shift was a relief to Jones, who claimed he had always lost money on the enterprise despite an increase in the subscription price from four dollars a year to five. It was "very gratifying" to act in the common good, but when subscribers failed to pay their bills, the cost of that privilege, Jones once said, "may be purchased at too dear a rate."[11] Without that burden, Jones was free to devote his energies to editorial duties.

In anticipation of the added importance his official position would give to the magazine, and to mark the Institute's formal connection, a

[10] Ibid., 5 (January 1828): iii. Others expected the same benefits. William Eichbaum, secretary of the Pittsburgh Mechanics' Institute, wrote Hamilton: "I sincerely rejoice with others on Doctor Jones's appointment to the superintendance of the Patent Office. I never thought Doctor Thornton fit for that situation, and I hope the F. Journal will improve in interest by the event as Mr. Jones will now have a fine field opened to him for the investigation of mechanical inventions" (William Eichbaum to the Actuary of the Franklin Institute, Pittsburgh, April 25, 1828, Journal Subscriptions, 1828, Franklin Institute Archives).

[11] *The Franklin Journal and American Mechanics' Magazine* 5 (January 1828): 72. It is a bit difficult to to sort out Jones's financial involvement in the *Journal*. He claimed that he had bought James Seaman's interest in the *American Mechanics' Magazine* and then reissued it under the revised title. But in August 1827, when the Institute's managers were looking for a way to absorb the journal and thus pay for an administrator, a committee concerned with the problem reported: "It appears that at present the Journal is in the hands of Messrs. [Judah] Dobson & [Jesper] Harding who pay to the editor Dr. Jones a certain sum for each number disposed of, as a compensation for his services." Apparently Jones purchased Seaman's subscription list and then subsequently allied himself with Dobson and Harding. In any event, collecting from distant subscribers was uphill work. At the beginning of 1828, Jones claimed that neither the editor nor the publisher had been compensated for their labors, and he warned those who had not paid: "Hereafter, we shall prune and lop, without hesitation, until we have removed all those branches which bear no fruit themselves, and injure those which do" (Report of the Committee on Publications, August 11, 1827; *Journal of the Franklin Institute* 5 [January 1828]: 72).

new series of the journal was started in 1828, and the name was changed to *Journal of the Franklin Institute of the State of Pennsylvania; devoted to the Mechanic Arts, Manufactures, General Science, and the Recording of American and Other Patented Inventions.* While preparing the July number of the new series, Jones was also in the process of moving his household, and he advised his readers:

The present number has passed through the press under circumstances very unfavourable to literary labour. The Editor's books, papers, ideas, and household stuff, have all been thrown into confusion, to be re-arranged in the city of Washington, an operation which the carpenter, the plasterer, and the house painter, have conspired to retard; a triumvirate too powerful for his control, and to whose government he is still compelled to submit, for although he is a member of the opposition, he is, unfortunately, in the minority.[12]

The result of Jones's domestic chaos was that articles for publication were "hastily selected." The inclusion of an article on rattlesnakes by John James Audubon brought an immediate storm of protest—one naturalist called it "a tissue of the grossest falsehoods"—and Jones was forced to admit in the next number that he had not read the article in manuscript or in proof.[13]

Relocation brought other difficulties, too. While Jones performed the editorial duties in Washington, the *Journal* was printed in Philadelphia, and one of the major problems had to do simply with the mechanics of transmitting copy and page proofs. Little more than six months after the new series was begun, Jones had fallen behind his publication schedule. In a bitter letter to William Hamilton, Jones complained about the printer:

Harding commenced the present number, i.e. the Octo'r No. early in the month, and to the present day I have had but five proofs: he has not waited a moment for copy, nor have I ever kept a proof a single night but have sent them back the day that I have received them. It is totally out of my power to have it out in time, and I do not think it worth while to write for any idle excuses.[14]

Geography created a handicap which time and experience failed to resolve. Jones continued to rail against delays in sending proof to him, and the *Journal* remained behind schedule. Petty Vaughan, the Insti-

---

12 *Journal of the Franklin Institute* 6 (July 1828), back cover notice "To Subscribers Generally."

13 Ibid., 6 (July 1828): 32–37; (August 1828): 144.

14 Thomas P. Jones to William Hamilton, Washington, September 27, 1828, Thomas P. Jones Letters, Franklin Institute Archives.

tute's London agent, collected foreign periodicals in exchange for the *Journal*, and he repeatedly sent anguished appeals for regularity. "I am attacked on all sides by those who give in exchange," he wrote in 1832, pleading for greater promptness.[15]

The geographic problem presumably was compensated by the prestige Jones's position at the capitol was expected to bring to the *Journal*. But he did not last long as superintendent of the Patent Office. A year after he took office, Jones was forced out by an administrative shake-up ordered by President Jackson. The Franklin Institute immediately launched an appeal on his behalf. A special committee drafted a memorial to be circulated among "the Scientific & Mechanic Institutes in the United States," urging their united efforts to bring about his restoration to the position for which he was so "eminently qualified."[16] Despite widespread sympathy for Jones in the mechanic community, the Institute's campaign failed. His friends mounted another effort in 1831, and Jones wrote to John Vaughan, at the American Philosophical Society, asking him to speak to Secretary of State Edward Livingston.[17] But nothing came of it, and Jones was left with the editorship of the *Journal* and the chair of chemistry at Columbian College, to which he had been appointed soon after his arrival in Washington. In 1836, Jones opened a patent agency in Washington, which he apparently closed about a year later, when he was made an examiner in the newly reorganized Patent Office under Commissioner Henry Ellsworth. He resigned that job after two years and in 1839 advertised that he had "resumed the business of Agent for applicants for Patents."[18]

[15] Petty Vaughan to Samuel V. Merrick, London, June 6, 1832, Petty Vaughan Letters, Franklin Institute Archives.

[16] Isaac Hays to P. S. Duponceau, Philadelphia, July 14, 1829, American Philosophical Society. Hay's letter to Duponceau, president of the Philosophical Society, included the "Resolutions & Memorial" drafted by the Institute on Jones's behalf. Similar memorials were sent to other societies in the mid-Atlantic and New England states. Minutes of a special meeting of the Franklin Institute, June 20, 1829, Franklin Institute Archives.

[17] Thomas P. Jones to John Vaughan, Washington, April 24, 1831, American Philosophical Society.

[18] Jones first advertised his agency to readers of the *Journal* in a notice inserted in the issue for October 1836: "The subscriber, formerly superintendent of the Patent Office, has determined to devote himself to the business of preparing specifications and drawings, and other transactions connected with the obtaining of patents for useful inventions. His acquaintance with theoretical and practical mechanics and chemistry, and with the progress of the useful arts, both at home and abroad, will enable him to pronounce with some confidence upon the novelty and utility of machines or processes which it is proposed to patent; a circumstance always of great

Whether in a private or public capacity, patents had great fascination for Jones, and his monthly series, "American Patents, with Remarks and Exemplifications, by the Editor," became one of the *Journal*'s most popular features. At an age when the lives of most men are settled affairs—he was fifty-four when he went to Washington —Jones was just beginning a new career as commentator to the nation on patent inventions. Since the government itself did not publish patent specifications until 1843, the *Journal* was the only source of such information, a feature which became historically significant when the Patent Office fire of December 1836 destroyed all records.[19]

Reporting on new inventions gave full play to Jones's wide knowledge, as well as his capacity for whimsy and sarcasm. He mercilessly flayed patent specifications which were shrouded in jargon or based on specious theoretical grounds. For example, by a special act of Congress in 1832, Horatio Spafford of Lansingburg, New York, was granted a patent for "Discoveries in Natural Philosophy, reduced to practice," a grand title for a sort of perpetual-motion prime mover, which Spafford's supporters believed would bring about "a new era in the progress of the useful arts." The invention contradicted the most elementary laws of motion, according to Jones, who wrote in disgust: "That any person having any pretensions to mechanical knowledge, should be, for a moment, deceived by such a plan of obtaining power, would be incredible." Some were, however, Jones noted sadly, and in such cases he felt obliged to act "as a public sentinel."[20]

The editor's often puckish language was also directed toward the

---

importance, but now rendered peculiarly so by the provisions of the new patent law." A cover advertisement in the number for October 1839 advised readers of the resumption of Jones's agency. See *Charge Addressed to the Graduates in Medicine, at the Commencement of the Medical Department of the Columbian College, D.C. March 10, 1830. By Thomas P. Jones, M.D. Professor of Chemistry and Dean of the Medical Faculty* (Washington, D.C.: Gales and Seaton, 1830); and Francis Fowler, "Memoir of Dr. Thomas P. Jones," *Journal of the Franklin Institute* 130 (July 1890): 1–7. George Escol Sellers, developer of an anthracite-burning furnace, was one of Jones's clients in 1836. Some details of their relationship are contained in the Peale-Sellers Papers, American Philosophical Society.

[19] Subsequent cover advertisements for complete sets of back issues of the *Journal* carried the notice: "These volumes contain the only account now extant of the Patents issued by the United States; the original records having been consumed at the recent conflagration of the Patent Office at Washington." The January 1837 number was without the editor's comments on patents, since all the papers were in his desk at the Patent Office. Jones lived near the Patent Office, and his house was also in imminent danger of the fire. Some sense of the nation's loss was suggested in a Senate report which Jones appended to his account of the event. *Journal of the Franklin Institute* 23 (January 1837): 22–28.

[20] *Journal of the Franklin Institute* 17 (February 1834): 149.

extravagant schemes advanced when patents were available merely by payment of a fee. He wrote of a steam-activated bedbug destroyer:

Woe to the bed-bugs, should these steam bug destroying machines become as numerous as washing, thrashing, and churning machines, of which there seems to be some danger. . . . As the bugs are doomed to destruction, it might be some consolation to them in their dying agonies, to know that their enemies will not be able to sustain the right which they claim to their 'infernal machines,' under the patent laws, the great seal to the contrary notwithstanding.[21]

Serious inventions of obvious utility received close attention from Jones, but he complained that the majority of patent specifications only added "extreme length to utter worthlessness in all respects."[22]

As a corrective to the propensity of Americans for reinventing things, in 1830 Jones began another special series in the *Journal*, entitled "Modern Antiques." It, too, embodied the editor's humor and his directly practical approach to patent practices:

Under this title we propose to furnish, occasionally, some palpable evidences of the forestalling disposition of our remote ancestors, who have, in numerous instances, deprived us and our contemporaries, of the honour of being the *true and original inventors, or discoverers*, of various improvements in mechanics, and other useful arts.[23]

Jones published four numbers in the series, devoted mainly to mechanical contrivances for the transmission of motion. His aim in each number was the same, namely, to make the *Journal* a source of useful information to artisans and inventors. Given the anarchic state of U.S. patent procedures prior to 1836, Jones's comments and publication of specifications provided an important service, and they were widely reprinted by other mechanics' magazines.[24]

The success of that feature of the *Journal* did not, however, alter the fundamental fact that the geographic separation of editing and

[21] Ibid., 19 (February 1835): 99.
[22] Ibid., 16 (July 1833): 16.
[23] Ibid., 9 (January 1830): 69.
[24] Subsequent installments of the series were published in ibid., 9 (May 1830): 353–55; and 10 (July 1830): 38–41, (October 1830): 279–81. All issues of the *Boston Mechanic, and Journal of the Useful Arts and Sciences*, which was published from 1832 to 1835, reprinted Jones's patent information, as did the New York *Mechanics' Magazine and Register of Inventions and Improvements*, although its editor was sometimes critical of Jones's selections—see, for example, vol. 1 (April 1833), p. 213.

publishing functions would ultimately demand some kind of resolution. If for no other reason, the Institute's financial stake dictated that the dominant voice in the periodical's affairs come from Philadelphia. And in a very short period of time, the Board of Managers was forced to recognize, as Dr. Jones's earlier experience had proved, that technical publication was a losing business. By the end of the first year of its proprietorship the magazine was over $600 in debt, and while the minutes of their meetings do not reveal it, the Board was considering an end to the venture. The evidence comes from a letter from Jones to Merrick:

The remark in your letter respecting the uncertainty of the board continuing to publish the Journal any longer, is a proof that you entertain the opinion that corporate bodies are without souls. I can scarcely conceive of an act more savouring of injustice, than would be such a determination, and I do not believe it possible for such a result to occur.[25]

Perhaps because of the Board's apparent ambivalence over the *Journal*'s future, publishing it in Washington appeared as an attractive alternative to Jones. Duff Green, publisher of the *Congressional Globe*, had suggested the possibility, and when the editor agreed with the idea, Green wrote James Ronaldson, inquiring the terms on which the Institute would transfer the magazine to him.[26] Green's interest caused the Board to reconsider the issue. In their opinion, the Institute was conducted as a "national" society, its periodical international in utility, and the "honour of publishing it" should remain in Philadelphia.[27] On those grounds, and with money loaned to it from the sinking fund—a reserve account to pay off the building loan—the *Journal* was continued.

In casting up accounts at the end of the second year, the results were less dismal—the *Journal* lost $170—but some sort of action was still required. The actuary's salary was an especially critical issue. Lacking the funds to pay Hamilton directly from the Institute's treasury, the managers had seen the *Journal* as a means by which they might indirectly afford his services. His compensation as agent for the magazine in 1829 came to $650; out of that sum he had to pay the

25 Thomas P. Jones to Samuel V. Merrick, Washington, January 3, 1829, Thomas P. Jones Letters.
26 Duff Green to James Ronaldson, Washington, May 17, 1829, Incoming Correspondence, Franklin Institute Archives.
27 Draft of a letter prepared to be sent to Duff Green in reply to his of May 17, Incoming Correspondence.

editor $500 and the janitor $100! Even if he had collected all of the *Journal*'s outstanding debts for the year, Hamilton's salary would not have amounted to $400.[28]

To resolve the problem, the Committee on Publications recommended that the editor's salary be one-half of the actuary's total compensation, with the Institute paying the janitor's salary. In their report, the committee admitted that the *Journal*'s "continued prospects of advantage to the Institute in a pecuniary point of view are by no means flattering." But they argued that the magazine printed subject matter of importance from the monthly meetings and the water-power investigation, which would increase future subscriptions. More to the immediate point, however, Jones accepted the committee's financial proposition, and the *Journal* gained another reprieve.[29]

The Board also sought Congressional aid for their publication. A general petition was drafted early in 1830, and supporting letters were sent to the city and state representatives in Congress. Three alternative forms of aid were proposed. The most direct proposal was simply a request for an appropriation to help defray the *Journal*'s expenses. Another was a suggestion that Congress take a subscription for 500 copies. The third alternative—and the most attractive from the Institute's point of view—was that the *Journal* become the "authorized medium" for patent information and that one-sixth of the patent fees be allowed the Institute so that it could more extensively print patent specifications and their accompanying illustrations. Their reasoning was that only about one-sixth of the total number of patents issued were worth publication.[30] All of the suggestions were based on the argument that patent information deserved wider dissemination and that the *Journal* was the most appropriate vehicle for that purpose.

The Institute's managers had some reason for hope. The Senate had passed a measure the previous year calling for a Congressional subscription to a privately-owned Washington journal which proposed to print patent specifications. With that precedent and the expectation that a nonprofit organization would at least merit equal consideration, the Board presented the Institute's case. In addition, they also relied on Dr. Jones, who claimed to have the support of "many of the influ-

28 Report of the Committee on Publications, 1829.

29 Ibid., January 7, 1830; Minutes of the Board of Managers, January 7, 1830, Franklin Institute Archives.

30 The Franklin Institute to the Honorable the Senate and House of Representatives of the United States, n.d.; The Committee on Publications to the Hon. J. B. Sutherland, n.d.; The Committee on Publications to Joseph Hemphill, February 5, 1830—all in the Franklin Institute Archives.

ential men of the dominant party."[31] Notwithstanding all efforts, government aid was not granted. During the course of the next year the *Journal* was the subject of a few sporadic and disconnected attempts either to renegotiate the arrangement with Jones or to connect it with another periodical. But as the Institute shifted its interests toward original research, the periodical came to have a new importance. To Bache and his circle, the value of publishing original material outweighed financial considerations, and termination of the *Journal* was never again seriously considered.

It was a relatively easy matter for the Committee on Publications gradually to assume a commanding role over both the content and the policies of the *Journal*. Simple logic argued the need for an Institute committee to superintend the details involved in putting together monthly issues. And because few members felt able to manage a literary enterprise, the committee was made up of essentially the same men over a period of years. Samuel V. Merrick was chairman from 1828 until 1831. Dr. Isaac Hays directed the group in 1832 and from 1837 to 1841; and Alexander Dallas Bache filled the post during the interval between Hays's terms. Merrick, Hays, and Bache effectively ordered the periodical's affairs after 1831, interchanging as chairman and forming the critical nucleus of the committee. Hays was a physician of more than ordinary accomplishment. In addition to his labors at the Institute, he had a strong interest in natural history. He was active in the Academy of Natural Sciences, serving for a time as its president, and was responsible for the resumption of its *Proceedings* in 1821.[32] Hays brought publishing experience to the committee, and he shared with Merrick and Bache the values of science. Their vision of the *Journal*, added to the logic of local management, moved the magazine in an important new direction.

The emergence of a strong Committee on Publications with its own ideas of technical journalism made conflict with Dr. Jones inevitable. Removed from the place of publication, Jones depended heavily on William Hamilton to oversee many of the details of printing. The cares of his duties in Washington also led him to turn to Hamilton and the committee for assistance in selecting and editing contributions for the *Journal*. An example is a paper submitted for publication by David H. Mason, entitled "Observations on the Inclined Plane, the Wedge, and

31 Thomas P. Jones to Isaac Hays, Washington, January 3, 1830, Thomas P. Jones Letters.
32 For information on Hays, see Edward J. Nolan, *A Short History of the Academy of Natural Sciences in Philadelphia* (Philadelphia: The Academy of Natural Sciences, 1909).

the Screw, as Mechanical Powers." After struggling with it for a time, Jones sent it back to Philadelphia, with a note to Merrick:

I have enough in all conscience to bear and endure here at present, and as all good Christians should bear each others burthens, I willingly shift mine in this way. Bye the bye tis a poor thing, or it would not have lain so long. I thought of remodelling it, but could not make a silk purse out of a sow's ear. Maybe you, or Dr. Hayes can.[33]

Notwithstanding such appeals, Jones never had any intention of relinquishing his editorial control over the magazine's subject matter, and he so informed Merrick late in 1830.[34] Despite his feelings, the committee's own interests and the exigencies of publication conspired against Jones. His initial complaints were relatively minor. "You would have done better to have selected a few short articles for the close of the number," he wrote Hamilton. He continued to urge nontechnical language in the *Journal*. Abstruse terms which might be clear to an author, he advised, were "dog latin to 99/100 of his readers."[35]

More abrupt conflict came when the Committee on Publications began to include significant amounts of content without consulting Jones. For instance, he quarreled with a report from the water-power investigation for its lack of editorial revision.[36] In the same fashion, when the committee printed a long article on meteorology by Espy, Jones claimed that anything over eight pages was "destructive" to the *Journal* and would not be read by a third of those who would have read it if it had been divided into parts. If the committee chose to print articles without first consulting him, Jones argued, they must bear the responsibility for it.[37]

None of Jones's complaints altered the committee's practices, and

[33] Thomas P. Jones to Samuel V. Merrick, Washington, April 16, 1829, Thomas P. Jones Letters. Mason's paper was published under that title in the *Journal* 7 (June 1829): 426–29.

[34] Thomas P. Jones to Samuel V. Merrick, Washington, December 6, 1830, Thomas P. Jones Letters.

[35] Thomas P. Jones to William Hamilton, Washington, March 25, 1829; June 18, 1831, ibid.

[36] Thomas P. Jones to William Hamilton, Washington, November 6, 1831, ibid.

[37] Thomas P. Jones to William Hamilton (1831), ibid. The editor of the *American Journal of Science* claimed that he liked to keep articles within fifteen pages. He ran longer pieces serially, which had the added advantage of increasing sales, since readers often then bought additional numbers in order to see the whole article. "This is a paltry consideration," he admitted, "but we are all the time sailing so near the wind that the least leeway is valuable to us" (Benjamin Silliman, Jr., to S. G. Morton, New Haven, October 8, 1846, Morton Collection, Library Company of Philadelphia).

when a long piece was printed on the steam-boiler investigation, Jones exploded. The article was too long by half, he wrote, and some of the unrevised parts were "disgraceful to the Journal." If the Committee on Publications insisted on printing material without the editor's prior consideration, the articles should be so identified. "The present number," Jones concluded, "shows that the body will let that pass which no individual would be willing to father."[38] His outburst brought an angry retort from the committee. The formal letter was written by Hamilton, but the draft is in Bache's hand. The editor was crisply notified that he was incorrect in his charges and improper in his conduct. "Dr. Jones is informed," Bache concluded, "that as the committee of the Institute are responsible to that body and to the public for their acts, they cannot receive such communications from the Editor of the Journal of the Institute as are referred to above."[39] With that exchange, the issue was clearly joined.

Over the course of the next year, Jones and the committee contended for power over the *Journal*. "I have never relinquished, and I never design to relinquish, the entire control," Jones wrote Hamilton. Once proofs left his hand, he argued, it was improper for any changes to be made without his approval. "I cannot believe," he further claimed, "that the committee of Publications, or any individual concerned, intend to contest my rights on points of this kind." Jones clearly stated what he believed to be the editor's responsibility and area of authority. None of his remarks was intended personally, he advised Hamilton, but "I am not inclined to make a stand capriciously, nor am I disposed to be driven from ground which I have a right to occupy."[40]

The committee outlined its position in a long letter which settled the dispute. Once Jones moved to Washington, they stated, it was clear that some sort of coeditorship arrangement was necessary for the *Journal's* survival. To that end, the committee sought original contributions from their friends and wrote articles themselves; they instituted regular meetings of the group and devised a plan for the arrangement of the magazine's contents. As a result of their efforts, the committee claimed, "the character of the Journal has been greatly elevated and the subscription list so enlarged as now nearly to pay the expenses of the publication." The editor's distance from the place of publication had necessitated their efforts, the committee continued.

38 Thomas P. Jones to William Hamilton (Received March 1, 1832), Thomas P. Jones Letters.
39 William Hamilton to Thomas P. Jones, Philadelphia, March 10, 1832, ibid.
40 Thomas P. Jones to William Hamilton, Washington, April 14; May 11, 1833.

Should circumstances become otherwise, they would "cheerfully abandon all superintendance of the Journal," and they assured Jones of their
regard for his labor.[41]

But behind the assurances, there was a hard note. The committee
pointed out that their authority came from the Institute's Board of
Managers. The committee had no intention of yielding to the editor's
"absolute control," and they hinted none too subtly that the *Journal's*
continuance depended upon the present arrangement. With the effective power in their own hands, the committee easily carried the dispute. In the future, Jones would be responsible for his articles and
selections and the committee for theirs, as well as for the "general
arrangement" and financial concerns of the publication.[42] What that
really meant was that Jones was limited to his comments on patents,
reading proof, and to whatever minor editorial aid he provided in
preparing indexes and tables of contents.

The dispute was not simply about the efficient management of the
periodical. Form and content were at the heart of the issue. While
Jones accepted the redefinition of his position, his continued comments
reveal the true cause of disagreement. He objected to a "heavy" article
on capillary attraction by John W. Draper on the grounds that "none
but a master in science will understand a page of it." Had he control
of the *Journal*, Jones wrote Hamilton, he would have referred the
article to Silliman's *American Journal of Science.*[43] In like spirit, he
wrote that an article by Walter R. Johnson was already overlong in
proof "and will be a blank to the general reader."[44] It was a gratuitous swipe, for he admitted that he was not responsible for its selection. When the Committee on Publications revised an article that he
had written himself, Jones flared up again, but only momentarily. The
committee exercised almost complete command, and Jones recognized
their power.

Bache, Merrick, and Hays used their control to make the *Journal* a
serious scientific and technical publication. Basically, there were
three elements involved in the changes they brought about. First, they
used the magazine to express their own professional interests and
standards. Second, they made a conscious attempt to link the *Journal's*
content with current scientific problems, as defined both in this country

---

[41] Draft of a letter to Dr. Jones, May 16, 1833, Thomas P. Jones Letters.
[42] Ibid.
[43] Thomas P. Jones to William Hamilton, Washington, August 4, 1834, ibid.
Draper's article, "Some Experimental Researches to determine the nature of Capillary
Attraction," was published in *Journal of the Franklin Institute* 18 (September 1834),
pp. 147–65.
[44] Thomas P. Jones to William Hamilton, Washington, October 8, 1834.

and abroad. Finally, they encouraged the talents of a rising generation of scientists and engineers by opening the periodical to their articles. In addition to these changes, all of which had as their objective the elevation of subject matter, the magazine's format was altered. And that change, too, reflected the shift in emphasis which characterized the *Journal* once the Committee on Publications gained solid control.

In the early 1830's the *Journal* relied almost entirely on members of the Institute's inner circle for its original articles. John W. Draper was the only outside contributor to come near their output. James P. Espy published his first observations on meteorology in the magazine, and he used it to solicit observers to provide him with weather information. When he and William C. Redfield fell into controversy over a theory of storms, the *Journal* provided a forum for their opposing views. Espy also published several articles stemming from his experiments in the water-power investigation, as did Johnson on his strength-of-materials research. Robert Hare, the eminent University of Pennsylvania chemist, also contributed heavily; in fact, Hare's was the leading article in five out of six issues in 1833. Until 1836, when the reports of the steam-boiler investigation filled its pages, Espy, Hare, Johnson, and Bache dominated the magazine with their articles. They were the principal sources of original research, the basic ingredient of a scholarly publication.

In addition to contributing articles to the *Journal*, Bache played another, more significant role: he connected the *Journal* with the world of science. When he communicated notice of Joseph Saxton's electromagnetic experiments in England, Bache compared them with similar experiments by Michael Faraday and called attention to the researches of Isaiah Lukens and Benjamin Say, who were working along the same lines in Philadelphia. All, in Bache's view, were linked in work on an international scientific problem.[45] In a similar way, Merrick and other members of the committee translated articles from foreign periodicals on subjects of wide technical interest.[46]

Bache also used the framework of international science as a setting for research in which the Institute had a direct interest. Meteorology was such a subject, and in an article on magnetic disturbances during an aurora, Bache noted "the beautiful connexion" which existed between meteorological phenomena and Faraday's research in electric-

---

[45] "Notice of Electro-Magnetic Experiments," *Journal of the Franklin Institute* 14 (July 1832): 66–72; see also 17 (March 1834): 155–56, (April 1834): 219–22.
[46] Ibid., 19 (February 1835): 119–25.

ity.[47] He concluded his article by observing that the subject had recently occupied meetings of the British Association for the Advancement of Science. Readers of the *Journal* were aware of the context in which Bache wrote; the magazine had published abstracts of the proceedings of the British Association since its first meeting in 1832.[48]

Scientific internationalism, in Bache's mind, was also combined with national pride. He and the Committee on Publications sought to make the *Journal* a first-rate periodical which would stand favorable comparison with any publication. To that end, the committee solicited contributions from the outstanding engineers and scientists of Europe and America. Bache wrote Joseph Henry, America's foremost physicist: "You must positively, lend your help to the Physical Science Department of our Journal."[49] Similarly, he forwarded from London Sir Charles Wheatstone's latest research for inclusion in the *Journal*, urging William Hamilton to publish it "as early as possible."[50]

National pride was also served by making the *Journal* the vehicle for American claims of scientific priority. Perhaps the best example is Bache's effort to persuade his friend Joseph Henry to publish the results of his electrical experiments. Henry was notoriously slow in publishing, and Bache prefaced an account of some of Henry's experiments with the remark: "Mr. Faraday having recently entered upon a similar train of observations, the immediate publication of the accompanying is important, that the prior claims of our fellow countrymen may not be overlooked."[51] Nor was Bache concerned only with scientific priority. Under his initials, the Committee on Publications published an article, "On the invention and progress of Medal ruling in the United States," primarily to advance the claim of Asa Spencer to a machine for engraving medals. John Bate, an Englishman, had called the invention his own, and worse for American pride, it had been displayed by Michael Faraday at a meeting of the Royal Institution. Bache pointed out the role of the *Journal* in setting such mistakes

[47] A. D. Bache, "Observations on the Disturbance in the Direction of the Horizontal Needle, during the occurrance of the Aurora of July 10th, 1833," *Journal of the Franklin Institute* 17 (January 1834): 1.

[48] Ibid., p. 9.

[49] A. D. Bache to Joseph Henry, Philadelphia, January 1836, Joseph Henry Private Papers, Smithsonian Institution Archives.

[50] A. D. Bache to William Hamilton, London, April 28, 1837, Incoming Correspondence.

[51] Joseph Henry, "Facts in reference to the Spark, &c. from a long conductor uniting the poles of a Galvanic Battery," *Journal of the Franklin Institute* 19 (March 1835): 169.

right: "America *has been* without her journals to put forth the claims of her ingenious men, and the credit of more than one invention has passed from her to those who have been able to give greater publicity to their designs."[52]

Another element in the reform of the *Journal* was the introduction of aspiring professional engineers and scientists to a national and international audience. For instance, the *Journal* printed articles on railroad-construction techniques by rising young engineers like John C. Trautwine. The aim was no longer to promote internal improvements, however; the articles were concerned with professional engineering. The *Journal* also sought to provide young scientists with a means of expression, and to encourage the submission of original articles, the committee offered "a liberal compensation" to authors.[53] On the eve of a brilliant career in physics, John W. Draper published his first scientific articles in the Institute's periodical, as did James P. Espy, Sears C. Walker, and Walter R. Johnson.[54] Discussions of engineering fine points or abstruse papers in physics were far from the plain talk for practical men which Jones had originally advocated for the *Journal*.

Professionalism was behind all of the changes with Bache and the Committee on Publications brought about. And the essence of professionalism, as Bache later pointed out, was specialization.[55] As with so many of his efforts to advance and elevate the character of American science, the idea had an earlier expression in Bache's work at the

[52] Ibid., 14 (September 1832): 145–47.

[53] Notices "To Readers and Correspondents" carried the message: "The Committee on Publications, anxious to render this work as valuable as possible, have determined to offer a liberal compensation for original articles on the subjects to which this Journal is devoted; and they accordingly invite mechanics and men of science to communicate their observations. Every article published will be liberally paid for" (vol. 11 [March 1831], p. 216). What the rate of compensation would be was never stated precisely, but from the *Journal's* financial records it appears the committee paid from three to four dollars, plus the cost of engravings, for an article of about the same number of pages. Joshua Shaw, for example, received three dollars and seventy-five cents for a four-page article on colors. Committee on Publications, Annual Statement, 1832, Franklin Institute Archives; *Journal of the Franklin Institute* 13 (January 1832): 10–12; 14 (October 1832): 224–25.

[54] For information on Draper, see the *Dictionary of American Biography* (New York: Charles Scribner's Sons, 1943), and Nathan Reingold, *Science in Nineteenth-Century America: A Documentary History* (New York: Hill and Wang, 1964), pp. 252ff. From his remote academic situation in Christiansville, Virginia, Draper depended on Hamilton for help with financial affairs as well as publication. Letters in Incoming Correspondence, Franklin Institute Archives, give some details of the relationship.

[55] A. D. Bache, "Address," *Proceedings of the American Association for the Advancement of Science* 6 (1851): xli–lx.

Franklin Institute. The germ may be found in his reorganization of the *Journal* in 1836. First, the periodical was given a new title, *Journal of the Franklin Institute of the State of Pennsylvania, and Mechanics' Register. Devoted to Mechanical and Physical Science, Civil Engineering, the Arts and Manufactures, and the Recording of American and Other Patented Inventions*. And behind the title was a new format. General science, a phrase incorporated in the *Journal*'s earlier title, reflected amateurism, and while the magazine had begun in that vein, Bache and his committee completely reordered its format and policies to meet their own professional ideals. The committee organized subject matter along disciplinary lines; and subcategories distinguished original material from that which was being reprinted. Original articles fell into three fields—"Physical Science," "Practical and Theoretical Mechanics and Chemistry," and "Civil Engineering." Abstracts and translations of current foreign and domestic work in those fields were published in corresponding sections under the headings "Progress in Physical Science," "Progress in Practical and Theoretical Mechanics and Chemistry," and "Progress in Civil Engineering." Foreign and domestic patent specifications, the editor's comments on American patents, and any other miscellaneous material of interest to artisans and manufacturers were gathered under a separate section entitled "Mechanics' Register."

The articles published during 1836 suggest the *Journal*'s new approach. Within each of the main subject divisions, the committee published the results of original investigation. For example, under "Physical Science" were articles by Bache on physics, chemistry, and meteorology; by Draper on chemistry and physics; by Sears C. Walker on astronomy; and by Espy on meteorology. "Practical and Theoretical Mechanics and Chemistry" included an article by Lt. T. S. Brown, of the Army Corps of Engineers, on "Experiments on the resistance of sand to motion through tubes," which incorporated the translation of a French work on the flow of sand together with his own results from trials at Ft. Adams in Newport, Rhode Island. There were other articles in the same section by Professor Cram, of West Point, on the strength of cast-iron beams; by James Frost on "Calcareous Cements"; and by Franklin Peale on machinery at the U.S. Mint in Philadelphia.[56]

The Institute's early interest in internal improvements still found expression in the "Civil Engineering" category, but the articles were written by professional engineers, and often as not, for other engineers. It included reports from various railroads, treatises on building

[56] All examples were selected from volumes 21 and 22 (1836).

materials, railroad-construction techniques, and pieces like John B. Jervis's report to the canal commissioners of New York. The non-original material in each of the main categories was selected—and, when necessary, translated—by the committee. Reprinted material reflected the committee's interests, too, and included reports from meetings of the British Association for the Advancement of Science, from Faraday's electrical researches, and abstracts from French technical literature. The new format also inaugurated, under the relevant disciplinary sections, critical reviews of recent publications. In the first year of the new style, G. W. Featherstonhaugh's *Geological Report of an Examination, made in 1834, of the Elevated Country between the Missouri and Red rivers* was subjected to a scathing attack, and James C. Booth wrote a lengthy analysis of Mitscherlich's *Compendium of Chemistry*. As Featherstonhaugh's reviewer pointed out, if the periodicals "whose particular province it is to be leaders and guides in matters of science" did not meet their duty:

It is time for America to abandon all pretensions to rivalry with Europe on such subjects, and sink at once into that station of mental inferiority, which has been sometimes so contemptuously and so unjustly assigned to her, by a certain class of transatlantic writers.[57]

Only in Dr. Jones's section was the mechanic free from algebra and chemical notation. Only there did he find a piece of straightforward humor. And the uncompromisingly serious tone which Bache and the committee set for the *Journal* brought occasional criticism from readers. Thomas W. Bakewell, a Cincinnati steam-engine manufacturer and a man of some learning, complained that the publication had "obtained a standing rather too 'correct and proper,' for those who are not veterans in science to adventure their speculations." The committee's response, however, was to doubt that the *Journal*'s readers "would desire its scientific tone to be lowered."[58] Their own efforts, certainly, were consistently directed toward elevating the magazine's form and content. The changes also had the wholehearted support of the Board of Managers, who reported in 1836:

The number & value of scientific articles is believed to be quite equal to that of journals devoted entirely to science, while the readers of practical & theoreti-

---

[57] *Journal of the Franklin Institute* 21 (March 1836): 190.

[58] Ibid., 19 (January 1835): 20. Actually, Dr. Jones's section was consciously seen as a relief measure: "The Mechanics' Register, attached to the Journal, is not *heavy* reading, and, when more solid articles tire, cannot fail to amuse as well as to instruct" (Ibid., 21 [June 1836]: 402).

cal mechanics have had their portion of matter rather increased than diminished.[59]

In fact, the transformation of the *Journal of the Franklin Institute* did not cause a decline in readers. Subscriptions increased after 1830, and the periodical came nearer to financial self-sufficiency than it ever had in earlier years. Experience helped correct some mistakes; press runs were trimmed to more realistic figures. But the committee also took steps to increase circulation. They actively searched out agents to handle subscriptions, and by 1836 there were sixty-three scattered throughout New England, the mid-Atlantic and Southern states, and as far west as Michigan territory.[60] The number of dealers was twice what it had been when the Institute assumed publication and even included representatives in London and Paris. Moreover, the 1836 reorganization increased the length of the magazine by about twelve pages, but, as the committee was pleased to announce, at no extra cost to readers.[61]

Since specific figures are unavailable, the increase in circulation can only be suggested by the money collected from subscribers each year. In the interval between 1832 and 1836, the amount almost doubled, from $1,200 to $2,100. In 1832, the press run was probably 1,000 copies, and while the corresponding run for 1836 is not known, it must have been nearly double that of the 1832 run.[62] But costs

[59] Fiftieth Quarterly Report of the Board of Managers, June 1836, Franklin Institute Archives.

[60] Names and addresses of agents were printed in cover advertisements for the *Journal*. In urban centers agents tended to be printers and booksellers, such as Light & Stearns, who distributed the work in Boston. In some areas engineers acted as agents. Alfred C. Jones, a civil engineer of Portsmouth, Virginia, who often contributed articles for publication, volunteered to serve without charge in that capacity. A. C. Jones to William Hamilton, Portsmouth, Virginia, September 22, 1835, Incoming Correspondence. In more remote areas, postmasters were usually agents for the magazine. Mail to distant parts had its own hazards. Jefferson Beaumont, the agent in Natchez, Mississippi, complained of not receiving the magazine, "as the mail after it arrives in Kentucky is carried principally on horseback & frequently gets very wet" (Jefferson Beaumont to Judah Dobson, Natchez, Mississippi, August 9, 1828, Incoming Correspondence).

[61] In a "Prospectus" for the new series, which appeared in the number for December 1835, the Committee on Publications noted: "For the additional matter thus furnished it is not proposed to make any additional charge, and should mechanics or men of science extend further patronage, the means which will thus be furnished will be applied to extend the amount of matter in the journal, and to carry out more fully the plan which will now be attempted."

[62] The report of the Committee on Publications, on August 11, 1827, inquiring into the expediency of an Institute journal, stated that the press run for that year had been two thousand copies. The Institute apparently began with a 1,500 copy run, which was reduced in two steps to 1,000. Report of the Committee on Publications (1829). In the July 1832 Report of the Committee on Publications, there is further suggestion of a press run of 1,000 copies.

increased, too. Payments to contributors and the more frequent use of illustrative material added to the *Journal*'s expense, even though the amount received by an individual author was quite modest. Over a nine-year period, for example, James P. Espy was paid $384, John W. Draper was paid $183, and Walter R. Johnson received $109.[63] And there were payments to others, as well, although Bache, who contributed the most heavily, gave his work at no charge.

In their annual reports, the Board of Managers constantly urged greater support for the publication, and in 1835 a special appeal was made to the Institute's membership. The Committee on Publications circulated a letter reiterating the original purposes for establishing the *Journal*. The first object, the dissemination of knowledge, had been achieved. The library, however still languished for funds. Nor had the actuary been paid fairly for his services. A great deal of time and effort had been devoted to the magazine, the committee claimed, and it had reached a high standing in the world, judging from "the copious extracts from it constantly found on the pages of the foreign journals." But members were advised:

Unlimited attention to details, and the most rigid economy, have alone enabled its conductors to struggle through a long period of discouragement; and after seven years' labor they find themselves involved in a debt which the entire collection of all their outstanding subscriptions will scarcely cover. Instead, therefore, of affording means of increased usefulness, the work scarcely pays the expense of publication.[64]

Most discouraging of all was that out of the 1,700 members of the organization only 103 subscribed to the *Journal*.

The appeal was not highly successful. Subscriptions increased slightly, and by the continued sales of back numbers some volumes finally became profitable. Through such a process, the volumes for 1836 were able to show a profit of four dollars and twelve cents by 1845. But the same factors which gave the periodical wide circulation and esteem also made it expensive to produce. Furthermore, when Bache left for Europe there was no one to take his place, or at least not gratuitously. John Griscom, who had figured in the earliest thoughts of an Institute publication, was therefore hired as an adjunct editor. Griscom later recalled the move: "I engaged to arrange and supervise

[63] The figures come from the annual statements of the Committee on Publications for the years indicated.

[64] *To the Members of the Franklin Institute, April, 1835*, Committee on Publications, Franklin Institute Archives.

the proof sheets. . . . It yielded me about $250 per annum, and continued for three or four years, to afford occupation for a portion of almost every day."[65] Actually, Griscom did more. He translated numerous articles for the magazine, wrote book reviews, and made selections of other material. Perhaps because of those extra labors, he really earned over $400 annually during the four years from 1837 to 1840.[66] His salary and the $500 paid yearly to Dr. Jones were further costs which the *Journal* had to bear, and it continued to depend upon deficit financing for its existence.

While the *Journal* was financially disappointing, it was in every other respect a brilliant success. It became unquestionably the nation's outstanding technical periodical and, as a result of Alexander Dallas Bache's influence, at least the equal of any other American journal publishing in the physical sciences. The Committee on Publications, with considerable acuteness to current problems and future needs, shaped the magazine into a voice for professional engineers and provided them with a model for high standards of technical journalism. By a studied policy to emphasize the publication of original research, the committee also made the *Journal* an important medium for aspiring scientists. It taught them the canons of intellectual excellence, too, and encouraged the specialization necessary to the development of American science.

Dr. Jones had devoted the magazine to the diffusion of knowledge among practical men, to whom, as he once said, "the philosopher is indebted for whatever is true in theory, and the arts for nearly everything that is correct in practice."[67] Bache, Merrick, and Hays turned that formula around and directed the work toward original research—to which science was obliged for its truth, and technology for its advancement. Their policies brought distinction to the *Journal*, prestige to the Franklin Institute and, at a time when it was sorely needed, international respect for the nation's science.

65 John H. Griscom, *Memoir of John Griscom, LL.D.* (New York: Robert Carter and Brothers, 1859), p. 259.

66 Annual Statement, Committee on Publications, for 1837, 1838, 1839, 1840. Griscom was also paid sixty-seven dollars for editorial services in 1836.

67 *The Franklin Journal and American Mechanics' Magazine* 1 (January 1826): 64.

IX THE FINANCIAL RACK

fettered as we are by the condition of our debt. . . .

Frederick Fraley to Bayes Newcomb, Esq.,
Philadelphia, September 27, 1841

As the *Journal of the Franklin Institute* clearly gained national status
and repute, the Board of Managers found several causes for congratu-
lation in their reports to the society's membership. Along with the
Institute's important original investigations, the *Journal* seemed proof
that the organization served national purposes, that in some measure
it had a responsibility for the reputation of American science and
technology. Philadelphians shared the Board's pride in the Institute's
accomplishments. They filled the hall for evening lectures, swelled the
membership rolls, and came to the biennial exhibitions in ever larger
crowds. By all appearances the Institute successfully blended a disparate
batch of interests in a program of varied appeal, and by 1835 it had
even achieved a modest prosperity.

The Institute's vigor and financial condition contrast sharply with
the traditional image of America's scientific and technical organizations in the first part of the nineteenth century. Scientists looking for
social position and research support frequently painted a bleak picture
of publication outlets, opportunities for experimentation, and of institutions comparable to those with which Europe seemed so richly supplied. But this country's societies have been little studied, and the validity of these assertions is open to question.[1] Certainly it is false that
America lacked for scientific journals; in the experience of the Institute's
Committee on Publications the need was for better articles, not more
magazines. Similarly, the Institute's history suggests that American
societies were not simply pallid imitations of European institutions. In
terms of membership or budget, the Philadelphia organization was de-
monstrably healthy. The issue confronting its leaders was how to maintain viability in a changing nation which offered scant precedent for

---

[1] For a recent study of scientific patronage in nineteenth-century America, see
Howard S. Miller, *Dollars for Research* (Seattle: University of Washington Press, 1970).

either private or public endowment. The difficulty for societies in the United States was not in getting born, but in staying alive.

When the Institute's establishment first captured public fancy, members paid their annual dues readily, so there was money for operating expenses, plus a surplus for the sinking fund to pay off the building loan. But as the novelty disappeared, dues were not so promptly paid. From 1827 to 1828, income from dues dropped by half, and when unexpected alterations were required in 1829, the treasury was reduced to a balance of sixty-nine cents.[2] Worse yet, in 1830 the district court reneged on its rental agreement. After discussions with court officers, the managers were able to negotiate a settlement for the remaining six years of the lease, but at an amount of $900 annually instead of the $1,500 in rent they had been receiving.

The Institute was able to absorb $250 of the loss by renting two of the rooms vacated by the court. The other space was converted into a library and reading room, where the mineral collection and inventor's models could be displayed. Since the society had long been without proper facilities for its books and other collections, as well as a place for conversational meetings, there was an important gain to the situation. On the treasurer's books, however, it still represented a cash loss, and further expenditures were required to alter the rooms to their new purpose.[3] The Board appointed successive committees in an attempt to find a way out of its financial difficulties, but there were no easy solutions. Indeed, in some cases the only answer seemed to be to take money out of one pocket and put it into another. The Institute's normal procedure was to allocate all income from rentals, the twenty-five-dollar life membership fees, and the extra sales of lecture tickets to women, minors, and visitors into the sinking fund. But the remaining income, a committee in 1829 reported, was not enough to pay the organization's bills. "To remedy the insolvency" the committee recom-

---

[2] Minutes of the Board of Managers, October 8, 1829, Franklin Institute Archives. The managers had earlier reported the decline: "In the formation of new institutions, there are, generally, a considerable number of persons who enrol their names on the list of members with a view of affording temporary aid, without designing to become permanent subscribers" (*The Franklin Journal and American Mechanics' Magazine* 4 [November 1827]: 331). For a published statement of the Institute's early financial condition see the Eighth Quarterly Report of the Board of Managers, January 19, 1826, published in *National Gazette*, January 26, 1826.

[3] The Board of Managers published a circular, in 1830, appealing to the Institute's members for donations of books and money, "as their funds are not, as yet, more than adequate to meet the necessary expenses of the other important branches of their operations" (Undated circular letter, Committee on the Library and Reading Room, Franklin Institute Archives). Judging from subsequent expenditures to fit out the rooms, the appeal was not greatly successful. Minutes of the Board of Managers, April 8, 1830.

mended that outstanding debts for building repairs and alterations be paid from the sinking fund.[4] That transaction replenished the treasury, but at a cost to the Institute's long-term obligations.

The basic problem the Institute faced was the same as that confronting most such societies in America at the time. Except in rare cases, private endowment funds were a dream of the future. So was public support from city or state governments. Even regular tax relief for nonprofit organizations was a concept for which governments were not quite ready.[5] Societies depended essentially on membership fees, voluntary labor, and whatever activities generated income. It was obvious that organizations prospered pretty much in direct relation to their success in touching public interest.

It was also apparent that there were balances to be struck. If a society owned a building, the choice was between rental income and the space needed for activities which sustained or generated support. Both the Franklin Institute and the American Philosophical Society counted on the revenue which came from rentals, and both were faced with such a choice.[6] The Institute had to make that kind of decision in 1830, when the district court moved out, and again in 1832, when Walter R. Johnson shifted his school to other quarters. Johnson had been paying an annual rent of $500, and when he left Bache wrote William Hamilton: "Mr. Johnson I observe has *moved*, & that out of our building. Pray *bestir* that we may have a suitable tenant for the large room & perhaps for the back room."[7] If normal income suddenly dropped, through nonpayment of dues, for instance, another choice had to be made. The scale of operations could be reduced in order to lower expenses to the level of income, but that would be a bit like mortgaging property in a real-estate game

---

[4] Minutes of the Board of Managers, October 8, 1829.

[5] In 1825, the Institute appealed to the state legislature for tax exemption, on the basis that the society's members came from throughout the state and that its exhibitions likewise served all portions of the Commonwealth. Petitions, Legislature, Franklin Institute Archives. Two decades later, a second memorial was planned, but on learning that other city institutions had decided against similar appeals, the Board dropped the idea. Minutes of the Board of Managers, February 17, March 17, 1847.

[6] At various times the American Philosophical Society rented space to Peale's Museum, the Athenaeum, the Agricultural Society, and other tenants. As Edward Conklin pointed out, "These rentals and the annual dues of members were for a long time the only regular income of the Society" ("A Brief History of the American Philosophical Society," *Year Book of the American Philosophical Society for 1959* [Philadelphia: American Philosophical Society, 1959], pp. 50–51). The Institute's tenants included the Army Corps of Engineers, while work was in progress on the Delaware Breakwater, and the Statistic Society; and offices were also rented for commercial purposes. Minutes of the Board of Managers, April 8, 1830; July 15, 1846.

[7] Alexander D. Bache to William Hamilton, West Chester, August 30, 1832, Incoming Correspondence.

and losing the chance to recoup losses. Understanding that, finance committees at the Institute consistently decided against retrenchment.

> The committee are of opinion that any reduction in the expenditures of the Institute at the present time would have a tendency to depress the spirit which now animates the public in its favour and be productive of more injury than the saving of a few dollars would repay.[8]

But the alternate choice also had disadvantages. It cost money to attract public interest, and expenses at the Institute always had a way of keeping up with income. An even more critical problem was that the principal committees had fallen into bad fiscal habits, and expanded activities badly strained the organization's accounting system. The committees responsible for the *Journal*, the water-power experiments, the library and reading room, and the sinking fund had fallen into bad fiscal habits. Records were often kept in only fragmentary fashion. Receipts and vouchers to cover income and expenditures were either unused or misused, in the sense that they were not cleared through a central accounting procedure.[9] It was not a matter of malfeasance or a lack of guidelines. The constitution described financial procedures, but committees developed an autonomous character over a period of time; carelessness became customary, and the society's original directives were neglected.

Frederick Fraley headed the committee which restored order to the Institute's fiscal operations. Fraley was one of the original members of the Institute and a childhood friend of Bache. As his later career was amply to demonstrate, he possessed considerable financial acumen and a great sense of responsibility for the city's intellectual and cultural institutions.[10] In his 1831 report to the Board of Managers, Fraley outlined a six-point program to centralize accounting practices and to insure that the Board knew with more certainty the state of its pocketbook. "Constant and unremitting exertions" would be required to make the Insti-

---

8 Minutes of the Board of Managers, January 7, 1830.

9 Report of the Committee on Finance, February 10, 1831, Franklin Institute Archives.

10 In addition to his long connection to the Franklin Institute, Fraley served as a director and president of Girard College, a trustee of the University of Pennsylvania, and president of the American Philosophical Society. He was a member of the state legislature for a time and a founder of the Union League Club and of the National Board of Trade, and he was particularly active in planning the Centennial Exhibition in 1876. Biographical sketches of Fraley are available in the *Public Ledger*, September 24, 1901; and the University of Pennsylvania's *Alumni Register*, vol. 5 (February 1901). See also *Proceedings at the Dinner to the Honorable Frederick Fraley on his Ninetieth Birthday* (Philadelphia: William F. Murphy, 1894).

tute's financial affairs "correspond with its high character as a scientific institution."[11] Fraley served as treasurer in 1831, and he continued to fill the post throughout the next decade. Gradually, the Institute's monetary position improved, and by 1835 he reported a total income of over $11,000. After the bills had been paid and more than $3,000 had been appropriated to the sinking fund, there was still a positive treasury balance in excess of $3,000.[12] It seemed as if the worst financial problems were over.

For men accustomed to fiscal stringency, prosperity was heady stuff, and they were tempted to think in expansive terms. With increased income as apparent proof of the Institute's value, and since existing quarters were already overcrowded, in the boom times of the 1830's the idea of a new building became irresistible. Early in 1835 the managers appointed a committee "to inquire what action it is expedient for this Board to take at this time in relation to extending the accommodations of the Institute."[13] Merrick and Fraley, who had moved the resolution, were named to the committee, along with Keating, Bache, and Alexander Ferguson. In June the committee learned that the Masonic Lodge was interested in selling its hall and building lot on Chestnut Street, between Seventh and Eighth Streets, for $110,550. Masonic Hall was one of Philadelphia's great gathering places, and the only one equipped with gas lighting. Furthermore, that part of Chestnut Street had become one of the city's most desirable locations, and real-estate prices, spurred by the inflationary character of the times, had been rapidly rising. It was a site "calculated to attract public attention," and the managers very quickly seized on the offer.[14] At a special meeting of the Board held on June 26, 1835, Merrick recommended that the Institute buy the property. To secure the membership's approval, a special meeting of the Institute was scheduled three days later, and the action was unanimously approved. The Board was also authorized to sell the Seventh Street building, if necessary, and to borrow additional money, pledging for its repayment "the faith, property, & revenue of the Institution."[15]

The purchase of Masonic Hall engaged the Franklin Institute in what was probably the most ambitious building project by a private society at that time in America. It involved a complex of three related structures containing over 32,000 square feet of floor space. The com-

[11] Treasurer's Annual Statement, January 10, 1831.

[12] Ibid., December 31, 1835.

[13] Minutes of the Board of Managers, February 18, 1835.

[14] Journal of the Franklin Institute 20 (September 1835): 154; J. Thomas Scharf and Thomas Wescott, 3 vols., History of Philadelphia, 1609–1884 (Philadelphia: L. H. Everts & Co., 1884), vol. 1, p. 643.

[15] Minutes of the Board of Managers, June 26, July 1, 1835.

mittee selected William Strickland to design a new building on the
Chestnut Street frontage, to house stores on the ground floor and a large
gallery on the second floor for the Institute's exhibitions. A new four-
story structure was planned for the center of the lot, which would provide more exhibition space plus rooms for the library, the mineral and
model collections, and a reading room. Masonic Hall was to be torn
down, and a new building was to be put up in its place, fronting on
Lodge Street. It would provide five rooms at ground level "suitable for
mechanics' shops of various descriptions," schoolrooms, and space for
laboratories and the apparatus of Institute lecturers. More rental space
was designed for the third floor. The second floor of the Lodge Street
building was wholly devoted to an auditorium capable of seating 1,200
persons. The committee reported that the Institute's Seventh Street lecture hall was already badly overcrowded. During the previous lecture
season, 478 tickets were sold to women and minors alone, "thus excluding nearly all the members" from attendance. In view of the fact that
there were over 1,800 members, a larger facility seemed to the committee
"indispensable."[16]

Plans to finance the project were equally ambitious. Strickland estimated the expense of construction to be $64,500. Together with the price
of the Masonic property, the total cost was put at $175,000. According
to the arrangement made with the Grand Lodge, the Institute was to pay
$15,000 on taking possession; $20,000 on January 1, 1836; and the remainder in three subsequent payments due January 1, 1838, 1840, and
1842. The last three installments were to constitute a loan from the
Masonic Lodge at a yearly interest of five percent. To meet construction
costs and the first two payments to the Masons, the committee—which
had been expanded to include Dr. Hays, Baldwin, Thomas Fletcher, and
John Struthers, a local builder—proposed to raise a loan of $100,000 by
the sale of stock certificates bearing interest at six percent annually and
unredeemable until 1856.

Interest payments on the debt to the Masons, on the new loan, and to
the stockholders of the Institute's original loan for the Seventh Street
building were all to be paid out of income. Receipts, too, in the committee's plan, were equal to the task. They outlined a system which had
worked well before. All rental income, life membership fees, extra lecture ticket sales, and "all legacies or bequests, and donations" would go
into the sinking fund, for ultimate redemption of the debt. By that kind
of allocation, the original sinking fund had grown to over $12,000 in

16 The entire plan was described at the Institute's general meeting on June 29,
1835, and was subsequently published in the *Journal of the Franklin Institute* 20
(December 1835): 380–82.

1835. Stockholders regularly collected their interest, and since the managers invested the fund, it collected interest too. It was a neat arrangement, especially appealing in this new application because the committee anticipated a rent income of $2,200 yearly from the old building and over $12,000 from space in the proposed project. By their reckoning, the Institute could meet all its annual interest payments out of sinking-fund income and still have almost $3,000 left over each year to pay off the principal.[17]

Altogether it was a bold scheme but different only in scale from other visions. The Academy of Natural Sciences was beginning to feel pinched in its quarters, and the American Philosophical Society was involved in a complicated arrangement to sell its headquarters and build anew on Chestnut Street at Ninth.[18] It was a prosperous time for Americans. Agricultural prices were high, industrial capacity was growing, and canals and railroads continued to reach further westward. It seemed only logical to the Institute's managers to capitalize on the same prosperity by purchasing a property "daily increasing in value."[19] It was only a sense of prosperity, however; in hardly more than a year the whole structure crumbled. There were signs of weakness even before the collapse. James Ronaldson, the Institute's president, donated $500 when the building plan was announced, but his example was not followed, and subscriptions to the new loan lagged. By contrast with the organization's first building loan, when most of the stock was immediately taken, the committee was forced to report in November 1835 that while the loan books had been kept open daily, "but little over $20,000 has been subscribed."[20]

Perhaps with a weather eye on stock sales, in the spring of 1836 the Masonic Lodge trustees requested that "fuller and more formal powers" be vested in the Institute committee with which they were negotiating.[21] Happily for the managers, who had hoped for a larger loan subscription, a delay in transferring title to their new property postponed the payment schedule. While the first $15,000 had been paid, the January 1836 installment was put off until the Institute took full possession. But by then the first ripples of the Panic of 1837 disturbed the city's commercial circles, and money was getting scarce. As if to assure prospective investors of its own financial stability, the Board published the treasurer's annual report

---

[17] *Journal of the Franklin Institute* 20 (December 1835): 382–84.

[18] Conklin, "A Brief History of the American Philosophical Society," p. 51; Edward J. Nolan, *A Short History of the Academy of Natural Sciences of Philadelphia* (Philadelphia: The Academy of Natural Sciences, 1909), p. 11.

[19] *Journal of the Franklin Institute* 20 (December 1835): 380.

[20] Minutes of the Board of Managers, November 18, 1835.

[21] Ibid., March 21, 1836.

—something they had not done for years.[22] In their April quarterly
report, the managers advised members that it had been "deemed prudent
under existing difficulties among mechanics" not to build on the new
site until some later time.[23] By October, the Committee on the New Hall
more explicitly reported the facts. Enough money to begin construction
had not been found, and the managers warned that it was even going to
be difficult to meet interest payments on the purchase money. However,
with the same energies which had brought the Institute through worse
times, the Board claimed, it would survive the present trial:

And in a few years more, endeared to the public as well by its important
services in the cause of education, as by its invaluable investigations of the most
important practical and scientific objects, the name of the Franklin Institute
will convey a highly exalted idea of national greatness, and stimulate our sister
institutions to a greater zeal in the promotion of the Arts and Sciences.[24]

Times were to get worse before they got better. Only $1,000 had been
paid on the second installment to the Masonic Lodge, and in the spring
of 1837 their trustees presented the managers with a formal demand for
the remaining $19,000. The Institute did not have the money, and the
Board offered an equivalent amount in stock certificates of the six-
percent loan or interest in that amount on the balance of the installment.[25] Since the stock had not proved of great commercial interest, the
Masons took the second option, solving the Institute's most immediate
problem. The managers were faced with another due date at the beginning of 1838, however, and without further stock sales, there was little
chance of constructing new quarters. In successive reports, the managers
continued to hope that better times would allow for the development of
the Chestnut Street property. But the critical issue was the Institute's
own survival, not expansion, and 1837 marked the beginning of a long
and desperate struggle to keep the organization alive.

The Panic of 1837 and its ensuing depression was the nation's first
major economic calamity, and the Institute was almost as overextended
as the country's land speculators and railroad promoters when it came.

---

22 *Journal of the Franklin Institute* 21 (March 1836): 193.
23 Ibid., 21 (June 1836): 402.
24 Ibid., 22 (December 1836): 387.
25 Minutes of the Board of Managers, April 19, 1837. Sidney George Fisher attended a Wistar party in the spring of that year, and afterwards he noted in his
diary: "The universal topic of conversation is the present distress, & melancholy
prospects of the commercial community" (Nicholas B. Wainwright, ed., *A Philadelphia Perspective: The Diary of Sidney George Fisher, Covering the Years 1834–1871*
[Philadelphia: Historical Society of Pennsylvania, 1967], p. 27).

Everywhere prices dropped, as trade and manufacturing came nearly to a standstill. And before the depression was over in 1843, many states, including Pennsylvania, defaulted on the bonds which they had issued to finance canals and railroads. English investors had put $35 million in Pennsylvania's state-financed transportation system. Their losses caused Sydney Smith, editor of the *Edinburgh Review*, to remark that he never met a Pennsylvanian "without feeling a disposition to seize and divide him."[26] In Philadelphia the crisis struck other organizations, too. The American Philosophical Society had begun a new building project at the same time as the Institute. The city had promised to buy the society's property, but when the depression came the offer was withdrawn. Meanwhile, the society had purchased a new site, mortgaging its real property as well as its scientific, artistic, and library collections in expectation of the city's pledge. At one point the sheriff was actually about to foreclose on the library; and the American Philosophical Society was saved literally at the last moment.[27]

The Franklin Institute was almost as close to disaster, but it, too, was rescued by its members. Fraley and Merrick, in particular, were most active in steering the organization through a tortured labyrinth of loans, stock certificates, and interest payments. The six-percent loan of 1835 sold badly and brought in only a little over $22,000. The principal on that amount was not due until 1856, but other obligations loomed darkly ahead. In addition to the 1838 payment to the Masons, plus another in 1840, the principal on the Institute's 1825 loan was due in 1840. To meet those payments, the managers sought another loan of $50,000 in 1836, through the sale of scrip "in such sums as can be obtained."[28] The idea behind the new plan was to encourage wide subscription by making it possible for those of limited means to buy stock through accumulated purchases of scrip. The new loan would pay five percent interest, and the principal would be available on demand any time after 1847.

Somehow the idea backfired. The managers blamed an erroneous report in one of the city's newspapers, but from whatever cause, doubts of the Institute's solvency were widespread and created, as it was delicately put, "a hesitancy among mechanics" to take the new issue.[29] The Board immediately recalled the notes and scheduled a special meeting

26 Thomas C. Cochran and William Miller, *The Age of Enterprise: A Social History of Industrial America* (New York: Harper & Brothers, 1961), p. 48.

27 Scharf and Wescott, *History of Philadelphia, 1609–1884*, vol. 2, p. 1193. Part of the society's help came from the city, in the form of a $2,500 loan. See S. C. Walker to Edward Olmstead, Philadelphia, January 2, 1842, Gratz Collection, Historical Society of Pennsylvania.

28 Minutes of the Board of Managers, May 17, 1837.

29 Ibid., June 6, 1837.

of the Institute to squelch the rumors. Fraley presented a financial report to the members, who voted a resolution of "undiminished confidence" in the organization's abilities to meet its obligations and carry through the building project. They also authorized the Board to make whatever arrangements it wished with the city's banks to borrow money for the 1838 payment to the Masons.[30] At a subsequent Board meeting, however, Fraley was forced to report that the Institute had been denied bank credit for any large sums. In one last effort to gain public support, the Institute issued fractional currency—in amounts of one dollar, fifty cents, twenty-five cents, and twelve and a half cents—payable in one year with six percent interest. The first notes were circulated in May 1837; additional issues were made in July, August, and September, the total of which was over $11,000.[31] Some of the notes were redeemed early, but in any event, it was not enough. From that point on, the Institute was forced to rely on its own exertions.

Over the next two years, the Board of Managers fought a hard rearguard action, allocating income to buy time. The Masonic Lodge accepted a delay, at five percent, in payment of the 1838 installment of the purchase price, which gave some breathing room. Through persuasion with their creditors, temporary loans from banks and friends, rental income from both its properties, and by tapping reserves in the sinking fund, the managers were able to juggle a mounting load of interest payments.[32] Their sole hope was that an upturn in the business cycle would bring renewed sales of the 1835 loan. But the depression continued, and at the end of 1839, the Board faced yet another installment of $25,000 to the Grand Lodge.

By that time, there was nothing left to mortgage, and credit was exhausted. The only other course was to sell the Chestnut Street building and lot. Even that turned out badly. Throughout 1840 the property remained on the market without a buyer. The Masonic Lodge trustees grew increasingly anxious for a settlement and secured a judgment on the Institute's Seventh Street hall. But in January 1841, in exchange for a payment of $1,500 on interest charges, they gave the managers an

---

[30] Ibid., June 14, 1837.

[31] Ibid., December 20, 1837.

[32] Quarterly reports of the Board of Managers in April and October 1838 claimed that rental income from the Chestnut Street property was "more than sufficient" to cover interest payments and that when temporary "embarrassments" passed, construction would proceed. But the treasurer's annual statements show an increase in the expenditures on the new hall and a decline in sinking fund revenue. Moreover, many organizations and business firms had issued fractional currency, to the extra chaos of the state's commercial situation, and the governor had recommended their redemption, which created an additional drain on the Institute's fluid reserves. Minutes of the Board of Managers, July 18, 1838.

additional six months to find a solution.[33] Fraley borrowed the money
from the Bank of the United States, and the society thus gained a little
more time. But the game was nearly up. Short of bankruptcy, there was
really only one hope, namely, that the Masons might take their property
back.

Merrick and Fraley approached the Grand Lodge with a proposition
along those lines in September 1841. The essence of their proposal was
that the Chestnut Street property revert to the Masonic Lodge in exchange for the $85,500 yet unpaid on the purchase price. For interest still
due—almost $10,000—Fraley and Merrick offered a second mortgage on
the Institute's hall, plus six percent annually on the unpaid balance.[34]
In a letter to one of the Masonic trustees, Fraley described the Institute's
past efforts to meet its obligations. "Every Dollar" had been strictly
employed to extinguish its indebtedness. The society had stripped its
treasury, but it was still confronted with claims for which it was "entirely
out of the power of the Institute at this time to make any provision."
The organization's very existence was at stake, Fraley claimed. Even the
proposed settlement would strain its resources to the utmost degree, and
in the spirit of the Golden Rule, he urged the trustees to accept it.[35]

Bankruptcy had no charm for either party, and the Grand Lodge
finally agreed to the proposition. When the Institute's obligations were
itemized, the truth of Fraley's prediction became evident. The society
had lost the $25,000 paid toward the purchase of the Chestnut Street
property. Interest payments and related expenses had drained away
another $11,000. But even more disastrous were the obligations which
had been incurred. Including back interest still due to the Masons, the
principal on the 1835 loan, its current interest, the repayment of bank
and personal loans, and the settlement of taxes, the Institute was over
$34,000 in debt. The whole melancholy adventure had cost the society
more than $70,000, not counting future interest payments. On top of

[33] At a meeting of the Board of Managers on April 15, 1840, the decision to sell
the property was announced—approval had been given at a general meeting of the
Institute on January 2, 1840. The property was placed in the hands of Isaac Elliott,
who was authorized to sell "the whole or in lots—either on Ground rent or in full."
No purchasers having appeared by November, C. J. Wolbert, the auctioneer, took
over the selling job and with broadside posters advertised a public sale of the property, to be held at the Philadelphia Exchange on December 10, 1840. The Board
apparently changed their mind about an auction, perhaps in fear that no selling price
could be realized "without great loss," and another effort was made to borrow money.
Minutes of the Board of Managers, November 18, 1840; January 20, 1841; January 19,
1842.

[34] Frederick Fraley to Bayes Newcomb, Philadelphia, September 27, 1841, Committee on the New Hall, Franklin Institute Archives.

[35] Ibid.

that, there was still $23,000, at interest, owed to the holders of the 1825 loan. The final indignity came at the 1842 exhibition, when a burglar carried off almost $600 from ticket receipts and all the prize medals.[36]

As it had done before, the Board of Managers empaneled a committee to study the Institute's financial prospects and began the painful climb back. Expenses were trimmed, and appeals were made to members for stock donations and to creditors for patience. Until the yearly burden of interest payments could be lightened, it was impossible to meet fully all outstanding obligations. Fraley's strategy, as chairman of the Committee on Finance, was "to satisfy as many of the creditors as possible" promptly and quietly. At the same time, he squeezed money out of income to pay off the principal and thus reduce the interest. Previous experience had proved the efficiency of "a small fund steadily applied," Fraley claimed.[37] The best and most immediate help, however, came from those closest to the Institute's plight. The professors voluntarily gave up their salaries, which added $1,000 to the treasury. James Ronaldson's son presented $1,000 in 1825 stock certificates. Harry Ingersoll donated $750. Merrick and Fraley each relinquished their $500 investments in the 1835 stock and made personal loans as well. Isaac P. Morris, of the Port Richmond Iron Works, did the same. Lukens, Baldwin, Bache, and others also made temporary loans or gifts of stock.[38] Economy, generosity, and the nation's recovery from depression gradually brought better times to the Franklin Institute. There were still long-term obligations, but by 1847 the managers were themselves looking for ways to invest their surplus cash, and William Hamilton was once again able to hire someone to help him with administrative duties.

[36] A thorough review of the efforts to forestall bankruptcy, as well as the Institute's financial situation at the end of the affair, was presented at a meeting of the Board for January 19, 1842, the minutes of which contain the details. John F. Frazer described the robbery in a letter to his friend Samuel S. Haldeman: "We were 'victimized' the other night to the tune of $600. in the coolest way imaginable. Some chap under our very noses walking into the Actuary's room non obstante the door lock, smashing the money-drawer, and borrowing our funds to that amount, without leaving any satisfactory security for repayment. The Institute are buzzing like a nest of disturbed hornets, but cui bono—Swain [William M. Swain, publisher of the *Public Ledger* and a great enthusiast for the powers of electricity] has a woman who being magnetized can describe the thief (I beg his pardon—I mean the transfer-clerk) but who the devil can produce the funds" (Frazer to Haldeman, Philadelphia, October 25, 1842, Manuscript Collection 211, Academy of Natural Sciences, Philadelphia).
[37] Minutes of the Board of Managers, November 15, 1843; Nineteenth Annual Report of the Board of Managers, January 1843, Franklin Institute Archives.
[38] Fraley listed some of the contributors in his draft of the Board of Managers' quarterly report for April 1842. For others, see Minutes of the Board of Managers, June 21, August 16, November 15, 1843. The managers also used life memberships in exchange for the settlement of some debts, or as an inducement for the payment of back dues. Minutes of the Board of Managers, November 15, 1843.

Throughout the entire crisis, the Board of Managers never considered a retrenchment in the program. There were economies, but never of a sort to curtail activities. The *Journal* continued to show a deficit, but there was no talk of reducing or suspending publication. Instead, the Board reached out to new projects, increased existing ones, and looked for alliances with other societies to broaden its claim to the public's interest. Financial pressure revealed even more sharply how the Franklin Institute functioned and in what ways it was different from other Philadelphia societies. Early experience had shown that the Institute's prosperity was directly related to its public estimation. In part, the relationship involved abstract considerations—the distinction the organization brought to the city, the state, or the nation, for instance. Some support must also have come to the Institute simply on the basis that it served a worthwhile educational cause. Those closest to the society undoubtedly gave it their time and money out of basically altruistic convictions. But a more generally operative consideration for the mass of people who paid membership dues, suscribed to the *Journal*, bought lecture tickets, sent their sons to Institute schools, and paid to see exhibitions of industry was that they expected something for their money. In other words, the activities which provided an income also demanded a service. There was the essence of survival.

Without any kind of endowment to provide a permanent income, the Institute was continually compelled to seek financial support. In that sense, it was forced into the marketplace, and the Board of Managers was inevitably cast in an entrepreneurial role. They had to find consumers for the organization's products—which implied a constant search for new products and new consumers. Furthermore, the Institute's multiple objectives gave its leaders considerable latitude in their search and perhaps reinforced the tendency to look for various sources of support. It was as if the advancement of the mechanic arts constituted a central pole around which the program might swing, depending on the attraction from any given quarter.

In the early years, the managers capitalized on the zeal for educational reform, and they placed most emphasis on lectures and schools. Those activities obviously remained important, but the dynamic center of interest shifted to internal improvements and annual exhibitions of domestic industry. In turn, research and publication promised a new kind of vitality and displaced earlier concerns as the dominant element. These rapid and successive alterations in the Institute's focus reflected the necessity for flexibility in the marketplace, the need to identify those particular activities which promised extra momentum. With a considerable acuity to fluctuations in demand, the Board of Managers initiated programs that seemed promising, terminated them when interest declined, and inaugurated others which suggested a greater return. Obviously, it was not simply a case of debits and credits, nor of profit for its own sake. In fact, there were even advantages to the situation. It was a challenging, stimulating role for the Institute's leaders which encouraged creativity. And since the Board consciously equated organizational vitality with public service, the Institute was probably more responsive to changing social needs than many better-established institutions. The managers saw the financial problem in dual terms and customarily looked for projects which promised both incoming revenue and social utility.

Depression and crisis gave further urgency to the habitual way of doing things, and along with the fiscal measures which the Board employed, they sought salvation in a variety of new enterprises. The most ambitious was the School of Arts. At a special meeting of the managers on November 24, 1837, when the Institute's financial difficulties had become apparent, Samuel V. Merrick presented the plan for the school. It was "the most favourable time for extending the usefullness of the Institute," Merrick claimed, and in order to make the details of the plan clear, he read a memorial which he and "a few gentlemen who are actively engaged in promoting Instruction" had drafted.[39] Cast in the form of a petition to the state legislature, the memorial emphasized the Institute's experience in education and research and the particular facilities of Philadelphia for such a school. From the conduct of its own lectures and schools, the Board of Managers had come "precisely to understand what kind of practical and scientific training is most required." In addition, the petitioners reminded legislators that the Institute had "in several instances been selected by the Government of the U. States and of this state, to examine points of importance, requiring the application of scientific research."[40]

Merrick and his associates argued that the organization's past efforts should alone warrant support, but they aimed to present also a "captivating picture of what it may do with expanded resources." The proposed school would be simply a logical extension of the existing state-supported common schools, but at an "auspicious" time to produce more advanced graduates capable of efficient and economic management of mines, factories, and plans of internal improvements. The key ingredients of their plan were the research capabilities of the Institute

[39] Minutes of the Board of Managers, November 24, 1837.
[40] *For the Establishment of a School of Arts. Memorial of the Franklin Institute, of the State of Pennsylvania, for the Promotion of the Mechanic Arts, to the Legislature of Pennsylvania* (Philadelphia: J. Crissy, 1837), pp. 4–5.

and the practical instruction available from the city's workshops. The
combination, according to the memorial, had great potential:

It is not difficult to foresee that a school of practical instruction, so assisted
would, itself, very soon become the birth place of valuable discoveries in the
arts, so that the state, if in no other way, might look to the solid benefits thus
arising to its citizens as a tenfold compensation for all that the proposed School
of Arts can cost it.[41]

The Institute's managers enthusiastically approved the idea. Merrick
and ten other members were named a committee to present the memorial
at Harrisburg and to take whatever measures they thought necessary "to
invoke the aid of public opinion in favour of the plan."[42] The proposal
for a School of Arts was exactly the sort which in the past had brought
prestige and prosperity. It was grand enough in scale to attract attention, it identified a demonstrable need, and it appeared perfectly suited
to the Institute's purposes and abilities. Best of all, the idea promised
funding and a revived sense of mission. The prospects for success looked
very good at first. Nicholas Biddle chaired a town meeting highly favorable to the proposal, and a memorial from the citizens of the city was
forwarded to the legislature. City authorities appropriated land for the
school, and the governor supported the project in his annual message.[43]
Merrick went to Harrisburg with Philadelphia's representative, Charles
B. Trego, to give the measure a further push. But in March 1838, Merrick reported that a bill to establish the school had been passed by the
House of Representatives and had then lost on a subsequent vote of
reconsideration. Hopes were still entertained for a similar bill before
the state's senate, but in May it, too, was defeated.[44]

Failure to secure public funding was a bitter blow to the Institute,
and in their minutes the managers hinted darkly of foul play "too well
known to the members of the Board to need recapitulation."[45] They

[41] Ibid., p. 5.

[42] Minutes of the Board of Managers, November 24, 1837. The committee consisted
of Merrick, Keating, Hays, Baldwin, John Wiegand, John S. Warner, Alexander
Ferguson, J. M. Linnard, John C. Cresson, C. B. Trego, and Alexander McClurg.

[43] Memorial of the Committee Appointed at the Town Meeting of the Citizens of
the City and County of Philadelphia, Held January 4, 1838, Praying for the Establishment of a School of Arts (Harrisburg: Packer, Barbett and Parke, 1838); Minutes of the
Board of Managers, January 24, 1838.

[44] Minutes of the Board of Managers, December 30, 1837; January 24, March 21,
May 8, 1838.

[45] Ibid., May 8, 1838. John Wiegand, Chairman of the Board of Managers, reported: "It is with extreme regret that the Board inform the Institute of the failure
of the Bill before the legislature for the establishment of a School of Arts under the
special care and direction of the Institute. The establishment of such a School could
not fail to be of incalculable advantage to the State at large. From the zeal with

were convinced, however, that public opinion was in favor of the school
and that a future appeal to the legislature would be successful. It is clear
that the managers saw the school as an important measure for the Institute's vitality. Fraley, who knew the finances as well as anyone, argued
that the society should itself take on the school and use Masonic Hall to
house it. The Board shared his opinion unanimously and placed $3,000
at the disposal of a committee made up of Fraley, Merrick, Keating,
Baldwin, Patterson, Isaac Hays, and Henry D. Rogers.[46]

Nothing was done immediately. Public support was worth waiting
for, and past experience may have suggested prudence. As a result, the
committee took no action for the remainder of 1838. The next year
the proposal was again presented to the legislature, but by that time the
state's own financial position had become desperate, and the second
appeal was also denied. There were still some who felt the Institute
should go ahead with the idea, and the subject was transferred to the
Committee on Instruction. Its chairman in 1839 was Alexander Dallas
Bache, who had just returned from an extensive tour of European educational institutions. Technical schools were more expensive than any
other kind, Bache warned, and few of the established schools of Europe
were self-sufficient. It was not a question of their value, he said:

The time is probably not distant when the importance of such schools will be
fully admitted among us: if they are a benefit in Europe they are a necessity in
the United States, where Mechanics hold so important a place in the social
organization.[47]

Until such time as public support was available, however, Bache was
certain that any Institute attempt to establish the school would prove a
failure.

---

which his excellency the Governor recommended the measure and from the spirit
with which all classes of the Community urged it upon the legislature the most
favourable results were confidently anticipated. The defeat of this bill is referrible to
other causes than lack of merit in the object, these causes, we hope, will not operate
with the next legislature" (Board of Managers, Fifty-seventh Quarterly Report, April
19, 1838, Franklin Institute Archives).

[46] Minutes of the Board of Managers, May 8, 1838. The connection between the
School of Arts and the Institute's standing in the country was suggested in the report
of the Committee on Premiums and Exhibitions, following the exhibition in the fall
of 1838. The school, together with expansion of the Chestnut Street property, would
give the Institute the "means of maintaining the primary stand it now holds among
the promoters of public improvement." But without those aids, the committee
warned, "other cities will soon have that precedence which is now due to our own"
(*Report of the Committee on Premiums and Exhibitions of the Tenth Exhibition of
Domestic Manufactures held by the Franklin Institute* [Philadelphia: The Franklin
Institute, 1838], p. 24).

[47] Report of the Committee on Instruction, September 19, 1839; Minutes of the
Board of Managers, September 18, 1839.

If indeed it was not already dead, Bache's observations killed the School of Arts. But it was not the only project which the managers pursued in their efforts to discover new clients and new sources of income. Late in 1838, a group of civil engineers hoping to establish an "Institution of American Civil Engineers" approached the managers to learn if the Institute would provide a home for their idea. The concept of a professional identification for engineers was not new to the Board. Since 1836, a specific section of the *Journal* had been set aside for articles on civil engineering, in a conscious attempt to make the publication a vehicle for professional interests. The School of Arts was to have included civil engineering within its plan of instruction. Furthermore, many of the organizers of the proposed association—William Strickland, Samuel H. Kneass, and Solomon W. Roberts, among others—were well known in Philadelphia. The managers seized upon the query with "anxious desire," as they put it, to cooperate in any possible way. They offered the engineers "all the accomodations they may desire," William Hamilton's aid, the use of the *Journal* for their transactions, and any other "assistance, advice, or services that may be required."[48]

Affiliation with a national society of civil engineers appealed to the Board's conception of the Institute as serving national purposes. There were also other attractions, including a probable increase in *Journal* subscriptions and the chance of additional income for William Hamilton. The engineers met at the Institute in April 1839 and drafted a constitution which called for location there. Other provisions suggest that the engineers were willing to merge some administrative offices and perhaps to publish their proceedings in the *Journal*. But it was a stillborn project. The engineers were split by internal dissension. Only six of the seventeen who had been appointed to draw up the constitution actually came to Philadelphia, and their results were not ratified by the others. The basic problem was that engineers were not sufficiently unified by common interests to support a nationwide organization, and it was not until 1867 that the American Society of Civil Engineers was permanently established.[49]

The notion that the Institute might subdivide its troubles by association with other groups, however, appealed to the Board of Managers even at the beginning of the financial crisis. Early in 1837, when the

[48] Minutes of the Board of Managers, December 31, 1838; January 16, 1839. Correspondence between the Institute and the engineers, as well as the proceedings of their initial meeting in Baltimore, was published in the *Journal of the Franklin Institute* 27 (March 1839): 160–67.

[49] For an analysis of these early efforts at professional organization, see Daniel H. Calhoun, *The American Civil Engineer: Origins and Conflict* (Cambridge, Mass.: The M.I.T. Press, 1960), pp. 182–86.

managers were still trying to find a market for the Masonic Hall loan, they opened negotiations towards a merger with the Mechanics' and Tradesmen's Exchange Company of Philadelphia. The Exchange was looking for quarters in which its members might meet for reading, conversation, and the conduct of business affairs. The managers agreed to the use of the reading room for those purposes, on the condition that members of the Exchange become members of the Institute. Union brought thirty-one new members, and in what must have been an attempt to reassure prospective loan stock investors, the Board reported that "a large and valuable accession of strength" had accrued to the Institute "by connecting with it some of our most respectable tradesmen and mechanics, and giving an additional warrant for the perpetuity and succession of our association."[50]

With Philadelphia's Athenian Institute the managers tried another approach. The Athenian Institute sponsored lectures on various subjects, customarily held in Masonic Hall. In 1838 Merrick wrote to Thomas U. Walter, the architect, with a proposition designed to benefit both societies. A building would be constructed on the Chestnut Street frontage, much along the lines of the structure outlined for that part of the property in the 1835 plan. The Athenian Institute would pay for the costs of construction, in return for which it would receive all the rental income. The Franklin Institute would be allowed free use of the building's lecture room for its own lecture programs. At the end of twenty years, Merrick's organization would buy the building at its original cost less depreciation. Walters was to notify Merrick if the proposal was acceptable to the managers of the Athenian Institute, so that a special meeting of the Franklin Institute might be scheduled to ratify the action.[51] But the Athenians decided against the plan, and the Board of Managers was forced to continue the search for ideas which might bring relief.

One recurring thought at the Institute was that there was still an unsatisfied demand for a publication more popular, and with wider circulation than the *Journal*. The managers may have been pushed in that direction by John Libby's short-lived magazine, *The Mechanics' Register*, which he published in Philadelphia during 1837 and 1838. In any event, they saw a market which financial stringency made attractive. At a Board meeting in June 1839, the managers appointed a committee to consider the subject of an "annual, or almanac, suitable for me-

---

[50] *Journal of the Franklin Institute* 24 (December 1837): 413–14. See also Minutes of the Board of Managers, February 15, May 18, 1837; Board of Managers, Fifty-fourth Quarterly Report, July 1837.

[51] Minutes of the Board of Managers, March 21, 1838; S. V. Merrick to Thomas U. Walter, Philadelphia, March 5, 1838, MSS Collection, Library Company of Philadelphia.

chanics."[52] John C. Cresson, Hays, Merrick, Isaac Morris, and Bache
made up the committee, and Bache, who had moved the resolution, was
named chairman. The following September, Bache presented the committee's report, which called for the publication of a "Mechanics' & Engineers Pocket Book and Annual of the Franklin Institute." In his report
Bache described the committee's idea of its contents:

Such a work should contain in a portable form, a calendar with suitable
astronomical & miscellaneous information, relating to Science & the Arts, with
mathematical, mechanical, engineering, chemical, & other miscellaneous scientific tables, registers of the meetings of the Institute & of its committees, general
commercial & other matters, with occasional popular articles of a scientific, or
practical character.[53]

With the remarkable kind of perception which characterized so many
ideas at the Institute, Bache's committee acutely recognized the need for
an engineer's pocket book years before they came into wide usage. But
with an eye to the marketplace, they meant also to make it of interest
to artisans and merchants, as well as to members of the Institute. Since
the annual would be time-consuming and expensive to produce, and
since it could only return a profit in subsequent editions, Bache argued
it was essential that it be done well. Some of the plates could be reused,
and that economy together with a high volume of anticipated sales made
the annual an attractive proposition. The managers appointed the Institute's best minds to the project—Bache, Cresson, Hays, Merrick, Morris,
Walker, Patterson, Lukens, Booth, Fraley, and Joseph Saxton, who had
recently returned from London—and aimed for an 1841 publication
date. In 1839, it seemed wise to devote effort and time to the production
of the annual. However, as the Institute slid toward insolvency, delayed
income lost its appeal. By 1841, the annual had been abandoned, and
the managers only briefly considered a weekly newspaper to take its
place.[54]

In other times, almost any of the projects to which the managers
turned might have proved valuable and rewarding. Many were evolved
from a shrewd evaluation of the country's needs, but they depended on
someone else putting up the energy and money or at least failed to provide immediately helpful income. The most successful measures to
generate additional clientele came not from new schemes but out of the

52 Minutes of the Board of Managers, June 20, 1839. The full title of Libby's
periodical was *The Mechanics' Register, or, Journal of the Useful Arts, Trades, Manufactures, Science, &c., &c.* Vol. 1, no. 1, was issued on February 8, 1837, and the magazine was apparently ended with vol. 1, no. 16, in December 1838.
53 Minutes of the Board of Managers, September 18, 1839.
54 Ibid., February 17, 1841.

strengths which the organization already possessed. Even if only modest, an expanded lecture schedule and frequent exhibitions—the original sources of prosperity—proved to be the best help.

In the early 1830's, when the lecture program was slimmed down to a hard core of evening courses in natural philosophy, chemistry, and technology (Booth's term for applied chemistry), volunteer lectures were jettisoned as excess baggage. It was always troublesome to line up speakers, and the miscellaneous nature of the talks seemed antithetical to the image the Committee on Instruction had of the program. When hard times came, volunteer lectures were restored, in a clear effort to increase ticket sales. Difficult as it would have been for the Board to admit, the Institute's treasury was better served by a program which filled the hall with outsiders; members were admitted to lectures at no charge, but nonmembers paid a fee. The managers began to think about extra lectures in 1839, and in the following year they reported that two additional courses of lectures had been scheduled for the coming season, in geology and in architecture and the fine arts. Those two series, plus the regular lectures, would occupy five evenings a week. Furthermore, the Board anticipated occasional lectures for the sixth evening, "on various interesting topics."[55]

A broadened offering was presented in 1840, as planned. John F. Frazer, a University of Pennsylvania graduate, Bache protégé, and Henry D. Rogers's assistant on the state geological survey, delivered the series on geology. Thomas U. Walter, one of the drawing school's earliest pupils and later the architect of the nation's capitol building at Washington, gave the course on architecture. In addition, there were occasional talks by J. S. Silver on the anthracite-coal regions of Pennsylvania. By 1841, the managers had decided to formalize their policy. Frazer was named to a new Institute professorship in geology, and Walter was likewise made professor of architecture. While academic titles suggested intellectual tone, it was still necessary to pitch the content in a manner appealing to a mixed audience. What that meant is indicated by Frederick Fraley's description of Walter's course. The professor instructed his class, Fraley noted, "in a proper appreciation of the beautiful in Building, but likewise connected that knowledge with the expressive and high wrought poetry with which the grand but crumbling monuments of ancient skill have been commemorated."[56] While Walter excited a sense of the sublime, others volunteered talks of a more practical nature. Ellwood Morris, one of the promoters of the stillborn Insti-

[55] Board of Managers, Sixty-third Quarterly Report, October 16, 1839; Sixty-sixth Quarterly Report, July 1840.
[56] Seventeenth Annual Report of the Board of Managers, January 20, 1841.

tution of American Civil Engineers, delivered a course on civil engineering. Another, on the theory and practice of mining, was given by Theodore Moss.

Expansion of the lecture program in other directions was also under consideration. Natural history lectures had been dropped after 1826, but in 1840 Frazer wrote his friend Samuel S. Haldeman, who later gained fame as a scientist of many talents: "If you want employment, come fill up an evening in the week with a Zoological course before the Franklin Institute."[57] Haldeman was apparently occupied with his family's Lancaster County ironworks and thus gave only a few volunteer lectures in 1841. But in the following year he agreed to a regular course and was named professor of zoology. Charles B. Trego, who along with Bache and Frazer had pushed Haldeman's nomination, wrote of his election:

So this matter is finished & you are now, *de jure* and *de facto*, one of our Professors. I need not recommend to you zeal, diligence, and every exertion within your power to render your lectures worthy of yourself and of the Institute; for I feel sure that you have the disposition to do this. Do not forget that a certain kind of *ad captandum* eloquence and manner of treating a subject is necessary in order to secure the *vox populi* of the groundlings. All this you understand, and will doubtless succeed in winning golden opinions; though in a Professorship without a salary they are about the only golden material you are likely to gain for the present. The Institute is not financially in a condition which will at this time warrant any increase of expenditure.[58]

Trego's words caught the matter nicely. The managers wanted lectures which would reflect properly on the Institute's standing, but popular enough to sell tickets. And without funds for salaries, they were forced to call upon their friends.

The frequency of exhibitions was increased in the same way, by depending more heavily on voluntary labor. The about-face in exhibition policy demonstrates even more clearly that in time of need the managers were forced to return to proven ground. In line with the shift in emphasis toward exhibitions which had taken place in the earlier years, none was planned for 1837, even though a biennial system called for one. The decision had been made early in the year, without reference to any other events. But as the depression settled over the city and sales of stock in the Institute's loan lagged, the absence of an exhibition suggested to some a decline in the organization's vigor and perhaps its life expectancy. The Board of Managers became aware of that attitude, and

[57] John F. Frazer to Samuel S. Haldeman, Philadelphia, December 6, 1840, Manuscript Collection 73, Academy of Natural Sciences.
[58] Charles B. Trego to Samuel S. Haldeman, Philadelphia, September 23, 1842, ibid.

in their annual report at the end of the year they carefully explained their policy. From a state of infancy, the mechanic arts had matured to the point that they no longer needed the encouragement of annual fairs. The Institute had originated the exhibitions "with a view to the benefit of the community," the managers claimed, and they "should be continued no longer than the interests of the society require."[59] Furthermore, instead of a one- or two-year interval, the Board argued that exhibitions every four or five years would better suit the Institute's purposes and industry's needs.

But just as financial pressure shaped other activities, the policy toward exhibitions was completely altered. Exhibitions were held in 1838, 1840, and again in 1842, following what the Board in 1840 claimed was its "fixed policy." In fact, the Institute's leaders were moving toward a revision in thinking. The managers sent a delegation to visit fairs sponsored by the Mechanics' Institute and the American Institute in New York in 1838, as well as one put on by the Massachusetts Charitable Mechanics' Association in Boston. Bache noted the point of such excursions in his draft of the managers' quarterly report in October: "The impression made by these visits is calculated to stimulate our own exertions in future exhibitions of the same kind."[60] The Institute's leaders were not concerned about competition or the possibility that other exhibitions might somehow detract from their own efforts; instead, it became apparent that industrial fairs were more popular than ever, and that they were profitable.

For the Institute, the 1842 exhibition proved the turning point. The only bright spot in its financial picture that year was that the exhibition resulted in a profit of over $1,300, even after the robbery. That was more than twice as much income as the previous exhibition had returned, and clearly it called for a new look at the issue of a biennial schedule. In their own report to the managers, the Committee on Premiums and Exhibitions put the matter plainly: "The embarrassed state of the Treasury presents the question of annual exhibitions in a new light which should have the early and earnest consideration of the Board of Managers."[61] There is no indication that lengthy deliberations were required, and in 1842 the Institute returned to annual exhibitions. Nor was it a quiet change, in submission to inexorable pressures. The managers em-

[59] Fourteenth Annual Report of the Board of Managers, January 18, 1838, also published in the *Journal of the Franklin Institute* 25 (February 1838): 104–6.
[60] *Address of the Committee on Premiums and Exhibitions*, 1840, p. 1; Board of Managers, Sixty-third Quarterly Report, October 16, 1839; see also *Journal of the Franklin Institute* 27 (August 1839): 143, for notices of fairs in Boston and New York.
[61] Minutes of the Board of Managers, November 16, 1842.

braced the new schedule eagerly. After the 1840 exhibition, fairs lasted
two weeks, concluding with a public ceremony featuring an address by
one of the Institute's prominent members. Frederick Fraley delivered the
first, on the connection between commerce and the mechanic arts, and
Alexander Dallas Bache gave the second.

For his speech at the 1842 exhibition, Bache drew upon his knowledge of European educational facilities. He sketched the accomplishments of Europe's endowed institutions, despite the limitations of
authoritarian governments, and the advance of English industry, notwithstanding the scanty educational opportunities of its artisans. As in
Britain, American institutions had developed along voluntary lines. The
Franklin Institute, Bache suggested, was an example of how much could
be attained by such associations. Only a national depression had checked
its career of usefulness, and "had the tide continued to rise, instead of
beginning to fall, we might have passed the shoal." Time would restore
the Institute, Bache claimed, but its own experience raised a fundamental issue. While the society labored for the common good, it was
supported by the efforts of only a few. No one believed any longer in
supporting a fire department by voluntary contributions, he said, and
then drew his parallel: *"Shall the principle be that what is for the good
of the whole, shall be supported by the whole?"* If education was to be
on a *"truly republican"* basis, no other conclusion was logical, and Bache
included all of Philadelphia's societies for promoting knowledge within
his definition of education. Diverse in their interests, all aimed to benefit the whole community, and they included in their membership all
classes of society. In that respect, the city's institutions were like the
federal union, and Bache urged Philadelphians to join them together in
*"a great system of public instruction, worthy the patronage and support
of a free and enlightened people."*[62]

Organized and tax-supported education, with provision for scientific
research was one of Bache's favorite concerns, and it continued to occupy
his mind in later years. But his experience at the Franklin Institute had
also given him a clear insight into the problems of voluntary educational
societies. They essentially depended on a small core of individuals to
sustain them. There were exceptions. The Academy of Natural Sciences
in Philadelphia enjoyed William Maclure's generosity and subsequent
donations from other wealthy members. But most institutions, including
the American Philosophical Society, could count on active support from
only a few members.

[62] *Address by Professor Bache, before the Franklin Institute, October, 1842*
(Philadelphia, 1842).

The Institute was different from other Philadelphia societies, however, and in some critical respects. To begin with, the Institute sought to serve a larger clientele. While the memberships of the Academy and the Philosophical Society each numbered about 300, only a portion of which lived in the city, the Institute's membership had climbed to 2,500 by 1839.[63] Moreover, the organization related to its membership in a different way. Although there were social implications to membership in the two other societies, the ostensible connection between member and society was a shared love of science. The affiliation might include a zeal to elevate the condition of American science and its practitioners, but it did not involve any kind of popular educational programs, exhibitions of science, or any of the other activities which formed the bond between the Franklin Institute and its members. There was another important difference. The Academy and the Philosophical Society never had egalitarian pretensions. The Franklin Institute, on the other hand, liked to think of itself as "a democratic learned society."[64] Because the Institute was oriented toward a larger public, it was forced to seek support for a broad and more expensive program. That need cast the Board of Managers into the marketplace.

Their own particular marketplace had inherent weaknesses, however. The areas in which the Institute operated—popular education, the promotion of manufactures and internal improvements, technical publication, and scientific research—were not financially profitable on a long-term basis. Mass education ultimately demanded tax support; science needed either public funds or private endowment; research and publication for industry and transportation companies returned scant income; and except for exhibition-gate receipts, the promotion of manufacturing had limited value as an issue of wide public concern. These areas had short-term potential for the Institute, and it served as a catalyst in clarifying issues worthy of support. It is a reflection on the innovative talents of the Institute's early leaders that so many of their ideas were brought into being. For the organization itself, however, the continuing demand was for creative leadership and the need to discover new sources of support and vitality.

[63] Fifteenth Annual Report of the Board of Managers, January 16, 1839.

[64] In his remarks at the celebration of the Institute's fiftieth anniversary, Coleman Sellers noted: "Our Franklin Institute was from the beginning a Mechanics' Institute, in one sense of the word. It taught by lectures, and sometimes by classes, but it was always more than was contemplated by the societies abroad. If I may express myself, it was, and still is, a democratic learned society; it is not exclusive." *Commemorative Exercises at the Fiftieth Anniversary of the Franklin Institute of the State of Pennsylvania for the Promotion of the Mechanic Arts* (Philadelphia: The Franklin Institute, 1874), p. 86.

X

IN SEARCH
OF A MISSION

Like all other institutions it
has had its day of novelty. . . .

Samuel V. Merrick, April 21, 1847

One of the Institute's strengths during the dark days of financial distress
was a sense of preeminence. In their most sanguine moments, its friends
and supporters envisioned the organization as the creative leader of
America's scientific and technical societies, destined to reflect "an exalted
idea of national greatness."[1] Even though fiscal misfortune had a
chastening effect on their optimism, the Board of Managers were still of
the conviction that theirs was the country's premier mechanics' institute,
with a special obligation to speak for all others in matters of general
interest to the mechanic arts. At the same time, experimental research
and cooperative work on scientific problems of wide concern gave the
managers a feeling of community with the nation's established and
prestigious scientific societies. In an era of nonspecialization, the Franklin Institute had become a general society *par excellence*. No other institution had so successfully mounted a program of such broad appeal,
encompassing the diverse interests of scientists and manufacturers, artisans and engineers, amateurs and professionals.

And yet, by the 1840's the organization faced a difficult situation. It
no longer occupied the unique position of earlier days. Other institutions were rising, especially within scientific fields, to claim professional
leadership and whatever support for research public funds might provide. The establishment of the American Association for the Advancement of Science, for instance, created a society more truly national in
scope, while the foundation of the Smithsonian Institution brought to
life an agency better equipped to support original research. Simply by
their existence, these two organizations raised important issues for the
future of the Franklin Institute.

[1] "Fifty-first Quarterly Report of the Board of Managers of the Franklin Institute," *Journal of the Franklin Institute* 22 (December 1836): 387.

One of the most important questions was whether government support would still be available for ongoing research interests. The meteorological observations were a case in point. The Institute had used state funds to mount an ambitious program. Standard sets of instruments were purchased; the barometers were carefully calibrated and compared to the standards of London and Paris observatories, with variations reduced to less than a hundredth of an inch; and instruments and printed reporting forms were then forwarded to observers throughout the state.[2] Volunteers were never found for some counties, and observations were not always consistently made in others. Charles B. Trego used the weight of his legislative position in Harrisburg to urge regular reporting from observers and acted as an intermediary for William Hamilton to keep them supplied with blank forms. Some instruments were lost, some were broken, and some puzzled their users. "I should be much obliged," one wrote, "for a brief explanation of the principles of the self registering thermometer."[3] William McLeod, the volunteer observer for Westmoreland County, had a different problem. He was prepared to begin observations, when the County Commissioners claimed authority for the project. "The Instruments are ours, unrestrictedly so," they argued, and they threatened suit when McLeod refused to hand them over.[4] Those were irksome details, but in fact, the project was a considerable success. Most observers felt a keen sense of participation in the "Cause of Science," often repairing instruments at their own expense and regularly forwarding their monthly reports to William Hamilton for collation and publication in the *Journal*.

Meteorology had been one of the favorite sciences of the "Young Institute." In 1842, however, the issue for the Board of Managers was whether or not to use its own money to continue the enterprise. With a nicety appropriate to present-day grant practices, all but $1.36 of the original $4,000 had been spent. When the Committee on Meteorology reported that only a small amount would be needed—for postage and blank forms—to maintain the project, the managers decided to continue. In Harrisburg, Trego managed to tack an amendment on the 1843 general appropriations bill, which gave the Institute another $300 for operating expenses over the course of the next decade. But if the Society was to do more than gather facts, if it was to reduce the mass of data

    [2] The Minutes of the Board of Managers for September 21, 1842, in the Franklin Institute Archives, contain a good summary of the meteorological project.
    [3] Wm. H. Johnson to Wm. Hamilton, Buckingham, February 1, 1844, Committee on Meteorology, Franklin Institute Archives. The same file also contains letters from other observers on equipment and the proper maintenance of weather records.
    [4] Report of the Committee on Meteorology, May 17, 1840, Franklin Institute Archives.

collected to some meaningful form, money was necessary. In 1859, the Institute appealed to the legislature for $2,500 in order to organize and publish the results of its work since 1839.[5] The appeal was apparently unsuccessful, and the Institute lost the opportunity to translate its efforts into a project of enduring vitality. Furthermore, during those two decades the national center of gravity in meteorological research shifted to Washington. Joseph Henry's ability to provide financial support for the analysis of data made the Smithsonian a natural focal point for meteorology, and he gradually pulled together the various programs of federal and state agencies, including the Institute's network, to form a nationwide system of weather observation and reporting.

The shift was symptomatic of the Institute's own changing position. Its meteorological investigations had demonstrated the value of simultaneous observations from a number of geographically scattered points. As the committee pointed out in its 1842 summation:

The information thus obtained is intimately connected with the Natural History of Pennsylvania, and along with the results of the Geological Survey now in progress, are calculated to reflect great credit upon the Commonwealth.[6]

The next logical stage of development was to expand geographic coverage and to centralize the analysis of data. While Joseph Henry's scientific interests included meteorology, his concern with the subject was more than personal. Meteorology fit the description of the work he thought the Smithsonian ought to do. In his mind, one of the institution's primary functions was to support scientific research, particularly that which could be defined clearly in terms of its aims and value. The example Henry had originally used to describe that kind of research was the Institute's steam-boiler investigation.[7] Meteorology fell into the same

<hr>

[5] A financial statement of the committee's disbursements is included in the Minutes of the Board of Managers, September 21, 1842. Trego wrote to Hamilton, after having scolded him for being late in sending results of the meteorological observations for his use in the legislature: "As an antidote to the croaking and complaining of my last letter, I now have the pleasure of informing you that on yesterday I succeeded in attaching an amendment to a section of the general 'Appropriation Bill' which grants $300 for the use of the meteorological observations. I have taken some pains to have the affair properly understood in the Senate, so that they may not strike it off" (Charles B. Trego to William Hamilton, Harrisburg, April 16, 1843, Committee on Meteorology). See the Minutes of the Board of Managers, December 15, 1859, and December 12, 1860, for further appeals to the legislature.

[6] Minutes of the Board of Managers, September 21, 1842. The managers had themselves argued for a nationwide program of meteorological observations, and they joined with the American Philosophical Society and the American Academy of Arts and Sciences in a petition for federal support. Minutes of Meetings, March 19, 1846, Franklin Institute Archives.

[7] W. J. Rhees, ed., *The Smithsonian Institution: Documents Relative to its Origin and History* (Washington, D.C.: Smithsonian Institution, 1879), p. 955.

category. The Smithsonian's income was slender, but by a continuous struggle to prevent its dissipation in other pursuits, Henry was able to finance scientific research. The Institute's leaders were unable to support their own program, however; and without state aid meteorological observations dwindled to an essentially local concern, conducted with a few remaining instruments on the roof of the hall.

Other research subjects of longstanding interest at the Institute also suffered from a decline in government patronage. The steam-boiler investigation had been a signal triumph for the organization, suggesting both past accomplishment and future potential. A dreadful disaster on board the *U.S.S. Princeton* in 1844 seemed to indicate that the Institute might still play the role of science advisor to the central government. The *U.S.S. Princeton*, which had been under construction at the Philadelphia Navy Yard from 1841 to 1843, incorporated several advances in naval technology. The engines, manufactured by Samuel V. Merrick and his partner John H. Towne at their Southwark Foundry, were designed to burn anthracite coal and employed a new kind of forced-draft boiler. Power was applied directly to the drive shaft; John Ericsson's new screw propellers were used, in their first application to a military ship; and all the machinery was located below the water line, out of reach of enemy shot. When completed, her captain, Robert F. Stockton, boasted that the ship was "the fastest sea going steamer in the world."[8] In addition, the *U.S.S. Princeton* featured a formidable battery of ordnance, also novel in design and construction. On the premise that a larger and stronger gun could be made of wrought iron—in place of the traditional cast-iron cannon—Stockton ordered a twelve-inch gun to be fabricated from bars of wrought iron welded together to form barrel and breech. Stockton's new weapon, the largest in the world, was dubbed the "Peacemaker." It promised great destructive potential because of its size, and great accuracy, since it also employed new fire-control mechanisms.

Altogether, the *U.S.S. Princeton* presaged a new era in naval construction and a technologically superior American Navy. Stockton had visions of a fleet of ships of his improved designs, and he used sea trials of the *Princeton* to publicize himself and his ideas. The culmination of his efforts came in February 1844, in an excursion to demonstrate the ship and its armament to high-ranking officials. Those on board for the occasion included President Tyler and his fiancée, the secretaries of

---

[8] Lee M. Pearson, "The *Princeton* and the 'Peacemaker': A Study in Nineteenth-Century Naval Research and Development Procedures," *Technology and Culture* 7 (Spring 1966): 173.

state and of the Navy, and a crowd of 300, including government officials, their wives, foreign ministers, and other prominent figures. It was a festive voyage, and Stockton counted on its effect to still any Congressional opposition to a new naval construction program. But on the third firing, the "Peacemaker" exploded, killing both Cabinet members, the chief of the Navy's Bureau of Construction, and three others.

The disaster obviously called for investigation, but as a recent student of the affair has pointed out, construction of the *Princeton* and the "Peacemaker" had been surrounded by political implications, personal ambitions, and confused lines of authority from the beginning.[9] In the wake of disaster the principal concern of many was to disassociate themselves from the calamity. But Stockton's ambitions and reputation were at stake, and he requested that a formal investigation be made by the Franklin Institute. The Committee on Science and the Arts appointed a subcommittee to conduct the inquiry, comprising Joseph Henry, Cresson, Merrick, Frazer, Patterson, John Agnew, S. W. Roberts, and John H. Towne. Because the committee lacked the legal power necessary to secure testimony on the methods of proving and firing the weapon, it restricted itself solely to an investigation of "the material and workmanship of the gun."[10]

Committee members studied details of the explosion and fragments of the cannon. Samples were cut for analysis on the Institute's materials-testing machine, and an additional set was carried to Boston for testing on a machine there. To learn the history of the gun's manufacture, the committee also addressed a series of questions to Ward & Company of New York, whose Hamersley Forge had produced the weapon. As a further basis for its inquiry, the committee had Walter R. Johnson's earlier report, which had established average tensile values for "good American iron." Samples from fragments and from that part of the gun which still remained on the *Princeton*'s foredeck were tested for tensile strength and subjected as well to several weeks of destructive testing that involved extremes of temperature variation and constant vibration.[11]

As a result of its analysis, the committee arrived at four conclusions.

9 Ibid., pp. 163–83.

10 "Report on the Explosion of the Gun on board the Steam Frigate 'Princeton,'" *Journal of the Franklin Institute* 38 (September 1844): 206.

11 The questionnaire sent to Ward & Co. was reprinted in the report of the Committee on Science and the Arts just cited. The destructive tests grew generally out of an interest in "the effect produced in a mass of iron by long heating, without cooling —by heating and cooling alternately—by subjecting the metal for several weeks to a constant vibration, &c." But the limits of the investigation, and probably a lack of funds, ended those experiments before any conclusive results were achieved. Ibid., p. 215.

First, the raw material, if properly worked, was capable of sufficient strength. Second, the iron had not, in fact, been adequately processed. Third, "as the metal existed in the gun it was, decidedly, bad." Finally, the manufacture of the gun itself was faulty. It was impossible, the committee claimed, to weld such a large mass of iron to the required degree of uniformity, and furthermore, welding required intense and prolonged heating, which drastically impaired strength. In the case of samples which they tested, the committee discovered that tensile strength had been reduced by half. As a result of those facts, the committee concluded: "In the present state of the arts, the use of wrought-iron guns of large calibre, made upon the same plan as the gun now under examination, ought to be abandoned."[12]

While the *U.S.S. Princeton* inquiry utilized the apparatus and results from the steam-boiler investigation, it differed from that earlier research in important respects. To begin with, it was carried out by the Committee on Science and the Arts, which Bache made the Institute's scientific arm, responsible both for the previous duties of the Committee on Inventions and for whatever new inquiries it wished to initiate itself. When he organized the committee in 1834, Bache conceived a largely autonomous body which would by its own initiative and energy sustain the major scientific work of the organization. But autonomy and confidentiality were critical, and thus the committee was usually removed from the ongoing life of the Institute, with a momentum much of its own. The investigation also differed from earlier research in the respect that it was conducted at the request of an individual rather than a government department, without the mandate for a complete investigation into all facets of the subject. Finally, despite the importance of the study, there were no federal funds to support the research.

Still, the *Princeton* disaster raised again the question of science and public policy, an issue of continuing relevance for steam-boiler explosions, too. Congressional timorousness had forestalled the opportunity to eliminate that problem; in fact, an increasing number of locomotive accidents only swelled the casualty lists. The Committee on Science and the Arts called attention to this troublesome problem in 1845, in a fashion which suggested another line of attack for the Institute, but this time in cooperation with the state government. Two fatal explosions that year—one in a locally built railroad locomotive and the other on board a Delaware River steamboat—were used by the committee to argue for a complete revision in the American procedure of conducting coroner's inquests. In Great Britain, the committee claimed, inquests

12 Ibid.

involved a thorough examination into the cause of death. Testimony was patiently collected, scientific opinion called into judgment, and the public fully informed. The results were definitive, and guilt or innocence was squarely assigned. In America, they said, the opposite was true:

It is needless to remark how different the system is in this country; how deplorable the remissness of juries, and the apathy of an injured, a defenceless, but too patient, and long suffering public, whom the newspapers almost invariably endeavor to assure that no blame can possibly be attributed to any of the parties concerned.[13]

From the Committee on Science and the Arts, the question was taken up by the Institute at large. Ellwood Morris addressed a meeting of the organization on the subject, presenting a set of resolutions to be sent to Trego for legislative enactment in Harrisburg. Morris reminded the legislators that the Franklin Institute had carried out extensive research in steam-boiler problems and that it had subsequently examined most of the explosions which had occurred in the vicinity of Philadelphia. The aim had been to discover means for preventing such accidents, Morris said, which called for further research. Coroner's inquests, which might properly be the source of valuable information, "are usually conducted with a carelessness which exceeds belief, and leave no trace behind them, except a verdict of *accidental death* when in many cases the most culpable negligence has existed."[14] To remedy the evil, Morris proposed that coroners be required to call before inquests "the nearest scientific and practical men"; that the causes of explosion be "minutely" examined; that the results of inquests be published in one Philadelphia newspaper, as well as in the local paper of the town in which the accident occurred; and finally, that coroners be directed to furnish the Institute with a printed record of the inquest.[15]

The legislature never acted on the Institute's proposal—it was perhaps naive to expect political appointees to yield power voluntarily. But the Board of Managers had intuitively perceived an important avenue to organizational viability. If the Institute were made an integral part of coroner's inquests in all boiler explosions, whether on land or

---

[13] "Address delivered by Frederick Fraley, ESQ., at the close of the Fourteenth Exhibition of American Manufactures held by the Franklin Institute of the State of Pennsylvania, for the Promotion of the Mechanic Arts, October 1844," *Journal of the Franklin Institute* 39 (January 1845): 34.

[14] Minutes of Meetings, January 16, 1845.

[15] Ibid.

water, it would have a significant and legitimate claim on public support. Furthermore, assignment of responsibility was but a step away from regulatory power—the essence of sustained income and authority, as later generations of government scientists were to discover.

The approach was the sort Bache would have hit upon. He had schooled the Institute in the ways science might be connected to large public interests. His influence is particularly evident in the work of the Committee on Science and the Arts, which consistently attempted to relate its investigations to national problems in science and technology. From the outset, the Committee on Science and the Arts took Bache's broad view of its mandate.[16] The first published report—on a telescope made by Amasa Holcomb, of Southwick, Massachusetts—led ultimately to a consideration of issues central to "the advancement of astronomical science in this country." Holcomb, a self-taught instrumentmaker, brought a six-foot reflecting telescope to Philadelphia for the committee's examination. Bache borrowed the University's telescope and two which were privately owned, and a comparative test was held on an open lot near the Pennsylvania Hospital. Holcomb's telescope bore favorable comparison with the others, but particularly noteworthy was his selling price, which was less than half the cost of imported instruments of equal performance.[17]

In three subsequent reports on improved models of Holcomb telescopes, the committee expanded the point. Published star catalogs allowed the investigators to compare Holcomb's telescopes with "the chefs d'oeuvre of British and German genius." The results demonstrated that "what the best telescopes in Europe can do upon stars distant 0".6., can be done upon stars distant 1".4., by instruments which are the work of

[16] The best source for the incredible variety of the more than 1,500 committee reports during the course of the nineteenth century is Percy A. Bivins, *Index to the Reports of the Committee on Science and the Arts of the Franklin Institute of the State of Pennsylvania, 1834–1890* (Philadelphia: The Franklin Institute, 1890). Most of the dramatic inventions of the period were examined by the committee, but more important, Bivins's *Index* reveals the extent to which technical advance depends rather upon a multitude of small improvements in technique.

[17] "Report on Amasa Holcomb's Reflecting Telescope," *Journal of the Franklin Institute* 18 (September 1834): 169–72. To preserve objectivity, committee members remained anonymous, and their published reports were issued over William Hamilton's name. In an autobiographical sketch written late in his life, Holcomb recalled that the committee consisted of "Mr. Patterson of the Mint, Alexander D. Bache superintendent of the Coast Survey, Dr. Robert Hare the chemist, James P. Espy, Sears C. Walker, Isiah T. Lukens and some others. These were among the first scientific men of America" (Robert P. Multhauf, "Holcomb, Fitz, and Peate: Three 19th-Century American Telescope Makers," *Contributions from the Museum of History and Technology* [Washington, D.C.: Smithsonian Institution, 1962], p. 163).

an unassisted, and almost neglected, American optician."[18] Given the progress which Holcomb had already shown, the committee confidently predicted that he would soon be able to equal the best European makers. However, the committee argued, Holcomb needed the patronage of those who customarily looked abroad for superior workmanship, and they noted:

The committee have been led to enlarge upon this subject, from a knowledge that one of our national institutions has, within a few years, imported into the country, at an expense of $2,500, a telescope which, though excellent in its kind, is inferior to that exhibited by Mr. Holcomb.[19]

The Holcomb reports constituted only one example of the committee's policy to address itself to major issues in the advancement of American science and technology. A report on the Coast Survey in 1849 was an even more direct effort to argue the case for scientific research and its application. Bache's organization was at that time under Congressional attack, and the committee framed a careful defense of science. They chose to emphasize three essential points—practical benefit, economy of operation, and "perfection" of organization.[20] The Coast Survey provided the useful information upon which a commercial nation depended, both by refining existing knowledge of the country's coastlines and by providing new information on hazards to navigation. Furthermore, the committee claimed, Bache's operations were conducted with an economy at least as great as that of surveying public lands, "while the results are much more to be relied on." Additional economy stemmed from the fact that land points fixed by the Coast Survey could be used by other levels of government, by triangulation, to solve their own measurement problems. Finally, the committee lauded the Survey's administration. Through a judicious employment of army and navy officers, as well as civilians, the talents of each were efficiently and harmoniously fused. Cooperation with schools and colleges also gave young men field training in important skills. The total result was "a great national scientific school" which made the U.S. Coast Survey the equal of any in the world.[21]

18 "Report on Holcomb's Reflecting Telescopes," *Journal of the Franklin Institute* 20 (July 1835): 13. The report is reprinted in Multhauf, "Holcomb, Fitz, and Peate." Two additional reports, on a telescope made for Newark College in Delaware, were published in volume 22 of the *Journal*, in the August and November issues.

19 Ibid.

20 "Report on the Survey of the Coast of the United States," *Journal of the Franklin Institute* 47 (March 1849): 209–14.

21 Ibid., p. 213.

The committee's defense of scientific research and the importance of America's scientific standing was also a lesson learned from Bache. From his earliest days in the Institute, Bache had argued for professionalism and high standards of research. His views found expression in the "club" which he, Joseph Henry, Sears C. Walker, Espy, and Henry D. Rogers had formed in the 1830's and in the United Bowmen "Toxies" of the following decade. In the 1840's the United Bowmen also shared membership in another Philadelphia clique, amorphous in form but with the same attitudes toward science. "Clique" was the word they used themselves. "Most affectionate regards to the clique!" Bache wrote John F. Frazer in 1851. "Tell Merrick that we must have been in Charleston within a day of each other."[22] The clique had no formal organizational structure; in many repects it was basically a local group. But by the late 1840's Bache had drawn some of its members into a movement for a national scientific establishment, supported by public funds, which would advise the government and would serve as a standard of excellence for American science. To push his ideas, Bache forged an alliance of government scientists in Washington, members of the Philadelphia clique, and faculty members at Harvard—who met together at meetings of the American Association for the Advancement of Science.

The American Association originated as the Association of American Geologists at a meeting at the Franklin Institute in 1840. The idea for the organization came primarily from Henry D. Rogers and others engaged in state geological surveys, and almost half of its founders were Institute men.[23] Two years later, the name was changed to the American Association of Geologists and Naturalists. Then in 1848, the final transition to a national scientific organization was made, and the newly styled American Association for the Advancement of Science held its first meeting, again, in Philadelphia. Bache and his group—which by that time included Louis Agassiz, the astronomer Benjamin Apthorp Gould, Harvard mathematician Benjamin Pierce, and, as always, Joseph Henry— soon saw the Association as a vehicle for influencing national scientific policies and eliminating amateurism in American science. Their aims

[22] A. D. Bache to J. F. Frazer, Washington, April 28, 1851. For an earlier mention of the clique, see Bache to Frazer, June 23, 1849. Both letters are in the Frazer Papers, American Philosophical Society. In an autobiographical sketch, Merrick's son John Vaughan Merrick recalled, "A. D. Bache, Fred'k Fraley, John F. Frazer, John Wiegand and my father were most intimate friends and constituted themselves a junto who met weekly at each other's houses. (A cocoanut sugar bowl in my possession was used by them; it is inscribed FIK for *Franklin Institute Clique* and was given to me by Mr. Fraley a few years ago)" (Mary Williams Brinton, *Their Lives and Mine* [Philadelphia: privately printed, 1973], p. 23).

[23] Joseph S. Hepburn, "Founding of Association of American Geologists," *Science* 129 (June 1959): 1750.

were pointedly expressed in a letter Agassiz wrote to Frazer prior to the Association's 1851 meeting: "Are you not going to Albany? Consider that if those who can raise the platform of science in this country will stay away deliberately, the humbug will take the stump & carry the day after all."[24]

Frazer was not fond of the Association meetings. He apparently suggested an alternative at one time, for Gould later reminded him:

Do you remember in one of our chronic fights of opinion about the "Am. Ass. Adv. Sci." (which does not signify Amazing Asses Adverse to Science) you broached an idea that more could be done by one good feed with decent fellows, than by an immensity of public howling.[25]

It had been done, Gould claimed, with Bache as "dictator." The group was to consist of nine men, but with no name, no officers, "no nothing except one good great happy annual winter feed." In fact, there was a name. They called themselves the Lazzaroni, and their search for a powerful scientific establishment ultimately led to the formation of the National Academy of Sciences.[26]

With all his connections to the city, Bache remained the critical link between the Philadelphia clique and America's scientific community. And his own program for the advancement of science carried a strong echo of his past experience in the Franklin Institute. Bache outlined the most pressing needs of American science in his address to the American Association for the Advancement of Science in 1851. As he had done in his speech at the closing of the Institute's exhibition a decade earlier, Bache argued that benefits to the community at large called for support from the entire community. Through governmental subvention, science could progress in America, with important practical results to repay "many times" the cost of such support. The examples he drew upon were familiar, too. A start had been made in meteorology, he claimed, but federal funding would be necessary to assemble more data, from which lasting principles could be derived. Bache also reiterated his 1836 argument to the secretary of the treasury, with reference to the steam-boiler investigation. The limits of those researches had been financial, he recalled, whereas in France scientists had been paid for similar labors. In Bache's mind, what

24 L. Agassiz to J. F. Frazer, Cambridge, August 7, 1851, Frazer Papers.

25 B. A. Gould to J. F. Frazer, Cambridge, November 22, 1856, ibid.

26 Ibid. As early as 1860, Agassiz argued to Maryland's Senator James Pearce the need for a "National Academy of Sciences" to examine critically "what is really worthy of publication, instead of allowing undigested performances to be printed at full length" (Louis Agassiz to the Hon. James Pearce, Cambridge, May 18, 1860, Miscellaneous Letters, Franklin Institute Archives).

America needed was a government-financed professional establishment of science in which specialists could pursue knowledge to logical conclusions and ultimate benefit.[27]

As Bache's ideas on the institutional needs of science in America developed, their relevance to the Franklin Institute changed. His scientific values had been tremendously important to the organization in the 1830's, and their influence continued in succeeding decades. During the 1840's and 1850's, however, Bache's model for the society failed to solve its real problems. Perhaps the greatest gap between ambition and actuality lay in the fact that the Institute could not directly finance the research of scientific professionals. Espy had gained $1,000 a year for his salary as meteorologist in the state-supported program which the Institute conducted. But otherwise the organization had been able to provide only modest and tangential aid to men who wanted a career in science. As a result, many of those who comprised what Bache once called "the Young Institute," the men who had given it prominence, were forced to seek their fortunes elsewhere.[28] Walter R. Johnson left in 1837, expecting to sail the Pacific Ocean. Espy moved to Washington in 1839, in search of an even larger corps of meteorological observers and federal subvention. Sears C. Walker, actuary in a local insurance company, exercised his interests in astronomy at the Institute and at Central High School, where he helped establish one of America's first observatories. But in pursuit of a scientific career, he went to the Naval Observatory in Washington, until 1847, when he joined the Coast Survey.[29]

Bache's relationship to the Institute also changed. In the summer of 1836, he was appointed president of Girard College, a new institution to be established in Philadelphia through the munificence of Stephen Girard.[30] That fall, Bache left on a two-year inspection tour of European schools. In Joseph Henry's opinion, institutional health was at best a fragile affair, and he predicted the consequences of Bache's trip:

[27] "Address of Professor A. D. Bache, President of the American Association for the Year 1851, on Retiring from the Duties of President," *Proceedings of the American Association for the Advancement of Science* 6 (1851): xli–lx.

[28] A. D. Bache to J. F. Frazer, Washington, April 18, 1844, Frazer Papers.

[29] As previously noted, the *Dictionary of American Biography* is the best single source of information for Walker, Espy, and Keating. For Johnson's subsequent career, see George Pettengill, "Walter Rogers Johnson," *Journal of the Franklin Institute* 250 (August 1950): 93–113.

[30] For information on Girard, see John Bach McMaster, *The Life and Times of Stephen Girard* (Philadelphia: J. B. Lippincott and Company, 1918). Fraley was one of the original directors of the college and later served as its president. The buildings were designed by Thomas U. Walter.

An absence from a place for a single year makes many changes and you will probably find, My dear Bache, that the two years you have been absent has made as great a change in the disposition of things which you once controlled as if you had been consigned to the grave during that period. Persons with whom you have associated and perhaps controlled have learned to do without you and measures and plans which you have laboured to advance are set aside for others not as good but carried into operation because of the production of others and those on the spot. . . . I think you will be somewhat displeased with several of the selections for the Franklin Journal since your departure.[31]

Bache's European tour sharpened his ideas about education and science. He easily resumed a dominant place in the society, but his energies were increasingly absorbed by other affairs. When the construction of Girard College was delayed, Bache took over the administration of Central High School, but in 1843 he resigned his Philadelphia engagements to direct the U.S. Coast Survey in Washington.

With Bache gone, a particular era in the Institute's history seemed to be over. In a sense it was, although not because his departure created any crisis of leadership. Instead, the hegira of scientists meant that in the future the Institute would have to depend for its intellectual standing on those who were Philadelphians first and then men of science. Others would channel their institutional efforts into organizations of more promise for professional advancement and would follow employment opportunities of greater potential to their financial needs and research interests. There were other important changes besides those of personnel. Without the encouragement of government funds and the feeling of relevance to national issues, the Institute was forced to turn to issues of local concern for the fiscal and moral support necessary for survival.

The organization's active figures during the 1840's and 1850's were especially well equipped to sense Philadelphia needs and opportunities. Unlike the times when most of the dominant personalities were young and just beginning their careers, the passage of time mixed men of varying age and experience. They were themselves, in a way, a mirror of the Institute's diversity. In 1840, William H. Keating died suddenly in London, where he had been trying to negotiate a loan for the Philadelphia and Reading Railroad, and John F. Frazer took the place he once occupied as professor of chemistry.[32] Samuel V. Merrick was elected to head the Society in 1841, when James Ronaldson, the

31 Joseph Henry to A. D. Bache, Princeton, August 9, 1838, Joseph Henry Private Papers, Smithsonian Institution.

32 Bache's resolutions, commemorating Keating's services to the Institute, are in the Minutes of the Board of Managers, June 27, 1840.

Society's first president and one of its "most consistent and devoted supporters," died.[33] Merrick transformed the office, giving it an authority Ronaldson had chosen not to exercise. Johnson's chair in natural philosophy was filled by John C. Cresson. Frederick Fraley continued to serve the Institute actively, as indeed he was to do for over another half-century. Merrick, Fraley, and Cresson were persons of substance, prominent in Philadelphia's industrial and financial circles. John C. Trautwine, Solomon W. Roberts, Ellwood Morris, and Thomas U. Walter were all members of a rising generation of engineers and architects. Frazer, Trego, Haldeman, Henry D. Rogers, and his brothers James B. and Robert E. Rogers were scientists and educators. Some, like Booth and Franklin Peale, touched several circles. All were distinguished by intellectual accomplishment or business success, and all were joined together by family ties, financial interests, or the bonds of personal friendship.

Fraley and Merrick, for instance, were elected to seats on the city council in order to fight for a city gaslight system. Merrick traveled to Europe to study facilities in use there and was responsible for the development of Philadelphia's gasworks. When he resigned its management, John C. Cresson, Fraley's brother-in-law, was named superintendent, reputedly at the urging of Merrick, Bache, and Keating.[34] Fraley, Cresson, and Merrick were prominent in the Western Savings Fund Society; and Fraley and Cresson were both interested in the Schuylkill Navigation Company, one of the important canals to Pennsylvania's coal regions. Their business connections touched the Institute in other ways. Cresson was president of the Mine Hill and Schuylkill Haven Railroad, which rented office space at the Institute. The Iron Association of Pennsylvania, which according to Fraley included "some of our active men," was another tenant.[35]

Early school associations also provided important bonds. Fraley and Bache had been friends since grammar school days. Cresson, John

[33] Bache presented a set of resolutions, on Ronaldson's death, which were copied into the minutes of a special board meeting on March 30, 1841.

[34] Frederick Fraley, "Obituary Notice of John C. Cresson," American Philosophical Society *Proceedings* 11 (1869–70): 584–97; "Obituary Notices of Members Deceased. Frederick Fraley, LL.D., President of the Society," ibid., 40 (1901): i–ix; *Philadelphia Gas Works News, Special Centenary Number, 1836–1936* (Philadelphia, 1936).

[35] *A Savings Bank Account: The Story of the Western Savings Fund Society of Philadelphia, 1847–1947* (Philadelphia: Western Savings Fund Society of Philadelphia, 1947). The Western Savings Fund was established as a savings bank for the laboring classes. Its directors also included John Wiegand, cashier at the Philadelphia Gas Works, and one of the Institute's managers for many years. Frederick Fraley to William Hamilton, Philadelphia, February 25, 1856, Incoming Correspondence, Franklin Institute Archives.

Cresson Trautwine, Solomon W. Roberts, and Ellwood Morris had all been pupils of Joseph Roberts at the Friend's School and had studied drawing together in one of William Mason's classes.[36] William Strickland's office provided further education for Trautwine, Morris, and Thomas U. Walter. Trautwine, Morris, Solomon W. Roberts, and Charles B. Trego were all inducted into the American Philosophical Society on the same day, an event Roberts later recalled as an instance of long and close friendship.[37]

The U.S. Mint in Philadelphia was another focal point for Institute men. Robert Patterson took his father's place as director of the Mint, which at various times also gave employment to Booth, Franklin Peale, Joseph Saxton, and William Kneass. Kneass's son Strickland had attended Espy's mathematical school with Trautwine, and another son, Samuel H. Kneass, had also been one of Trautwine's officemates under William Strickland.[38]

Frazer, Trego, Haldeman, and Booth had their own set of associations. All had served with Henry D. Rogers on the Pennsylvania geological survey.[39] Together with Franklin and Titian Peale, all were

---

[36] "Obituary—John C. Trautwine," *Journal of the Franklin Institute* 116 (November 1883): 390–96; Eugene S. Ferguson, ed., *Early Engineering Reminiscences [1815–40] of George Escol Sellers* (Washington, D.C.: Smithsonian Institution, 1965), p. 54.

[37] Agnes Addison Gilchrist, *William Strickland, Architect and Engineer, 1788–1854* (Philadelphia: University of Pennsylvania Press, 1950), pp. 11, 22; Solomon W. Roberts, "An Obituary Notice of Charles B. Trego," American Philosophical Society *Proceedings* 14 (1874–75): 357.

[38] Ferguson, *Early Engineering Reminiscences*, pp. 61–78, contains information on the Mint and the various Institute men who were connected with it. For Booth's work at the Mint, see Edgar F. Smith, *James Curtis Booth, Chemist, 1810–1888* (Philadelphia: privately printed, 1922); and the obituary in *Journal of the Franklin Institute* 126 (July 1888): 67–69. Additional details on Peale are available in Sister St. John Nepomucene, "Franklin Peale's Visit to Europe in the U.S. Mint Service," *Journal of Chemical Education* 32 (March 1955): 156–59; and Robert Patterson, "An Obituary Notice of Franklin Peale," American Philosophical Society *Proceedings* 11 (1869–70): 597–604.

[39] The Institute had provided much of the impetus for the state geological survey, even before it became involved in the meteorological work of the survey. In 1826, Peter A. Browne called a public meeting in Philadelphia to agitate for a statewide survey, the results of which were published as *An Address, Intended to Promote a Geological and Mineralogical Survey of Pennsylvania* (Philadelphia: P. M. Lafourcade, 1826). Since the legislature proved unwilling at that time to support a survey, the Institute began one of its own in 1831, in the form of a manufacturing census. The Board aimed to discover "the number and condition of all the manufacturing establishments and mechanic Institutions in this State," an effort which they hoped would reveal "the physical power and resources" of the Commonwealth. A circular was sent to each member of the legislature, and printed forms for tabulating raw data were also distributed throughout the state. The effort was an almost total failure— there were only five responses, all from Philadelphia—but the idea persisted that "a correct knowledge of our resources & advantages" remained an important need.

members of the United Bowmen, which, as earlier noted, was an arch-
ery club made up of young men of scientific disposition.[40] Frazer,
Booth, Sears C. Walker, and Cresson were all at one time or another
on the faculty of Central High School or otherwise active in its affairs.
Three of the Rogers brothers—Henry, James, and Robert—as well as
Frazer, Booth, Trego, and Haldeman, were faculty members at the
University of Pennsylvania, where Cresson and Fraley were trust-
ees.[41] In addition to their connections to Central High School and the
University, all of these men were influential members of the American
Philosophical Society, and many were also active in the affairs of the
Academy of Natural Sciences in Philadelphia.

The fact that the city's scientific and educational institutions were
to a large degree managed by the same men gave them a certain
cohesiveness. They stuck together, at least with respect to the outside
world. When Benjamin F. Greene, director of the Rensselaer Polytechnic Institute, wrote to inquire whether the Franklin Institute would
be interested in having the school moved to Philadelphia—an action
which, in hindsight, might have been wise—the managers responded
negatively, since the University was about to establish a School of
Arts.[42] The city's organizations also came to Titian Peale's aid when
he sought a position in the Patent Office. The post of examiner had
fallen vacant, and Peale wrote to Frazer: "Now as the Franklin Institute must be a great mechanical lever, can't you fix a fulcrum for me
in that quarter?"[43] Bache and Henry took up his nomination with the
commissioner of patents, while Frazer wrote Haldeman, who had some
political influence: "So try what you can to keep a clever fellow from

Fraley and Trego carried the fight to Harrisburg and in 1836 succeeded in pushing
through an appropriation for the state geological survey. Information on the Institute's census efforts, including committee reports and sample forms, is available in
the Franklin Institute Archives. See also Minutes of Meetings, October 19, November
24, December 22, 1831; January 19, 1832; and Henry D. Rogers, Annual Report of the
Geological Survey of Pennsylvania (Harrisburg, 1836–46).

40 For information on the United Bowmen, see Jessie Poesch, Titian Ramsay
Peale, 1799–1885, And His Journals of the Wilkes Expedition (Philadelphia: American
Philosophical Society, 1961).

41 An excellent survey of the varied accomplishments of the remarkable Rogers
brothers is available in W. S. W. Ruschenberger, "A Sketch of the Life of Robert E.
Rogers, with Biographical Notices of his Father and Brothers," American Philosophical Society Proceedings 23 (1886): 104–46. For the University of Pennsylvania, see
Edward P. Cheyney, History of the University of Pennsylvania, 1740–1940 (Philadelphia: University of Pennsylvania Press, 1940).

42 Minutes of the Board of Managers, March 20, 1850.

43 T. R. Peale to J. F. Frazer, Washington, May 22, 1848, Frazer Papers.

being compelled, after a long life spent in science and for the Government, to emigrate with his family to California."[44]

A more important use for whatever political power Philadelphians possessed came when Bache's Coast Survey was threatened. Early in 1849 Bache reported to Frazer that *Hunt's Merchants Magazine* had printed a vicious assault on the Survey, written by a dismissed employee and published anonymously. The problem came when Congressional foes prepared to use the article against him, and Bache wrote, using a figure of speech from his military training days:

Your particular friend Col. Benton is inquiring in the Senate of your other particular friend the Prest. about how the Coast Survey gets on. Your third particular friend the Sec. Treas. has recommended that I should furnish myself with the opinions of the most excellent Amer. Philos. & Franklin Inst. as to the progress & character of the work so that in case of attack there may be grape on hand.[45]

He had already written Patterson at the Philosophical Society, Bache said, and he asked Frazer to meet with him and "with Merrick Fraley & Co." to plan concerted action.

Political maneuvering was one reflection of group consciousness. A more basic expression was the comradeship of men joined by a mutual love of science. Frazer, Trego, and Haldeman were great friends from geological survey days, and their letters overflow with the pleasures of nature walks together. Trego enjoyed putting those occasions in purple tones:

Though sensible that I was but a clog upon the soaring flights and bold excursions of nobler spirits and more vigorous minds, yet I did not the less admire their vigorous sallies into the worlds of wisdom and of wit, of science and of sentiment. Though myself but a mere candidate for initiation, a neophyte in the arcana of science, having scarcely entered the vestibule of her noble temple, yet I love to be near those who, like yourself and our friend, have been admitted

44 John F. Frazer to S. S. Haldeman, Philadelphia, April 17, 1848, Manuscript Collection 73, Academy of Natural Sciences. By mistake, Bache recommended Peale for the post of assistant examiner. Peale was too mortified to say anything to Bache about the error; he wrote Frazer instead, hoping to clear up the matter indirectly. There were eighty applicants for the job, Peale said, "and some expecting office will be offered without applying, in which party W. R. Johnson is included" (T. R. Peale to J. F. Frazer, Washington, May 21, June 2, 1848, Frazer Papers).

45 A. D. Bache to J. F. Frazer, Washington, June 2, 1849, ibid. Peale had also urged Frazer to use the Institute's influence in securing the position of Commissioner of Patents for Thomas Ewbank, when he came before the Senate for confirmation. T. R. Peale to J. F. Frazer, Washington, May 9, 1849, ibid.

to a knowledge of her mysteries, and who stand as ministrants within the penetralia of that august shrine.[46]

Haldeman was more direct. As he once said to Frazer, "I would make some sacrifices to get to Phila., both to be among my friends, & to have the facilities for studying which the various institutions of your city afford."[47]

It is difficult to know what place the Franklin Institute occupied in the spectrum of Philadelphia's scientific societies. In the heyday of the Bache era the Institute was probably the most vital of all, even though it lacked the established prestige of the Academy of Natural Sciences and the Philosophical Society. But all of the city's societies were subject to fluctuations in their vitality, as suggested by a remark Haldeman once made: "The Philosophical is rising & so is the Academy, whilst the Institute is a most excellent place to pass an evening."[48] Frazer had a different opinion. In his judgment the Academy had declined sadly, and he told Haldeman: "I am done expecting anything from them as a Scientific Society."[49] Differences in basic purposes distinguished the three to some extent, although there were still large areas of overlap. In their relations with each other, there were also differences. The Institute's closest links were with the American Philosophical Society and the University of Pennsylvania. Irrespective of their differences, however, the city's institutions and their influential men constituted a powerful force in the nation's engineering and scientific circles.

The alliance represented all of those who were closely linked by business, intellectual, and social ties, and it was a potent array to outsiders. Charles Ellet, a civil engineer with large ideas for river improvements on the Ohio, in 1857 became engaged in a dispute with W. Milnor Roberts over the merit of his plans. Since they depended on federal appropriations, Ellet's principal concern was that Roberts had the support of the "Philadelphia Clique" and therefore political influence. Ellet defined the clique as the men behind the Franklin Institute, the Erie Railroad, the Pennsylvania Railroad, the Schuylkill

[46] C. B. Trego to S. S. Haldeman, Harrisburg, June 23, 1842, Manuscript Collection 211c, Academy of Natural Sciences.

[47] S. S. Haldeman to J. F. Frazer, June 14, 1847, Frazer Papers.

[48] Ibid. For the state of the American Philosophical Society during the same era, see Whitfield Bell, Jr., "The American Philosophical Society as a National Academy of Sciences, 1780–1846," Ithaca 9 (1962): 165–67.

[49] J. F. Frazer to S. S. Haldeman, Philadelphia, September 6, 1840, Manuscript Collection 73, Academy of Natural Sciences.

Navigation Company, and the Smithsonian Institution.[50] The combination was not as unlikely as it might seem. Edward Miller, one of the Pennsylvania engineers in the 1839 attempt to form an engineering society in conjunction with the Institute, was chief engineer on the Erie. Samuel V. Merrick, the first president of the Pennsylvania Railroad, was followed by Edgar Thompson, who had done his apprenticeship in Strickland's office with Trautwine.[51] Fraley and Cresson were affiliated with the Schuylkill Navigation Company, and at the Smithsonian Joseph Henry still maintained his old Philadelphia friendships from Princeton days.

Helping friends and opposing enemies came easily to a group as tightly linked as these men were. Their dedication to the city and its institutions was also a valuable aid to the Franklin Institute as its managers searched a variety of avenues for the means to insure the society's health and usefulness. One idea was to create a technological museum, which illustrates how the organization moved from a broad-gauge conception characteristic of an earlier era to an activity of ultimately local significance. The Institute had always solicited inventors for models of their devices and manufacturers for samples of goods from the exhibitions. Other additions to the Institute's collections had come through gifts, purchases, or arrangements such as that with the Maclurean Lyceum, which brought natural history specimens. By such a process, the organization acquired over a period of time a collection of mechanical models, mineralogical specimens, and a miscellaneous array of manufactured goods.

In 1837, the Board decided to create a Museum of Arts and Manufactures, by organizing the collections into some system which would serve educational ends and would also preserve the "records of national ingenuity and skill" against the possibility of another Patent Office fire.[52] The 1838 School of Arts proposal incorporated a museum as part of its teaching facilities, and in 1840 Trego, Bache, Henry D. Rogers, Frazer, Booth, Joseph Saxton, John H. Towne, and Henry Troth, a manufacturing chemist, were named a committee to prepare and report a plan for a "Technological Collection." When the managers accepted their report, the same group was subsequently trans-

50 Gene D. Lewis, Charles Ellet, Jr., The Engineer as Individualist, 1810–1862 (Urbana: University of Illinois Press, 1968), p. 148.

51 Gilchrist, Strickland, p. 22; Daniel H. Calhoun, The American Civil Engineer: Origins and Conflict (Cambridge, Mass.: The M.I.T. Press, 1960), pp. 82, 92; Daniel R. Goodwin, "Obituary Notice of Samuel Vaughan Merrick, Esq.," American Philosophical Society Proceedings 11 (1869–70): 590–91.

52 Cover advertisements in the Journal throughout 1837 carried notices of the collection and solicited donations to it.

formed into the Committee on the Cabinet of Arts and Manufactures.[53]

Bache suggested that the museum be patterned after European institutions. In his speech at the close of the 1842 exhibition, he asked:

Why should not provision be made in the ordinary and regular working of the Institution for a constant exhibition? Why should all these products once collected be dispersed, never again to be reunited? Like the Conservatory of Arts, of Paris, or the Trade Institute, of Berlin, we should find such a collection a chronicle of the history of each art in our country.[54]

To achieve something in the direction of that vision, the managers refitted rooms on the third floor to house the Cabinet of Arts and Manufactures, and it was opened freely to the public. Almost inevitably, the collection came to include pickled snakes, elk horns, and a souvenir brick from the Colosseum in Rome, but its principal strength lay in the models and mineral collections. Since Peter A. Browne's days in the Institute, there had been an interest in geology and mineralogy, and that collection was further swelled in 1848, when the specimens from the state geological survey were deposited in the cabinet.[55]

The conception of a technological museum was novel for America, and a creative use for the Institute's collections. In time, the cabinet became a popular resort for Philadelphians with out-of-town guests. Robert Hare deposited his electrical apparatus for display, the committee bought more mineralogical specimens, and gifts came in large number. By 1855, the collections had assumed sufficient value that the managers doubled the Institute's insurance on them.[56] Together with the library, the cabinet came to occupy an important place among the Board's concerns. Without any supporting educational system in which to integrate the museum, however, its teaching function was essentially passive. And since the collections played no part in the city's pub-

[53] As chairman, Trego presented the report, which noted: "The Committee believe that no successful attempt has been hitherto made to establish such a Collection in America; though in Europe, some extensive and highly curious and useful Cabinets of the kind have been for some time in existence, which afford much instruction and gratification to the scientific and practical examiner. It would seem to be peculiarly the province of the Franklin Institute to take the first step forward introducing such collections into this country, inasmuch as such a measure so well comports with the original design of the Association" (Report of the Committee on a Technological Cabinet, n.d., Miscellaneous Reports, Franklin Institute Archives).

[54] *Address by Professor Bache, before the Franklin Institute, October, 1842* (Philadelphia, 1842), p. 9.

[55] Minutes of Meetings, April 19, 1848.

[56] Minutes of the Board of Managers, November 15, 1855. Among the collections which had been acquired by that date was a "Complete Geological Suit" of 700 specimens selected and arranged by the "Mineralogical Institute" of Heidelberg, purchased by friends of the Institute and donated to the cabinet in 1852. Minutes of Meetings, January 15, 1852.

lic schools, they had no access to public funds. The real potential of a technological museum as a vitalizing new mission for the Institute and a source of patronage still lay in the future.

Another Board plan for promoting new local sources of vitality was a design school for women. Just as in earlier times, the training of Americans for new roles in an emerging industrial nation still called for imaginative solutions. Early in 1850, it dawned on the Board that educational opportunities might also be created for women. In the spring of that year, Mrs. William Peter, wife of the British consul at Philadelphia, approached the managers for their support of a school of design for women which she had been conducting informally for the past few years.[57] They directed the Committee on Instruction to take up the subject, and at a subsequent meeting of the Board the committee reported that the establishment of such a school could not fail "to be of great value to the Community." But Mrs. Peter, a woman of substantial determination, wanted more than approbation, and the managers themselves became increasingly attracted to the idea of a school of industrial design conducted under the Institute's auspices. Merrick, Fraley, Frazer, Thomas U. Walter, Dr. Charles M. Wetherill, and David S. Brown were appointed a committee to study the question and to report the mode by which the organization could "best forward the project of a School of Design for Women."[58]

In June, Merrick presented the committee's report at a meeting of the Institute. There were compelling reasons to establish the school, Merrick said. First, it would provide a new and valuable type of employment for women. Second, it would advance manufactures "by giving them that originality of design of which they are now deficient." Finally, Merrick claimed, the Franklin Institute had a special mission with respect to the school, because of its own position "in regard to the Industrial Arts of our City" and because the community expected the Institute to provide direction in that field. It was "in the highest degree desirable" that the school be established under the organization's supervision, but equally imperative, Merrick warned, that it not drain any of the Institute's own funds.[59]

What Merrick's committee therefore recommended was a straightforward resort to benevolence—a public appeal should be made for an endowment. As soon as contributions produced an annual income of $2,000, the school would be opened. In no way, however, was it to be a charge on the Institute. Bitter experience had tempered the Board's

---

[57] Minutes of the Board of Managers, April 17, 1850.
[58] Ibid., May 15, 1850; Minutes of Meetings, May 16, 1850.
[59] Minutes of Meetings, June 20, 1850.

enthusiasm for new educational projects. The committee responsible
for the school's management were expressly forbidden to contract any
debts exceeding income, and if at any time funds were insufficient for
operation, the school was to be suspended immediately. Management of
the proposed facility was confined to a committee of three men and
three women appointed by the Board of Managers. "The Ladies of said
Committee," the report continued, "shall be specially charged with the
examination of the moral character & circumstances of the applicants
for admission," and they were also to oversee the operation of the
school.[60] The function of the male members of the committee was less
explicitly stated, but as befitted the Board's conception of its role, they
occupied a more generally supervisory position.

The School of Design for Women had many of the ingredients
necessary to make it interesting to the Institute and to philanthropic
Philadelphians. It promised value to manufactures at a time when
Americans were becoming conscious of industrial design. Probably as
important, it opened new avenues of employment to young women
who might otherwise be tempted into less wholesome occupation.
Morality was an issue, even if submerged, since the school was pointed
toward young women who, because of social and economic circumstance, would probably not attend the classically-oriented Normal
School, which had opened in Philadelphia two years earlier. Instead of
education in the liberal arts, the School of Design aimed to provide useful knowledge and decent employment. Alonzo Potter, Episcopalian
Bishop of Pennsylvania, became one of its supporters, and so did
Elliott Cresson, Joseph R. Ingersoll, and others known for their charitable impulses. Despite their aid, however, the fund drive failed to
secure the endowment necessary for the school to live off its income.
But the idea had gained enough momentum that the managers decided
to begin anyhow, on the premise that a year's trial would prove the
school's value. On that basis, the Franklin Institute School of Design
for Women was opened in December 1850, in space rented on the third
floor of a building at 70 Walnut Street.[61]

Instruction was divided among three departments: drawing, from
elementary principles to original compositions; the "Industrial Department," in which textile, furnishings, and furniture design were taught;
and a department of wood engraving and lithography. Anne Hill, "one
of the most accomplished instructors in drawing," was named principal,
Charles Parmalee taught engraving, and Thomas W. Braidwood was in

60 Ibid.
61 Minutes of the Board of Managers, July 17, December 18, 1850.

charge of industrial design. The school was an immediate success; during the first year almost a hundred girls were enrolled. The committee admitted about one-third of the students free of the quarterly four-dollar tuition fee, but by a novel arrangement some of the cost was regained. Once a girl reached sufficient skill, she was allowed to execute work for sale. One quarter of the proceeds from the sale of her goods was retained by the school, and the remainder was given to the student. In their first annual report, the managing committee noted that institutions on the same plan had also begun in New York and Boston, both of which were reputed to be "handsomely endowed."[62]

Since the trial year proved an undoubted success, the committee decided to continue the school, and they appealed once again for financial aid:

No one claiming a spark of philanthropic feeling, can witness the limited means at the command of women for obtaining a livelihood by labor, without a deep sense of regret, and a consciousness that something should be done to extend those means.[63]

The second canvas was more successful, and by the spring of 1853, $17,000 had been subscribed for an endowment. Beneath the surface, however, was a growing conflict between Mrs. Peter and the Board of Managers. Mrs. Peter was a strong personality—indeed, John F. Frazer had early felt the weight of her opinions and had resigned his connection with the school because of it. Mrs. Hill, the principal, was the harmonizing element among patrons, students, and the Institute, but in the summer of 1852 she was killed in a fire on the steamboat Henry Clay.[64] Meanwhile, Mrs. Peter had visited similar establishments in Europe, and she returned with ideas which Institute committee members found impossible to accept. As they explained to the Board: "The Committee have labored with great earnestness to render this branch of the Institute worthy of it, but have been thwarted by

---

[62] Journal of the Franklin Institute 53 (March 1852): 208–11. Advertisements for the design services of the school were couched in terms to appeal both for the need of worthwhile employment for "estimable women" and to the value of design in industry. "Unless, as Americans, we can compete, in matters of taste, with European artists," manufacturers were advised, "we must forever be subject to the mortification of FOLLOWING where we should LEAD,—and content ourselves with lower prices and heavier drudgery of coarser fabrics, while the skill and taste of other nations bear away Prizes which we could easily have made our own." The quotation comes from notices of the school, which appeared on covers of the Journal throughout 1852.

[63] Journal of the Franklin Institute 53 (March 1852): 211.

[64] Ibid., 54 (September 1852): 216. For Frazer's relation to the project and some indication of why he may have wanted out of the project, see Sarah Peter to [John F. Frazer], n.d., Frazer Papers, American Philosophical Society.

internal dissentions in the school which paralyzed their efforts and destroyed its usefulness."[65]

Once it became apparent that an impasse was unavoidable, the committee reported, there were two options available to the Board. They could reorganize the school without Mrs. Peter or abandon it "to her and her friends."[66] Since Mrs. Peter had originated the idea, it seemed appropriate to choose the latter course, which they did. They transferred the entire property to a new group of trustees and completely severed the Institute's connection. Under an independent charter, the school was continued. It later merged with the Moore Institute of Art, Science and Industry, and thus formed the basis for the present Moore College of Art in Philadelphia.

With respect to its schools, the Institute seemed always the bridesmaid. Except for the drawing school, which continued to attract students and regularly paid its way, the other attempts at formal, classroom education were all stillborn or short-lived. And at least in historical perspective, there is something ironic about those efforts. Even though none of them succeeded in giving the Institute an unequivocal educational mission or providing a lasting source of support, in another regard they were quite successful. Each effort rested on a far-sighted awareness of educational needs and a perception of gaps in the existing system. Each effort, in one form or another, ultimately led to permanent establishments. It was the Institute's particular destiny to invent educational solutions rather than perpetuate them, but the readiness with which such new ideas were seized upon suggests that there were few things the Board of Managers wanted more than the attachment of some kind of formal school. The seasonal rites of graduating one class and then welcoming a new one to take its place had the quality of life itself, and the Board saw it in just those terms.

It was clear to the Institute's leaders that future vitality depended on new recruits with a predisposition to carry on the work. Local boys would be the ideal choice, and Merrick proposed Central High School graduates as the logical candidates. The organization and the high school had always been closely connected, and Merrick suggested a formal relationship to legitimize the bonds. A committee which he headed to study the idea presented their reasons for union at an 1847 meeting of the Board.[67] The Institute was essentially a popular organization. As all such institutions, "it has had its day of novelty and participated largely from its novelty in the public patronage." Large

[65] Minutes of Meetings, May 19, 1853.
[66] Ibid.
[67] Minutes of the Board of Managers, April 21, 1847.

and interesting collections had been accumulated, along with an extensive and valuable library. "But now," Merrick argued, "it must put forth deeper roots." His concern was for those who would come afterward to manage and sustain the society. "The field of labor is among the young," he said, "and in order to reach them we must see where the opening has to the most extent been made ready for our grafting."

Graduates of Central High School were clearly the most suitable inheritors, and Merrick sketched a relation which fully displayed the Institute's hopes:

The Committee acting upon the suggestions of the President, the author of the resolution under consideration, is unanimously in the opinion that the most suitable body of young men with which to begin the experiment is to be found in the alumni of the High School. They seem to form the most appropriate connexion between our body and the workshops of the country. As they leave the valuable institution in which they have been instructed in Physical Science, distinguished by its honors, they will feel more than those in ordinary life the necessity of keeping the links bright that connect them [to] the great mechanical Philosophers of the day, whose books have been their companions for years, and in whose path they must tread should they desire to be distinguished. Some of them after a short trial may give way, but if we can, out of the hundred who will in a few years look to the High School as their Alma Mater, attach to our body a tenth part of it, [they] will form a body active and vigorous to sustain the Franklin Institute and they may be taught to regard it as the Alma Pater, who has taken them from nurse and made them the fit & able associates of *men*. . . . They will in fact become our adopted children, succeed to our inheritance and we trust carry our Institution with honor to coming generations.[68]

To carry the plan into effect, Merrick and his fellow Board members gave Central High School graduates under twenty-one years of age all the privileges of membership save the right to vote. They could attend lectures freely, participate in the monthly conversational meetings, and serve on committees. In the following year, the same favor was conferred on University of Pennsylvania science graduates.[69] Both measures were designed with the hopes of insuring a continuing source of vitality for the Institute. The organization had depended for its past energy upon those with a "desire to be distinguished," to use Merrick's words. In his view, the future rested no less on ambitious young men whose voluntary labors would bring reputation to them and honor to the Institute. But there was more at stake than preserving a patrimony. The organization had reached a difficult point in its history, and the Board recognized a multilayer set of problems.

[68] Ibid.
[69] Ibid., May 19, 1847; June 21, 1848.

The Board of Managers could no longer suggest, with the intimation of uniqueness, that the Franklin Institute was the most obvious resource whenever government needed scientific expertise. There were still such jobs to be done, and in 1843 the society prepared a report on street-paving techniques, at the request of city officials.[70] But at the national level, by the 1840's there were other organizations equally or better equipped to act the role of science advisor. In any event, since the relationship was unofficial there were always distinct limits. The Institute's talents were called into play only when government saw fit to use them; the organization had no effective power to shape policy or to secure a steady flow of patronage. Indeed, the managers were forced repeatedly to plead to city, county, and state officials for tax relief, with only mixed results.[71] The failures were all the more critical at a time when the Institute needed some tangible reminder of its usefulness.

Benefactions came to the society to be used to encourage research. Elliott Cresson, a Philadelphian generous in many causes, gave the Institute $1,000 in 1846, the principal of which was to provide gold medals to reward "extraordinary merit" in inventiveness.[72] Uriah Boyden, of Boston, donated $1,000 in 1859, as a prize to the American experimentalist who could determine to the Institute's satisfaction whether known physical rays had equal velocities.[73] But scientific

---

[70] Ibid., January 19, 1843. The investigation into street-paving techniques was published at the city's expense, under the title *Report of the Franklin Institute of the State of Pennsylvania, for the Promotion of the Mechanic Arts, on the Best Modes of Paving Highways* (Philadelphia, 1843). In a forty-page survey, the committee summarized major historical developments in paving, current European practices, and the relationship of roadbed and drainage to paving material.

[71] See, for example, Minutes of the Board of Managers, February 17, 1847; November 9, December 14, 1853.

[72] Minutes of Meetings, April 15, 1847. Terms of award for the Cresson Medal are in William H. Wahl, *The Franklin Institute of the State of Pennsylvania for the Promotion of the Mechanic Arts: A Sketch of its Organization and History* (Philadelphia: The Franklin Institute, 1895), pp. 88–89.

[73] Minutes of the Board of Managers, April 13, 1859. In his letter offering the award, Boyden wrote: "I wish said Institute to award this money to such person as shall by researching in North America, prove to the satisfaction of said Institute whether all the rays which may be known, have or have not equal velocities of transmission. I do not know that I can offer any rule as to the accuracy with which such determination of comparative velocities should be made; or that I can offer any other guide in this matter, which would not be liable to embarass the Institute instead of being useful." In lieu of any directions from Boyden, the managers appointed Cresson, Frazer, and A. D. Bache a committee to define the terms of award. There were few competitors for the prize, and in 1862, the original time limit was extended for a year. None of the subsequent entries, in the committee's opinion, constituted a sufficient contribution to physics to merit the award. In that somewhat awkward circumstance, the committee—which in 1863 consisted of Bache, Joseph Henry, and

investigations no longer provided any direct impulse to the society's affairs. Extraordinary events, such as the *Princeton* disaster, momentarily stirred an interest in original research, and the Committee on Science and the Arts was continuously active and valuable. Its numbers included the Institute's best minds, but unlike the steamboiler investigation, their hidden labors could not infuse the organization with a spirit of dramatic accomplishment.

Perhaps the most sensitive problem was that the Institute had to turn, time and again, to the same small group of men to carry on its business. They were all closely connected and were in common dedicated to the city and the society. As their own careers developed, however, many of them found it increasingly difficult to give as much time as they had in the past. Annual exhibitions, for instance, were an important source of income and a public reminder of the Institute's usefulness. But they required an enormous effort to stage, and as the displays became larger, the need to oversee details grew in proportion. The *Journal* also demanded constant attention, especially after Dr. Jones's death in 1848. And in 1847, the Board decided that its lecture program needed revision, in a way that put further strain on an already overloaded administrative structure.

It was all rather anomalous. The Franklin Institute was the country's most distinguished technical society, and its activities were widely imitated.[74] Yet it struggled with a heavy burden of debt, lived in cramped quarters, and as the institutional structure of American science and technology changed, faced a less than certain mission. Bache's scientific interests and values had played an important part in raising the organization to national prominence. But with the passage of time his objectives lost their relevance for the Institute, and it was led back to its local community in search of purpose, support, and longevity.

Frazer—wrote to Boyden, asking his pleasure in the matter. The best solution, Boyden said, was to extend the deadline again, and he noted: "I do not know any cause which should induce the Franklin Institute to change its way of managing this business" (Minutes of the Board of Managers, March 11, 1863). There the affair stood, and for the next half-century the Boyden Premium remained unawarded.

[74] The editor of *The American Repertory of Arts, Sciences and Manufactures*, in vol. 1 (June 1840), pp. 346–47, described the Institute's monthly meetings as "peculiarly beneficial and worthy of imitation," noting that the New York Mechanics' Institute had begun the same practice. The same society later formed a Committee on Arts and Sciences to examine and report on new inventions. *Appleton's Mechanics' Magazine and Engineers' Journal* 1 (November 1851): 658.

A CENTER OF INDUSTRY

In the nineteenth century, smoke from factory chimneys signaled prosperity. Advertisements of Philadelphia industrial concerns always showed busy smokestacks. Multilingual advertisements also reflected the fact that the city's products competed in an international marketplace. Baldwin's Locomotive Works grew to be the largest in the world, and William Sellers's machine tools consistently won the major prizes at international industrial exhibitions. Indeed, by mid-century manufacturing had replaced commerce as the principal avenue to riches and reputation in Philadelphia. The new industrial elite built mansions on fashionable Rittenhouse Square or suburban retreats in Germantown. They suppported the cultural and benevolent societies, which traditionally depended on the wealthy.

Men like Samuel V. Merrick, Frederick Fraley, and William Sellers were also the key figures in Philadelphia's civic life. They were as active in the city's financial institutions as they were in its educational establishments. They rallied public support for the Pennsylvania Railroad in the 1840's and for the Union cause in the 1860's. With the experience gained from decades of Institute exhibitions, they organized Sanitary Commission fairs during the Civil War, and when the time came to celebrate the centennial of American independence, they organized an exhibition for that purpose, too.

The Institute's Twelfth Exhibition of American Manufactures, 1842, at the Chinese Museum (courtesy of the Franklin Institute).

A view of the foundry and machine works of Merrick & Son, 1850 (courtesy of the Free Library of Philadelphia).

A nineteenth-century engraving of the industrial plant of Powers & Weightman (courtesy of the Free Library of Philadelphia).

A view of the foundry and machine works of Neall, Matthews & Moore, 1850 (courtesy of the Historical Society of Pennsylvania).

Lithographic advertisement for the Morris Iron Works (courtesy of the Historical Society of Pennsylvania).

INDUSTRIAL WORKS,

Callowhill Street, between Twentieth and Twenty-First, Philadelphia.

CASTINGS,

Heavy or Light.

Cylinders, Pumps, Retorts, Rosin Stills, Soap Kettles, Large Fly Wheels and Pulleys, and all such Castings as are made in

LOAM,

WITHOUT PATTERNS.

ROLLING MILL WORK,

ROLLS Cast and Finished. Strict attention given to use Iron suitable to the work.

PATTERNS made to order.

SHAFTING,

Of the best quality.

PULLEYS,

OF ALL DIAMETERS AND FACES.

HANGERS,

From any of their various patterns, being the fullest and most complete assortment of Hangers with Self-Adjusting Boxes to be found. All Shafting furnished at short notice, finished in the best style and guaranteed.

BEMENT, DOUGHERTY & THOMAS,

CONSTRUCTING ENGINEERS,

TOOL BUILDERS AND IRON FOUNDERS,

Are prepared to make Designs and Drawings for Mills, Machine Shops and Foundries, and to furnish all the necessary Machinery, Tools, Cupolas, Fans, Cranes, &c. and to estimate for the same complete.

MACHINISTS' TOOLS. Lathes to swing any diameter, from 12 inches to 10 feet, any length of shear required. Planers to plane from 18 inches square by 4 feet long; to 10 feet square by 40 feet long. Shaping, Slotting, Wheel-Quartering and Boring Machines; Horizontal and Upright Drills, Wheel-Cutting and Screw Cutting Machines, with improved Taps and Dies, Punching and Shearing Machines, Scroll Chucks, &c.

Advertisement for the Industrial Works (courtesy of the Free Library of Philadelphia).

Wm. Sellers & Co., Philadelphia (courtesy of the Free Library of Philadelphia).

Pascal Iron Works, Philadelphia (courtesy of the Free Library of Philadelphia).

A view of the Baldwin Locomotive Works, 1872 (courtesy of the Free Library of Philadelphia).

Residence of Joseph Harrison, Esq., Rittenhouse Square (courtesy of the Historical Society of Pennsylvania).

Left, Frederick Fraley, 1804–1901 (courtesy of the Free Library of Philadelphia); *right*, William Sellers, 1824–1905 (courtesy of the Free Library of Philadelphia).

XI

INDUSTRIAL TECHNOLOGY AND THE FRANKLIN INSTITUTE

Philadelphia Tools unquestionably surpass those
made elsewhere in this country, in *strength*,
proportion, and *workmanship*.

Edwin T. Freedley,
Philadelphia and its Manufacturers, 1857

Although it was not yet clear in the 1840's, the Franklin Institute's
future vitality rested on an identification with the demands of industry,
not science—or at least not science the way Bache defined it. Like
science, technological advance depended on specialized education and
specialized practitioners. In a way also analogous to science, technology needed research and publication, within an institutional context,
which would define relevant problems and acceptable answers. Aside
from those parallels, however, there were important differences; and a
certain amount of rhetorical rubble had to be cleared away to get at
them. The Institute's earlier experimental researches had done part of
the job by demonstrating that it was the methods and not the principles
of science which were important to technology. Other distinctions
remained to be discovered.

The Institute found some of the answers in the emergence of
Philadelphia's industry. Two of the city's favorite sons, John F. Frazer
and William Sellers, played important and complementary roles in
the process. Frazer was particularly able to influence the society's
activities as a result of an administrative reorganization which made
him a salaried executive officer—a position new to America's scientific
and technical societies. Fraley proposed the idea in April 1847, at the
same Board meeting which adopted Merrick's proposal for an alliance
with Central High School graduates. It was a time for reflection, and
while a popular society obviously required fresh recruits to maintain
its vigor, the managers also recognized that the Institute's affairs

demanded a degree of attention which voluntarism could not provide. Fraley argued for the creation of a single office to integrate fiscal operations, publication of the *Journal*, and superintendence of exhibitions.[1] In keeping with one of the organization's primary concerns, Fraley suggested the office of treasurer as a logical choice for the new position, and he resigned to make room for the new appointee. After a brief skirmish among Board members on the constitutionality of the issue, Charles B. Trego was named treasurer, at an annual salary of $1,000.[2] Trego's tenure was brief, however, and the following year he was replaced by John F. Frazer, who held the office for the next sixteen years.

Frazer brought distinction to the position in an important way. He was a man of science and direct heir of the Bache tradition at the Institute. In fact, Bache had turned him away from a career in law toward a scientific one, and he followed his tutor's footsteps. After an elementary education, which included a year at Captain Partridge's quasi-military academy in Connecticut, Frazer entered the University of Pennsylvania, where he became Bache's laboratory assistant. Although he also studied law and was admitted to the bar, Frazer never took up a legal practice. Instead, in the years immediately after graduation, he assisted Bache in the observations of terrestrial magnetism made at Girard College, served with the state geological survey, and filled the chair of natural philosophy at Central High School.[3] Then, in 1844, Frazer was named to Bache's place in the chair of natural philosophy and chemistry at the University. "I have therefore acquired the right," he joked to his friend Samuel Haldeman, "of instilling into the minds of some 80 or 90 juveniles the sublime mysteries of all kinds of physical science."[4] But the position was important to Frazer, and one he had eagerly sought.

Frazer had other attributes which were valuable to the Institute. He was a confirmed Philadelphian, devoted to Philadelphia's social life and its institutions. In a city celebrated for status distinctions, family wealth and position gave Frazer an assured place. He belonged

[1] Minutes of the Board of Managers, April 21, 1847, Franklin Institute Archives.

[2] Ibid., June 16, 21, 1847. Ostensibly, the issue was over the Board's right to accept the resignation of an officer and to fill the vacancy. But the opposition was led by Matthias Baldwin, who consistently took exception to constitutional tinkering.

[3] Frazer deserves a full-length biography, but none exists. The best single source of information is John L. LeConte's "Obituary Notice of John F. Frazer," American Philosophical Society *Proceedings* 13 (1872): 1–8.

[4] John F. Frazer to Samuel S. Haldeman, Philadelphia, April 7, 1844, Manuscript Collection 73, Academy of Natural Sciences.

to those associations—the First City Troop, for instance—which defined a man's standing in the city.[5] Frazer was also one of the Institute's inner circle. After Keating and Mitchell, he was named professor of chemistry in 1840, and he served continuously on the Board of Managers from 1844 until shortly before his death in 1872. He was active as well in the American Philosophical Society, where he was elected secretary and then vice president. But best of all, Frazer was a man of great vitality and intellectual keenness. His learning and interests were broad, his talent in communicating knowledge celebrated. "His mind was quick in its action, and penetration beyond example," one friend remembered. "No man ever mastered a subject more rapidly, or could explain it more clearly or gracefully to others."[6] Whether in terms of social position or mental prowess, civic interest or personal vigor, Frazer was the ideal executive for the Institute.

The *Journal,* in particular, needed supervision. It had gone through a series of administrative realignments in an attempt to find some satisfactory replacement for the personal efforts Bache devoted to it when he was chairman of the Committee on Publications. John Griscom's editorial and translating labors provided a temporary solution, but when they ended in 1840, another alternative was required to link Dr. Jones, William Hamilton, and the printer. The next experiment, begun with a new series of the *Journal* in 1841, was to divide editorial labors among a group of "Collaborators"—Cresson, Booth, Frazer, Bache, Griscom, Walker, Merrick, Fraley, Ellwood Morris, and Solomon W. Roberts—each responsible for a specialized field of interest. Roberts responded to the idea in a letter to William Hamilton. He had long been concerned with the Institute's prosperity, he wrote, "and did what I could in trying to establish a Society of Civil Engineers in connection with it." He was also aware, he said, "of the impor-

---

[5] For a guide to the hallmarks of a proper Philadelphian, see E. Digby Baltzell, *Philadelphia Gentlemen: The Making of a National Upper Class* (Glencoe, Ill.: The Free Press, 1958).

[6] "In Memorium John F. Frazer, LL.D.," *Proceedings at the Public Inauguration of the Building Erected for the Departments of Arts and Science, October 11, 1872* (Philadelphia, 1872). Frazer's friends worried about his pace and its effects on his health. Haldeman once wrote: "I think you sit up too late for yr own good, you seem to sleep too little & work too much, between yr two or three professorships (that in the Univ'ty being in itself double) your introductories & occasional lectures, your lectures instead of recitations; your trouble & labor beyond what seems necessary, to prepare a good (& smooth) course for yr students, yr treasureship, editorship, committeeship, exhibition superintendence, secretaryship, proofreading, &c. &c. &c. would at least kill half a dozen like me, whatever the effect upon you" (Samuel S. Haldeman to John F. Frazer, April 18, 1848, Frazer Papers, American Philosophical Society).

tance of a proper management of the Engineering portion of the Journal" and offered his assistance to that purpose.[7]

The real problem was not proper management—Jones and Hamilton took care of the details—the need was for a continuous supply of original articles and the selection, and translation if necessary, of foreign material worth republication. The Committee on Publications stressed that point in an "Address to the Subscribers to the Journal of the Franklin Institute, and to the Public, generally," which prefaced the first number of the new series in January 1841. American engineers were urged "to contribute the results of their practice"; mechanics to submit information on "practical matters"; and men of a philosophic turn to furnish "original articles in chemical and physical science."[8] The role of the collaborators was spelled out even more clearly in the Board's annual report of January 20, 1841. The Committee on Publications, it was noted, "have recently made arrangements with several gentlemen of distinguished ability, to furnish contributions regularly for its pages."[9] Over a period of time, collaborators and the subject areas they represented were shifted about, but finding original material for the Journal required constant effort. "I have not yet been able to raise any Civil Engineering for the Sept. number," Hamilton wrote Frazer in 1852. "If you have any translations I can use them."[10]

Other changes suggested alterations in management. For two years the Journal was conducted under the joint editorship of Jones and James J. Mapes, of New York.[11] Mapes had edited a magazine called the American Repertory. In 1842, however, he opened a consulting engineering office, and to escape the whole burden of publication, and

[7] S. W. Roberts to Wm. Hamilton, Philadelphia, April 5, 1841, Incoming Correspondence, Franklin Institute Archives. Initially, the collaborators were variously grouped under the specialities "Practical and Theoretical Mechanics," "Practical and Theoretical Chemistry," "Architecture," "Physical Science," "Commerce and Manufactures," and "Civil Engineering."

[8] "Address to the Subscribers to the Journal of the Franklin Institute, and to the Public, generally," Journal of the Franklin Institute 31 (January 1841): 2.

[9] "Seventeenth Annual Report of the Board of Managers of the Franklin Institute of the State of Pennsylvania for the Promotion of the Mechanic Arts," Journal of the Franklin Institute 31 (February 1841): 96.

[10] William Hamilton to John F. Frazer, Philadelphia, August 4, 1852, Frazer Papers. The changing order of collaborators and of the subject areas represented can be followed on the front covers of the Journal.

[11] Mapes was corresponding secretary of the New York Mechanics' Institute and lectured on chemistry and natural philosophy in the city. In association with William A. Cox, he advertised himself as a consulting engineer, analytical chemist, patent agent, and instructor "in the several branches of knowledge necessary to an Engineer" (Cover advertisement, Journal of the Franklin Institute 35 [May 1843]).

perhaps some of its costs, he approached Jones with a proposal to merge the two magazines. Jones recommended the idea to Merrick: "The union would, undoubtedly, so far increase the list of subscribers as to render the *Journal* a source of profit, instead of one of loss."[12] With the same hope, the managers agreed to the plan, and in 1842 they changed the title of their periodical to read *Journal of the Franklin Institute and American Repertory of Mechanical and Physical Science, Civil Engineering, the Arts and Manufactures, and of American and Other Patented Inventions.* Actually, the change was made for economic reasons. Mapes played no apparent role in the editorial process, and his name was dropped from the title page at the end of 1843. The *Journal* continued with the revised subtitle until 1847 and then dropped it as well.

Dr. Jones, on the other hand, seemed to go on forever. As in earlier days, he quarreled with the Committee on Publications over Griscom's assumption of editorial functions, and he was always quick to react to what he considered intrusions into his own sphere. He continued his vendetta against quacks who hid their trumpery behind grand language, maintained his patent agency, and still entertained hopes that he would someday be restored to the superintendence of the Patent Office.[13] Jones never let anyone forget that he was alive, but in fact his health was declining. In 1845, Charles M. Keller, an examiner in the Patent Office, took over the job of reporting new inventions for the *Journal.* For the next two years, Jones continued to read proof, organize the magazine's contents, and to make up indexes and tables of contents. He had long before lost effective control over policy, but he still considered the *Journal* his own creation, and even minor editorial tasks were valuable reminders of the connection. When he died in 1848, the last vestige of external editorial interest disappeared.

By that date, Frazer had been named treasurer and, by the new arrangement, was responsible for the management of the *Journal.* In 1850, by way of officially confirming an existing state of affairs, the Board made him editor. Frazer had previously been chairman of the Committee on Publications and had contributed significantly to the periodical's pages. In 1839, for instance, he translated Daguerre's account of a new photographic process—the first American publication of the invention. On one hand, it was the beginning of a long interest in photography at the Institute, but on the other, it revealed

---

[12] Thomas P. Jones to Samuel V. Merrick, Washington, February 26, 1842, Thomas P. Jones Letters, Franklin Institute Archives.

[13] For examples, see Thomas P. Jones to William Hamilton, Washington, February 15, 1841; April 30, 1842, Thomas P. Jones Letters.

the more important process by which European advances were made available to Americans.[14] It required no small amount of labor to read the European journals, select articles worth republication, and translate them accurately. Frazer devoted his editorial lifetime to that effort. The task was fundamentally anonymous; articles were prefaced by the simple statement "Translated for the Journal of the Franklin Institute." But his friends recognized the importance of the work and cited the *Journal* as the best monument to Frazer's scientific contributions.[15]

Like Bache, Frazer also managed to enlist others to supply articles and translations of significant foreign science. Booth and his industrial-research-laboratory partner Martin H. Boyè translated material from Liebig's chemical investigations. Ellwood Morris provided original articles based on his civil-engineering experiences, translations of French experiments on Fourneyron's new water turbines, and the results achieved with local versions of the foreign wheel. John C. Trautwine also wrote articles on a variety of engineering problems, including a report on his route survey for a ship canal through the Panamanian isthmus.[16] Two of Trautwine's *Journal* articles—one on laying out railroad curves and another on calculating earth removal —were published as separate studies by the Institute.

There was precedent for the idea. The managers planned to issue the results of their water-power experiments in book form, and the reports of the steam-boiler investigation were published individually after having been printed in the *Journal*. Furthermore, in 1838 the Institute published Colonel Joseph Totten's *Essays on Hydraulic and Common Mortars and on Lime-Burning*, a translation of a French

---

[14] *Journal of the Franklin Institute* 27 (November 1839): 303–11. Frazer's translation led immediately to efforts at duplicating the process, one of which was Joseph Saxton's daguerreotype of Central High School, taken in 1839 from a window in the U.S. Mint. See Beaumont Newhall, *The Daguerreotype in America* (New York, 1961).

[15] See the obituaries cited in nn. 3 and 6 above, both of which make the same point.

[16] Liebig's "Theory of Saponification" appeared in translation in the *Journal of the Franklin Institute* 34 (July 1842): 58–62. Ellwood Morris's "Remarks on Reaction Water Wheels used in the United States; and on the Turbine of M. Fourneyron, an Hydraulic Motor, recently used with great success on the continent of Europe" appeared in vol. 34, in the issues for October (pp. 217–27) and November 1842 (pp. 289–304). Morris pointed out that Americans probably did not adopt the turbine sooner because its virtues were "locked up from many in a foreign language." Trautwine's various papers on civil engineering are best discovered through the index of the *Journal*. The first installment of his "Rough Notes of an Exploration for an Interoceanic Canal Route by way of the Rivers Atrato and San Juan, in New Granada, South America" appeared in vol. 57 (April 1854), pp. 217–31, and was continued in succeeding numbers.

work on the subject combined with the results of experiments Totten had conducted at Fort Adams.[17] The essays were issued serially in the *Journal* and were then gathered between separate covers. There is no evidence which clearly indicates that the Board of Managers actively conceived a program to publish specialized studies which might not find a commercial market. And yet, Totten put the issue very much in those terms. "I do not know a sound treatise on the subject in our language," he wrote Hamilton. "I have some doubt whether there would be adequate sale to cover the expenses, & I have no money to lose—but still I should regret if the country were deprived of the benefits which I think must flow from a publication."[18] Totten therefore proposed that the manuscript be published in the *Journal* and then, using the same plates, printed as a book.

The Institute followed the same procedure with Trautwine's books, and as with the Totten study, William Hamilton acted as sales agent, using advertisements in the *Journal* to publicize the books. Both of Trautwine's works were popular. *The Field Practice of Laying Out Circular Curves for Railroads*, originally published in 1851, went through six editions by 1869. His other study, *A New Method of Calculating the Cubic Contents of Excavations and Embankments*, was first issued in 1852 and was in its third edition by 1869. Both books were conceived in terms of joint publication in the *Journal*. As early as 1838 Trautwine had a railroad book in mind, but he wrote Hamilton, "I find it requires as many *years* to prepare it, as I had thought months."[19] Trautwine apparently planned to use the fee paid by the Committee on Publications for original articles to finance extra paper and printing costs. In that fashion, he hoped to publish his book without great personal expense, and in a scheme which would also further the Institute's interests. "If the *Journal* chooses to father it," he told Hamilton, "we will probably strike a bargain."[20]

Once published, the Institute became the copyright proprietor of Trautwine's books, as it had of Totten's study. The exact nature of the

[17] The full citation of the published work is J. G. Totten, *Essays on Hydraulic and Common Mortars, and on Lime-Burning. Translated from the French of G. Treussart, M. Petot, and M. Courtois. With brief observations on Common Mortars, Hydraulic Mortars, and Concretes, and an Account of Some Experiments made therewith at Fort Adams, Newport Harbor, Rhode Island, from 1825 to 1838* (Philadelphia: The Franklin Institute, 1838).

[18] Joseph G. Totten to William Hamilton, Newport, May 31, 1837, Incoming Correspondence. The work was published serially in the *Journal* in vols. 24 (October 1837), p. 229, through 26 (September 1838), p. 145.

[19] John C. Trautwine to William Hamilton, Knoxville, October 15, 1838, Incoming Correspondence.

[20] Ibid.

financial relationship between author and publisher is not clear. Trautwine responded to one inquiry that the books "have been placed entirely under the control of Mr. Hamilton, Esq., Actuary of the Franklin Institute, to whom I must refer you for any information respecting them."[21] Hamilton received a commission on sales, which was also the arrangement employed with B. H. Bartol's *A Treatise on the Marine Boilers of the United States,* published in Philadelphia in 1851. Bartol's book consisted of a descriptive listing of the machinery in sixty-four American-made steamboats, and he apparently paid for its printing costs himself.[22] But the Institute's internal operation made book sales and distribution a relatively easy matter. Hamilton regularly handled orders for the *Journal,* whose subscribers constituted a logical audience for technical books. Lack of funds made any extended program of book publication impossible. By using the *Journal* to absorb printing expenses, however, the Institute was indirectly able to publish a few specialized technical studies.

Publication had the same implications for engineers that it had for scientists. It was both a measure of talent and a means to advance one's career. Bache based his 1836 reorganization of the *Journal* on the assumption that professionalization and specialization hinged on publication, and he created a separate section of the magazine for original articles in civil engineering. As a result, the periodical became an important medium for engineers who hoped to establish a reputation for expertise by publishing technical articles. Trautwine, for example, sent reprints of his article on Southern internal improvements to state legislatures throughout that area. Stephen H. Long, a former Army engineer, used extra notices of his bridge improvements in much the same way.[23] By 1850, when Frazer became editor, new types of engineers were emerging, and he slanted the *Journal* to their needs and interests. While neither chemical engineering nor mechanical engineering had yet been defined as an occupational speciality, it was becoming evident that each demanded a particular kind of knowledge. With the same kind of sensitivity which characterized the Institute's earlier years, the *Journal* became an important outlet for these new fields.

21 John C. Trautwine to Henry C. Baird, Philadelphia, March 10, 1853, Historical Society of Pennsylvania.

22 Advertisements for Bartol's book appeared on *Journal* covers throughout 1852, listing Hamilton as one of several sales agents. It was briefly reviewed in the *Journal,* in vol. 53 (February 1852), p. 144.

23 See John C. Trautwine to William Hamilton, Knoxville, December 28, 1838; S. H. Long to William Hamilton, Marietta, December 24, 1839, Incoming Correspondence.

Frazer had studied and taught chemistry himself, and to some degree his own interests may have influenced the selection of material for publication. But the increasing number of *Journal* articles on chemistry and its applications also reflected the growth of the chemical industry in Philadelphia. The manufacture of industrial chemicals, paints, and pharmaceuticals was well begun in the city by the first decade of the nineteenth century. John Harrison, Samuel Wetherill, and John Price Wetherill were among the city's manufacturing chemists who joined the Institute on its founding. Harrison had studied with Joseph Priestley, but most Philadelphia chemical manufacturers came out of an empirical tradition.[24] By the 1830's, however, particularly with European advances in chemistry, specialized training became important. More than any other single person in Philadelphia, James C. Booth introduced the analytical methods of science to industrial chemistry. According to one of his biographers, Booth returned from study in Europe with the idea that "the laboratory should be a miniature factory and the factory a mammoth laboratory."[25] To provide a more direct link between academic study and practical application, in 1836 Booth opened a laboratory for teaching and analytical services to industry. Americans were becoming aware of the commercial value of applied chemistry, and Booth's laboratory illustrated the trend. Louis Agassiz visited the city in 1846 and wrote back to Switzerland in some surprise:

During my stay in Philadelphia, there was also an exhibition of industrial products at the Franklin Institute, where I especially remarked the chemical department. There are no less than three professors of chemistry in Philadelphia, —Mr. Hare, Mr. Booth, and Mr. Frazer.[26]

By 1848, Martin Hans Boyè had opened his own laboratory for "chemical analysis and instruction in practical chemistry," and retail merchants in the city found it profitable to sell chemical apparatus of the same type "as used by Liebig, Berzelius, and other continental chemists."[27] Boyè emigrated to Philadelphia from Denmark, served

24 Baltzell, *Philadelphia Gentlemen*, p. 97. See also William Haynes, *American Chemical Industry*, 6 vols. (New York: D. Van Nostrand Company, 1954), vol. 1, pp. 175ff.

25 Edgar F. Smith, *James Curtis Booth, Chemist, 1810–1888* (Philadelphia: privately printed, 1922), p. 4. Booth's original enterprise survives in Philadelphia today as Booth, Garrett, and Blair.

26 Elizabeth Cary Agassiz, *Louis Agassiz: His Life and Correspondence*, 2 vols. (London, 1885), vol. 2, p. 419.

27 Advertisements, on inside and outside covers of the *Journal* are a rich source of information but have usually been lost in the process of binding. Edward N. Kent, who styled himself a "practical chemist," advertised his chemical apparatus on *Journal* covers in 1848 and 1849, and Boyè called attention to his laboratory for industrial analysis and instruction in the same way.

in the state geological survey, and in the 1840's was one of an active and creative circle of chemists in community which included Frazer, the Rogers brothers, Booth, Campbell Morfit, and Charles M. Wetherill, one of the city's early European-trained Ph.D.'s. Booth and Boyè were for a time partners in Booth's laboratory, and Morfit coauthored with Booth *The Encyclopedia of Chemistry, Practical and Theoretical*.[28] As one student of Philadelphia's history has pointed out, chemical manufacturing and the related business of sugar-refining formed the basis of several family fortunes in the city. By the 1850's the industry involved a capital investment estimated at $2.5 million, making Philadelphia an important national center for the production of a wide variety of chemicals, drugs, paints, and allied manufactures.[29]

Steam engineering was another branch of study and practice which fit Frazer's ideas for the *Journal*. The Navy was then engaged in a conversion to iron ships and steam propulsion, a shift which created a new field of engineering practice and a market of great potential for Philadelphia industry. Navy officials early realized that steam power called for a new type of officer, and the Academy at Annapolis, established in 1845, was partly designed to fill that need. Since specialized knowledge was an obvious requirement for officers with technical responsibilities, naval engineers soon developed professional attitudes not unlike those of the Army's Topographical Engineers, and they placed a similar emphasis on publication.[30] The *Journal* became their voice. Benjamin Franklin Isherwood is a case in point. Isherwood had strong career ambitions, ultimately realized in his appointment as first chief of the Navy's Bureau of Steam Engineering. Throughout the 1850's the *Journal* printed a steady stream of Isherwood's articles on the performance tests of various steamships, different forms of paddlewheels and screw propellers, and the efficiency of different boiler types. Much of the comparative data Isherwood collected was incorporated in a two-volume study, *Engineering Precedents for Steam*

[28] For information on Boyè see Edgar F. Smith, *Martin Hans Boyè, 1812–1909, Chemist* (Philadelphia: privately printed, 1924).

[29] Baltzell, *Philadelphia Gentlemen*, pp. 96ff.; Edwin T. Freedley, *Philadelphia and its Manufactures; a Hand-Book of the Great Manufactories and Representative Mercantile Houses of Philadelphia, in 1857* (Philadelphia: E. Young & Co., 1860), pp. 206ff.

[30] Monte Calvert provides information on the professional aspirations of naval engineers in his *The Mechanical Engineer in America, 1830–1910* (Baltimore: The Johns Hopkins Press, 1967).

Machinery, published in 1859.[31] He also became absorbed with the general problem of steam-engine efficiency, and early in 1860 he began a series of experiments into all facets of steam engineering. The results of those trials were also assembled for publication. Commercial publishers, fearing a limited market, declined to take the work. But with financial support from other engineers to help cover costs, the Franklin Institute published the first volume of Isherwood's *Experimental Researches in Steam Engineering* in 1863. The second volume was published by the Institute in 1865, after Gideon Welles, Secretary of the Navy, authorized the subscription of 300 copies by his department. By that time the Institute was itself engaged in planning, along with the National Academy of Sciences and the Navy Department, a series of experiments on the expansion of steam.[32]

The Institute's interest in Isherwood's work was perhaps made easy by the precedent publication of earlier specialized studies and the predilection for new fields of investigation worth exploitation. But as with the *Journal*'s interest in chemistry, there were local implications which undoubtedly shaped editorial considerations. By the 1850's Philadelphia had become a focal point for the manufacture of machinery in America. And more to the point, several of the Institute's most prominent figures were heavily involved in the industry. Samuel V. Merrick was one of them.

Merrick's enterprise went through several permutations in the transition from a small fire-engine factory to a large-scale industrial complex. Under the firm name S. V. Merrick and Company, Merrick and his partner John Agnew manufactured a variety of hand-operated fire engines throughout the 1820's. In 1835 the business was called the Franklin Works. Rufus Tyler had joined the firm, and the three advertised themselves as "Engineers, Machinists & Brass Founders" in the production of fire engines and "machines in general."[33] Tyler's association was brief, and in the following year Merrick and Agnew were again advertised as the active partners, but in a new location. By 1837 a foundry had been added and the line of products expanded to include high- and low-pressure steam engines, machine gearing, and fire engines. The business continued under the name Franklin Works at least until 1838. In 1839 Merrick formed a partnership with John H. Towne, and a new concern, styled the Southwark Foundry,

31 For Isherwood's career, see Edward W. Sloan III, *Benjamin Franklin Isherwood: Naval Engineer* (Annapolis: U.S. Naval Academy, 1965).

32 Ibid., pp. 92–95.

33 Cover advertisement, *Journal of the Franklin Institute* 20 (November 1835).

was established. Agnew remained "at the old established stand" and continued to build hand-operated fire engines. Merrick's ambitions were considerably larger, however, and his new firm advertised the manufacture of steam engines of all types, a wide variety of mill machinery, and general foundry work.[34]

In the years that followed, the Southwark Foundry became one of Philadelphia's most important firms in an industry in which the city was preeminent—the production of heavy machinery. Towne left the business in 1849, and Merrick was joined by his sons J. Vaughan Merrick and William Merrick. As Merrick and Sons, the firm "constructed almost all the machinery for the steamers of the U.S. Navy."[35] Perry's ship to Japan, the *U.S.S. Mississippi*, was powered by Merrick engines, as were the *Princeton*, the *San Jacinto*, the *Wabash*, the *Susquehanna*, and the *Saranac*. Merrick also built the machinery for two of Bache's Coast Survey ships and for a number of private contractors. The construction of marine engines gave Merrick's company a direct interest in the problems which concerned Isherwood, and the connection was reinforced by the fact that the Philadelphia Navy Yard soon emerged as the principal source for the service's steam-powered vessels. Marine engineering demanded the ability to cast and machine large masses of metal, a talent which many of Philadelphia's foundries developed in the years before the Civil War. Those who celebrated the city's industrial advance claimed that its workshops were responsible for "some of the largest Engines and Machines, as well as largest Castings, ever made in this country."[36]

The concentration of a number of firms with basically similar abilities led to a certain amount of specialization. For example, the city had early become a center for locomotive manufacturing. Philip Garrett, a machinist engaged in making lathes, presses, and other machinery, formed a partnership in 1835 with Andrew M. Eastwick to produce locomotives, an association which continued until 1839. The Norris Locomotive Works grew out of an 1831 agreement between William Norris, Stephen H. Long, and Dr. Richard Harlan, a Philadelphia naturalist. By 1857, the firm had constructed almost a thousand engines, many of them for use in Great Britain, Europe, and Latin

---

[34] Cover advertisements, *Journal of the Franklin Institute* 28 (October 1839).

[35] Freedley, *Philadelphia and its Manufactures*, p. 327. For more accurate details on the builders of Navy steamships, see Charles B. Stuart, *The Naval and Mail Steamers of the United States* (New York, 1853).

[36] Freedley, *Philadelphia and its Manufactures*, p. 326.

America.[37] Eastwick and Harrison was another of the city's locomotive firms which gained international repute. Joseph Harrison, Jr., became Eastwick's partner after Garrett retired, and the two produced railroad and stationary steam engines, as well as general machinery work. In 1843, Eastwick and Harrison contracted with the Russian imperial government to build the locomotives and rolling stock for the St. Petersburg and Moscow Railway, a considerable engineering accomplishment which brought wealth and fame to its builders.[38]

The most celebrated Philadelphia locomotive builder was Matthias W. Baldwin. From his original partnership with David H. Mason, Baldwin's firm grew steadily over the years, both in size and in the estimation of civil engineers. "Hurra Baldwin!!!" John C. Trautwine once wrote from Tennessee. "His iron horses rank as No. 1 down this way; I consider them the best in the world."[39] Charles Ellet, the engineer in charge of construction of the Virginia Central Railroad, claimed that the performance of Baldwin's locomotives over the Blue Ridge Mountains "confirmed the claim of the American Locomotive, in climbing steep grades, to unrivalled pre-eminence."[40] Specializing exclusively in locomotives came only with time, however. Until shortly before the Civil War, and under varying partnership arrangements, Baldwin's firm also produced stationary and marine steam engines, machine tools, pumps, sugar-mill machinery, blowing apparatus for furnaces, hydraulic presses, and general machine work. While the bulk of his effort was directed toward locomotives—he had built 1,500 by 1866—Baldwin also engaged in a varied foundry practice.[41]

[37] Information on Garrett and Eastwick is available in a report on their locomotives by the Committee on Science and the Arts, *Journal of the Franklin Institute* 22 (September 1836): 179–80. For Norris, see Henry Hall, ed., *America's Successful Men of Affairs*, 2 vols. (New York: The New York Tribune, 1895). For a good account of the city's locomotive builders, see Joseph Harrison, Jr., "The Locomotive Engine, and Philadelphia's share in its Early Improvements," *Journal of the Franklin Institute* 93 (March 1872): 161–74; (April 1872): 233–48.

[38] *The Biographical Encyclopedia of Pennsylvania of the Nineteenth Century* (Philadelphia: Galaxy Publishing Company, 1874), pp. 380ff, contains information on Harrison, as does Hall, *America's Successful Men of Affairs*, vol. 2, p. 369. Better still is Coleman Sellers, "An Obituary Notice of Mr. Joseph Harrison, Jr.," American Philosophical Society *Proceedings* 14 (1874–75): 347–55. A report from the Committee on Science and the Arts, concerning locomotives of Eastwick and Harrison, appeared in the *Journal of the Franklin Institute* 28 (June 1839): 383–85; and additional notice of their locomotives is in volume 35 (January 1843), pp. 15–19.

[39] John C. Trautwine to William Hamilton, Knoxville, October 15, 1838, Incoming Correspondence.

[40] As quoted in Freedley, *Philadelphia and its Manufactures*, p. 308.

[41] In addition to those sources of information on Baldwin cited in previous chapters, see *The Biographical Encyclopedia of Pennsylvania of the Nineteenth Century*,

Since the capital equipment of Philadelphia's ironworkers was basically similar, and since their techniques were essentially the same, it was usual for them to specialize out of general foundry and machine work. The Port Richmond Iron Works, operated by I. P. Morris and Company, tended to emphasize the construction of large stationary steam engines, primarily to power the pumps of urban water systems and to provide air blasts for iron furnaces. In 1858 it was claimed that the firm had built "the largest Engines ever constructed for making Iron with *Anthracite coal*."[42] The Morris concern also produced marine steam engines and iron lighthouses. Merrick's Southwark Foundry specialized in iron lighthouses, too, some of which were reputedly the largest in the world.[43] Merrick's gasholder frame, which he built for the Philadelphia Gas Works, was also said to hold a world's record. In fact, the manufacture of gas apparatus was another of the city's mechanical specialties. In addition to Merrick, Morris, Tasker, and Morris's Pascal Iron Works produced machinery and equipment for the manufacture of lighting gas, and there were a number of other firms engaged in making meters, governors, and related devices.[44]

Besides the companies which dominated the fields of steam-engine manufacture, locomotive construction, and the general production of heavy industrial machinery, by the 1850's Philadelphia had also become the center of the American machine-tool industry. Machineworking was an established tradition in the city. Since the early years of the nineteenth century, ingenious mechanics, such as Isaiah Lukens, David Mason, Rufus Tyler, and others, had constructed their own special-purpose tools and manufactured them for sale. By the 1840's the industry was well developed in the city. George Fletcher and Company advertised for sale their rose-turning engines, lathes, and related machine tools; Baldwin produced lathes and planing machines; and Merrick's firm became the sole U.S. licensee for Nasmyth's patented

---

p. 342; Hall, *America's Successful Men of Affairs*, vol. 2, p. 51; and the firm's cover advertisements in the *Journal* during the 1840's and 1850's.

42 Freedley, *Philadelphia and its Manufactures*, p. 327; *The Manufactories and Manufacturers of Pennsylvania of the Nineteenth Century* (Philadelphia: Galaxy Publishing Company, 1875), pp. 24–26.

43 Freedley, *Philadelphia and its Manufactures*, p. 327. For related information, see J. Vaughan Merrick, "On the History and Construction of Iron Lighthouses," *Journal of the Franklin Institute* 61 (March 1856): 145–50.

44 *The Manufactories and Manufacturers of Pennsylvania of the Nineteenth Century*, pp. 509–10.

steam hammer.[45] Specializing in machine tools, however, became particularly the province of two firms by the 1850's—Bement and Dougherty and William Sellers and Company.

William Bement learned his skills in the Amoskeag Machine Shop in New Hampshire and the Lowell Machine Shop in Massachusetts, two important New England centers of machinemaking. In 1851, Bement moved to Philadelphia, where he formed a partnership a few years later with James Dougherty, a local ironfounder, and the two established the Industrial Works, a firm second only to William Sellers & Company.[46] Sellers came directly out of Philadelphia's tradition in the mechanic arts. Family connections linked him to a number of prominent machinists. He apprenticed at an early age to an uncle, whose Wilmington, Delaware, machine shop provided an introduction to machinebuilding. He then joined another family-connected machine shop, in Providence, Rhode Island, for three years before returning to Philadelphia in 1848.[47] From that date until the Civil War, Sellers concentrated his efforts on the production of mill gearing and shafting, heavy machinery, and on the manufacture of machine tools. Both Sellers and Bement made "severely plain" unadorned machines, in a conscious effort to emphasize their engineering design and the quality of their materials. "Philadelphia Tools," it was claimed in 1858, "unquestionably surpass those made elsewhere in this country, in *strength, proportion,* and *workmanship.*"[48] The manufacture of special-purpose machines—lathes of exceptional size, railway turntables, and large boring machines, for instance—seemed to contemporary observers the capstone of the city's leadership in ironworking. As Joseph Harrison, Jr., remarked in 1872, "for nearly forty years Philadelphia skill has been sought for to fill responsible places in all parts

[45] Eugene S. Ferguson, ed., *Early Engineering Reminiscences [1815–40] of George Escol Sellers* (Washington, D.C.: Smithsonian Institution, 1965), is the best source of information on Philadelphia's early mechanical vitality. And again, cover advertisements in the *Journal* give some indication of the productions of Tyler, Fletcher, Merrick, and others. Philadelphia's emergence as the center of the American machine-tool industry in the years before the Civil War is described in Joseph Wickham Roe, *English and American Tool Builders* (New York: McGraw Hill, 1926).

[46] *The Manufactories and Manufacturers of Pennsylvania of the Nineteenth Century*, pp. 12–14.

[47] Sellers and his industrial activities are treated in all of the nineteenth-century biographical works mentioned just above in connection with Bement, Baldwin, Harrison, and Norris. In addition, see E. C. Savidge and William Anderson, eds., *A Gallery of Eminent Men of Philadelphia* (Philadelphia: Henry L. Everett, 1887); the obituary published in the *Journal of the Franklin Institute* 159 (May, 1905): 365–81; and Roe, *English and American Tool Builders*.

[48] Freedley, *Philadelphia and its Manufactures*, p. 314.

of the United States, in the West Indies, in South America and in Europe, and even in British India."[49]

Besides its influence in shaping *Journal* policies, the expansion of industry in the Quaker City during the 1840's and 1850's had several important effects on the Franklin Institute. One of the most immediate was to give additional impulse to the organization's exhibitions of domestic manufactures. While exhibitions brought in valuable revenue, the Board of Managers was also caught up with the idea that exhibitions were particularly significant as a measure of the nation's growing industrial prowess. From the decision in 1841 to hold annual fairs, exhibitions grew steadily in size. As in earlier days, the Committee on Exhibitions urged manufacturers to submit working machinery, because of its popular appeal, and employed other techniques to attract visitors. A newspaper, *The Fair*, published daily at the 1844 exhibition contained poetry appropriate to the occasion, news items, and advertisements by exhibitors. As the exhibitions grew larger, the committee was forced to seek expanded quarters. Dunn's Chinese Museum was used until it was destroyed by fire in 1854. Subsequent fairs were held in a hall constructed by Dr. David Jayne, famous for his patent medicines. By that time, from 75,000 to 100,000 visitors were attending the Institute's exhibitions.[50] To accommodate them, the exhibition for 1858—which, as it turned out, was the last one before the Civil War—was held in the State Armory.

Since 1838, the practice of defining award categories in advance of exhibitions had been discontinued. But prizes were still given to articles in a variety of classes, and to mark the importance of advancement in industrial progress, the managers increased the number and value of awards. In 1845 a gold medal called the Franklin Premium was introduced to reward "extraordinary" merit, in addition to the regular silver and bronze medals. By the 1850's the number of awards was further swelled by "recall" gold and silver medals, to convey special distinction on manufacturers whose products were consistently

49 Harrison, "The Locomotive Engine," *Journal of the Franklin Institute* 93 (April 1872): 247.

50 By the 1840's, exhibitions had assumed much of their modern character. Besides working machinery and public displays of the efficiency of domestic apparatus, manufacturers used attendants to explain their wares, and local restaurateurs set up branch establishments to purvey food and drink. The records and published reports of the Committee on Exhibitions contain details of each fair. For information on Dunn's Museum and Dr. Jayne's hall, see J. Thomas Scharf and Thomas Wescott, *A History of Philadelphia, 1609–1884*, 3 vols. (Philadelphia: L. H. Everts & Co., 1884), vol. 2, p. 948; and Baltzell, *Philadelphia Gentlemen*, p. 100.

of award quality.[51] As in prior exhibitions, there were complaints from disgruntled competitors and false claims of prize awards which the committee was forced to deny. But in 1851, a more serious assault was made on the Institute's leadership. A small group of people apparently angered at premium policies called for a change in management. In January an anonymous advertisement in the city's newspapers appealed to members of the society "who wish to see it the Pride of Mechanics and Scientific Men" to vote "in favor of a reformation of the many abuses existing for late years" by electing a reform slate of candidates.[52] The advertisement appeared on January 16th, the day of the Institute's annual election, too late for any counteraction by the Board of Managers, and the opposition gained ten seats on the Board. Reaction came at the next meeting of the Institute. A motion was made to consider the accusations and to discover on whose authority the advertisement had been published. The motion was discreetly tabled, however, and the issue quietly simmered for a year.[53] As the election for 1852 approached, the Institute's established leadership was better prepared. A circular endorsed by the organization's most distinguished figures was sent to all members, calling upon them to support the "Regular Ticket." Members were advised that "a strenuous effort" would be made at the coming election "to remove a majority of the present management." The opposition, according to the circular, was motivated by "dissatisfaction with premiums awarded at former exhibitions," and members were urged to vote "a prompt and decided rebuke to an effort which thus strives to pervert our noble society to the promotion of private instead of public advantage." The appeal was successful, and at a "very large" meeting of the Institute, the regular ticket was elected.[54]

Looking back now, it seems surprising that a quarrel over prize awards should serve as a basis for a wholesale attempt to overthrow the Institute's government. But in the nineteenth century, industrial exhibitions played a role of considerable economic importance, and

51 Minutes of Meetings, April 17, 1845, Franklin Institute Archives. As exhibitions grew larger there was a natural tendency to escalate premium awards. By 1852, for example, the lighting-fixtures firm of Cornelius, Baker & Company had over the years won every prize the committee offered and was therefore awarded a "Special Premium." *Report of the Twenty-third Exhibition of American Manufactures, held in the City of Philadelphia, from the 18th of October, to the 3d of November, 1853, by the Franklin Institute, of the State of Pennsylvania, for the Promotion of the Mechanic Arts* (Philadelphia: Barnard & Jones, 1853).

52 As quoted in Minutes of Meetings, February 20, 1851.

53 Ibid.

54 Circular letter, dated Philadelphia, January 5th, 1852, Franklin Institute Archives; Minutes of Meetings, January 15, 1852.

they were liable to some of the features of marketplace competition. Product displays directly served exhibitors in two ways. The award system served as a guide to consumers at a time when they received scant protection from any public agencies; and a prize therefore constituted an objective and authoritative seal of approval which gave a distinct market edge to the producer. Equally important, exhibitors expected direct sales at the Institute's annual fairs. A premium award conveyed a significant economic advantage in that respect, too. As a consequence, the competition for prizes was sharp.

From the beginning the Board of Managers hoped for exactly those results. Exhibitions were originated in a self-proclaimed effort to change American buying habits in order to create an atmosphere favorable to the consumption of domestic goods and the improvement of home industry. By 1850 it was clear that American manufacturers were more than capable of meeting domestic demand. And as industry became aware of its growing power, it recognized, too, the potential of an international marketplace.

The Crystal Palace exhibition in London in 1851 made explicit the outlines of an emerging international industrial competition. The occasion brought together for the first time the productions of the world's manufacturing countries, and comparisons of national styles were unavoidable. For Americans, industrial consciousness always carried an ideology, and it found expression in the Institute's exhibitions. "May we not indulge the hope," Thomas Balch addressed his audience at the closing ceremonies of the twenty-fourth exhibition in 1854, "that the mission of the American people is to free man from the necessity of mechanical drudgery, and leave him at liberty to give his powers, both of mind and body, to labor which requires intelligence?"[55] Balch's remarks, predicated on assumptions of "national disposition," came easily after the London exhibition. Since the managers of the Franklin Institute considered themselves the "pioneers" in American industrial fairs, it was also easy for them to assume that the Institute's displays somehow carried the burden of showing national disposition. In their report on the society's own 1851 exhibition, the committee noted that it was glad "to learn from persons who have had the opportunity of judging correctly, that our display has very much surpassed that made in the American department of the

[55] Report on the Twenty-fourth Exhibition of American Manufactures, held in the City of Philadelphia, from November 14, to December 2, 1854, by the Franklin Institute of the State of Pennsylvania, for the Promotion of the Mechanic Arts (Philadelphia: Barnard & Jones, 1855), p. 84.

great World's Fair."[56] While the remark has a parochial flavor, the Board had attempted a cooperative scheme with the Massachusetts Charitable Mechanics' Association to provide for proper American representation in London.[57] Three decades of exhibition experience had given the managers a sense of certainty about the direction and purpose of the nation's industry.

Ironically, while the Crystal Palace exhibition gave a new impetus and relevance to the Institute's exhibitions, the Board of Managers had already decided that industrial demands for sophisticated technical knowledge made its own educational program obsolete. In 1847, the Board terminated its traditional faculty appointments and the lectures in physics, chemistry, and technology. In place of the regular courses, John F. Frazer presented a totally new scheme. There would be about eighty lectures, he said, "divided into suitable courses, on subjects of general interest connected with the natural sciences."[58] Frazer's idea was that each series might last around ten weeks and that lecturers would be paid $100 for a course. At the same time, Frazer also moved a resolution to admit graduates of the University of Pennsylvania's newly created technical school, the Department of Arts, to membership in the Institute on the same terms as Central High alumni.

Both resolutions were connected. The Department of Arts was part of a movement in the United States toward advanced technical education which spelled the end of the Institute's traditional educational aims. Both Harvard and Yale also created new departments to teach the practical applications of science in 1847, the same year that William Barton Rogers published *A Plan for a Polytechnic School in Boston*, which ultimately led to the establishment of the Massachusetts Institute of Technology. In the 1840's, Americans concerned with technical education, and with European advances in that field, had already concluded that industrial competition between nations required specialized university-level institutions pointed toward the training of a new technical-managerial class.[59] Those ideas had been incorporated

[56] *Report of the Twenty-first Exhibition of American Manufactures, held in the City of Philadelphia, from the 21st of October to the 1st of November, inclusive, 1851, by the Franklin Institute of the State of Pennsylvania, for the Promotion of the Mechanic Arts* (Philadelphia: R. W. Barnard & Sons, 1851).

[57] Minutes of Meetings, July 18, 1850. A concern, if somewhat faint, continued about the apparent lack of effectiveness of America's exhibit at the Crystal Palace. There was some brief thought of an Institute investigation into the question, but it was not pursued. Minutes of Meetings, March 21, 1850; June 19, 1851.

[58] Minutes of the Board of Managers, April 21, October 20, 1847; June 21, July 19, 1848.

[59] For a brief discussion of the evolution of technical training in the United States, see Bruce Sinclair, "The Promise of the Future," in *Science in Nineteenth-*

in the Institute's 1838 School of Arts proposal, and they surfaced again in 1847 at the University of Pennsylvania.

By that date, too, the Institute's managers perceived that in a new era of technical training their own faculty and the old course structure consituted an anachronism. Speakers at the organization's annual exhibitions reiterated the point made by Lyon Playfair, one of the English commissioners at the Crystal Palace, that "industry must, in future, be supported, not by a competition of local advantages, but by a competition of intellect."[60] The London exhibition conclusively demonstrated the need for advanced technical schools especially directed toward international industrial competition. Alfred Kennedy, a European-trained chemist who established the Polytechnic College of the State of Pennsylvania in Philadelphia in 1853, argued the need for his new school on the same grounds. "Professional Miners, Engineers, and Directors of farms and factories, have not as yet existed as a class in this country," Kennedy claimed. Without such specialization, the United States faced incompetence, wasted capital, and what he called "a loss of position before the art-tribunal of nations."[61]

The Franklin Institute had been one of the key agencies in a vital revolution of American education. It had pointed out the need for systematic technical training—in place of older empirical or apprenticeship methods—for the rational exploitation of natural resources, the construction of transportation systems, and the industrial applications of chemistry. But the organization's original educational role was essentially a transitional one, and newer institutions emerged to train civil engineers, geologists, and chemists in a more direct way than provisional night school efforts could ever have done. These schools therefore received a level of support never enjoyed by the Institute, and it was thus continually impelled to seek new educational terrain.

John F. Frazer, who was actively engaged in the planning and organization of the University's new Department of Arts, perceived a local opportunity. The existence of Central High School, Booth's analytical laboratory, Kennedy's Polytechnic College, and the proposal for a science department in the University made the spectrum of

---

Century America: A Reappraisal, edited by George H. Daniels (Evanston: Northwestern University Press, 1972), pp. 249–72.

[60] *Report of the Twenty-third Exhibition of American Manufactures* . . . (Philadelphia: Barnard & Jones, 1853), p. 9.

[61] *Second Annual Announcement of the Polytechnic College, of the State of Pennsylvania* (Philadelphia: Inquirer Book Press, 1854), p. 6.

formal training appear reasonably complete.[62] However, an evening program of general interest slanted toward a mixed audience, largely emphasizing scientific subjects but without career implications, served a purpose. No one called Frazer's plan adult education because the term had not yet acquired its present usage, but more than anything else, that is what it was. Public expressions about the Institute's lectures always held out the prospect of a budding new Franklin who might be inspired by a popular talk on science. Undoubtedly, the lectures did serve to introduce some to science who might not otherwise have discovered its attractions. But by the 1850's, the educational program was more significant as one of the cultural opportunities of a large city.

The courses for the 1849–1850 season reveal Frazer's conception. John C. Cresson gave five lectures on the nature of sound; Charles M. Wetherill delivered ten on chemistry; and ten were devoted to mechanics. Fraley presented five lectures on the "Internal Improvements of Pennsylvania"; a course on hygiene occupied five evenings during the season; fifteen lectures were given on physiology; ten on the history of the Continental Congress; five on volcanic action; and ten lectures "On the Aboriginal Antiquities of America" completed the program.[63] More explicitly than when volunteer lectures on miscellaneous subjects were solicited to bring in money during the depressed days of 1841, the Committee on Instruction redirected the Institute's educational efforts. In time, William Sellers would recognize that the interests of large-scale manufacturing and the problems of mechanical engineering opened new avenues of educational value. Until then, evening lectures at the Institute were slanted toward general intellectual improvement.

The Institute's library came to fill the same kind of role. For many years the library occupied a modest position in the Board's hierarchy of concerns. It had served as one of the justifications for publishing a journal, but it was not until 1830 that the library acquired space of its own in the Institute. Thereafter it lived a quiet existence. It provided no direct income, nor was it immediately involved in those activities which gave the organization public notice. There was always a small group of men devoted to the library's interests, however, and their book donations, appropriations from the Board, plus the constant accretion

62 Saul Sack, *History of Higher Education in Pennsylvania*, 2 vols. (Harrisburg: Pennsylvania Historical and Museum Commission, 1963), provides information on technical and scientific education at the University of Pennsylvania.

63 Report of the Committee on Instruction, March 13, 1850, Franklin Institute Archives.

of periodical literature through exchanges with the *Journal* gradually produced a substantial technical library. The Board of Managers
regularly set aside funds for book purchases. In the early years, the
amounts were small—$60 in 1830, $76 in 1831—but the figure rose in
succeeding years. In 1836 almost $1,000 was appropriated, although
over $700 of that amount consisted of a special allocation to Bache, for
book purchases in Europe.[64] In the wake of the Masonic Hall disaster, book budgets fell to the 1831 level. As in times past, committee
members felt a proprietary interest in the library, assessing themselves for additional funds, and in 1844, digging into their own
pockets for an index to the collection. The committee published a catalog of the library in 1847—a project Frazer pushed to completion.[65]
The event marked the library's emergence to a position of importance
among the Institute's concerns and also indicated a shift in the
Board's interests.

The Franklin Institute had become an educational resource of a
somewhat different kind than originally anticipated. Its collections of
books, models, and minerals comprised a valuable adjunct to the class-
rooms of other educational agencies and to individuals of whatever age
no longer engaged in the process of organized instruction. The Board
of Managers recognized the possibilities of a new approach directed
less toward career advancement and more toward cultural improvement. Evening lectures were reoriented to that purpose. The library
was open six days a week, from ten in the morning until ten in the
evening. Space was expanded for more books, and then it opened an
hour earlier, at nine. More specimens were purchased for the technological cabinet, and the managers made building alterations to
render it more accessible to visitors.[66] When the Board doubled the
value of its insurance policies in 1855, the action constituted a tangible
recognition that museum and library collections had become a central
feature of the Institute's existence.

Larger collections pressed hard on the society's space, however, and
the Board of Managers once again turned to ideas for a new building.
As in 1835, the Board also visualized a structure large enough to house
its industrial exhibitions. Annual displays required an expansive atti-

64 See the annual reports of the treasurer for 1830, 1831, and 1836.
65 Minutes of the Board of Managers, November 20, December 18, 1844; January
15, 1845; February 18, December 16, 1846. The catalog was published under the title
66 Minutes of the Board of Managers, March 20, 1850; July 14, 1852.
*Catalogue of the Books belonging to the Library of the Franklin Institute of the
State of Pennsylvania, for the Promotion of the Mechanic Arts* (Philadelphia: S. D.
Steele, 1847).

tude in any event, but the demand for more space, the Committee on Exhibitions reported in 1856, "has convinced all parties that the period has arrived when the Institute should possess such a hall as will fully and fairly accommodate all future exhibitions of American skill and labor."[67] Other factors also led the managers to think about new quarters. Their building was thirty years old and needed repairs, including a fireproof roof, since its wooden shingles had several times been set ablaze by sparks from neighborhood fires. In the Board's mind, it was altogether a proper moment to reconsider moving the Institute, and in the spring of 1856 a committee was appointed to study the question.

Undoubtedly, the city's prosperity swayed the managers. Philadelphia's industrialists, talented and experienced, sent their machinery and steam engines to all parts of the United States and to an increasing number of foreign consumers. An elaborate system of canals and railroads strategically connected the city to nearby coal regions and gave it direct access to burgeoning markets in the West and South. Furthermore, iron shipbuilding, commenced in the 1850's, became so concentrated on the Delaware that it was described as the "American Clyde."[68] In the expansive mood of the day, the committee charged with looking into the matter of new quarters reported "a great disposition in the Community to assist the Institute in accomplishing that object."[69] In February 1857, the Board appointed George Erety, Merrick, Cresson, Frazer, and John Addicks a new committee to draft a plan for financing the construction of a new hall—fireproof and of sufficient size to house the society "in all its Departments." At a Board meeting the following month, however, John C. Cresson, who had assumed the presidency in 1856, when Merrick's industrial and railroad interests forced him to decline reelection, notified the managers that an anonymous friend of the Institute was prepared in a short time to offer "accommodations that would answer all their purposes."[70]

Just as it seemed the society was finally to receive the benefaction due long and honorable service, the Depression of 1857 fell like a dark cloud. Its financial consequences were as severe as those of 1837, and at

---

[67] *Report on the Twenty-fifth Exhibition of American Manufactures, held in the City of Philadelphia, from the 11th to the 29th Day of November, 1856, by the Franklin Institute of the State of Pennsylvania, for the Promotion of the Mechanic Arts* (Philadelphia: Barnard & Jones, 1857).

[68] For a study of iron shipbuilding in and near the city, see David B. Tyler, *The American Clyde: A History of Iron and Steel Shipbuilding on the Delaware from 1840 to World War I* (Newark, Del.: The University of Delaware Press, 1958).

[69] Minutes of the Board of Managers, December 10, 1856.

[70] Ibid., March 11, 1857.

the Institute another economic calamity brought a replay of events distressingly familiar. Income dropped, and the search for ways to economize began anew. Additional privileges were granted to the children, wards, and apprentices of members, in an effort to stimulate dues income. At the same time, the Board voted to charge Central High and University graduates for the benefits they enjoyed. Frazer relinquished $600 of his salary, and lecturers gave up their fees. The first wave of crisis did not, of course, reveal the problems yet to come. "Owing to the financial distress," the managers did not hold an exhibition in 1857, but in the following year they made ambitious plans for one and secured the State Armory to make a larger display than ever before. It was not a financial success, however, and in that respect only contributed to a worsening situation. Moreover, the anonymous friend apparently changed his mind. Subsequent plans for a new building, centering around an idea proposed by Joseph Harrison, Jr., bogged down in what appears to have been personality conflict.[71]

Meanwhile, the Institute's economic circumstances grew steadily more grave. Normally, operating expenses were met out of current income and exhibition receipts were allocated to meet interest payments and debt liquidation. There was little margin in the formula, but in good times—from the late 1840's into the 1850's—exhibitions yielded a profit, and even after paying running costs, the treasurer often had a modest balance. However, the 1856 exhibition only netted about $200, depression cut receipts, and the 1858 fair lost money.[72] That meant no funds for interest charges and revenues not always equal to ordinary expenses. By 1860, an examination of the Institute's financial condition revealed debts of $1,700, not counting interest or principal on old loans, and receipts scarcely sufficient for current bills.

71 Harrison was something of an embarrassment to his fellow industrialists in Philadelphia. He had grown wealthy from his Russian contracts, and he returned to the city with ambitious plans for its beautification and cultural improvement. But the single-mindedness which had proved such an asset in building Russian railroads was apparently a liability in matters of taste and judgment. Harrison's ideas for a new Institute building, the records indirectly suggest, fell into the same category as his other plans, and he left for an extended European tour in 1860, feeling that his motives had been misconstrued and unappreciated. Sellers, "An Obituary Notice of Mr. Joseph Harrison, Jr."; Minutes of the Board of Managers, January 26, February 9, 1859.

72 The 1848 exhibition, for instance, returned $4,200 to the sinking fund and provided an additional $1,200 for general appropriation. Minutes of the Board of Managers, February 16, 1848. In their report, the Committee on Exhibitions attributed the loss in 1858 to the Armory's location, "the position being too far from the centre of population." Report of the Twenty-sixth Exhibition of American Manufactures, held in the City of Philadelphia, from October 15, to November 13, 1858, by the Franklin Institute of the State of Pennsylvania, for the Promotion of the Mechanic Arts (Philadelphia: William S. Young, 1858).

The situation obviously required action, and once again the managers appointed a special Committee on the Financial Condition of the Institute. In March 1860, the committee presented its recommendations at a special meeting of the society. John M. Gries, chairman of the committee, had pointed out, in a circular to the members prior to the meeting, that its purpose was to raise money, and attendance was unusually large. By careful management, Gries claimed, the Institute's old debt had been reduced from $50,000 to $30,000. But interest charges represented "a sad clog" on the organization's ability "to increase its already valuable Library" or to pursue "scientific investigations and experiments, such as have heretofore added so much to its usefulness, and its standing in the community."[73] Gries and his committee proposed a straightforward appeal to generosity in an effort to raise the entire amount of indebtedness. Their approach was aimed at both heart and head. On one level, the appeal stressed the Institute's long and distinguished career of service and called upon a sense of civic pride:

Surely in a city like Philadelphia, distinguished by so many Literary, Scientific, and Charitable monuments of her liberality distinguished, too, by being the great centre of Arts and Manufactures in our country, the sum of thirty thousand dollars will be raised without difficulty.[74]

On a less abstract plane, Gries emphasized the organization's practical value to local industry. Let the debt be removed, he claimed, and all the Institute's resources could be brought to bear "upon the continued advance of the manufacturing interests of our city; By common consent considered its greatest source of present prosperity."[75]

The committee's plea, seconded by further remarks from Frederick Fraley, caught the spirit of the special meeting, and well over $4,000 was subscribed on the spot. Two thousand copies of a circular appeal were distributed to the members, urging them individually to solicit donations, and the fund was almost doubled in a month. To induce further contributions, the Board of Managers offered free admission to a season's lectures for a one-dollar donation and the addi-

---

[73] Report of the Special Committee on the Financial Condition of the Institute, March 11, 1860; Circular to members of the Institute from John M. Gries, March 26, 1860, both in the Franklin Institute Archives.

[74] Circular appeal "to the members of the Institute, and to their fellow citizens generally," from John M. Gries, John E. Addicks, John Agnew, Frederick Fraley, and William Sellers, April 6, 1860, Franklin Institute Archives.

[75] Report of the Special Committee on the Financial Condition of the Institute, March 11, 1860.

tional use of the library and reading room for a year with a three-dollar pledge.[76]

Financial pressure also forced the managers to look long and hard at the *Journal*'s expenses. It always lost money. By charging the value of periodicals received in exchange against the library's budget, the treasurer could make it appear that the magazine gained income for the Institute. But the balance was only on paper. By 1855 the publication had built up a net deficit of almost $5,000. Over a period of time, the Committee on Publications tried various strategies to increase revenue. In 1846, for instance, readers were offered free postage if subscriptions were paid in advance. In 1853, the committee reduced the price of multiple copies—five dollars for one copy, eight dollars for two copies, or ten dollars for three copies. More special offers came as deficits continued to mount. In 1855, Institute members were allowed a year's subscription at half price, provided that their membership dues were paid up.[77]

Hard times made more imperative the need to either reduce the *Journal*'s costs or increase its receipts. The managers pressured the committee on both counts, suggesting alterations in format or pricing and the possibility of getting its patent reports from *Scientific American* at a lower price than was paid Keller.[78] By 1860, the committee had reduced its coverage of patents to a simple listing, and in the following year it eliminated even that feature. Simultaneously, the press run was trimmed by 250 copies. Ironically enough, at the same time patent coverage was terminated, advertisements to encourage new subscriptions emphasized the fact that the *Journal* provided in its back issues "a complete record" of American patents granted since 1826. None of the committee's efforts brought a significant change in the *Journal*'s finances, and by 1863 the Board decided to sell back issues —which, given enough time, had always produced an income—at the price paid for waste paper.[79]

The managers had no time. More compelling events absorbed the attention of Americans, and from 1861 on the Institute's fortunes fell

[76] Minutes of Meetings, March 29, April 12, 19, 1860.

[77] Cover advertisements in the *Journal* detail the changing terms of subscription over a period of time. See also Minutes of the Board of Managers, November 10, 1852, and January 10, 1855; and the Records of the Committee on Publications, Franklin Institute Archives.

[78] Minutes of the Board of Managers, March 24, 1858; January 12, 1859; May 8, 1861.

[79] See the "Prospectus" published on back covers of the *Journal* in 1861 and 1862. With the outbreak of war, of course, the magazine lost all its Southern subscribers, to the further embarrassment of its funds.

steadily downward to their lowest ebb. The fund drive raised over $11,000 in pledges by the spring of 1861, but "owing to the unsettled state of business," the campaign was temporarily halted and then dropped when the Civil War broke out.[80] The conflict added its own particular problem to the Institute's burden. Nineteenth-century scientific and technical societies had no clear role to play in wartime. No administrative mechanism existed to link their expertise to the crisis, nor was there any precedent for a connection. If anything, tradition ran in the opposite direction; science was conceived as something which transcended boundaries and adversaries.[81] Individually, men were caught up in the contest. Many of the Institute's leaders were active in the formation of the Union Club, and their business firms were of considerable importance to the Union cause. Some were involved in the measures to defend the city against rebel attack, and some went off to war. In the society's records, however, only a brief notice of the death of Major John Gries, "from the effects of a wound received in the service of his country," suggested the existence of wartime.[82] The Institute and similar organizations in the city otherwise remained detached and remote from the great drama.

Without any clear relevance to the war and thus a direct call on the attention of its community, the organization's already precarious situation worsened. Fraley presented a new plan in the fall of 1861, in another effort to save the society. The previous year's attempt to raise money by direct contribution had failed, Fraley said, and he proposed instead a stock system, which would give its holders certificates of marketable value and a proprietary interest in the Institute. Other societies had used such a mechanism to establish themselves, and it seemed to Fraley all the more appropriate "for the relief of an old and useful Institution having already in its possession Real Estate, Library and Cabinets of great value."[83] His idea involved an issue of 5,000 shares at ten dollars each, the total estimated worth of all the society's holdings. The stock was divided into two categories. Holders of the first-class stock received a share for ten dollars, payable in quarterly installments and transferable at will for a small charge. If, by their purchase, they wished simply to aid the Institute, no further payments were required, and Fraley's scheme incorporated a series of devices to

---

[80] Minutes of the Board of Managers, March 13, 1861.

[81] Joseph Henry, for example, while personally involved in wartime activities, attempted to keep the Smithsonian neutral and aloof from the "exciting subjects of the day" A. Hunter Dupree, *Science in the Federal Government: A History of Policies and Activities to 1940* (Cambridge, Mass.: Harvard University Press, 1957), p. 131.

[82] Minutes of the Board of Managers, July 9, 1862.

[83] Ibid., May 8, 1861.

maintain its par value. Holders of second-class stock were eligible, for an annual payment of two dollars, to enjoy all the educational facilities, plus free admission to exhibitions, and to vote each share of stock at annual elections. First-class stock could be converted to the second class upon payment of the requisite fees, but once converted it remained in that class. Since the stock constituted a proprietary share in the Institute's physical assets, it paid no interest, nor was there any provision for its redemption. For someone already interested in the society, Fraley's plan offered a greater sense of identification, and to holders of second-class stock a share in its affairs. For anyone else, who could in any event buy a regular membership for three dollars, the idea had no compelling attractions.

Nor did it solve the immediate financial problem. Against a melancholy background of gratuitous lectures and personal loans, the Board of Managers shuffled and reshuffled the Committee on the Debt Fund and tried to think of ways to make meetings more interesting to members and to find money for badly needed building repairs.[84] And the Civil War was a much more pressing concern, except to the most loyal members. Furthermore, they had been in harness a long time and had already seen the Institute through one financial crisis. While Merrick had removed himself from the organizations center in 1855, he continued on the Board of Managers, adding yearly to his prolonged concern for the society. Cresson was of the same generation. His membership stretched back twenty-five years, during most of which time he served as chairman of the Committee on Science and the Arts, performed other important committee duties, and for a decade filled the professorship of mechanics and natural philosophy. Fraley had fought many long years to keep the organization's financial balance. And John F. Frazer—lecturer, *Journal* editor, exhibition supervisor, and the active spirit at monthly meetings—was plagued with a recurring illness which forced him to take long recuperative vacations. The Institute needed the dynamism of new leaders, and the older generation knew it.

[84] The Board was forced to seek a personal loan of $500, in May 1861, to meet current expenses, and another in December for the same reason, and in October 1862 it had to appeal once more to its friends for immediate aid. In hopes of attracting members, refreshments were reintroduced at monthly meetings, a practice which had been discontinued twenty years earlier in the interest of economy. Cresson, Frazer, Fairman Rogers, and others continued to lecture without pay. Minutes of the Board throughout the period are ample testimony of the society's fiscal difficulties.

XII

CONSOLIDATING A TECHNICAL COMMUNITY

... the Institution under the impulse of the
younger and more active members who are now
to guide its destiny will put forth its strength in a
long career of increasing usefulness.

John C. Cresson, January 21, 1864

For years, the Institute's managers had talked about the day a new generation would take over. When the time finally came, it was hardly triumphant. Cresson set the stage for a transition with an announcement at the December 1863 meeting of the organization that he wanted to step down. To fill his place he nominated William Sellers. Simultaneously, in the interest of an "infusion of new spirit," Fraley resigned as corresponding secretary.[1] Other officers and Board members followed, and in the ensuing election, an almost totally new slate of officers and managers was installed. The change was not accompanied by an air of conspiracy; nor were the new faces unknown. It was a conscious effort at regeneration. Sellers was elected president, and John H. Towne and Fairman Rogers were elected vice-presidents. Rogers, professor of civil engineering at the University of Pennsylvania, was a man of wealth and learning who had studied with Frazer at the University, worked with Bache in the Coast Survey, and lectured at the Institute. Along with Frazer, he was also one of the original members of the National Academy of Sciences.[2] Robert Briggs, elected to Fraley's place as corresponding secretary, immediately took an active role in the Institute's proceedings. Briggs was a Bostonian who had come to Philadelphia in 1860 as superintendent and engineer of the Pascal Iron Works.[3] New members of the Board included B. H. Bartol, superin-

[1] Minutes of Meetings of the Franklin Institute, December 17, 1863, Franklin Institute Archives.

[2] For biographical information on Rogers, see the privately printed obituary, *F.R., 1833–1900* (Philadelphia, 1903).

[3] "Memorial of Robert Briggs," *Journal of the Franklin Institute* 115 (1883): 229–36.

tendent of the Southwark Foundry; Charles H. Cramp, of the iron
shipbuilding firm; J. Vaughan Merrick, who took his father's seat on
the Board; Coleman Sellers, an associate of his cousin in William
Sellers & Company; and James Dougherty, of Bement and Dougherty.

More than any previous Board of Managers, the new men bore the
stamp of industrial power and success. They were leaders in the emerging field of mechanical engineering and directly concerned with
attempts to systematize manufacturing processes. They provided, therefore, both a new sense of direction and a potential new source of income
for the Institute. Further, they came to office with a self-imposed task.
Never before had a meeting of the Board of Managers taken the
ceremonial form that it took for the first meeting under the new administration, especially to mark a changing of the guard. Robert Briggs
made a handsome speech to express the society's gratitude to those who
had gone before. "The Institute," Briggs said, "represented not only
the relations between the mechanic and the scientific man in Philadelphia, but was beyond that, the representative institution of the connexion of mechanics with Science for the Country." No other similar
organization in the world had its reputation, he claimed, and its position was directly the result of those who, with Cresson, had labored
so long on its behalf. The retiring president responded in kind, concluding with the hope "that the Institution under the impulse of the
younger and more active members who are now to guide its destiny
will put forth its strength in a long career of increasing usefulness."[4]

The new leaders stepped in immediately and firmly. They had been
called upon to save the organization, and by their actions they clearly
meant to do so. Sellers set in train a series of steps designed to reorganize the Institute. The first and most obviously critical job was to raise
money, either by stock sales or "by absolute donations, of unconditional
character."[5] There was still some question about the legality of the
stock issue, however, which called for constitutional changes. Since
charter amendment required action by the state legislature, Sellers also
used the occasion to revise the society's bylaws. A special committee
was formed for that job. At the same time, two other committees were
named to report on building alterations and on ways to upgrade the
quality and interest of monthly meetings.[6] When an amended charter
passed the legislature in May 1864, the way was clear for the internal
changes Sellers had in mind, for sales of the new stock, and for a vigorous campaign to eliminate the debt problem.

[4] Minutes of Meetings, January 21, 1864.
[5] Minutes of the Board of Managers, January 24, 1864. Franklin Institute Archives.
[6] Ibid., February 10, March 9, 1864.

The Institute's records are silent about the work of the Committee
on the Debt Fund, which Sellers had reorganized. But the nature of
stock purchases speaks eloquently. By the end of the year, Sellers and
J. Vaughan Merrick reported to the Board that between them they had
garnered subscriptions to the first-class stock of one hundred shares each
from twenty-seven individuals and business establishments, for a total
of $27,000.[7] In little over six months almost the total amount of the
institution's debt was wiped out, and contributions were still coming
in. Furthermore, the money had not been raised by an appeal for one-
dollar donations or by an appeal to those who might have subscribed
for the additional privileges of membership. The money came largely
from Philadelphia's industries and industrialists, who by a change in
the stock plan were able to vote shares of the first class.

Financial solvency was only one of several dramatic transformations
Sellers brought about at the Institute. The new bylaws centralized
power in the organization. In 1843, when the managers first struggled
with the burden of the Masonic Hall debt and interest charges, Fraley
and Samuel V. Merrick pushed through a number of constitutional
revisions to engage the membership more directly in the society's affairs.
Over the strong objections of Baldwin and others on the Board, Fraley
argued that if the Institute did not have the active interest of its membership, no plan for its financial security would succeed.[8] His changes
gave members authority previously wielded by the managers in the
make-up of committees and control over the procedures for admitting
new members. Sellers reversed those decisions. Under the terms of the
new bylaws, the president was also made chairman of the Board,
whereas previously the managers had elected the chairman from their
own number. The Board itself was rearranged so that one-third of the
managers were subject to reelection or replacement each year.

And there were other changes. While Sellers gathered control of the
organization back into the Board's hands, he moved to upgrade intellectual activities. Professorships in chemistry, natural philosophy, and
mechanics were reestablished. Monthly meetings were restructured to
reduce the amount of business and to increase informational content.
The Board appointed a new Committee on the Scientific Proceedings of
the Institute to reform membership meetings. Papers, the subjects of
which were to be announced in advance, would be delivered at future

---

[7] Ibid., January 19, 1865.
[8] See Fraley's draft of the Nineteenth Annual Report of the Board of Managers,
January 1843. In their conscious attempt to lower the Board's profile in the society,
Fraley and Merrick made the historian's job a bit more difficult, since quarterly and
annual reports from the Board ceased in 1843.

meetings, and the committee would accept for presentation only those new inventions or discoveries germane to the society's purposes. By implication, at least, members could no longer anticipate such sensations as the "singing mouse" introduced at an earlier meeting.[9] Two decades before the establishment of the American Society of Mechanical Engineers, Sellers refashioned the Franklin Institute into something like a professional engineering society to serve the technical interests of manufacturers, with the same centralized structure which characterized both industry and later the American Society of Mechanical Engineers.

As a direct example of the style of meetings he had in mind, Sellers personally presented the first paper. It was modestly entitled "A System of Screw Threads and Nuts," but the topic once again connected the Institute back to technical issues of national consequence. No uniform system of screw threads existed in America, Sellers pointed out, nor had any "organized attempt" been made to establish one. Instead, manufacturers tended to work out whatever combination of form and dimension seemed best suited to their own interests. Such chaos threatened America's industrial advancement, Sellers warned, and he advised his audience that so radical a defect should be allowed to exist no longer."[10]

English engineers had long before recognized the importance of a standard system and by common agreement had adopted a uniform set of proportions, proposed by Joseph Whitworth, so that a bolt of any given diameter always had the same form of thread and the same number of threads per inch.[11] Since the two countries shared the same unit measurements of length, Sellers suggested, it might well be argued they should also share the same thread system. He outlined for his audience

---

[9] From the time of Bache's reorganization of monthly meetings, they constituted an important mechanism for the discussion of scientific and technical issues. Bache and Joseph Henry used them to explain the principles and use of the dew-point hygrometer. Walter Johnson presented the results of his investigations at monthly meetings, and over a period of years, Frazer contributed information on a wide variety of scientific discoveries. Generally, meetings considered topics in the physical sciences, such as Frazer's explanation of Foucault's pendulum experiment to demonstrate the earth's rotation or such technical questions as steam-boiler incrustation. In time, however, the quality of discussion declined. Members at the September 16, 1847, meeting listened to the singing mouse "with much attention," and William Hamilton recorded the fact that "it excited considerable interest." But the topic was not one for the kind of discussion Bache originally had in mind.

[10] Minutes of Meetings, April 24, 1864. The proceedings of the meeting, including Sellers's paper, were also published in the *Journal of the Franklin Institute*, vol. 77 (May 1864), pp. 343–51. For further details, see Bruce Sinclair, "At the Turn of a Screw: William Sellers, the Franklin Institute, and a Standard American Thread," *Technology and Culture* 10 (January 1969): 20–34.

[11] *Journal of the Franklin Institute* 77 (May 1864): 344.

the essential features of Whitworth's standard, as compared with the one he proposed for American usage. Except for a slight difference in a few sizes, both systems employed basically the same range of pitch, that is, the same number of threads per inch. Building to his argument, Sellers again noted that pitch differences were not substantial enough to call for a separate American standard, "providing the other peculiarities of the English system should meet our approval."[12] Then he turned to the matter of thread form.

Whitworth's thread, based on a shape averaged from samples of the best English shop practice, consisted of sides sloping at an angle of fifty-five degrees, with the apex of each angle, top and bottom, rounded to a curve of set dimension. There Sellers leveled his objections to the English system. First, he claimed, the fifty-five-degree angle was difficult to verify without special gauges made by special tools. Next, in normal practice the rounded top and bottom threads of nuts and bolts could not easily be made to fit each other. As in the case of the angle, the question was not that the English thread was impossible to make but rather that consistently accurate production was difficult. The details of thread-cutting constituted Sellers's third objection. Because Whitworth's thread form was more complicated to shape, it was also more costly. It required "three kinds of cutters and two lathes to perform what with our practice requires but one cutter and one lathe."[13]

Simplicity and economy were powerful arguments for the system Sellers proposed for American usage, and he capped his plan with a simple gauge to insure uniformity and a standard for nut sizes and shapes. The need for some kind of system was compelling and widely felt. Just the previous year, the editor of *Scientific American* had claimed: "If there is any one thing in the transactions of the machine shop more incomprehensible than another, it is the want of some settled size or number for screw threads."[14] Nuts and bolts of the same diameter but made in different places would not fit each other. Repairs or replacements demanded that thread be cut especially to match the original. And some manufacturers purposely used threads of unusual design to prevent outside repairs of their machinery. It was, as Sellers had said, a radical defect.

It was also a problem particularly amenable to a Philadelphia solution, since the city's industrialists were accustomed to thinking in terms of standardization. Ten years earlier, George Wallis, one of the British commissioners to New York's 1853 imitation of the Crystal Palace

12 Ibid.
13 Ibid., p. 346.
14 *Scientific American* 9 (October 10, 1863), p. 233.

exhibition, visited Philadelphia's industrial establishments. Included
in his observations was notice of a uniform system already in use:

The gas-works of the city of Philadelphia are celebrated for the perfection to
which the manufacture of gas is carried, and the thorough scientific principles
upon which every detail of the establishment is carried out, not the least important of which is the uniform gauge of all fittings; so that any part becoming
defective is at once repaired without trouble, and, of course, at a less expense
than when a constant variation in the gauge of the fittings is permitted.[15]

Uniformity was equally important in machine-tool manufacture. Sellers
had introduced it in his own plant, in which "all the parts are made to
standard gauges, whereby each will fit its corresponding part in a hundred tools."[16] He applied the same approach to screw threads and was
already using the system he proposed to the Institute, as were Merrick,
Bement and Dougherty, and the Philadelphia Navy Yard.[17] Furthermore, Sellers had developed an automatic screw-cutting machine, a
device of great utility in a standardized system.

The rationality of a national system was a convincing argument for
action, and the Institute immediately began a campaign to establish
the Sellers thread as the American standard. Copies of his paper were
forwarded to other societies for their consideration and support. The
managers also appointed a special committee whose purpose was to
present "a proper system of screw threads, bolt-heads, and nuts, to be
recommended by this Institute, for the general adoption of American
engineers."[18] Representatives of Philadelphia's ironworking establishments dominated the committee. William Bement was named chairman.
Charles T. Parry and Edward Longstreth were, respectively, superintendent and foreman at Baldwin's Locomotive Works, which also
employed standardized manufacturing processes;[19] James Moore was
associated with the Matthews and Moore machine shop; Algernon

[15] Nathan Rosenberg, ed., *The American System of Manufactures. The Report
of the Committee on the Machinery of the United States 1855 and the Special Reports
of George Wallis and Joseph Whitworth* (Edinburgh: The University Press, 1969), p.
276.

[16] Edwin T. Freedley, *Philadelphia and its Manufactures; a Hand-Book of the
Great Manufactories and Representative Mercantile Houses of Philadelphia, in 1857*
(Philadelphia: E. Young & Co., 1860), p. 315.

[17] A list of most of the country's major machinery firms, with the thread system
each employed, is printed in *Report of the Board to Recommend a Standard Gauge
for Bolts, Nuts and Screw Threads for the United States Navy, May 1868* (Washington, D.C.: Government Printing Office, 1880), pp. 7–13.

[18] *Journal of the Franklin Institute* 77 (May 1864): 351.

[19] John H. White, Jr., *American Locomotives: An Engineering History, 1830–1880*
(Baltimore: The Johns Hopkins Press, 1968), p. 25.

Roberts represented the Pencoyd Iron Works; John H. Towne, who by that time had become a partner in I. P. Morris, Towne and Company's Port Richmond Iron Works, was on the committee; J. Vaughan Merrick and B. H. Bartol represented the Merrick interests; and finally, both Coleman and William Sellers were also named to the investigation.

From the outset, the committee's direction was clear. Bement made the point explicit when he advised *Scientific American*'s editor that his committee welcomed the opinions of "all good *practical* mechanics."[20] The magazine picked up Bement's emphasis and remarked that it was a matter of good fortune that such a vital question had not fallen "into the toils of schemers and theorists who would have confused instead of making the subject plain and practical."[21] Since almost any system would presumably have been an advance over the prevailing anarchy, "practical" obviously had special connotations to American machinists. When the committee presented its report in December 1864, those implications were laid bare. The sixty-degree angle of Sellers's thread was "more readily obtained" than any other form. A flat top was easier to produce than a rounded one, which not only required more machining but an entire set of gauges, since the radius of each curved top would vary with thread size. In other words, "practical" meant something an ordinary workman would do with ordinary equipment at the least expense. As the committee put it, a national standard should be based on "such a form of thread as would enable any intelligent mechanic to construct it without any special tools."[22]

The system which met all those prerequisites was the one Sellers had proposed. In their report, the committee did not explicitly identify it as his, but their own proposal incorporated unchanged the same ideas. Without widespread acceptance, however, a standard was certainly not a standard. The Institute took upon itself the job of securing national conformity to the plan. The society passed two resolutions aimed at unification. First, an appeal was directed at governmental agencies—the Quartermaster General, the Navy's Bureau of Steam Engineering, and the Army Corps of Engineers—to push conformity by requiring the Institute's system in all new contracts. Then railroad companies were urged to do the same. Copies of the committee report were also sent "to all Mechanical and Engineering Associations or Institutes, and the principal Machine and Engine Shops in the country,

20 *Scientific American* 11 (October 29, 1864): 278.
21 Ibid., 12 (March 4, 1865): 151.
22 Minutes of Meetings, December 15, 1864. The report was also published in the *Journal of the Franklin Institute* 79 (January 1865): 53–57.

with a request that they will use their influence in the proposed
system."[23]

In one respect, uniform sizes and shapes for nuts and bolts was the
concept of interchangeable-parts manufacture simply carried a logical
step further. But the idea demonstrated the maturity of industry. By
1865, the private sector had grown to the stage that it could think of
its own interests and needs—on a technical level—in national terms.
The campaign also marked an important watershed in the Institute's
development. In contrast to an earlier time, when the organization
habitually looked to the public sector for a sense of its worth, the matter
of a screw-thread standard was determined by private industry. Initially, the managers approached governmental agencies, and the
Bureau of Steam Engineering investigated the question carefully.
Indeed, it recommended the Sellers system for naval use. But it did so
on the basis that private industry was more likely to employ his standard than Whitworth's.[24] There was no hint that government should use
its authority to compel conformity. In fact, the argument was carried
largely by entrepreneurially-oriented technical associations, and in
time the system came to be known as the Sellers, or Franklin Institute,
standard.[25]

Sellers's plan for a national screw-thread standard gave the Institute
a vital and creative new mission. American industry was already powerful enough to compete with the world's established manufacturing
nations. In that sense, it no longer needed the society's fostering care.
But future profits demanded rationalization and organization on a
larger scale. Systematizing the shape and dimensions of nuts and bolts
was only one of many possibilities. The committee on screw threads
suggested as much when it noted that uniformity in one sphere would
demonstrate benefits "so manifest as to induce reform in other particulars of scarcely less importance." But even before their report was
presented, Robert Briggs proposed that the Institute should investigate
the weights, measures, and coinage of the United States "with regard to
the proposed introduction of the decimal system."[26] Another committee
took up the question of standardizing railroad signals, an issue with
significant implications for public safety and the expeditious movement

[23] Ibid., p. 56.
[24] Report of the Board to Recommend a Standard Gauge for Bolts, Nuts and
Screw Threads for the United States Navy, May 1868, p. 30.
[25] The Master Car-Builder's Association argued "Uniformity can only be secured
by the general adoption of a correct standard," and it instructed its standards committee "to urge all railroad companies to adopt the Sellers' or Franklin Institute system for all new work" (American Machinist 5 [September 9, 1882]: 3).
[26] Minutes of Meetings, February 18, 1864.

of passengers and freight. And there were clearly other subjects which similarly called for rational analysis and conformity—constants to measure everything from units of horsepower to sizes for plumbing supplies.

In the search for a standard screw thread, the Franklin Institute found its door to the future. No other agency existed to perform the same functions. National engineering societies, which might address themselves to questions of uniform practice, did not exist. Nor was the federal government disposed to act—the National Bureau of Standards was not created until the twentieth century. But it was an ideal role for the Institute. The organization had reputation, an important ingredient in securing widescale conformity to standards. In the *Journal* it had a national voice. And the society was located at the center of America's machine and machine-tool industries. Furthermore, the new mission also defined a new clientele for the organization, adding the attractions of support to its zeal for usefulness.

Those two elements—funding and sense of mission—were critical to the Institute's regeneration. It was not simply that money solved all problems. In times past, momentum had existed with only slender financial resources, and there were societies which were solvent but indolent. In Sellers's administration, support and objectives were positively linked. A clear feeling of purpose brought vitality to all of the organization's proceedings. Members came to meetings in larger number. New lectures were planned. New lines of investigation were started. The Navy's request for Institute representation on a special board to conduct experiments on the nature of steam power and its effective use gave further impulse to the society.[27] Relief from debt amplified the same spirit. Money was finally available for new seats in the lecture hall, in place of the "exceedingly uncomfortable" old benches which a generation of audiences had painfully endured. The building was painted, and other repairs and alterations were possible.

[27] Early in March 1864, Sellers received a letter from Gideon Welles, Secretary of the Navy, asking for the appointment of a three-man committee "especially conversant with the theory and practice of steam and the Steam Engine." The Institute's group along with similar committees from the Navy and the National Academy of Sciences would form a Commission on the Expansion of Steam, to "conduct, witness and report upon" a jointly formulated course of experiments. Sellers appointed John H. Towne, J. Vaughan Merrick, and Richard A. Tilghman to the Institute's committee. The Commission met periodically during the next two years, but only a few progress reports were issued, and nothing further was ever accomplished. Minutes of Meetings, March 17, April 24, 1864; A. Hunter Dupree, *Science in the Federal Government: A History of Policies and Activities to 1940* (Cambridge, Mass.: Harvard University Press, 1957), p. 146.

Money was available for the library, too, and the Board allocated $1,500 for books that had gone unpurchased in poorer times.

Sellers also renovated the Institute's administration. The revised bylaws did away with the offices of the recording and corresponding secretaries, substituting in their place a single secretary. But the new position was invested with those qualities Frazer had embodied as treasurer and executive. The secretary, as the revised rules put it, "shall be a person of scientific and literary attainments," charged with the regular duties of the office plus that of keeping the organization informed of important advances in science, engineering, and industry.[28] Frazer was moved to a third vice-presidency—another result of constitutional revision—and Fraley returned to the office of treasurer, which once again held responsibility simply for finances.

Sellers also ended the complicated commission arrangements by which William Hamilton gained an income, and he was paid a straight salary of a $1,000 annually. The new position of secretary demanded a larger sum, since it was to be filled by a man of science who, in addition to his administrative duties, would intellectually represent the Institute. The Board determined on $1,500 annually for his salary and in January 1865 named Henry Morton to the post. A University of Pennsylvania graduate in chemistry, Morton was headed toward a bright career in technical education.[29] His nomination insured the connection between science and practice which the organization had always seen as its essential contribution to the mechanic arts.

By 1865, as the country turned from civil warfare to the task of reconstructing a nation, the Franklin Institute was itself pulled back together again. And just as its official records were unmarked by the outbreak of conflict, peace also arrived unheralded. In a quiet way the Institute resumed its former connections with Southern friends. "Over four sad and eventful years have passed since we parted," William McNeill wrote from Virginia. "My usual kind feelings towards your

28 Minutes of Meetings, June 16, 1864.

29 Morton first gained notice in Philadelphia for his remarkable talent as a popular science lecturer. An 1865 series of talks on "Light," "Sound," and related topics was delivered at the Academy of Music in order to accommodate larger audiences than the Institute's hall could seat. Crowds swarmed to the lectures, which received very wide publicity, and Morton repeated them in New York, Baltimore, Providence, and New Haven. He became editor of the *Journal of the Franklin Institute* in 1867 and professor of chemistry at the University of Pennsylvania in 1869. In 1870 Morton accepted the presidency of Stevens Institute, a new technical school specializing in mechanical engineering, where he enjoyed a long and distinguished career. Coleman Sellers and Albert R. Leeds, eds., *Biographical Notice of Pres't Henry Morton, Ph.D., of the Stevens Institute of Technology* (Hoboken, N.J.: Stevens Institute, 1892).

noble old Institute and its worthy members still continue," he said, "political changes do not affect, happily, the good feelings which generally exist among men who devote themselves to science." In a reflective mood, however, McNeill could not help remembering bygone days and "the pleasant hours I used to spend in the 'Old Franklin.' "[30] For the Institute, too, it seemed almost as if past and future were momentarily cast in high relief. Its history clearly defined an important phase in America's material development, yet it was equally apparent that the years ahead would be different.

The organization had been dominated by the idea that a positive connection existed between technology and America's destiny and that the society served national purposes. Inevitably, such a conviction led to the assumption that government should encourage technical advance. In that vein, it seemed perfectly logical to appeal for Congressional aid for the *Journal*, to argue in favor of an equivalent coinage between Great Britain and the United States, or to consider experiments on the durability of iron ships, "provided the Government will defray the necessary expenses of materials and labor."[31] In short, it was consistent with the Institute's self-image to think in terms of a public role, either with regard to the solution of specific technical problems or with reference to the formulation of governmental policy in technical matters. Indeed, in the period before the Civil War, it seldom occurred to the Board of Managers that it might somehow be improper to speak to issues of political consequence or that certain questions might better be left to the private sector for solution.

Since the Board of Managers pictured the Franklin Institute as an agency of public utility, it followed naturally that they should also think of public support. Bache vocalized the idea best in his 1842 exhibition speech—benefit to the whole called for financial assistance from the whole. Spokesmen for the Institute frequently, and with a measure of pride, described how much the organization had accomplished without any direct subvention from the public purse. But implicitly, if not explicitly, the managers expected public aid for those contributions. Years in advance of the widespread acceptance of a managerial conception of government, the Institute's leaders argued that technical expertise was a normal expense of efficient proceeding in public affairs, justifiably purchased with tax dollars.

Industry, conversely, had come clearly to appreciate the importance

---

[30] T. E. McNeill to W. Hamilton, Lynchburg, Virginia, July 7, 1865, Incoming Correspondence, Franklin Institute Archives.

[31] Minutes of the Committee on Science and the Arts, February 11, 1847, ibid.

of skilled technical management. Men like Briggs, C. T. Parry, Bartol, and Longstreth filled engineering and supervisory positions in the city's leading mechanical establishments, which had grown to a scale and complexity beyond the supervision of original proprietors. The need for technical knowledge was itself not new, of course. Even before the Institute's founding, particularly through the unfortunate experiences of men such as John Fitch, Philadelphians were aware that ignorance of European advances was the greatest single stumbling block to inventive progress.[32] And, after all, the organization had been started partly to remedy the deficiency. What distinguished 1865 from 1824 was that by 1865 Americans had learned from science the most effective means of securing, diffusing, and advancing technology.

The search had begun with essentially eighteenth-century precedents, principally the use of prizes to stimulate ingenuity. Europeans and Americans devised a great many institutions, in the period before 1824, to advance technology by inducements to the skillful to improve upon their skills. The mechanics' institute movement meant, through educational reforms, to open new avenues of progress to the craftsman. And in the United States, particularly, a democratic ideology gave special force to the vision that the philosopher's principles and the mechanics's skills might even be joined in the same person, who would then attain his rightful place in the new republic. As Bishop Alonzo Potter once put it: "I give but utterance to the spirit of our institutions, and to the views of all good and wise men, when I say, that in this land we are, or at least ought to be, *all workingmen* and *all gentlemen.*"[33]

The idea that in America science would be redeemed from its historic subjugation to class and privilege, both by its connection to practical skill and by its application to the common good, was a widely popular theme. Indeed, most historical interpretation of the Franklin Institute's significance has cast its role in somewhat that light. But the organization's crucial relationship to science was not in encouraging the uninformed to a "contemplation of the sublime," to use Perry Miller's phrase, even if introductory lectures were often delivered in that mood.[34] Nor was it in the union of theory and practice, at least as those ingredients were originally conceived. The Institute's importance

[32] Carroll W. Pursell, Jr., *Early Stationary Steam Engines in America* (Washington, D.C.: Smithsonian Institution, 1969), p. 20.
[33] As quoted in Daniel H. Calhoun, *The American Civil Engineer: Origins and Conflict* (Cambridge, Mass.: The M.I.T. Press, 1960), p. 198.
[34] Perry Miller, *The Life of the Mind in America from the Revolution to the Civil War* (New York: Harcourt, Brace & World, 1965), p. 275.

came from its formulation of a scientific style for technology, fortified by intellectual standards and based on original research and publication.

It has also been assumed that the solitary inventor, depending on native ingenuity, a bit of luck, and his own tireless labor, was the central figure in American technical development until the closing decades of the nineteenth century, when he was finally pushed from the stage by corporate-financed industrial research teams. The Institute's history suggests some modification of that idea. By the 1840's the complexity of a variety of industrial pursuits was already beyond most inventors. Despite Dr. Jones's persistent efforts to elevate the level of inventive activity, for instance, the vast majority of patents were worthless. Moreover, it is clear that in the years before the Civil War, the critical work in certain areas of technical activity took place within the context of a community, whether tightly knit in the prosecution of cooperative experiments or more loosely structured in the assumption of shared interests and values, which identified mutual concerns and promoted a common methodology.

The mechanics' institute movement provided a basis for the new approach, particularly in its emphasis on open knowledge and a group consciousness, instead of the individualistic practices of craft secrecy. But science offered an even more explicit model of a community whose labors were characterized by detailed, precise, systematic investigation into carefully restricted problems. Alexander Dallas Bache recognized the value of those methods in solving technical questions. From its beginnings, the Franklin Institute's leaders visualized a national position for the organization, but with his administrative talents and his own broad definition of science, Bache perceived most clearly the nature of that role.

On a popular level, Americans might boast that "the whole world must, ere long, acknowledge the superiority of American ingenuity" and in that spirit little heed Sidney Smith's famous barb, "Who reads an American book?"[35] But Bache and others like him felt the sting of foreign criticism. Their concern was that creative work, whether in the disinterested investigation of natural phenomena or in the solution of practical problems, be a genuine contribution to knowledge and that American contributions in either sphere stand favorable comparison with European labors. In his view, with its explicit intellectual standards, Bache could link science and its applications without any sense of

[35] *Mechanics' Register* 1 (February 1837): 15; *Edinburgh Review* 33 (January 1820): 79.

contradiction, without any feeling that applied science was somehow a depreciated currency. The enemy was "mere empiricism," a cut-and-try methodology just as harmful for technology as for science.

The Institute's water-power tests and the investigation into steam-boiler explosions were models of the new style and suggested to American technical men a paradigm for creative attack on a variety of problems. Samuel V. Merrick's study of European methods for producing illuminating gas reveals some aspects of the approach. Merrick was sent abroad in 1834, at public expense, to discover the best plan for the city to employ in its own projected gasworks. When he arrived in England, however, Merrick discovered considerable variation in processing techniques, since, as he put it, manufacturers there often conducted their business "without any definite idea of the principle to be aimed at."[36] In that situation, a descriptive account of English technical practices would have served little point. Instead, Merrick conducted a series of experiments in several establishments, using the specific gravity of the gas produced as a standard against which to measure the efficiency of different methods of production. His report described those experiments and their results, giving Philadelphia a clear plan for its own works and gas producers throughout the country an analytical basis for judging their performance.

Formulating a rational basis for the production of lighting gas was an important stage in Merrick's own career, too. Before he went abroad, Merrick's fire-engine factory was an essentially modest concern. But when he returned, he and his firm played a central role in the design and construction of the city's new plant. That activity netted him a considerable profit, and he expanded his operations and entered into new lines of manufacturing. The first was in the production of gas apparatus, but with his new foundry capacity, Merrick went on to the construction of sugar-mill machinery, iron lighthouses, and marine machinery—all enterprises in which his company became famous. There appeared to be a link between a scientifically-inspired technology and business success, and in Merrick's case it is traceable back to his investigation into methods of making lighting gas. Even his acquisition of sole U.S. rights to manufacture Nasmyth's steam hammer, a tool of vital importance in working large masses of iron, stemmed from an engineering connection made during that 1834 visit abroad.[37]

36 S. V. Merrick, *Report, upon an Examination of Some of the Gas Manufactories in Great Britain, France, and Belgium* (Philadelphia, 1834), p. 8. Another edition of the report was published in Pittsburgh the following year.

37 Mary Williams Brinton, *Their Lives and Mine* (Philadelphia: privately printed, 1973), pp. 27–28.

Thaddeus B. Wakeman, long-time secretary of the American Institute in New York, once described the process which Merrick's career illustrated: "Science has at last entered the factory, and the shop, and a new era in productive labor has commenced." A new breed of philosopher mechanics "weighed, measured, and analyzed." "Everything," he claimed, "is submitted to the ordeal of experiment."[38] Wakeman's remarks were designed to uplift; they came during a lecture on the promotion of American manufactures. But he caught the spirit of an approach to technological advancement which the Franklin Institute had done much to foster. Merrick's industrial activities epitomized the new style, and it was reflected in the way he trained his son. J. Vaughan Merrick was sent to Central High School, under Bache, and was kept there an extra year for further study. When he then went to his apprenticeship in the family business, it was not on the shop floor, where he spent a minimal time, but in the design department to sharpen his engineering skills.[39]

Merrick and Sellers were entrepreneurs of a new type which would become increasingly familiar to Americans; they capitalized on technical knowledge. The Institute and its community provided an ideal incubator for industrialists and engineers. The introduction of Fourneyron's new water turbine, for example, was essentially a Philadelphia story. Ellwood Morris had learned of French improvements in reaction water wheels and became convinced of their utility in the United States, where most industry still depended on water power. But in addition to the conservatism surrounding the use of traditional water wheels and the language barrier posed by foreign technical literature, some unsuccessful early trials had prejudiced many mill operators against the technique. Convincing Americans to use turbines was a little like demonstrating the true causes of boiler explosions. Both demanded the clear presentation of data solidly based on experimental evidence.

First, Morris translated French tests of Fourneyron's turbines for the *Journal of the Franklin Institute*, and using the society's water-power investigation as a baseline, he argued for the superiority of the new technique. Then he drew up plans for a turbine, which Merrick manufactured at his Southwark Foundry, and installed several of them in nearby industrial establishments. Experiments were made with those wheels, and the results were published in the *Journal*.[40] Morris

[38] *Mechanics' Magazine, and Register of Inventions and Improvements* 5 (February 1835): 80.

[39] Brinton, *Their Lives and Mine*, pp. 22–23, 25–27.

[40] Early French and American turbine efforts are described by Louis C. Hunter in "Origines des Turbines Francis et Pelton," *Revue d'Histoire des Sciences et de leurs Applications* 17 (July–September 1964): 209–42. Morris's article was published serially

worked within a well-developed community. He had access to the Institute's collection of foreign periodicals, to its conversational meetings, to Merrick's foundry, and as one of its collaborators, to the *Journal*. Industrial power and its transmission within a factory were issues of wide geographic importance which engaged the efforts of engineers in various localities. But like the research into the strength of materials, which also served as a point of departure for the development of a remarkable sophistication in that field, the Franklin Institute provided a focus for the systematic examination and solution of important technical problems.[41]

These examples, even if the details are yet uncertain, say some important things about industrial technology in pre-Civil-War America. That history has most often been described in terms of light industry and has emphasized the emergence in New England of mass production techniques using systems of interchangeable parts. But in the 1840's and 1850's, the United States also developed a substantial heavy industry, centered in the mid-Atlantic states. Nor did the freedom with which Americans experimented in prime movers or used materials in new and often surprising ways spring wholly from an unfettered ingenuity. Whether building steam engines for the Navy, cannons for the Army, or machines of all description for the private sector, heavy industry

---

in the *Journal of the Franklin Institute* 34 (October 1842): 217–27; (November 1842), 289–304. See also Ellwood Morris, "Experiments on the useful effect of Turbines in the United States," *Journal of the Franklin Institute* 36 (November 1843): 377–79; idem, "On the Friction Dynamometer, or Brake, of M. de Prony, a cheap, simple, and effectual instrument, for measuring the actual power developed by machines," in vol. 35 of the *Journal*, pp. 225–38; and Ellwood Morris, trans., "Experiments on Water-Wheels, having a vertical axis, called Turbines. By Arthur Morin, Captain of Artillery, Professor of Machinery in the School of Artillery, &c., &c," in vol. 36, pp. 234–46 (October 1843); 289–302 (November 1843); and 370–77 (December 1843).

41 See, for instance, the article on transmitting power by systems of belts and shafting by Ithamar Beard, an engineer and at that time agent for the *Journal* in Lowell, Massachusetts, in *Journal of the Franklin Institute* 15 (January 1833): 6–15. James B. Francis also published on the subject of power transmission in the *Journal*, in vol. 83 (June 1867), p. 379, and conducted fundamentally important research on water power which appeared in his *Lowell Hydraulic Experiments* (New York, 1855).

The history of materials testing in America has yet to be written, but it appears that at least by the 1850's, if not earlier, American ironworkers had developed considerable skill in that branch of engineering science. Locomotive manufacturers, for example, used cast iron in ways that always surprised European observers. White, *American Locomotives*, pp. 30–31.

And in 1853, John Anderson, inspector of machinery for Great Britain's Board of Ordnance, argued that the use of testing machines had so advanced the quality of American metals that its cast iron had twice the tenacity of similar English goods. In England, Anderson said, "nothing is done to ascertain the precise conditions of the metal in tenacity, transverse strength, compressibility, and torsion" (Rosenberg, *The American System of Manufactures*, p. 158).

depended upon engineers who read and contributed to the technical literature, who carried on experimental and testing programs, and who thought of themselves as joined in interests and labors with a community of coworkers.

These men gave new meaning to the old idea that technical progress would flow from a union of theory and practice. When Dr. Jones spoke of teaching the principles of science to workingmen, he gave no clear indication of the way a craftsman would actually use them. Neither Dr. Jones nor anyone else who invoked that catch-phrase knew precisely how the union was to be effected. Nor could they, since it represented an ideological stance rather than a program. Industrialists like Merrick and Sellers had a firm faith in the practical understanding which on-the-job training provided but an equally deep distrust in rule of thumb methods. What sounded like a combination of theory and practice, however, was actually Bache's approach translated in terms of production and efficiency. By 1865, "theory" defined a body of engineering knowledge and the ability to use it; "practice" meant the rational manipulation of power and materials in an industrial context.

Even in this revised definition, the old formula still had some ideological potency. Harrison, who started as a poor apprentice, returned from his Russian railroad contracts a man of great wealth. Baldwin, whose beginnings had been equally humble, came to command the largest locomotive factory in the world. In an earlier day, money from mechanical pursuits was a social liability in Philadelphia. By the time of the Civil War, a new industrial elite collected art, patronized music, supported churches, and left money for the poor when they died.[42] Sellers and Merrick were men who began life with advantages. But the city's industrial capacity had grown so greatly in the years after 1824, and there were enough other examples to support the case, that it was easy to think there was a connection between the Institute's ideals and personal success in industrial enterprise. At least it seemed that the men who took over in 1864 were of that powerful and assured self-made type. They were all workingmen and all gentlemen. In a way that unified past and present, their own careers apparently justified the Institute's earliest efforts.

They rescued the organization from financial disaster for more than sentimental reasons, however. Many had grown up with the society, and while they may have seen something of themselves in its history,

[42] For an insight into the cultural and charitable activities of prominent Philadelphia industrialists, see Coleman Sellers's sketch of Joseph Harrison, Jr., American Philosophical Society *Proceedings* 14 (1874–75): 347; and J. Vaughan Merrick's autobiographical account in Brinton, *Their Lives and Mine*, pp. 15–47.

they perceived its future value in a different light. Sellers, in particular, recognized a new role for the Institute in the private sector. The proposal for a standardized system of screw threads pointed to a rising generation of technical issues. Those questions, as Sellers and other engineers made clear, would be dominated by a concern for uniformity and the perfection of machines "to utilize unskilled labor."[43]

Sellers thought of mechanical industry in national terms, and he defined the coming tasks of engineers in the same way. For a time, financial crisis and the Civil War blunted the Institute's sense of purpose and obscured its worth. But Sellers saw that the organization already constituted a technical community sensitive to the interests of industry. His own ideas were a logical outgrowth of the Franklin Institute's earliest aims, and he recognized in its history a new mission for the future.

[43] William Sellers & Co., *A Treatise on Machine-Tools, etc. as Made by William Sellers & Co.* (Philadelphia: William Sellers & Co., 1877), p. 113. For a later version of the same approach, see George R. Stetson, "Standard Sizes of Screw Threads," *Transactions of the ASME* 1 (1880): 125.

BIBLIOGRAPHY

PRIMARY SOURCES

Manuscripts

The Franklin Institute's own manuscript records constituted the most significant documentary resource for this study. The amount of records is substantial, but because the material is housed in various locations within the Institute, it is difficult to estimate the quantity.

The manuscripts can be grouped into three major categories: minutes of meetings; committee reports; and correspondence. Minutes of meetings themselves fall into two categories: minutes of meetings of the membership and minutes of meetings of the Board of Managers. Both types of minutes are complete for the period covered by this study. Minutes of membership meetings are housed in the Institute's archives; those of the Board of Managers are located in the office of the Secretary of the Institute. A few remaining notebook fragments suggest the manner in which minutes were recorded. After 1828, William Hamilton, the actuary, kept minutes for almost all meetings, whether of the membership, the Board of Managers, or special committees. Hamilton made a rough draft of the minutes in small notebooks. In the case of membership and Board meetings, he then transcribed his notes into larger bound volumes as the official record. Few of his notebooks have survived, but the formal record is voluminous and continuous.

Committee reports, except for the records of the Committee on Science and the Arts, which are maintained in that committee's office, are filed alphabetically in the Institute's archives. They vary considerably in bulk. The files from the Committee on Premiums and Exhibitions are full and rich. By contrast, the records of committees which performed special investigations and therefore acted most independently are thin. For instance, Alexander Dallas Bache apparently took some of the records from the water-power investigation to Washington, where they were only recently discovered among Joseph Henry materials at the Smithsonian Institution by Nathan Reingold.

The Institute's correspondence is housed in its archives. For the period of this study, the correspondence consists of incoming letters only, except for the years from 1824 to 1826, when the corresponding secretary, Peter A. Browne, recorded his outgoing correspondence in a separate letterbook. Three important groups of letters—those from Alexander Dallas Bache, Thomas P. Jones, and Petty Vaughan—have been removed from the general incoming correspondence and are filed separately. Bache's letters, about forty-five in number, span the period from 1829 to 1863. Jones's correspondence, which began with his removal to Washington in 1828 and continued until his death in 1848, contains a wealth of detail on the publication of the *Journal of the Franklin Institute*. His letters are supplemented by a sizeable correspondence relating to *Journal* subscriptions. Petty Vaughan acted as the Institute's London agent, and most of his correspondence relates to exchanges for the *Journal*.

In addition to these large groups of records, the Institute's archives contain a great deal of miscellaneous material. There are reports from temporary committees concerned with finance, with construction of the new hall in 1826, with the building-expansion plans of 1835, and with a wide variety of other issues. The quarterly and annual reports of the Board of Managers are also filed in the archives, as are treasurer's reports. Dr. A. Michal McMahon is currently directing a National Science Foundation-sponsored effort to make the Institute's archival materials more available to scholars.

I used a number of other manuscript collections in Philadelphia repositories. They included the Frazer Papers, the Peale-Sellers Papers, and the papers of Alexander Dallas Bache at the American Philosophical Society; the S. S. Haldeman correspondence at the Academy of Natural Sciences, whose collections also contain material pertaining to Walter R. Johnson and Peter A. Browne; and the Dreer, Gratz, and Stauffer Collections, plus the Poinsett, Vaux, and Peter A. Browne Papers in the Historical Society of Pennsylvania. At the National Archives, Record Groups 56 and 217 contain material on the Institute's steam-boiler investigation. Joseph Henry's papers and correspondence at the Smithsonian Institution also contain relevant materials.

Periodicals

Dr. Thomas P. Jones's *Franklin Journal, and American Mechanics' Magazine* (1826–28), subsequently renamed *Journal of the Franklin Institute* (from 1828 to the present), was also a major source of information for this study. Both in editorial comment and in specific articles, it provided significant primary material. An examination of its contents amply proved Frank Luther Mott's comment that it is "a most valuable repository of information concerning scientific (and especially engineering) subjects." His *History of American Magazines, 1741–1850* (Cambridge, Mass.: Harvard University Press, 1939) sets the *Journal* into the larger framework of American scientific and technical publication. I also sampled issues of *The Young Mechanic* and the *Boston Mechanic, and Journal of the Useful Arts and Sciences,* two periodicals which grew out of Timothy Claxton's efforts to elevate the mechanic arts in Boston, as well as early issues of the *American Journal of Education* (subsequently retitled *American Annals of Education*), which began publication in Boston the same year Dr. Jones commenced his *Journal.*

Printed Materials

The following list does not include all the references cited in footnotes to the text, and it contains some sources not cited in footnotes. My aim, here and in the selection of secondary sources which follows, is to provide a check list of printed materials which might be of interest to someone generally concerned with the subject of this book. When the distinction between primary and secondary printed materials proved difficult to draw, I used a publication date of 1900 as the dividing line.

Address by Professor Bache, before the Franklin Institute, October, 1842. Philadelphia, 1842.

Address of the Committee of Instruction of the Franklin Institute of Pennsylvania, on the Subject of the High School Department attached to that Institution. Philadelphia: The Franklin Institute, 1826.

Address of the Committee on Premiums and Exhibitions of the Franklin Institute of the State of Pennsylvania, for the Promotion of the Mechanic Arts: with a List of the Premiums offered to Competitors at the Eighth Exhibition to be Held in October, 1833. Philadelphia: T. W. Ustick, 1833.

Address of the Committee on Premiums and Exhibitions of the Franklin Institute of the State of Pennsylvania, for the Promotion of the Mechanic Arts: with a List of the Premiums offered to Competitors at the Ninth Exhibition, to be Held in October, 1835. Philadelphia: T. W. Ustick, 1835.

Address of the Committee on Premiums and Exhibitions. Philadelphia, 1840.

Address to the Manufacturers of the United States. Philadelphia, 1828.

Bache, A. D. "Address of Professor A. D. Bache, President of the American Association for the Year 1851, on Retiring from the Duties of President." *Proceedings of the American Association for the Advancement of Science* 6 (1851): 41–60.

———. *Anniversary Address before the American Institute of the City of New York.* New York: Pudney & Russell, 1857.

———. [Obituary of James P. Espy] *Annual Report of the Board of Regents of the Smithsonian Institution, showing the Operations, Expenditures, and Condition of the Institution for the Year 1859.* Washington, D.C.: Thomas Ford, 1860.

Barnard, Henry. *Memoirs of Teachers, Educators, and Promoters and Bene-factors of Education, Literature and Science.* 2 vols. New York: F. C. Brownlee, 1859.

Bigelow, Jacob. *A short reply to a pamphlet published at Philadelphia entitled "A defence of the experiments to determine the comparative value of the principal varieties of fuel used in the United States, and also in Europe . . . By Marcus Bull . . ." By one of the committee of the American Academy.* Boston: Hilliard, Gray, Little and Wilkins, 1828.

―――. *Elements of Technology, Taken Chiefly from a Course of Lectures Delivered at Cambridge, on the Application of the Sciences to the Useful Arts.* Boston: Hilliard, Gray, Little and Wilkins, 1829.

The Biographical Encyclopedia of Pennsylvania of the Nineteenth Century. Philadelphia: Galaxy Publishing Company, 1874.

"Biographical Notice of Prof. Alexander Dallas Bache." *Journal of the Franklin Institute* 87 (May 1869): 352–60.

Bishop, J. L. *A History of American Manufactures from 1608 to 1860.* 3 vols. Philadelphia: E. Young, 1861–68.

Bivins, Percy A. *Index to the Reports of the Committee on Science and the Arts of the Franklin Institute of the State of Pennsylvania, 1834–1890.* Philadelphia: The Franklin Institute, 1890.

Bolmar, Antoine. *A Collection of colloquial phrases, on every topic necessary to maintain conversation.* Philadelphia: Carey & Lea, 1830.

―――. *Key to the first eight books of the adventures of Telemachus, the son of Ulysses.* Philadelphia: P. M. Lafourcade, 1828.

Booth, James Curtis. *The Encyclopedia of Chemistry, Practical and Theoretical: Embracing its Application to the Arts, Metallurgy, Mineralogy, Geology, Medicine, and Pharmacy.* Philadelphia: H. C. Baird, 1850.

―――. *The Phonographic Instructor; being an introduction to the corresponding style of phonography.* Philadelphia: E. H. Butler and Co., 1849.

―――, and Morfit, Campbell. *On Recent Improvements in the Chemical Arts.* Washington, D.C.: Smithsonian Institution, 1851.

Browne, Peter A. *A Lecture on the Oregon Territory.* Philadelphia: United States Book and Job Printing Office, 1843.

―――. *An Address, Intended to Promote a Geological and Mineralogical Survey of Pennsylvania, the Publication of a Series of Geological Maps, and the Formation of State and County Geological and Mineralogical Collections. To which are prefixed, the Resolutions of the Meeting before which it was read.* Philadelphia: P. M. Lafourcade, 1826.

―――. *An Essay upon the Theory and Operation of the Steam Engine.* Philadelphia: I. Ashmead and Co., 1837.

―――. *A proposal to establish & maintain 1 uniform system of weights, measures & coins among all civilized & commercial nations.* New York, 1851.

―――. *The Classification of Mankind by the Hair and Wool of their Heads, with the Nomenclature of Human Hybrids.* Philadelphia: J. H. Jones, 1852.

―――. *To the Freemen of Philadelphia.* Philadelphia, 1825.

Carey, Matthew. *Reflexions on the Proposed Plan for Establishing a College in Philadelphia*. Philadelphia: Carey & Lea, 1826.

Catalogue of Philosophical Apparatus Manufactured and Sold by Claxton & Wightman, No. 33 Cornhill, Boston. Boston, 1835.

Catalogue of the Books belonging to the Library of the Franklin Institute of the State of Pennsylvania, for the Promotion of the Mechanic Arts. Philadelphia: S. D. Steele, 1847.

Charter, Constitution, and By-Laws of the New-York Mechanic and Scientific Institution. New York: New-York Mechanic and Scientific Institution, 1822.

Circular, Fourth Exhibition of the Kentucky Mechanics' Institute, Louisville, September and October, 1856. Louisville, 1856.

Claxton, Timothy. *Concise decimal tables, for facilitating arithmetical calculations*. Boston, 1830.

―――. *Hints to Mechanics on Self-Education and Mutual Instruction*. London: Taylor and Watton, 1839.

―――. *Memoir of a Mechanic, Being a Sketch of the Life of Timothy Claxton, Written by Himself, Together with Miscellaneous Papers*. Boston: George W. Light, 1839.

Commemorative Exercises at the Fiftieth Anniversary of the Franklin Institute of the State of Pennsylvania for the Promotion of the Mechanic Arts. Philadelphia: The Franklin Institute, 1874.

Communications Received by the Committee of the Franklin Institute on the Explosion of Steam Boilers. Philadelphia: The Franklin Institute, 1832.

Contributions of the Maclurean lyceum to the arts and sciences. Philadelphia: J. Dobson, 1827–29.

Daly, Charles P. *Origin and History of Institutions for the Promotion of Useful Arts*. Albany: American Institute, 1864.

A Description of the Patent Improved Fire Engines and other Hydraulic Machines, Invented by Jacob Perkins, and Manufactured by S. V. Merrick & Co. Philadelphia, n.d.

Directions for Making Meteorological Observations for the Committee on Meteorology, Constituted by the Franklin Institute of the State of Pennsylvania for the Promotion of the Mechanic Arts. Philadelphia: Barnard & Jones, 1854.

Espy, James P. *Hints to Observers on Meteorology*. Philadelphia: The Franklin Institute, 1837.

―――. *Report of the Committee on Meteorology to the Franklin Institute of the State of Pennsylvania, for the Promotion of the Mechanic Arts*. Philadelphia, 1838.

―――. *The Philosophy of Storms*. Boston: Little and Brown, 1841.

Evening Schools and District Libraries: An Appeal to Philadelphians, in Behalf of Improved Means of Education and Self-Culture, for Apprentices and Young Workmen. Philadelphia: King & Baird, 1850.

Everett, Edward. *Importance of Practical Education and Useful Knowledge*. Boston: Marsh, Capen, Lyon and Webb, 1840.

F[airman]. R[ogers]., *1833–1900*. Philadelphia: privately printed, 1903.

Fiftieth Anniversary of the Ohio Mechanics' Institute, 1828–1878, Historical Sketch. Cincinnati, 1878.

First Annual Report of the Proceedings of the Franklin Institute of the State of Pennsylvania, for the Promotion of the Mechanic Arts. Philadelphia: J. Harding, 1825.

For the Establishment of a School of Arts. Memorial of the Franklin Institute, of the State of Pennsylvania, for the Promotion of the Mechanic Arts, to the Legislature of Pennsylvania. Philadelphia: J. Crissy, 1837.

Fraley, Frederick. "An Essay on Mechanics and the Progress of Mechanical Science—1824 to 1882." *Transactions of the American Society of Mechanical Engineers* 3 (1881): 213–19.

————. "Obituary Notice of John C. Cresson." American Philosophical Society *Proceedings* 11 (1869–70): 584–97.

Freedley, Edwin T. *Leading Pursuits and Leading Men. A Treatise on the Principal Trades and Manufactures of the United States*. Philadelphia: E. Young, 1856.

————. *Philadelphia and its Manufactures; a Hand-Book of the Great Manufactories and Representative Mercantile Houses of Philadelphia, in 1857*. Philadelphia: E. Young & Co., 1857.

General Report on the Explosions of Steam-Boilers, by a Committee of the Franklin Institute of the State of Pennsylvania for the Promotion of the Mechanic Arts. Philadelphia: C. Sherman, 1836.

Goodwin, Daniel R. "Obituary Notice of Samuel Vaughan Merrick, Esq." American Philosophical Society *Proceedings* 11 (1869–70): 584–97.

Gould, James. *An Oration, Pronounced at New Haven, before the Connecticut Alpha of the Phi Beta Kappa Society, September 13, 1825*. New Haven, 1825.

Graff, F. "Notice of the Earliest Steam Engines Used in the United States." *Journal of the Franklin Institute* 55 (April 1853): 269–71.

Griscom, John. *Address Delivered before the Newark Mechanics' Association, on their Third Anniversary, January 25, 1831*. Newark: William Tuttle, 1831.

————. *A Discourse, on the Importance of Character and Education in the United States, Delivered on the 20th of 11th Mo. (November), 1822, Introductory to a Course of Lectures, on Experimental Philosophy and Chemistry*. New York: Mahlon Day, 1823.

————. *Monitorial Instruction. An Address, Pronounced at the Opening of the New-York High-School*. New York: Mahlon Day, 1825.

Griscom, John H. *Memoir of John Griscom, LL.D., late professor of chemistry and natural philosophy; with an account of the New York High School; Society for the Prevention of Pauperism; the House of Refuge; and other institutions. Compiled from an autobiography and other sources*. New York: Robert Carter and Brothers, 1859.

Gross, Samuel W., and Gross, A. Haller, eds. *Autobiography of Samuel D. Gross, M.D., with Reminiscences of his Times and Contemporaries*. 2 vols. Philadelphia: W. B. Saunders, 1893.

Hale, Benjamin. *Catalogue of the Officers and Students of Gardiner Lyceum, with an Address to the Public. October, 1824.* Gardiner, Maine: P. Sheldon, 1824.

Hall, Henry, ed. *America's Successful Men of Affairs.* 2 vols. New York: The New York Tribune, 1896.

Harrison, Joseph, Jr. *The Iron Worker and King Solomon. With a Memoir and an Appendix.* 2nd ed., rev. Philadelphia: J. B. Lippincott & Co., 1869.

————. "The Locomotive Engine, and Philadelphia's share in its Early Improvements." *Journal of the Franklin Institute* 93 (March 1872): 161–74; (April 1872): 233–48.

————. *The Locomotive Engine, and Philadelphia's share in its Early Improvements.* Rev. ed. Philadelphia: G. Gebbie, 1872.

Henry, Joseph. "Eulogy on Prof. Alexander Dallas Bache, Late Superintendent of the United States Coast Survey." *Annual Report of the Board of Regents of the Smithsonian Institution, showing the Operations, Expenditures, and Condition of the Institution for the Year 1870.* Washington, D.C.: Government Printing Office, 1872.

————. "Memoir of Joseph Saxton, 1799–1873." National Academy of Sciences *Biographical Memoirs* 1 (1877): 287–316.

Holbrook, Josiah. *American Lyceum of Science and the Arts, Composed of Associations for Mutual Instruction, and Designed for the General Diffusion of Useful and Practical Knowledge.* Worcester, Mass.: S. B. Manning, 1826.

————. *American Lyceum, or Society for the Improvement of Schools, and Diffusion of Useful Knowledge.* Boston: T. R. Marvin, 1829.

Hole, James. *An Essay on the History and Management of Literary, Scientific & Mechanics' Institutions.* London: Longman, Brown, Green and Longmans, 1853.

Howe, Henry. *Memoirs of the Most Eminent American Mechanics: Also, Lives of Distinguished European Mechanics; together with Anecdotes, Descriptions, etc., etc., Relating to the Mechanic Arts.* New York: A. V. Blake, 1844.

Hudson, J. W. *History of Adult Education.* 1851. Reprint. London: The Woburn Press, 1969.

"In Memorium John F. Frazer, LL.D." *Proceedings at the Public Inauguration of the Building Erected for the Departments of Arts and Science, October 11, 1842.* Philadelphia, 1872.

"James Curtis Booth." *Journal of the Franklin Institute* 126 (July 1888): 67–69.

Johnson, W. R. "On the Combination of a Practical with a Liberal course of Education." *Journal of the Franklin Institute* 6 (July–December 1828): 108–113, 116–69, 275–78, 353–55, 367–79.

Jones, Henry Bence. *The Royal Institution: Its Founder and Its First Professors.* London: Longmans, Green, and Co., 1871.

Jones, Thomas P. *Charge Addressed to the Graduates in Medicine, at the Commencement of the Medical Department of the Columbian College, D.C.* Washington, D.C.: Gales and Seaton, 1830.

————. *New Conversations on Chemistry, adapted to the Present State of that*

Science; wherein its elements are clearly and familiarly explained. Philadelphia: J. Grigg, 1831.

————. *Observations upon the Automaton Chess Player of von Kempelen, and upon other Automata and Androides, now exhibiting in the United States, by Mr. Maelzel.* Philadelphia: J. Dobson, 1827.

Keating, William H. *Considerations upon the Art of Mining, to which are added, Reflections on Its Actual State in Europe, and the Advantages which would Result from an Introduction of this Art into the United States.* Philadelphia: M. Carey and Sons, 1821.

————. *Conversations on Chemistry; in which the Elements of that Science are familiarly explained and illustrated by experiments.* Philadelphia: T. De Silver, 1824.

————. *Syllabus of a course of mineralogy and chemistry, as applied to agriculture and the arts.* Philadelphia, 1822.

Lardner, Dionysius. *Popular Lectures on the Steam Engine, in which its Construction and Operation are familiarly explained; with an Historical Sketch of its Invention and Progressive Improvement.* London: J. Taylor, 1828.

LeConte, John L. "Obituary Notice of John F. Frazer." American Philosophical Society *Proceedings* 13 (1872): 1–8.

Letter from the Corresponding Secretary of the Franklin Institute of the State of Pennsylvania, for the Promotion of the Mechanic Arts. Philadelphia, December 15, 1824.

Lloyd, James T. *Lloyd's Steamboat Directory and Disasters on the Western Waters.* Cincinnati: J. T. Lloyd & Co., 1856.

The Manufactories and Manufacturers of Pennsylvania of the Nineteenth Century. Philadelphia: Galaxy Publishing Company, 1875.

"The Mechanics' Institute of the City of New-York." *The Mechanics' Magazine and Register of Inventions and Improvements* 3 (September 1834): 180–82.

Memoir of Josiah Holbrook. Hartford, Conn.: F. B. Perkins, 1860.

Memorial of a Committee appointed at the town meeting of the citizens of the City and County of Philadelphia, Held January 4, 1838, Praying for the Establishment of a School of Arts. Harrisburg: Packer, Barbett and Parke, 1838.

Memorial of Matthias W. Baldwin. Philadelphia: privately printed, 1867.

"Memorial of Robert Briggs." *Journal of the Franklin Institute* 115 (March 1883): 229–36.

Merrick, J. Vaughan. "On the History and Construction of Iron Lighthouses." *Journal of the Franklin Institute* 61 (March 1856): 145–50.

Merrick, Samuel V. *Report, upon an Examination of Some of the Gas Manufactories in Great Britain, France, and Belgium.* Philadelphia: City Councils, 1834.

Millington, John. "Address on Civil Engineering." *Southern Literary Messenger* 5 (1839): 592–95.

————. *An Epitome of the Elementary Principles of Natural and Experimental Philosophy.* London: privately printed, 1823.

————. *Elements of Civil Engineering.* Philadelphia: J. Dobson, 1839.

Morehead, L. *A Few Incidents in the Life of Prof. James P. Espy.* Cincinnati: R. Clarke & Company, 1888.

Nystrom, John W. *On technological education and the construction of ships and screw propellers, for naval and marine engineers.* Philadelphia: H. C. Baird, 1866.

"Obituary—John C. Trautwine." *Journal of the Franklin Institute* 116 (November 1883): 390–96.

"Obituary Notice of the Late Isaiah Lukens." *Journal of the Franklin Institute* 42 (December 1846): 423–25.

"Obituary Notices of Members Deceased. Frederick Fraley, LL.D., President of the Society." American Philosophical Society *Proceedings* 40 (1901): i–ix.

"Observations on the Rise and Progress of the Franklin Institute." *The Franklin Journal and American Mechanics' Magazine* 1 (February 1826): 66–71; (March 1826): 129–34.

Patterson, Robert. "An Obituary Notice of Franklin Peale." American Philosophical Society *Proceedings* 11 (1869–70): 597–604.

Pennsylvania Polytechnic College, Philadelphia. *Historical Record, 1st ed., 1853–1890.* Philadelphia, n.d.

Percy, John. *The Manufacture of Russian Sheet-Iron.* Philadelphia: Henry Carey Baird, 1871.

Proceedings at the Dinner to the Honorable Frederick Fraley on his Ninetieth Birthday. Philadelphia: William F. Murphy, 1894.

"Proposed Polytechnic and Scientific College, in Philadelphia." *Franklin Journal and American Mechanics' Magazine* 1 (March 1826): 189–91.

"Recollections of a Cinquegenarian." *Philadelphia Sunday Dispatch,* March 27, 1859.

Renwick, James. *Treatise on the Steam Engine.* New York: G. & C. & H. Carvill, 1830.

"Report in Relation to Weights and Measures in the Commonwealth of Pennsylvania." *Journal of the Franklin Institute* 18 (July 1834): 13.

Report of a Plan for Extending and More Perfectly Establishing the Mechanic and Scientific Institution. New York, 1824.

Report of the Board to Recommend a Standard Gauge for Bolts, Nuts, and Screw-Threads for the United States Navy. May, 1868. Washington, D.C.: Government Printing Office, 1880.

Report of the Committee of the Franklin Institute of the State of Pennsylvania, for the Promotion of the Mechanic Arts, on the Explosions of Steam Boilers. Part I, Containing the first Report of Experiments made by the Committee, for the Treasury Department of the U. States. Philadelphia: John C. Clark, 1836.

Report of the Committee of the Franklin Institute of the State of Pennsylvania on the Explosions of Steam Boilers, of Experiments made at the request of the Treasury Department of the United States. Part II. Containing the report of the sub-committee to whom was referred the examination of the

strength of the materials employed in the construction of Steam Boilers.
Philadelphia: Merrihew and Gunn, 1837.

Report of the Committee on Premiums and Exhibitions of the Tenth Exhibition of Domestic Manufactures held by the Franklin Institute. Philadelphia:
The Franklin Institute, 1838.

Report of the Franklin Institute of the State of Pennsylvania, for the Promotion of the Mechanic Arts, on the Best Modes of Paving Highways. Philadelphia:
City Councils, 1843.

Report of the Second Annual Exhibition of the Franklin Institute of the State of Pennsylvania for the Promotion of the Mechanic Arts. Philadelphia: The
Franklin Institute, 1825.

Report of the Seventh Annual Exhibition of the Franklin Institute of the State of Pennsylvania for the Promotion of the Mechanic Arts. Philadelphia:
J. Harding, 1831.

Report of the Twenty-first Exhibition of American Manufactures, held in the City of Philadelphia, from the 21st of October to the 1st of November, inclusive, 1851, by the Franklin Institute of the State of Pennsylvania, for the Promotion of the Mechanic Arts. Philadelphia: R. W. Barnard & Sons, 1851.

Report of the Twenty-third Exhibition of American Manufactures, held in the City of Philadelphia, from the 18th of October, to the 3d of November, 1853, by the Franklin Institute, of the State of Pennsylvania, for the Promotion of the Mechanic Arts. Philadelphia: Barnard & Jones, 1853.

Report on the Twenty-fourth Exhibition of American Manufactures, held in the City of Philadelphia, from November 14, to December 2, 1854, by the Franklin Institute, of the State of Pennsylvania, for the Promotion of the Mechanic Arts. Philadelphia: Barnard & Jones, 1855.

Report on the Twenty-fifth Exhibition of American Manufactures, held in the City of Philadelphia, from the 11th to the 29th day of November, 1856. By the Franklin Institute, of the State of Pennsylvania, for the Promotion of the Mechanic Arts. Philadelphia: Barnard & Jones, 1857.

Report on the Twenty-sixth Exhibition of American Manufacturers, Held in the City of Philadelphia, from October 15, to November 13, 1858. By the Franklin Institute, of the State of Pennsylvania, for the Promotion of the Mechanic Arts. Philadelphia: William S. Young, 1858.

Rhees, W. J., ed. *The Smithsonian Institution: Documents Relative to its Origin and History.* Washington, D.C.: Smithsonian Institution, 1879.

Roberts, Solomon W. *An Address, Delivered at the Close of the Sixteenth Exhibition of American Manufactures, held in Philadelphia, by the Franklin Institute of the State of Pennsylvania.* Philadelphia: John C. Clark, 1846.

————. "An Obituary Notice of Charles B. Trego." American Philosophical
Society *Proceedings* 14 (1874–75): 356–58.

Ruschenberger, W. S. W. *A Notice of the Origin, Progress, and Present Condition of the Academy of Natural Science of Philadelphia.* Philadelphia: T. K.
and P. G. Collins, 1852.

————. "A Sketch of the Life of Robert E. Rogers, with Biographical Notices of his Father and Brothers." *American Philosophical Society Proceedings* 23 (1886): 104–46.

Sanderson, John. *Remarks on the Plan of a College (About to be established in this City).* Philadelphia: J. Maxwell, 1826.

Sartain, John. *Reminiscences of a Very Old Man.* New York: Merrymount Press, 1900.

Savidge, E. C., and Anderson, William, eds. *A Gallery of Eminent Men of Philadelphia.* Philadelphia: Henry L. Everett, 1887.

"Scientific Societies, Aims and Activities." *American Journal of Science* 10 (1826): 373–74.

Second Annual Announcement of the Polytechnic College, of the State of Pennsylvania. Philadelphia: Inquirer Book Press, 1854.

Sellers, Coleman. "An Obituary Notice of Mr. Joseph Harrison, Jr." American *Philosophical Society Proceedings* 14 (1874–75): 347–55.

————, and Leeds, Albert R., eds. *Biographical Notice of Pres't Henry Morton, Ph.D., of the Stevens Institute of Technology.* Hoboken, N.J.: Stevens Institute, 1892.

Sellers, William, & Co. *A Treatise on Machine-Tools, etc. as Made by William Sellers & Co.* Philadelphia: William Sellers & Co., 1877.

Sharpless, John T. *Report of the Transactions of the Maclurean Lyceum of the Arts and Sciences of Philadelphia, from its commencement in 1826 to January, 1830.* Philadelphia: The Maclurean Lyceum, 1830.

Simpson, Henry. *The Lives of Eminent Philadelphians Now Deceased.* Philadelphia: William Brotherhead, 1859.

Steamboat Disasters and Railroad Accidents in the United States. Worcester, Mass.: Warren Lazell, 1846.

Stewart, Frank H. *History of the First United States Mint.* Camden, N.J.: privately printed, 1924.

Strickland, William. *Reports on Canals, Railways, Roads, and other Subjects, made to the Pennsylvania Society for the Promotion of Internal Improvement.* Philadelphia: Carey and Lea, 1826.

Stuart, Charles B. *Lives and Works of Civil and Military Engineers of America.* New York: D. Van Nostrand, 1871.

Tappan, Henry P. *Review by Rev. H. P. Tappan of his connection with the University of Michigan.* Detroit, 1864.

Torrey, Jesse. *The Herald of Knowledge; or, An Address to the Citizens of the United States, Proposing a New System of National Education.* Washington, D.C.: A. Way, 1822.

To the Citizens of the City and County of Philadelphia. Philadelphia, 1826.

Wahl, William H. *The Franklin Institute of the State of Pennsylvania for the Promotion of the Mechanic Arts: A Sketch of its Organization and History.* Philadelphia: The Franklin Institute, 1895.

"William Sellers." *Journal of the Franklin Institute* 159 (May 1905): 365–81.

SECONDARY SOURCES

Allen, Henry Butler. "Alexander Dallas Bache and His Connection with the Franklin Institute of the State of Pennsylvania." *American Philosophical Society Proceedings* 84 (May 1941): 145–49.

Bailyn, Bernard. *Education in the Forming of American Society: Needs and Opportunities for Study.* Chapel Hill: University of North Carolina Press, 1960.

Baltzell, E. Digby. *Philadelphia Gentlemen: The Making of a National Upper Class.* Glencoe, Ill.: The Free Press, 1958.

Bates, Ralph S. *Scientific Societies in the United States.* 3rd ed. Cambridge, Mass.: The M.I.T. Press, 1965.

Bathe, Greville, and Bathe, Dorothy. *Jacob Perkins.* Philadelphia: Historical Society of Pennsylvania, 1943.

———. *Oliver Evans: A Chronicle of Early American Engineering.* Philadelphia: Historical Society of Pennsylvania, 1935.

Bell, Whitfield J. *Early American Science: Needs and Opportunities for Study.* Chapel Hill: University of North Carolina Press, 1955.

———. "The American Philosophical Society as a National Academy of Sciences, 1780–1846." *Ithaca* 9 (1962): 165–77.

Bennett, Charles A. *History of Manual and Industrial Education up to 1870.* Peoria, Ill.: The Manual Arts Press, 1926.

Bernstein, Leonard. "The Working People of Philadelphia from Colonial Times to the General Strike of 1835." *Pennsylvania Magazine of History and Biography* 74 (July 1950): 332–39.

Binder, Frederick M. "Anthracite Enters the American Home." *Pennsylvania Magazine of History and Biography* 82 (January 1958): 82–99.

Bode, Carl. *The American Lyceum: Town Meeting of the Mind.* New York: Oxford University Press, 1956.

Bradsher, Earl L. *Matthew Carey: Editor, Author and Publisher.* New York: Columbia University Press, 1912.

Bridenbaugh, Carl, and Bridenbaugh, Jessica. *Rebels and Gentlemen: Philadelphia in the Age of Franklin.* New York: Oxford University Press, 1965.

Brinton, Mary Williams. *Their Lives and Mine.* Philadelphia: privately printed, 1973.

Burke, John G. "Bursting Boilers and the Federal Power." *Technology and Culture* 7 (Winter 1966): 1–23.

Burn, D. L. "The Genesis of American Engineering Competition, 1850–1870." *Economic History* 2 (January 1931): 292–311.

Burr, Anna Robeson. *Weir Mitchell: His Life and Letters.* New York: Duffield & Company, 1930.

Calhoun, Daniel H. *The American Civil Engineer: Origins and Conflict.* Cambridge, Mass.: The M.I.T. Press, 1960.

Calvert, Monte. *The Mechanical Engineer in America, 1830–1910.* Baltimore: The Johns Hopkins Press, 1967.

Cheyney, Edward P. *History of the University of Pennsylvania, 1740–1940*. Philadelphia: University of Pennsylvania Press, 1940.

Clark, Malcolm C. "The Birth of an Enterprise: Baldwin Locomotive, 1831–1842." *Pennsylvania Magazine of History and Biography* 90 (October 1966): 423–44.

Clark, Victor S. *History of Manufactures in the United States*. 2 vols. Washington, D.C.: Carnegie Institution, 1928.

Clark, Walton. "Franklin Institute and the State." *Journal of the Franklin Institute* 178 (August 1914): 221–25.

Clopper, Edward N. "The Ohio Mechanics' Institute: Its 125th Anniversary." *Bulletin of the Historical and Philosophical Society of Ohio* 11 (July 1953): 179–91.

Cochran, Thomas C., and Miller, William. *The Age of Enterprise: A Social History of Industrial America*. New York: Harper & Brothers, 1961.

Conklin, Edward. "A Brief History of the American Philosophical Society." *Year Book of the American Philosophical Society for 1959*. Philadelphia: American Philosophical Society, 1959.

Coulson, Thomas. "The First Hundred Years of Research at the Franklin Institute." *Journal of the Franklin Institute* 256 (July 1953): 1–25.

———. *The Franklin Institute from 1824 to 1949*. Philadelphia: The Franklin Institute, 1949.

———. "The Journal of the Franklin Institute: Its First One Hundred and Twenty-Five Years." *Journal of the Franklin Institute* 251 (January 1951): 1–10.

———. "Some Prominent Members of the Franklin Institute 1. Samuel Vaughan Merrick, 1801–1870." *Journal of the Franklin Institute* 258 (November 1954): 335–46.

———. "Some Prominent Members of the Franklin Institute 2. Joseph Saxton, 1799–1873." *Journal of the Franklin Institute* 259 (April 1955): 277–91.

———. "Some Prominent Members of the Franklin Institute 3. Matthias William Baldwin, 1795–1866." *Journal of the Franklin Institute* 212 (September 1956): 171–84.

Dictionary of American Biography. New York: Charles Scribner's Sons, 1943.

Dupree, A. Hunter. *Science in the Federal Government: A History of Policies and Activities to 1940*. Cambridge, Mass.: Harvard University Press, 1957.

———. "The History of American Science: A Field Finds Itself." *American Historical Review* 71 (April 1966): 863–74.

Eberlein, Harold D., and van Dyke Hubbard, Cortland. "The American 'Vauxhall' of the Federal Era." *Pennsylvania Magazine of History and Biography* 68 (1944): 150–74.

Eckhardt, George H. "Isaiah Lukens, 'Town Clock Maker and Machinist.'" *Antiques* 25 (February 1934): 46–48.

Edmonds, Franklin Spencer. *History of the Central High School of Philadelphia*. Philadelphia: J. B. Lippincott, 1902.

Ekirch, Arthur A., Jr. *The Idea of Progress in America, 1815–1860*. New York: Columbia University Press, 1944.

Fagan, George V. "Alexander Dallas Bache, Educator." *The Barnwell Bulletin* 18 (April 1941): 1–46.

Fee, Edward M. *The Origin and Growth of Vocational and Industrial Education in Philadelphia to 1917.* Philadelphia: privately printed, 1938.

Ferguson, Eugene S., ed. *Early Engineering Reminiscences [1815–40] of George Escol Sellers.* Washington, D.C.: Smithsonian Institution, 1965.

———. "On the Origin and Development of American Mechanical 'Know-How.'" *Midcontinent American Studies Journal* 3 (Fall 1962): 3–15.

Fisher, Marvin. *Workshops in the Wilderness: The European Response to American Industrialization, 1830–1860.* New York: Oxford University Press, 1967.

Fowler, Francis. "Memoir of Dr. Thomas P. Jones." *Journal of the Franklin Institute* 130 (July 1890): 1–7.

Frazer, Persifor. *Notes and Papers of or Connected with Persifor Frazer in Glasslough Ireland and his son John Frazer of Philadelphia 1735 to 1765.* Philadelphia: privately printed, 1906.

———. "The Franklin Institute: Its Services and Deserts." *Journal of the Franklin Institute* 165 (April 1908): 245–98. The article was also published separately under the same title by the Franklin Institute in 1908.

Frazier, Arthur H. "Joseph Saxton's First Sojourn at Philadelphia, 1818–1831, and His Contributions to the Independence Hall Clock." *Smithsonian Journal of History* 3 (Summer 1968): 45–76.

Gibbons, Chester H. *Materials Testing Machines.* Pittsburgh: Instruments Publishing Company, 1935.

Gilchrist, Agnes Addison. *William Strickland, Architect and Engineer, 1788–1854.* Philadelphia: University of Pennsylvania Press, 1950.

Goode, George Brown. "The Origin of the National Scientific and Educational Institutions of the United States." *Annual Report of the American Historical Association for the Year 1889.* Washington, D.C.: Government Printing Office, 1890.

Goodrich, Carter, ed. *Canals and American Economic Development.* New York: Columbia University Press, 1961.

Greene, John C. "Science and the Public in the Age of Jefferson." *Isis* 49 (1958): 13–25.

Hartz, Louis. *Economic Policy and Democratic Thought: Pennsylvania, 1776–1860.* Cambridge, Mass.: Harvard University Press, 1948.

Haynes, William. *American Chemical Industry.* 6 vols. New York: D. Van Nostrand Company, 1954.

Hepburn, Joseph S. "Notes on the Early Teaching of Chemistry in the University of Pennsylvania, the Central High School of Philadelphia, and the Franklin Institute of Philadelphia." *Journal of Chemical Education* 9 (1932): 1577–91.

Hindle, Brooke. *Technology in Early America: Needs and Opportunities for Study.* Chapel Hill: University of North Carolina Press, 1966.

———. *The Pursuit of Science in Revolutionary America.* Chapel Hill: University of North Carolina Press, 1956.

Hudson, D., and Luckhurst, K. W. *The Royal Society of Arts 1754–1954.* London: Murray, 1954.

Hunter, Louis C. "Heavy Industries before 1860." in *The Growth of the American Economy,* edited by Harold F. Williamson. New York: Prentice-Hall, 1944.

———. "Origines des Turbines Francis et Pelton." *Revue d'Histoire des Sciences et de leurs Applications* 17 (July–September 1964): 209–42.

———. *Steamboats on the Western Rivers: An Economic and Technological History.* Cambridge, Mass.: Harvard University Press, 1949.

Jackson, Joseph. *Early Philadelphia Architects and Engineers.* Philadelphia: privately printed, 1923.

Kaser, David. *Messrs. Carey & Lea of Philadelphia; A Study in the History of the Booktrade.* Philadelphia: University of Pennsylvania Press, 1957.

Katz, Michael B. *The Irony of Early School Reform: Educational Innovation in Mid-Ninetenth Century Massachusetts.* Cambridge, Mass.: Harvard University Press, 1969.

Kelly, Thomas. *A History of Adult Education in Great Britain from the Middle Ages to the Twentieth Century.* Liverpool: At the University Press, 1962.

———. *George Birkbeck, Pioneer of Adult Education.* Liverpool: At the University Press, 1957.

Layton, Edwin T. "Mirror Image Twins: The Communities of Science and Technology in Nineteenth-Century America." *Technology and Culture* 12 (October 1971): 562–80.

Lewis, John F. *History of Apprentices' Library of Philadelphia, 1820–1920.* Philadelphia, 1924.

Lively, Robert A. "The American System: A Review Article." *Business History Review* 29 (1955): 81–96.

Livingood, James W. *The Philadelphia-Baltimore Trade Rivalry, 1780–1860.* Harrisburg: The Pennsylvania Historical and Museum Commission, 1947.

Lurie, Edward. *Louis Agassiz, A Life in Science.* Chicago: University of Chicago Press, 1960.

McCadden, Joseph J. *Education in Pennsylvania, 1801–1835, and its Debt to Roberts Vaux.* Philadelphia: University of Pennsylvania Press, 1937.

McCreary, George W. *The Ancient and Honorable Mechanics Company of Baltimore.* Baltimore: Kahn and Pollock, 1901.

Macfarlane, John J. *Manufacturing in Philadelphia, 1683–1912.* Philadelphia: Philadelphia Commercial Museum, 1912.

Meier, Hugo. "American Technology and the Nineteenth Century World." *American Quarterly* 10 (Summer 1958): 116–30.

———. "Technology and Democracy, 1800–1860." *Mississippi Valley Historical Review* 43 (March 1957): 618–40.

Miles, Wyndham D. "A Versatile Explorer: A Sketch of William H. Keating." *Minnesota History* 36 (1959): 294–99.

———. "William H. Keating and the Beginning of Chemical Laboratory Instruction in America." *Library Chronicle* 19 (Winter 1952): 1–34.

———. "With James Curtis Booth in Europe, 1834." *Chymia* 11 (1966): 139–49.

Miller, Howard S. *Dollars for Research.* Seattle: University of Washington Press, 1970.

Miller, Perry. *The Life of the Mind in America from the Revolution to the Civil War.* New York: Harcourt, Brace & World, 1965.

Muir, James. *John Anderson: Pioneer of Technical Education and the College he Founded.* Glasgow: John Smith & Son, 1950.

Multhauf, Robert P. "Engineering in Philadelphia, 1775–1825." In *Pennsylvania's Contributions to the Professions,* edited by Homer T. Rosenberger, pp. 60–67. Waynesboro, Pa., 1964.

————. "Holcomb, Fitz, and Peate: Three 19th-Century American Telescope Makers." *Contributions from the Museum of History and Technology.* Washington, D.C.: Smithsonian Institution, 1962.

Nepomucene, Sister St. John. "Franklin Peale's Visit to Europe in the U.S. Mint Service." *Journal of Chemical Education* 32 (March 1955): 156–59.

Nolan, Edward J. *A Short History of the Academy of Natural Sciences in Philadelphia.* Philadelphia: The Academy of Natural Sciences, 1909.

Oberholtzer, E. P. *Philadelphia: A History of the City and its People.* 4 vols. Philadelphia, 1911.

Odgers, Merle M. *Alexander Dallas Bache: Scientist and Educator, 1806–1867.* Philadelphia: University of Pennsylvania Press, 1947.

100 Years of Mechanics' Institute of San Francisco, 1855–1955. San Francisco: Mechanics' Institute of San Francisco, 1955.

"Outline History of the United States Patent Office." *Journal of the Patent Office Society* 18 (July 1936): 1–251.

Paniagua, Evelyn S. "American Inventors' Debt to the Institute." *Journal of the Franklin Institute* 247 (January 1949): 1–6.

Pearson, Lee M. "The *Princeton* and the 'Peacemaker': A Study in Nineteenth-Century Naval Research and Development Procedures." *Technology and Culture* 7 (Spring 1966): 163–83.

Pessen, Edward. "The Workingmen's Movement of the Jacksonian Era." *Mississippi Valley Historical Review* 43 (December 1956): 428–43.

Pettengill, George. "Walter Rogers Johnson." *Journal of the Franklin Institute* 250 (August 1950): 93–113. This article provides excellent information on Johnson, including a full bibliography of his writings.

Pharo, Elizabeth B. *Reminiscences of William Hazell Wilson, 1811–1912.* Philadelphia, 1937.

Philadelphia Gas Works News. Special Centenary Number, 1836–1936. Philadelphia: Philadelphia Gas Company, 1936.

Poesch, Jessie. *Titian Ramsay Peale, 1799–1885, And His Journals of the Wilkes Expedition.* Philadelphia: American Philosophical Society, 1961.

Pursell, Carroll W., Jr. *Early Stationary Steam Engines in America.* Washington, D.C.: Smithsonian Institution Press, 1969.

Rae, John B. "The 'Know-How' Tradition: Technology in American History." *Technology and Culture* 1 (1960): 139–50.

Reingold, Nathan. "Alexander Dallas Bache: Science and Technology in the American Idiom." *Technology and Culture* 11 (April 1970): 163–77.

————. *Science in Nineteenth-Century America: A Documentary History.* New York: Hill and Wang, 1964.

————, ed. *The Papers of Joseph Henry. Volume I, December 1797–October 1832. The Albany Years.* Washington, D.C.: Smithsonian Institution Press, 1972.

Rezneck, Samuel. *Education for a Technological Society: A Sesquicentennial History of Rensselaer Polytechnic Institute.* Troy, N.Y.: Renssalaer Polytechnic Institute, 1968.

————. "The Rise and Early Development of Industrial Consciousness in the United States, 1760–1830." *Journal of Economic and Business History* 4 (August 1932): 784–811.

Roe, Joseph Wickham. *English and American Tool Builders.* New York: McGraw Hill, 1926.

Rosenberg, Nathan, ed. *The American System of Manufactures. The Report of the Committee on the Machinery of the United States 1855 and the Special Reports of George Wallis and Joseph Whitworth 1854.* Edinburgh: The University Press, 1969.

Ross, Earle D. *Democracy's College; the Land-Grant Movement in the Formative Stage.* Ames: Iowa State College Press, 1942.

Sack, Saul. *History of Higher Education in Pennsylvania.* 2 vols. Harrisburg: Pennsylvania Historical and Museum Commission, 1963.

Sanford, Charles L. "The Intellectual Origins and New Worldliness of American Industry." *Journal of Economic History* 18 (1958): 1–16.

A Savings Bank Account: The Story of the Western Savings Fund Society of Philadelphia, 1847–1947. Philadelphia: Western Savings Fund Society of Philadelphia, 1947.

Sawyer, John E. "The Social Basis of the American System of Manufacturing." *Journal of Economic History* 14 (December 1954): 361–79.

Scharf, J. Thomas, and Wescott, Thompson. *History of Philadelphia, 1609–1884.* 3 vols. Philadelphia: L. H. Everts and Co., 1884.

Shaw, Ralph R. *Engineering Books Available in America Prior to 1830.* New York: The New York Public Library, 1933.

Shelling, Richard J. "Philadelphia and the Agitation in 1825 for the Pennsylvania Canal." *Pennsylvania Magazine of History and Biography* 62 (April 1938): 175–204.

Sinclair, Bruce. "At the Turn of a Screw: William Sellers, the Franklin Institute, and a Standard American Thread." *Technology and Culture* 10 (January 1969): 20–34.

————. *Early Research at the Franklin Institute: The Investigation into the Causes of Steam Boiler Explosions, 1830–1837.* Philadelphia: The Franklin Institute, 1966.

————. "Gustavus A. Hyde, Professor Espy's Volunteers, and the Development of Systematic Weather Observation." *Bulletin of the American Meteorological Society* 46 (December 1965): 779–84.

————. "The Promise of the Future." In *Nineteenth-Century American Sci-*

ence: A Reappraisal, edited by George Daniels, pp. 249–72. Evanston: Northwestern University Press, 1972.

Skeen, John R. "The Origin and Influence of Major Technical Libraries in Philadelphia." *Journal of the Franklin Institute* 250 (1950): 381–90.

Sloan, Edward W., III. *Benjamin Franklin Isherwood: Naval Engineer*. Annapolis: U.S. Naval Academy, 1965.

Smith, Edgar F. *Franklin Bache, 1792–1864, Chemist*. Philadelphia: privately printed, 1922.

————. *James Curtis Booth, Chemist, 1810–1888*. Philadelphia: privately printed, 1922.

————. *John Griscom, 1774–1852, Chemist*. Philadelphia: privately printed, 1925.

————. *Martin Hans Boyè, 1812–1909, Chemist*. Philadelphia: privately printed, 1924.

Spiess, Philip D. "Exhibitions and Expositions in 19th-Century Cincinnati." *Cincinnati Historical Society Bulletin* 28 (Fall 1970): 171–92.

Spitz, Armand N. "Meteorology in the Franklin Institute." *Journal of the Franklin Institute* 237 (April–May 1944): 271–87, 331–57.

Stanton, William. *The Leopard's Spots: Scientific Attitudes toward Race in America, 1815–59*. Chicago: University of Chicago Press, 1966.

Swank, James M. *History of the Manufacture of Iron in All Ages*. Philadelphia: The American Iron and Steel Association, 1892.

Talbot, Hamlin. "Some Greek Revival Architects in Philadelphia." *Pennsylvania Magazine of History and Biography* 65 (April 1941): 121–44.

Temin, Peter. "Steam and Waterpower in the Early Nineteenth Century." *Journal of Economic History* 26 (June 1966): 187–205.

Thomson, Elihu. "Address on the Occasion of the Observance of the Centenary of the Founding of the Franklin Institute." *Journal of the Franklin Institute* 198 (November 1924): 581–98.

————. "One Hundred Years of the Franklin Institute." *Science* 60 (1924): 343–51.

Tylecote, Mabel. *The Mechanics' Institutes of Lancashire and Yorkshire before 1851*. Manchester: Manchester University Press, 1957.

Tyler, David B. *The American Clyde: A History of Iron and Steel Shipbuilding on the Delaware from 1840 to World War I*. Newark, Del.: The University of Delaware Press, 1958.

————. *The Wilkes Expedition*. Philadelphia: American Philosophical Society, 1968.

Wainwright, Nicholas B., ed. *A Philadelphia Perspective: The Diary of Sidney George Fisher, Covering the Years 1834–1871*. Philadelphia: Historical Society of Pennsylvania, 1967.

Warner, Sam Bass, Jr. "Innovation and the Industrialization of Philadelphia." In *The Historian and the City*, edited by Oscar Handlin and John Burchard, pp. 63–69. Cambridge, Mass.: The M.I.T. Press and Harvard University Press, 1963.

————. *The Private City: Philadelphia in Three Periods of its Growth*. Philadelphia: University of Pennsylvania Press, 1968.

Watson, Paul Barron. *The Tragic Career of Commodore James Barron, U.S. Navy (1769–1851)*. New York: Coward-McCann, 1942.

Welter, Rush. "The Idea of Progress in America; An Essay in Ideas and Method." *Journal of the History of Ideas* 16 (1955): 401–15.

White, John H., Jr. *American Locomotives: An Engineering History, 1830–1880*. Baltimore: The Johns Hopkins Press, 1968.

Wickersham, James P. *A History of Education in Pennsylvania*. Lancaster, 1886.

Wright, Sidney L. *The Story of the Franklin Institute*. Philadelphia: The Franklin Institute, 1938.

INDEX

Academy of Natural Sciences, 48n, 58, 205, 223, 239–40, 258; and Institute scientific circle, 135, 256

Academy of Sciences (France), 157, 180, 181

Adams, John Quincy, 43, 44

Adams, William, 127

Agassiz, Louis, 153, 250, 251 and n, 288

Agnew, John, 4n, 144, 245, 290, 291

American Academy of Arts and Sciences, 8, 243n

American Association for the Advancement of Science, 241, 250–51

American Association of Geologists and Naturalists, 250

American Chemical Society, 117

American Institute, 91, 137n, 238, 322

American Journal of Education, 11, 12

American Journal of Science, 206n, 208

American Lyceum of Science and the Arts, 10

American Mechanics' Magazine (New York), 54, and n, 57, 198n

American Philosophical Society, 8, 29–31, 48n, 58, 136, 240; finances of, 219 and n, 223, 225, 239; and Institute scientific circle, 135, 255–58, 282; interest in meteorology, 116, 156–57, 243n

American Society of Mechanical Engineers, 310

Anderson, John, 323n

Anderson's Institution, 6, 30

Appleton, Nathan, 144

Ashley, General William, 91

Athenian Institute, 112, 234

Audubon, John James, 199

Bache, Alexander Dallas, 147, 221, 228, 235, 266n, 281, 301, 324; advocates scientific professionalism, 188, 195, 208, 211–12, 250–53, 320; biographical details, 149–51; calls for creation of technological museum, 259–60; and Committee on Science and the Arts, 151, 246, 248 and n; conducts study of weights and measures, 192–93; and exhibition policy, 102–3, 238; heads U.S. Coast Survey, 189, 249, 253, 257; and Institute educational program, 115–18, 129–30, 132, 219, 232–33, 237, 259–60; and Institute scientific circle, 135–36, 136n, 152–54, 191, 205, 250n, 257n; and Journal of the Franklin Institute, 205–13, 215, 282, 285, 287; plays leading role in Institute, 105–6, 150, 160; portrait of, 169; as principal of Central High School, 123, 322; reorganizes Institute membership meetings, 104, 311n; and research at the Institute, 156, 158, 173, 175–78, 180–83, 185–87; urges public support of science, 189, 239, 251

Bache, Franklin, 118, 135

Bache, Hartman, 63n, 64n

Bacon, Francis, 5, 6

Bakewell, Thomas W., 176, 213

Balch, Thomas, 297

Baldwin, Matthias W., 31, 85, 102, 135, 222, 228, 310; participates in Institute technical investigations, 144, 174–77, 192; and Philadelphia mechanic community, 28, 55 and n; portrait of, 80; and School of Arts, 231n, 232

Baldwin Locomotive Works, 292–93, 313; engraving of, 277

Barron, Commodore James, 64

Bartol, B. H., 287, 308, 314, 319

Barton, John, 62

Beard, Ithamar, 323n

Bement, William, 294, 313–14

Bement and Dougherty, 294, 309, 313. See also Industrial Works

Biddle, Nicholas, 33, 231

Binney, Horace, 44 and n

Birkbeck, George, 6 and n, 12

Bolmar, Antoine, 126 and n

Bonney, Jonathan, 97

Booth, James C., 135, 213, 235, 259, 282; biographical details, 254–56; career in industrial chemistry, 160, 285, 288–89; member, United Bowmen, 154n; portrait of, 169; and revision of Institute lecture program, 116–17, 119

Boston Lyceum, 16

Boston Mechanics' Institution, 12, 16, 18
Boston Mechanics' Lyceum, 17, 18
Boyden, Uriah, 266 and n
Boyè, Martin H., 285, 288–89
Braidwood, Thomas W., 262
Brandywine millers, 142–43
Bridport, Hugh, 47, 120, 121
Briggs, Robert, 308–9, 315
British Association for the Advancement of Science, 147, 149, 157, 210, 213
Brown, David S., 261
Brown, Lt. T. S., 212
Browne, Peter A., 12, 20, 32, 71, 105, 135; aids establishment of Franklin Journal, 51–58; architectural interests of, 47 and n, 48n; charged with patent fraud, 61–62; controversy with Patent Office, 42–45; as early Institute leader, 35, 41n, 48, 51, 63; geological interests of, 255n, 260; and Institute lectures, 35–36, 110–11, 114–15; and Institute schools, 39, 65–69, 123–24, 131; portrait of, 26
Buchanan, Senator James, 157
Bull, Marcus, 89 and n, 90
Burke, Edmund, 490

Cabinet of Arts and Manufacturers, Committee on the, 260. See also Technology: museum of
Caldwell, Captain Thomas, 64n
Canby, James, 143
Carey, Matthew, 34, 37n, 52, 92, 105, 135, 136n; and controversy over Institute high school, 67 and n, 68, 123; forms Pennsylvania Society for the Encouragement of Internal Improvements, 58
Carpenters' Hall, 38, 46, 94, 120
Central High School, 256, 281, 285n, 299, 322; Alexander Dallas Bache at, 132, 253; alumni and Franklin Institute, 264–65, 298; astronomy at, 252
Chapman, Dr., 136n
Chappell, James, 97
Chemistry: industrial, 117, 288–89; Institute professorship in, 114n, 118; lectures, by John K. Mitchell, 113
Civil War, 306–7, 317–18
Claxton, Timothy, 6n, 15–18, 38, 109 and n
Clay, Henry, 43, 44
Clinton, De Witt, 48 and n
"Clique," 250 and n
Cloud, Joseph, 172
"Club," 250

Colburn, Warren, 142, 144 and n
Coleman, William and Company, 89
Colt, John, 143
Colton, Oren, 31
Commission on the Expansion of Steam, 316 and n
Connecticut Academy of Arts and Sciences, 9
Cooper, Dr. Thomas, 172
Craig, John, 14, 135
Cram, T. J., 212
Cramp, Charles H., 308
Cresson, Elliott, 262, 266
Cresson, John C., 20, 231n, 245, 266n, 282; biographical details, 254–56, 259; as Institute president, 307–9; as Institute professor of natural philosophy, 254; lectures on sound, 300; portrait of, 27
Crystal Palace Exhibition, 100, 297–99

Daguerre, 284
Dallas, A. J., 64n
Darrach, Dr. William, 111
Dearborn, Henry A., 144
Debt Fund, Committee on the, 307, 310
Delaware breakwater, 143
Depression of 1857, 302–5
Dobson, Judah, 198n
Dougherty, James, 294, 309
Draper, John W., 208, 209, 211–12, 215
Dry docks, 64
du Pont, E. I., 143

Earle, Anthony, 143
Eastwick, Andrew M., 291–92
Education: controversy over Institute plans for, 66–67, 123–25; monitorial system of, 124–25; and organization of Institute schools, 120, 130; public support for, 131–32; scientific, 129–30, 133; technical, 66, 122–23, 130–34, 298–99; tuition for, in Institute schools, 120–21, 124; for workingmen, 9, 11–12, 18, 66, 68–69, 129. See also Instruction, Committee on; Lectures, Committee on
Eichbaum, William, 198n
Ellet, Charles, 258, 292
Emerson, Dr. Gouveneur, 116
Engineering: chemical, 287; civil, 131, 233, 286–87; mechanical, 287, 309; training in, 131–34, 230, 299
Engineers' pocket book, 235
Ericsson, John, 244
Erie Railroad, 258, 259

Espy, James Pollard, 248n; biographical details, 154–58; career in meteorology, 110, 116, 154–58, 160, 209, 252; and Institute scientific circle, 152–53, 250; as mathematics teacher, 122, 255; portrait of, 169; publishes in *Journal of the Franklin Institute*, 206, 209, 211–12, 215; and steam-boiler investigation, 175–76; and water-power experiments, 144, 150

Evans, Oliver, 28, 31, 143, 147, 175n

Everett, Edward, 5 and n

Ewbank, Thomas, 257n

Examiners, Board of, 61–62. *See also* Inventions, Committee on

Exhibitions, 228, 303; and American industrial progress, 100, 295–98; effort required to sponsor, 100–101; first of Institute industrial, 39–41, 85; popularity of, 93–94, 99, 295; prize award policy at, 86–88, 94; proposal for joint, with Maryland Institute, 101–2; shifts in policy of, 100–103, 237–39; special awards at, 94–96, 295; value of prize awards at, 97–98, 296

Fairbanks, E. & J., & Co., 97

Fairmount Waterworks, 44n, 141, 142

Faraday, Michael, 113, 138, 209, 210, 213

Featherstonhaugh, G. W., 213

Ferguson, Alexander, 221, 231n

Financial Condition of the Institute, Committee on the, 304

Fisher, Sidney George, 44n, 112

Fletcher, George, and Company, 293

Fletcher, Levi, 121–22

Fletcher, Thomas, 31, 73, 222

Fourneyron, M., 285, 322

Fox, George, 174–75

Fraley, Frederick, 102, 119, 192, 232, 235, 257, 282; biographical details, 151, 220, 250n, 252n, 254, 256, 259, 268; gives lecture on the mechanic arts, 239, 247n; and Institute financial condition, 220–21, 228, 304, 306–7; and lecture program, 236, 298, 300; portrait of, 279; and purchase of Masonic Hall, 221, 225–28; and reorganization of Institute, 280–81, 308, 310, 317; and School of Design for Women, 261

Francis, James B., 323n

Franklin, Benjamin, 4, 9, 28, 30, 33, 41n, 47, 73, 106, 129, 152

Franklin Almanack, 56–57

Franklin College, 66

Franklin Institute: administration of, 69–70, 280–82, 308–11, 317; advises state on weights and measures, 192–93; assumes control of *Franklin Journal*, 70–71, 198–99; attempts census of manufactures, 255n; basis for support of, 229; Board of Managers, 50, 65, 69–72, 102, 229–30, 296, 308–10; building projects of, 38, 46–48, 221–28, 301–2; as career base for scientists and engineers, 158, 160, 194, 210–11, 252; and Central High School, 264–65; committee structure at, 50–51, 63; compared with other mechanics' institutes, 18–19; compared with other Philadelphia societies, 240, 258; constitution of, 31–33; as consultant to government, 191–94; drawing school at, 38–39, 46, 111, 120–21, 121n, 129–30, 236, 264; election controversy at, 296; English school sponsored by, 129–30; evening lectures at, 35–38, 109–19, 236–37, 298–300; financial condition of, 46, 218–28, 302–7; forms Committee on Science and the Arts, 151; founding of, 3–5, 29–33; high school at, 65–69, 123–28; industrial exhibitions sponsored by, 39–41, 93–105, 295–98; and the *Journal of the Franklin Institute*, 195–216 passim; library of, 46, 70–71, 218, 300–301; mathematics school of, 65 and n, 111, 121–23, 129; membership in, 45, 128, 218; membership meetings of, 103–4, 119; meteorological observations conducted by, 155–56, 242–44; museum of technology at, 259–61; professorship in, 37–38, 109, 236–37, 310; and protective tariffs, 91–93; publications of, 51–56, 234–35, 285–87; School of Arts proposed by, 132–34, 230–32, 259, 299; School of Design for Women, 261–64; scientific circle of, 152–53; standard for American screw threads, 311–15; steam-boiler investigation by, 173–91; study of street-paving methods, 266; water-power experiments performed at, 140–49

Franklin Journal and American Mechanics' Magazine: concern with internal improvements, 63–64, 89; egalitarian objectives of, 196–97; format and contents of, 56–58, 74–78, 81, 195–97; as national periodical, 58; renamed *Journal of the Franklin Institute*, 70, 199; Thomas P. Jones as editor of, 53, 70

Franklin works. *See* Merrick, S. V., & Company

Frazer, John F., 117, 228*n*, 245, 259, 307 and *n*, 308; biographical details, 254–58, 281–82, 282*n*; and Boyden prize, 266*n*; as Institute administrator, 280–82, 303, 317; and *Journal of the Franklin Institute*, 160, 282–83, 284–85, 287–89; and lecture program, 236–37, 253, 282, 298–300; and membership meetings, 311*n*; portrait of, 169; prepares catalog of Institute library, 301; and School of Design for Women, 261, 263; and scientific professionalism, 250–51

Friend's Academy, 123, 255

Gardiner, R. H., 143
Garrett, Philip, 291, 292
Gas lighting, 221, 254
Geddes, John, 48 and *n*
Geological survey, 117, 255*n*, 260
Geology: lectures in, 114, 116–17, 236, 260; training in, 133
Germantown Academy, 123, 126
Girard College, 252, 253, 281
Glascow Mechanics' Institution, 6, 7, 11
Godman, John, 110–11
Gould, Benjamin Apthorp, 250–51
Graff, Frederick, 141, 144, 172, 175
Green, Duff, 203
Greene, Benjamin F., 256
Gries, John M., 304, 306
Griffith, Dr. Robert, 111
Griffith, Eli, 126
Griscom, John, 8*n*, 9, 52, 215–16, 282, 284
Gross, Samuel, 110

Haines, Samuel, 144
Haldeman, Samuel S., 228*n*, 281, 282*n*; biographical details, 254–58; Institute lectures in zoology by, 237; member, United Bowmen, 154*n*
Hamer, John, 36
Hamilton, William, 97, 100, 107, 176, 187, 228; appointed actuary, 71; and *Journal of the Franklin Institute*, 205–8, 210, 282–83, 286–87; and meteorological observations, 242, 243*n*; portrait of, 27; salary of, 203–4, 233, 317
Harding, Jesper, 198, 199
Hare, Robert, 136*n*, 175, 248*n*, 260; chemistry professor at University of Pennsylvania, 30, 117, 288; lectures at the Institute, 110–11; publishes in

Journal of the Franklin Institute, 197, 209

Harlan, Dr. Richard, 291
Harrison, John, 288
Harrison, Joseph, Jr., 292, 294, 303 and *n*; lithographic view of residence of, 278
Haviland, John: architect of Institute's building, 46; biographical details, 47 and *n*; Institute professor of drawing, 29, 120–21; supports technical college, 67
Hays, Dr. Isaac, 136*n*, 205, 216, 222; and the School of Arts, 231*n*, 232, 235
Henry, Joseph, 136 and *n*, 184, 256, 311; and Boyden prize, 266*n*; heads investigation of *U.S.S. Princeton* disaster, 245; and publication of steam-boiler explosion report, 186–88; and scientific professionalism, 153–54, 195, 250, 252; at Smithsonian Institution, 158, 243–44, 259
Hill, Anne, 262–63
Holbrook, Josiah, 10, 16, 17
Holcomb, Amasa, 248–49
Humphreys, J., 64*n*
Hunt, Uriah, 56

Industrial art, 261–64
Industrial Works, 294; engraving of, 274. *See also* Bement and Dougherty
Industry: coal, 86–87, 89–91, 94–95, 133, 236; iron and steel, 86–91, 133; promotion of American, 86–87, 91–93, 295–98; Russian sheet iron, 95–96; textile, 88, 93, 143
Ingersoll, Harry, 228
Ingersoll, Joseph R., 262
Ingham, Samuel D., 176–77
Institution of American Civil Engineers, 233, 282
Instruction, Committee on: admits women to lectures, 112; alters lecture program, 116–19, 300; considers expansion of Institute schools, 65–66; and controversy over high school, 127–28; establishes English school, 129–30; and mathematics school, 121–23; proposes Institute high school, 67–69, 123–24; reforms membership meetings, 104; replaces Committee on Lectures, 65; and School of Design for Women, 261–64
Internal improvements, 34–35, 58–60, 63–64, 84, 89, 141, 212, 230, 300

Inventions, Committee on, 61, 92, 139–40; aims of, 60–61; controversy with Patent Office, 42–45; formation of, 63; replaced by Committee on Science and the Arts, 151

Iron Association of Pennsylvania, 254

Isherwood, Benjamin Franklin, 289–91

Jackson, Patrick Tracy, 144

Jefferson Medical College, 114n, 135

Jervis, John B., 213

Johnson, Walter R.: appointed to U.S. Exploring Expedition, 184–85, 252; biographical details, 126, 135, 152–53, 155, 185, 257n, 311n; conducts study of American coal, 185; portrait of, 169; as principal of Institute high school, 124–28, 219; publishes in *Journal of the Franklin Institute*, 208–9, 211, 215; strength-of-materials research by, 160, 175, 181–84, 245; teaches natural philosophy, 115, 118, 254

Jones, Dr. Thomas P., 49, 73, 89n, 98, 114, 139, 175, 320, 324; appointed superintendent of U.S. Patent Office, 71, 197–98, 200; biographical details, 4n, 9, 47n, 54–55, 135; conception of technical journalism, 195–97, 206; and controversy over Institute high school, 67–68; and controversy with Committee on Publications, 205–8; as editor of *Franklin Journal and American Mechanics' Magazine*, 51–58; as editor of *Journal of the Franklin Institute*, 198–208, 213, 216, 282–84; as patent agent, 200 and n; portrait of, 80; promotes internal improvements, 63–64, 89, 92; proposed as Institute administrator, 70; as science lecturer, 10, 54 and n, 55, 111

Journal of the Franklin Institute: and Bache scientific circle, 106, 209–10, 216; editorial collaborators in, 282; finances of, 203–4, 214–16, 305; format altered, 212; Institute assumes control of, 70–71, 198–99; John F. Frazer as editor of, 284–85, 287–89; John Griscom performs editorial tasks for, 215–16, 282, 284; joint editorship plan for, 283–84; meteorological register in, 155; patent specifications published in, 200–202, 284, 305; payment to authors, 211 and n, 215; and Philadelphia industry, 288–95; subscription agents for, 214 and n; Thomas P. Jones as editor of,

198–208, 213, 216, 282–84; translates European technical studies, 284–86, 322

Keating, William H., 20, 36, 52, 102, 118, 192, 253; as chemistry professor at University of Pennsylvania, 117, 135; and founding of Franklin Institute, 5, 29–34; lectures at Institute, 36, 109–11; and Masonic Hall purchase, 221; portrait of, 27; and steam-boiler investigation, 173–77; and water-power experiments, 144

Keller, Charles M., 284, 305

Kennedy, Alfred, 299

Kentucky Mechanics' Institute, 13

Kirk, Caleb, 142, 143

Kneass, Samuel H., 59, 69, 233, 255

Kneass, Strickland, 255

Kneass, William, 29, 255

Lancaster, Joseph, 124

Lazzaroni, 153, 251

Lectures: in America, for workingmen, 109; for British workingmen, 6–7; at Institute, organization of, 110–13; natural history, 110, 237; popular, in science, 9–10, 109–11; shift in Institute policy for, 115–20, 236–37

Lectures, Committee on: established, 35–38; proposes appointment of Institute faculty, 38; recommends establishment of drawing school, 38–39, 120; replaced by Committee on Instruction, 65

Lehman, Samuel, 139

Lesley, Mr., 136n

Levering, John, 144

Libby, John, 234

Library: at Institute, 70–71, 218 and n, 260, 300–301, 317; scientific, proposed in Boston, 11

Liebig, Justus, 285

Linnard, J. M., 231n

Livermore, Daniel, 143

Liverpool Mechanics and Apprentices' Library, 8n

Locke, John, 14, 135

Locks and Canals Company, 142, 143

London Mechanical Institution, 16

London Mechanics' Institute, 6–7, 12

Long, Stephen H., 63, 287, 291

Longstreth, Edward, 313, 319

Lukens, Isaiah, 135, 141, 228, 235; conducts electromagnetic experiments, 153, 209; and examination of new in-

Lukens, Isaiah (*Continued*)
ventions, 61 and *n*, 248*n*; and Philadelphia mechanic community, 28, 55 and *n*, 73, 293; portrait of, 80; and steam-boiler investigation, 175, 177
Lyceum movement, 10

Macauley, Isaac, 92
McClurg, Alexander, 231*n*
McLeod, William, 242
Maclure, William, 34*n*, 150, 239
Maclurean Lyceum, 150
McNeill, William, 317–18
Magazine of Popular Science (London), 186
Malin, Joshua, 90
Mapes, James J., 283–84
Maryland Institute, 12, 13, 101–2, 136
Mason, David H., 31, 55*n*, 61, 73, 85, 177, 205, 293
Mason, William, 28, 73, 177, 255; Institute professor of drawing, 121; teacher in Institute high school, 127
Mason and Tyler: engraving of machine tools of, 76
Masonic Hall: exhibitions in, 94; Institute purchases, 221–27
Massachusetts Charitable Mechanics' Association, 238, 298
Matthews and Moore, 313; lithographic view of, 272
"Mechanics' and Engineers Pocket Book and Annual of the Franklin Institute," 235
Mechanics' and Tradesmen's Exchange Company, 234
Mechanics' Institute movement: in America, 4–5, 7–8; in Great Britain, 5–6, 11–12
Mechanics' Magazine (London), 6, 51 and *n*, 54, 147
Mechanics' Register (Philadelphia), 234
Merrick, George, 175 and *n*
Merrick, John Vaughan, 250*n*, 291, 309, 310, 314, 316*n*, 322
Merrick, Samuel Vaughan, 15, 20, 52, 63, 92*n*, 143, 228, 234, 235, 307; and administration of Institute, 70, 105–6, 253–54, 310; biographical details of, 29–30; and Central High School, 264–65; and exhibition policy, 101–3; and founding of Franklin Institute, 4, 29–34; ideas of, for Institute high school, 67–68, 123–24; and *Journal of the Franklin Institute*, 203, 205–6, 208–9,

216, 282; as member of Institute scientific circle, 135, 152–53, 191, 250 and *n*, 257; participates in steam-boiler investigation, 174–78; portrait of, 27; as president of the Pennsylvania Railroad, 259; proposes School of Arts, 230–32; and purchase of Masonic Hall, 221, 225–28; and School of Design for Women, 261; studies lighting gas manufacture, 152, 254, 321; and *U.S.S. Princeton* disaster, 244–45; views on technological advancement, 322, 324; and water-power experiments, 141; and weights-and-measures study, 192
Merrick, S. V., & Company, 55, 73, 313–14, 322; engraving of fire engine of, 79; establishment of, 4*n*, 290; manufactures lighting gas apparatus, 293, 321; produces marine engines, 244, 291
Merrick and Sons, 291; lithographic view of, 270. *See also* Merrick, S. V., & Company
Meteorology: Institute interest in, 152–56, 209, 242–44; lectures on, 110, 112; public funding of research in, 156, 242–44; reports published in *Journal of the Franklin Institute*, 242; at Smithsonian Institution, 243
Middlesex Manufacturing Company, 97
Miller, Edward, 259
Millington, John, 116 and *n*
Mills, Robert, 61
Mine Hill and Schuylkill Haven Railroad, 254
Mitchell, Dr. John K., 113, 114*n*, 125, 135, 175, 185, 282
Mitchell, S. Weir, 117
Models, Committee on, 37, 69
Moore, James, 313
Morfit, Campbell, 289
Morris, Ellwood, 282, 285 and *n*; biographical details, 254–55; lectures on civil engineering, 236–37; and prevention of locomotive boiler explosions, 247; and water-turbine experiments, 322
Morris, I. P., & Co., 293, 314; lithographic advertisement for, 273
Morris, I. P., Towne and Company, 314
Morris, Isaac P., 228, 235
Morris, Tasker and Morris, 293
Morton, Henry, 317 and *n*
Moss, Theodore, 237

Nasmyth, James, 321

National Academy of Sciences, 106, 151, 251, 290, 308, 316n
New Castle and Frenchtown Turnpike and Railroad Company, 95–96
New England Society for the Promotion of Manufactures and the Mechanic Arts, 143, 144
New York Mechanic and Scientific Institution, 7, 8, 9, 13, 30, 39 and n, 51
New York Mechanics' Institute, 13, 238
New York Society for Mechanics and Tradesmen, 14
Niles, Hezekiah, 91, 92
Norris, William, 291
Norris Locomotive Works, 291
North American Coal Company, 59

Ohio Mechanics' Institute, 14, 135
Olmstead, Denison, 153

Panic of 1837, 223–25
Parker, J. W., 186–88
Parmalee, Charles, 262
Parry, Charles T., 313, 319
Pascal Iron Works, 293, 308; engraving of, 276. See also Morris, Tasker and Morris
Paterson, New Jersey Mechanics' Society, 13
Patterson, Robert M., 61n, 63, 135, 235, 245, 248n, 257; and controversy over Institute high school, 66–68, 123; director of U.S. Mint, 255; and School of Arts, 232; science lectures of, 35–36, 38, 109–12; and steam-boiler investigation, 175 and n; and study of weights and measures, 192
Peale, Charles Willson, 115
Peale, Franklin, 115, 154n, 212, 254–55
Peale, Titian, 154n, 251n, 254–56
Pencoyd Iron Works, 314
Pennsylvania: economic development of, 84, 86–87; geological survey of, 117, 255 and n; and Panic of 1837, 134, 225; and public support for education, 131, 134, 230–32; weights and measures of, 192–93
Pennsylvania Railroad, 258, 259
Pennsylvania Society for the Promotion of Internal Improvements, 34–35, 58–59, 63n, 84, 89
Percy, John, 99
Perkins, Jacob, 4n, 28, 55, 89n, 172, 179
Peter, Mrs. William, 261–64
Philadelphia: Arcade, 47n; chemical industry in, 288–89; dry-dock facilities of, 64; educational system of, 67, 122–23, 125–26; intellectual quality of, 136; lighting gas manufacture in, 254 and n, 313, 321; machinery manufacture in, 290–95, 313; machine shops of, 28; mechanic community of, 28 and n, 29, 73, 234; and Panic of 1837, 225; and Russian sheet iron industry, 99; and School of Arts, 230–31; scientific men of, 253–59; Select and Common Councils of, 103; Stone Cutters Company of, 95; street lighting of, 95; street paving of, report on, 266 and n; water-works, 141
"Philadelphia Clique," 258
Philadelphia Gas Works, 293, 313
Philadelphia High School, 128
Philadelphia Navy Yard, 244, 291, 313
Phillips, Hardeman, 91
Phillips, John S., 61
Phillips and Company, 86
Pierce, Benjamin, 250
Pittsburgh Mechanics' Institute, 198n
Playfair, Lyon, 299
Polytechnic and Scientific College, 68
Polytechnic College of the State of Pennsylvania, 299
Port Richmond Iron Works, 228, 293, 314
Potter, Alonzo, 262, 319
Poughkeepsie Screw Company, 97
Powers and Weightman: engraving of, 271
Premiums and Exhibitions, Committee on, 88–89, 93, 95, 98, 101–4, 238
Priestley, Joseph, 30, 54, 288
Providence, Rhode Island Mechanics' Institute, 113
Publications, Committee on, 52, 186, 204; assumes control over Journal of the Franklin Institute, 205–8; efforts to publish original articles, 283

Rafinesque, Constantine, 111, 114
Ralston, Gerard, 63n
Randel, John, 64n
Redfield, William C., 153, 157
Reeves, Benjamin, 73, 141, 150, 192n; and steam-boiler investigation, 175–78
Rennie, George, 147
Rensselaer Polytechnic Institute, 256
Renwick, James, 64n, 176
Research: industrial, 96–97, 97n, 140; Institute financing of, 252; laboratory at Institute, 138–39; public funding

Research: industrial (*Continued*)
  for, 191; scientific, 136–37; technical,
  33–34, 128. See also Steam-boiler ex-
  plosions; Water power
Richardson, John, 70
Roberts, Algernon, 314
Roberts, Joseph, 255
Roberts, Solomon W., 99, 233, 245, 254–
  55, 282–83
Roberts, W. Milnor, 258
Rogers, Fairman, 307n, 308
Rogers, Henry D., 154, 156, 232, 254–55,
  259, 289; lectures on geology, 116–17;
  and Pennsylvania geological survey,
  236, 250
Rogers, James B., 254, 289
Rogers, Robert E., 254, 289
Ronaldson, James, 20, 37n, 62–63, 92n,
  102, 175, 228; biographical details, 34
  and n; and Institute founding, 31–32;
  portrait of, 26; as president of Frank-
  lin Institute, 106, 203, 223, 253–54
Royal Institution, 113, 116, 138, 210
Royal Society of Arts, 39 and n
Rush, James J., 31, 61n, 144, 175 and n
Rush and Muhlenburg, 31, 89, 144, 175n

Sanderson, John, 67
Saxton, Joseph, 85, 153, 209, 235, 255,
  259, 285n
Say, Benjamin, 209
Schuylkill Navigation Company, 254,
  258–59
Science: and democratic ideology, 2–3,
  17, 48, 137–38, 196, 319, 324; government support of, 185, 191, 194, 240,
  244, 248, 251–53; professional standards
  for, 115–16, 149, 159, 195, 211–12, 250
Science and the Arts, Committee on:
  Bache's conception of, 246, 248; in-
  vestigation of *U.S.S. Princeton* disaster,
  245–46; and locomotive boiler ex-
  plosions, 246–48; replaces Committee
  on Inventions, 151; report on Amasa
  Holcomb telescopes, 248–49; report on
  U.S. Coast Survey, 249; resolutions on
  meteorology, 155; study of telegraph
  systems, 193–94
Scientific American, 305, 312, 314
Scientific mechanic, 5, 14–15
Scientific Proceedings of the Institute,
  Committee on the, 310
Scott, John, 103
Scott Legacy, 103
Screw threads: English system of, 311–

12; need for American standard of,
  312; system of, proposed by William
  Sellers, 311–13
Seaman, James, 54 and n, 57, 198n
Sellers, Coleman, 240, 309, 314
Sellers, George Escol, 28, 55
Sellers, William, 280, 294, 300; elected
  Institute president, 308; as entre-
  preneur, 322–25; portrait of, 279; pro-
  poses standard for American screw
  threads, 311–15; reorganizes Institute,
  309–11, 317
Sellers, William, & Company, 294, 309;
  engraving of, 275
Sergeant, John, 44
Shaw, Joshua, 61
Siddall, James, 142
Silliman, Benjamin, 10 and n, 152, 153,
  184
Silver, J. S., 236
Sims, Edward, 90
Smeaton, John, 146
Smith, Daniel B., 125
Smith, George W., 63n, 64n
Smith, Seth, 129
Smithsonian Institution, 241, 259; mete-
  orology at, 158, 243; scientific research
  at, 243–44
Society for Establishing Useful Manu-
  factures, 143
Southwark Foundry, 244, 290–91, 293,
  309, 322. See also Merrick, S. V., &
  Company
Spencer, Asa, 210
Standardization, 313–16
Steam-boiler explosions: British parliamentary inquiry into, 179; early Philadelphia investigation of, 172–73;
  government role in the problem of,
  174, 189; hazards of, 171; prize for
  solution of, 88; in railroad locomotives,
  246–48; and steamboat regulation,
  189–90
Steam Boilers, Committee on: controversy with W. R. Johnson, 181–83;
  experimental apparatus used by, 160,
  164–65, 178; formed, 175; *General Report of*, 186–89; plan of experiments
  by, 176–80; publications of, 181–83,
  185–89, 190–91; receives federal financial aid, 176–77
Steam engineering, 289–90, 316 and n
Stewart, Charles, 64n
Stockton, Robert F., 244–45

Strength of Materials, Committee on: apparatus used by, 160, 166–68, 178, 183, 245; experimental results of, 183, 323; report of, 181–83

Strickland, George, 121

Strickland, William, 34–36, 38, 105, 121, 135; architect of proposed Institute building, 222; engineering pupils of, 255, 259; and Institution of American Civil Engineers, 233; lectures, 109–10, 115; and Society for the Promotion of Internal Improvements, 59–60, 89

Struthers, John, 222

Swain, William M., 228n

Technology: dangers of, 171–72; demand for informed, 142; lectures in, 119–20, 236; museum of, 259–61; relation of science and, 6, 15, 170–71, 219–20, 280; value of cooperative research in, 148–49

Telegraph systems, 193

Thompson, Edgar, 259

Thornton, William, 42–45, 198n

Tilghman, Richard A., 316n

Totten, Colonel Joseph, 285–86

Towne, John H., 244–45, 259, 290–91, 308, 314, 316n

Trautwine, John C., 211, 254–55, 259, 285–87, 292

Trego, Charles B., 154n, 231 and n, 237, 247, 281; biographical details of, 254–58; and Institute meteorological project, 242–43, 243n; and School of Arts, 231 and n; and technological museum, 259, 260n

Troth, Henry, 125, 259

Tyler, John, 244

Tyler, Rufus, 28, 55, 61n, 73, 141, 192, 290, 293

Union Club, 306

United Bowmen's Company of Philadelphia, 154 and n, 250, 256

University of Pennsylvania, 30–31, 38, 66, 68–69, 105, 117, 123, 135, 149, 256, 258, 281; Department of Arts, 256, 265, 298–99

Ure, Andrew, 6

U.S. Army: Corps of Topographical Engineers, 63, 149, 212, 219n, 289, 314; Quartermaster General, 314

U.S. Coast Survey, 106, 151, 249, 257, 291

U.S. Exploring Expedition, 182, 184–85

U.S. Mint, 29, 116, 212, 255

U.S. Navy, 185, 244–45, 289–91, 313–16, 316n

U.S. Patent Office, 42–45, 71, 140, 197–98, 256, 257n, 284

U.S.S. Princeton, 244–46

Van Buren, Martin, 109

Vaughan, Benjamin, 30

Vaughan, John, 4, 30 and n, 136n, 200

Vaughan, Petty, 30 and n, 199–200

Vaux, Roberts, 125

Wakeman, Thaddeus B., 137n, 322

Walker, Sears C., 156, 192, 211–12, 235, 248n, 282; and Institute scientific circle, 250, 252, 254; teaches mathematics, 122, 127, 155

Wallis, George, 312

Walter, Siegfried, 126

Walter, Thomas U., 234, 236, 252n, 254–55, 261

Ward & Company, 245

Warder, John R., 64

Warner, John S., 231n

Water power, 87; Institute experiments on efficiency of, 140–49

Water turbines, 285, 322

Water Wheels, Committee on: experimental apparatus employed by, 144–45, 160, 161–63; financial support for experiments of, 142–44; report of published, 148

Webb, Benjamin, 143

Welles, Gideon, 316n

Western Savings Fund, 259 and n

West Point, U.S. Military Academy at, 108n, 132 and n, 149

Wetherill, Charles M., 261, 289, 300

Wetherill, John, 52

Wetherill, John Price, 288

Wetherill, Samuel, 288

Wheatstone, Sir Charles, 187, 210

Whitworth, Joseph, 311–12, 315

Wickham, M. R., 31

Wiegand, John, 231n, 250n, 254n

Wilson, John, 63n, 64n

Wirt, William, 44

Wistar parties, 136 and n

Wood, Samuel R., 31, 62, 63

Woodbury, Levi, 181, 182

Young, Andrew, 141

Young Mechanic (Boston), 17